HOLOCAUST HOLIDAY

HOLIDAY

One Family's Descent into
Genocide Memory Hell

RABBI SHMULEY BOTEACH

WICKED SON

A WICKED SON BOOK
An Imprint of Post Hill Press
ISBN: 978-1-64293-780-0
ISBN (eBook): 978-1-64293-781-7

Holocaust Holiday:
One Family's Descent into Genocide Memory Hell
© 2021 by Rabbi Shmuley Boteach
All Rights Reserved

Cover Design by Matt Margolis

This is a work of nonfiction. All people, locations, events, and situations are portrayed to the best of the author's memory.

Post Hill Press
New York • Nashville
posthillpress.com

Published in the United States of America
1 2 3 4 5 6 7 8 9 10

To my father, Yoav Boteach,
who passed away while I was completing the manuscript of
this book, at eighty-seven years old. I am in the midst of the
eleven-month recital of the Kaddish mourners' prayer, three
times a day for my father, a haunting and beautiful Jewish
ritual that was denied the six million of the Holocaust.
and to
Sheldon Adelson,
Global Jewish philanthropist and mega-donor and one of
modern Jewish history's most consequential figures, who
partnered with me in fighting genocide and preserving
the sacred memory of the six million. Sheldon, Israel's
tireless defender, passed away just weeks before this
book's publication, also, at eighty-seven years old.
And to
Yisrael "Zoli" Zoltan Wiesner, HY"D
my wife Debbie's great-uncle who was murdered
at Auschwitz, at just twenty-two years old.
May their memories be an eternal blessing.

CONTENTS

FOREWORD

BY AMB. GEORGETTE MOSBACHER

When you have visited Auschwitz once, it's hard to go a second time. When I revisited the site as United States Ambassador to Poland in 2019 with Vice President Mike Pence, I could barely make it past the gate.

Being there makes the horror feel so real. You are forced to absorb what you cannot properly digest. I didn't believe I could do it again. And yet, I believe every person must make the pilgrimage, because it's the only way to truly understand what actually happened to the Jews of Europe between 1939 and 1945.

Like many, I had heard the rallying cry of "Never Again." But I had never fathomed its true meaning. Being on the ground where humanity's greatest crime was committed, and knowing full well it could happen again, made me understand, at last, just how deeply the Holocaust affects us.

This was the slaughter that forced the global community to take its staff and draw an international line against hatred. The Holocaust summons all of us to wage endless war against anti-Semitism and any other form of bigotry—wherever it finds embodiment in the intentions, words, or actions of others.

That moment for me was an epiphany that has framed my outlook on life with a permanent urgency. Auschwitz awakened within me a new sense of responsibility to recognize the suffering of others, whether in the past, present, or future. I knew then that it was down to me to end or prevent injustice. It is also down to you, and each and every one of us. But the duty is mine as far as *I'm* concerned.

I first visited Auschwitz a few years before my appointment as Ambassador to Poland, the land where the Germans built their machinery of death. A land where millions of Jews had lived and died, and where today only a few thousand remain.

It was 2013, and the Polish government had joined some private donors in opening a Museum of Jewish History in Warsaw. One of my close friends was a benefactor. He was not Jewish, yet he believed it to be his responsibility to make sure a temple was erected to the Jewish communities eradicated on Polish soil, to enshrine their memory forever.

He had paid a visit to the extermination camps. At that time, I had not. I had never been to Poland.

I knew I had to see the camps. There are few sites as essential to the story of humanity than these searing monuments to what humans are both capable of doing and enduring. My journey to that sacred ground was non-negotiable.

We traveled to Krakow, where Europe's greatest rabbinic minds had once held forth on the precepts of Halacha and the secrets of Kabbalah. Today, its Jewish community is dwarfed by its number of Jewish graves. And yet, I witnessed a small but vibrant Jewish community being reborn—an eternal people who refuse to die.

From there we traveled to the small town of Oswiecim, the namesake of the nearby camp, Auschwitz-Birkenau, a name that has come to personify unimaginable evil.

We arrived amid the bitter cold of the Polish winter, which pressed through my coat and shoes.

We began to walk through the concentration camp, a center of mass Jewish enslavement. I thought of the Jews who lived there without coats or shoes, receiving meager amounts of food. Jews whose only crime was being born a Jew.

We walked on to the extermination camp and its crematoria, whose rubble still lies strewn about in horrifying heaps of bricks and steel. The Germans, I was told, had exploded them in hopes of burying their crimes, even as their victims were never buried but turned to ash and dust and blown into forest mounds. Each was an airtight structure designed to murder thousands of men, women, and children a day with poison gas. Mothers and fathers clutching their children; poets, craftsmen, and sages; murdered with methods of German heavy industry—one million at Auschwitz alone.

As the biting breeze increasingly chilled us, I thought of what those incarcerated here had endured, and whose last moments were a toxic blend of confusion, loss, and pain. My mind reeled to think that human beings could create these massive factories of death. Not just here at Auschwitz-Birkenau, but in more than 900 other camps erected across Europe.

Even seventy years later, I could hardly bear to witness the physical evidence of these crimes. How could anyone be a willing participant in this evil design? Where was it in the human genome to have the capacity for a systematic slaughter of such magnitude? Is the center of the human soul just an utterly unlit, vacuous black hole?

Yet this capacity exists somewhere inside of us, which means it could happen again. Things would never be the same for me. I had seen the world through a new lens, one I didn't know existed—and one I wish never did. I decided then and there to commit myself to the principle the Holocaust taught us: Never Again.

Six years later, I returned. This time, I arrived in a different capacity as the representative of the mightiest country on earth, the very nation that had been decisive in defeating Hitler's evil.

Beside me was Vice President Pence. Accompanied by a team of diplomats, aides, and advisors, we walked toward the notorious gates, with their infamous message of false hope: *Arbeit Macht Frei*. Like nearly all of what was spoken by the Germans, the promise that "Work Makes Freedom" was a shameless, heartless lie. Only death would free the prisoners who came here.

That was as far as I could make it.

"Would it be wrong," I asked the vice president, "if I only went as far as the gate?"

I knew the protocols. As Ambassador I was meant to escort the vice president everywhere. But, seared by my previous visit, I could not walk one step further.

He and the rest of the group said they understood. But it was only after they returned that I believed them.

Growing up in a steel-town in Indiana, I knew many Jews. Yet I never really knew what anti-Semitism truly meant. I had never been exposed in a personal sense to the depths of its evil, nor the devastation it has wreaked on Jewish communities for millennia. Nor to the potency with which it still rages today.

My trips to Auschwitz burst my bubble, forcing me to realign my conscience and clarify a nobler mission here on earth.

With a national platform and the power and moral weight of the United States behind me, I set out to make the difference I know the world needs: the difference I alone could make.

As America's ambassador, I represented my country on a range of geopolitical, economic, and strategic matters. But none were as crucial as helping Poland, the United States, and the world at large eternalize the memory of the Holocaust in the land where the bulk of its horrors took place.

My earliest briefings by the State Department were on the subject of the controversial Polish "Holocaust Law," a parliamentary decision to criminalize any allegations of Polish collaboration with the Nazis. While there could be no question that the Holocaust was planned, executed, and carried out by Germans, many Jewish leaders and historians perceived this law as an attempt to whitewash some undisputed Polish crimes. Poland was invaded by the Nazis and bravely resisted their brutality throughout the war. But a not insignificant number of Poles chose to collaborate in Nazi atrocities against the Jews. Justice demanded that the law be opposed.

At my Senate confirmation hearing, a lawmaker asked me if I believed the law encouraged anti-Semitism. "Frankly," I answered, "I do."

I hadn't even returned to my office when I was notified that Poland had lodged a formal complaint against me with the State Department—not exactly the start a new ambassador wants. I knew their perspective wasn't without merit. Poland had never ceased fighting against Germany and bore a terrible share of the Nazi terror. And yet I felt strongly that the world needed to know the truth, without any crimes redacted.

The very next day, Poland accepted my credentials.

As a nation, the United States made it crystal clear: there would be no discussions until the Holocaust law was fixed. The Polish president, Andrzej Duda, even had a visit to Washington postponed until the matter was resolved.

Months of diplomacy and dialogue would bring Poland to defang the controversial law, and the dispute seemed ripe to subside by the time I arrived in 2019. But there was still an outlying issue, with Holocaust researchers in Poland refusing to share their findings with the Holocaust Museum in Washington, D.C., lest their work be misconstrued or otherwise misunderstood. Yet this was a malfeasance we could not overlook.

I forced a meeting between the top Polish Holocaust researcher and our own, and told them both that I would be there. "There will be an agreement," I insisted, "or there will be consequences. This is at the White House level." It took my threats to get it done, but they came to an agreement.

Poland would also host a global security summit to advance our goals of countering the Iranian threat to the wider region and its genocidal intent against Israel, an event that I and my team arranged and coordinated. It was during that conference that I accompanied Vice President Pence to the camps—or more precisely, to the gates.

I also witnessed Poland's efforts to preserve the memory of the Holocaust and teach the truth of what occurred, and saw how my own nation not only channeled time and focus into Holocaust education and memory, but the funds that made the difference.

That April, I wished Jews a happy Passover in Polish. Shockingly, a wave of furious comments ensued. Of course, I also wished the Poles a happy Easter, but I was still accused of offending Poland, which (as far too many pointed out) was a predominantly Roman Catholic country.

The anti-Semites behind this offensive commentary apparently did not know that Mosbacher is my married name. They assumed that I was Jewish—and I may as well have been.

In response, I told my staff that we would be proudly tweeting warm wishes in Polish before every single Jewish holiday. "Get a Jewish calendar," I said. "Don't miss a single Jewish special day!"

I would not be intimidated—that much had to be clear. These people did not know me, yet they felt they could attack me with impunity, based on the assumption I was Jewish. I determined to plant my feet and take a stand.

It was not the first time I had been forced to do so. Back in 1991, at a London dinner party where a group of socialites were gathered, some decided to posit publicly that Israel was behind the first Gulf War against Saddam Hussein. Not his mass murder of innocent Kurds and Sunnis. Nor his unprovoked invasion of Kuwait, an act of wanton aggression that was, and had to be, opposed by the entire world. No—it was the Jews who were behind it; so they claimed. For anti-Semites, the Jews always are.

Indignantly breaking decorum, I slammed my fists down on the table. "Here's the real truth," I told them. "You're all just anti-Semites, try as you might to pretend you aren't."

They just couldn't keep it below the surface. Hatred always shows.

My experiences, of course, are those of a non-Jew on the outside looking in. Jewish pain and suffering is something I could never fully understand.

But realizing that such manifestations of hatred persist never fails to hit me at my core.

Which is why I intend to end it, hand in hand with all good people across the globe.

It was my privilege and honor to accept Rabbi Shmuley and The World Values Network's "Champion of Holocaust Memory" Award at their annual gala at Carnegie Hall in New York City in March, 2020, just days before the global lock-downs brought on by the coronavirus pandemic.

It is likewise my honor to contribute a foreword to his important book, in which he details the excruciating journey he took with his wife and children in the summer of 2017 to the killing fields of Europe—a pilgrimage which every person of conscience should attempt at least once in their lifetime.

It is our universal obligation to dedicate ourselves to the memory of the martyred six million, just as it is our obligation to confront and defeat genocide wherever it rises. We must continue to give voice to the victims and dedicate ourselves, now and forever, to the eternal motto of "Never Again."

Georgette Mosbacher
International Holocaust Remembrance Day
January 27, 2021

CHAPTER 1

HEY, KIDS! WE'RE GOING ON VACATION TO VISIT CONCENTRATION CAMPS

I was ten years old the first time I saw pictures of the bulldozers at Buchenwald pushing the bodies into mass graves. As a Jewish kid in Miami and Los Angeles, I knew of the Holocaust from an early age. Everywhere, there were survivors. They were part of our communities, part of our minyan—the quorum of ten needed for prayer services. You saw people all the time whose forearms were tattooed with numbers.

I was born November 19, 1966, just two decades after the Holocaust, and yet it still felt like a thousand years ago. People like Anne Frank lived in a colorless, black-and-white era before ours. There's no way you could comprehend, as a kid growing up in LA or Miami, the extent of these horrors, and it seemed there was no way they could have happened just twenty years before I was born.

My elders knew better. This had all happened in their memory. No Jewish child born in the twentieth century can escape the Holocaust. I heard about it all the time, and read all sorts of books, but my knowledge felt abstract and theoretical. I became a rabbi and met Elie Wiesel, the author of *Night*; and the great Nazi hunter Simon Wiesenthal. But it only became real to me when I met Anne Frank's best friend from childhood. Her name is Jacqueline van Maarsen, and she's a Holocaust survivor living in Amsterdam. I was shocked to hear that anyone knew who Anne Frank's best friend was, and even more amazed to hear she was still alive.

Yves Kugelmann of the Anne Frank Foundation introduced me. My wife and I went to a modest apartment in Amsterdam and met a warm and hospitable elderly couple. They spoke near perfect English, with an accent, and at one point in our conversation, Jacqueline turned to her husband, Ruud Sanders, and asked, "Do you think we should show them?" And he said, "Why not. They seem like nice people."

He went into the bedroom and returned with something like a shoebox. Inside were postcards from Anne Frank to Jacqueline, pictures of Anne on the beach in Holland, notes from school. I'm looking at this and trying to compute it. I always knew, of course, that Anne Frank was a real person. But is this real? People who went to school with *Anne Frank*? Are you kidding me? Notes that she passed in class. It hit me as I sat there that Anne didn't live in the Dark Ages or during ancient Byzantium. Anne was a little girl who lived just a short time ago. Had she not been murdered, she would likely still be alive today. And here was a woman who had played with her.

I felt compelled to be a witness to the places of our people's destruction. I wanted to completely immerse myself in the full horrors of the Holocaust, and I did not want to wait months or years. The survivors are dying every day, and too many people are like I was as a child, unable to comprehend the magnitude of the genocide directed at the Jewish people. There is some need in us modern Jews, I suppose, to see it as some ancient event, like the destruction of the Jerusalem Temple two thousand years ago, by the Romans. But that was all over for me after I met Jacqueline. The Holocaust had become fresh and immediate, and I decided I wanted to see as much of it as I could before it was too late. I also wanted my children to understand the Holocaust occurred during the lifetime of people they had met.

It was June 2017. My children had just finished school, and they were free all summer. I started thinking of a plan, one I worried they might hate.

Every summer, my wife and I round up our nine children, and we go on a trip. We've been to the battlefields of the Civil War, the National Parks. We have been to Israel, the Jewish homeland. We RV'd in Alaska. These trips tend to be joyful, a reprieve from the stress of the school year. But this year, I decided my children needed to learn about the Holocaust more than they needed a break.

I was reminded of the ads they used to run at the end of the Super Bowl, when someone would say to the star of the game, "You've just won the Super Bowl. Now what are you going to do?" And they would answer, "I'm going to Disney World!"

In my case, it was more like, "All right, kids. You've just finished school. Guess what we're going to do now? Go to visit concentration camps!"

Our family trip, however, was *logistically* uneventful. That is, if you can call moving a family of eight—with all of its luggage, need for kosher food, last-minute housing, and time spent in a tightly packed car together—uneventful. The trip was nightmarish, however, in an entirely different and more profound way. We were not visiting the beautiful sites of Europe. Our goal was not museums, art galleries, shopping districts, and nightlife. Our mission, rather, was to explore the darkest places in Jewish and world history: where a monster named Adolph Hitler was born; where the Final Solution was formulated; where the ghettoization, deportation, and extermination of six million Jews was conducted; and where the last remnants of Eastern European Jewry subsist.

This was also not a trip planned for years, or even months in advance. I decided on a family *vacation*, a Holocaust holiday, at the end of June, largely because of a trip I'd taken to Poland in March, with my daughters Shaina, Baba (Rochel Leah), and Chana, for the March of the Living, and at the invitation of my friend Elisha Wiesel, the only son of Elie Wiesel. It was during that pilgrimage to sites of the Holocaust that I made up my mind to pay tribute to Elie and the survivors and victims of the Holocaust by bearing witness to the places where the Final Solution was planned and implemented.

My desire to honor the world's best-known Holocaust survivor, human rights champion, and symbol of the Jewish community was inspired by my decades-long friendship with Elie, whom I always affectionately called *Reb Eliezer,* and who would, in turn, call me, *Reb Shmul.* Our relationship began while I was rabbi at Oxford, where my wife and I ran a renowned Jewish student organization called The Oxford University L'Chaim Society, which we had started in 1988. I had been an avid student of Elie Wiesel's works for years. His books took me back to a terrible time where my people were starving for food, battling disease, fighting for survival, fearing deportations, and searching desperately for any trace of the God within, with whom they had laid their faith.

Elie was awarded the Nobel Peace Prize in 1986, and used his renown and influence to enshrine the memory of those for whom help never came, and to campaign to help save those being victimized today. It was Elie who pushed President Jimmy Carter to commission the United States Holocaust Memorial Museum, and who would speak truth to power by telling President Reagan he should not lay a wreath at the German cemetery in Bitburg because it has SS graves.

Elie was committed to the welfare of all humanity—not just Jews—which he exemplified in his plea for President Clinton to protect those being slaughtered in Kosovo and the Balkans, and implored him not to have the United States stand by while a genocide was taking place in Rwanda.

I hosted one of his last public appearances, where he joined me in speaking out in the United States Senate, against the nuclear agreement President Obama was negotiating with Iran. The next day, I took him to the Capitol for the speech Israeli Prime Minister Benjamin Netanyahu made to a joint session of Congress. The capitol rotunda was closed, but we got special permission to enter. It was moving to be alone in this citadel of democracy, and the photo I have of the four of us, including my wife, Debbie, alone in the capitol rotunda is one I cherish.

Elie gave a voice to the silenced, a face to the nameless, and a story to each of the six million Jews martyred in the Holocaust. He became the living representative of those lost, and dedicated his life to ensuring that their deaths were not in vain, that the world never forget the suffering that befell his people, and that others never share their fate. Elie represented the most fundamental values of the Jewish people: faith and struggle, strength and pride, righteous indignation, and the courage to always remember.

Hosting him at Oxford, which I did twice, would prove to be one of the greatest honors of my eleven years there as rabbi. From there, Elie and I would embark on a special friendship of nearly thirty years. During that time, we worked together to bring attention to genocides that had been perpetrated in places such as Rwanda, Armenia; and to raise the alarm when fanatics, such as the leaders of Iran, threatened the Jewish people with annihilation.

After Elie's death, I told Elisha that I wanted to honor his memory by writing a Torah in his father's name and the memory of the six million who perished. Elisha was moved by the gesture, and approved the idea. We commissioned a scribe to write a special Torah scroll of a unique size that would make it portable, amid the serious laws governing the transport of Judaism's holiest object.

This beautiful Sefer Torah would accompany us throughout our trip—a small but powerful beacon of light amid the sea of darkness into which we would be diving.

I hate traveling without my family. I wrote a book about parenting, where I argued the best way to be a parent is to act like a camp counselor. Parents need to give children constant activities, mental stimulation, and passions. I have this little camp that consists of my kids, and I do stuff with them. Always, we learn together. This summer would be our Holocaust holiday.

I began to piece together an itinerary, one that would take us from where the Holocaust originated in Germany, throughout the lands where it was carried out. In the first leg of the trip, I would seek to understand the Nazi machinery of death that perpetrated the Holocaust. We would visit the site of the Holocaust's conception in Wannsee before seeing the places from where it was ordered in the Nazi offices still standing in Berlin. I wanted to stop in Dresden, too, to understand the Nazis' devotion to the cause, along with the sheer amount of force required to stop them. Prague, I knew would offer clues to the size and scope of European Jewry at the time of WWII, alongside the totality of the slaughter intended by the Nazis. There, we could also trace the steps of the heroic Czech resistance fighters who assassinated Reinhard Heydrich, and find in the Nazi reprisals the secret to their power: the combination of unmatched ambition with unprecedented brutality.

From there, we would head into Poland to understand the Holocaust as it was experienced on the ground by its victims, the Jews. By visiting the grand Jewish community of Warsaw, we'd understand just how enormous Poland's Jewish community was before the war. By visiting Krakow, we would get a taste of just how formidable Jewish Talmudic scholarship had been for centuries, before being extinguished by the Nazis. From there, we'd see the slave camps in Płaszów that they were herded into, and where Schindler made his list. Then we'd drive to the very epicenter of the Holocaust, the camps at Auschwitz-Birkenau, and from there, to the ghettos in Białystok and Łódź. On the way, we'd stop by the notorious death camp of Treblinka, and then seek out the other Holocaust epicenters of the environs of Warsaw, Lublin, Bratislava, and Budapest. From there, I knew the kids would be saturated with sadness and probably in need of something lighter. Still, it would be heavy: I decided that, in the last leg of the trip, we would loop back into Austria and Bavaria, where the evil that brought about the Holocaust found itself a fan base.

It was an itinerary of great intensity, and yet I wanted my kids to come along. Even the little kids. I wanted them to learn firsthand about the

Holocaust, to go beyond what they can read in books or glean from movies. I wanted them to learn everything that transpired so they would understand the meaning of *never again,* and commit themselves to preserving Jewish identity and values, fighting anti-Semitism, and standing up for Israel's right to exist and defend itself. I wanted them to appreciate the sanctity of human life. Most importantly, I wanted us as a family to honor the memory of the six million Jewish people who had been murdered.

It's not like they're shielded from horrors. They went through the pain, confusion, and horrible daily news of the coronavirus. They see news stories about police being gunned down, or race riots in places like Charlottesville. They see Hollywood movies with a lot of violence, and no matter how we try to protect them with PG-13 ratings, so much still slips through, especially on the Internet. I am not saying this is good. It's not. But I did not believe, that as a parent, I could say they were not ready to go to places of Jewish memory where terrible things happened. They know about the Holocaust, and they know about my work to speak out against genocide and Hitler-like threats.

Thankfully, my wife, Debbie, was supportive of this plan. Unlike me, she is a second-generation child of survivors. My own grandfather left Poland in about 1905, and worked to bring his brothers and sisters over. My grandmother left Lithuania and came to the United States as a baby at the turn of the 20th century. So thank God I never knew of any close relatives who had perished in the Holocaust.

Debbie was just the opposite. Her mother's family came from Slovakia. She had a twenty-two-year-old uncle who was taken away by the SS and never seen again. He was murdered at Auschwitz in May of 1943. Debbie has a great aunt who was forced into slave labor for the SS, and her great-grandfather owned a bakery that supplied the Slovakian army with bread. Debbie's grandparents hid as non-Jews, in Budapest and Prague. Her other set of great-grandparents and many other family members were murdered by the Nazis. So she was much more directly affected by the Holocaust than I was, and she was raised with stories about the family that survived, and those who did not.

I'm much more consumed with the Holocaust than she is. For her, it's more about her family story. For me, the trip was about what these monsters did to my people, and our responsibility to always remember the victims. I'm unusual for a Jew my age, because I don't have any family members who died in the Holocaust, even though I did have family from Poland and Lithuania. My wife's family was decimated. So the trip would be far more emotional for Debbie. For me, the emotions were more collective, borne against the genocidal destruction of the Jewish people.

Some of my friends thought I had lost my mind. A friend of ours contemplated joining us on the trip, but her ex-husband thought the idea of taking small children on such a trip was so outrageous that she dismissed it out of hand.

Debbie also was hesitant about taking the younger children. I was not reluctant at all. We resolved that we would only let them see the actual places, the trains, the boxcars, but we would keep them away from any graphic pictures. Those, they could see when they were older.

The kids were, understandably, less enthusiastic.

I have, thank God, nine children. The three oldest children did not join us. Mushki, at the time, was twenty-eight and married with three kids. Chana, twenty-six, said her last trip to Poland with me for the March of the Living was more traumatic than being under missile fire as a member of the Israeli Defense Forces. My daughter Shterny, twenty-five, is also married, and was living in Jerusalem at the time, with her medical-student husband. My eldest son, Mendy, was living in Israel and serving in the Israeli army. He joined us for the second part of the trip, after we had gone to the absolutely horrible places.

The next eldest daughter, Shaina, was twenty-two. She was a student at Stern College, but spent a semester six months earlier studying the Holocaust at George Washington University in Washington, DC. At the same time, she interned for Israeli Ambassador Ron Dermer. Earlier, she had spent a year in a real hardship post—Honolulu—where she ran adult educational programs for Chabad of Hawaii. She'd had a wild and engaging year of activism and study, and I wasn't sure if a trip to concentration camps was how she wanted to top it off. But she was game. She loved the course she took at GW on the Holocaust, with Professor Jeffrey Richter, who had been a historian in the Justice Department's Nazi-hunting unit, the Office of Special Investigations.

During the class, she developed a deep interest in the Holocaust, and realized that as much as she thought she knew, there was so much more to learn. She said it drove her insane to think about how it happened. When she contemplated the number of deaths, and then the number of people murdered daily, Shaina became obsessed with writing a paper on the Warsaw Ghetto Uprisings. She chose that topic because the Jewish revolts against the Nazis was one of the least publicized aspects of Holocaust history. She said that they did not use a textbook for the class. They read journals that told the stories of people's experiences, which made her feel more connected. At last, I had at least one.

Rochel Leah, who we call Baba, was nineteen and had a very different reaction than Shaina. She had spent the previous year studying in a Chabad seminary in Jerusalem, called Mayanot. She was on a spiritual high, as so often happens in Israel. She was writing essays about the Torah portion of the week, and the Lubavitcher Rebbe's talks, before I asked her to join our family vacation to the camps. Baba said it was like living in a bubble in Jerusalem. That bubble would burst during our trip.

Both Shaina and Baba came with me on March of the Living, and like Chana, each vowed never to return to Poland afterward. They pleaded with me not to go back. I told them it was a family trip that was deeply connected to my work in fighting genocide. They came along reluctantly, and planned to stay for only a few days. But I asked them to extend their trips, and they didn't leave until they were completely drained, three weeks later. While Mendy missed the horrible parts of the trip and got to participate in the more enjoyable tour of Italy, the girls had the opposite experience. It was shattering for both in different ways.

Yosef, my sixteen-year-old son, only spent the first week with us in Germany. He returned home to go on a three thousand-mile cross country bike ride in the United States—cycling one hundred miles per day—to raise money for Chabad's Friendship Circle program for special-needs children.

My youngest son, Dovid Chaim, was eleven and had learned some basic facts about the Holocaust, in school. He loves history, like I do, because he also believes it helps him understand the world better. After the trip, he admitted that he had no idea what he was in for. "My father said we would go to Germany for about a week and see a couple of Holocaust sites. I thought that would be cool. Then we went to Wannsee. Then we stayed and went to more terrible places. I didn't realize it would keep going on." He said if he had known, he probably would not have wanted to go.

Perhaps the person who had the most challenging visit was my youngest, Cheftziba, who began the trip when she was just eight years old. Assimilating all the information and sites was overwhelming because of her youth. But what made it even more difficult was that her birthday, July 3rd, coincided with the trip. Imagine hearing these words from your child: "Please, Tatty, don't let us spend my birthday in Auschwitz." She said it over and over.

How could I be unmoved? And besides, what kind of father would force a child to celebrate their ninth birthday in an extermination camp? A piece of me, however, couldn't help thinking that one point of the trip was to put ourselves in the shoes of the children and parents who lived through Hitler's reign of terror. Altogether, more than 1.5 million Jewish children were murdered by the Nazis. How many children did not live to see their ninth birthday? How many children had birthdays in Auschwitz, or the other camps? How many were lucky enough to survive to celebrate their next birthday?

Questions like these arose throughout the trip, and to be honest, many would never have occurred to me before. I also must admit that I did not fully prepare the kids for the intense journey that we were about embark upon. Some other people go on family trips to see their origins in Eastern Europe, and they visit one or two of the concentration camps. But we were going to be visiting four or five killing fields a day. I also did not anticipate the tension this immersion would create within the family, especially between Baba and me.

Once the decision was made to go to Germany, Poland, Slovakia, the Czech Republic, Austria, and Italy, we had to confront the huge matter of logistics. It is no easy task to organize a family of six, transport them from place to place, find lodging and kosher food, pack and unpack repeatedly, and keep to a semblance of a schedule. Somehow, we managed. But things did not always go smoothly, and I cannot tell you how grateful I am for the patience each child demonstrated, not to mention my wife.

Given the size of our entourage, we had to keep costs as low as possible. One way we did this was to do all our own driving. On the one hand, this gave us a lot of flexibility to come and go as we pleased. On the other hand, it created certain hardships. It's much more relaxing when you can sit back and let someone local and knowledgeable do the driving in a private car or a bus, especially around Eastern European countries whose terrain and topography are unfamiliar and often poorly paved. A local driver also knows how to keep you safe. We spent a lot of time getting lost, or taking a less than optimal route. We also did not have the benefit of a local guide's expertise about the sites we visited, or the interaction about life today. Then there is a lasting feeling of unease for Jews visiting remote places where our people were annihilated. Going it alone also added to the sense of being foreign, lonely, and vulnerable. Even without my beard, *yarmulke*, and *tzitzit*, we would have felt like aliens.

While my family might have felt more comfortable with a driver or guide, I was not looking to minimize the feeling of foreignness. After all, the Jews were singled out for persecution because of their *otherness*, which effectively made them strangers in their birthplaces.

With all this in mind, we departed for Germany on June 25, 2017, with a mixture of excitement and trepidation.

CHAPTER 2

WANNSEE: THE PLAN FOR THE FINAL SOLUTION

As we waited for our luggage at Berlin-Tegel Airport, an Israeli security guard—who had been contracted to protect a Jewish group who would be visiting Berlin—walked over to me and told me that my sons and I should take off our *yarmulkes*. He said that it was dangerous to wear them, and that I was being an irresponsible father for putting my children at risk.

He had good intentions, but I obviously ignored him. Orthodox Jewish men cover their heads as a symbol of being God-fearing. The very word *yarmulke* means *Yoreh Malkah*, fear of the King. It is an important sign of piety and religious devotion. It is also an identifiable sign of Jewish identity and connection. I will never teach my children to be afraid to be Jewish, or to show the world they're Jewish. But this was to happen over and over again: locals coming over to us in Germany, Poland, France, and other countries, pleading with us, for our own sake, not to wear our *yarmulkes*.

We were exhausted from the overnight flight, had not showered, and were generally unkempt. But we didn't want to waste any time. We rented a van, packed it up, and set out for Wannsee, directly from the airport. I was determined to see as much of the history of the Holocaust as was humanly possible in the time allowed. Wannsee, where the Final Solution of the Jewish question was discussed by senior officials of the Third Reich, was the place to start.

Wannsee is a wealthy suburb of Berlin, situated on picturesque Lake Wannsee, about a half-hour drive from Tegel. The mansion overlooks the lake, and is surrounded by beautiful gardens where walkers, joggers, and cyclists come to enjoy the serenity. It is the former stately home of a German industrialist, in a lovely residential neighborhood that gives no clue as to the monstrous decisions that were made there.

The wheels for genocide had actually been set in motion much earlier. Some might say that the first turn of the wheel was the enactment of the Nuremberg Laws in 1935, and the increasing persecution of the Jews that followed in succeeding years, leading up to *Kristallnacht*, November 9–10, 1938, when, over the course of less than forty-eight hours, at least ninety-six Jews were killed; thirty thousand more were rounded up and sent to concentration camps; 7,500 Jewish businesses were destroyed; and countless Jewish cemeteries, schools, and synagogues were vandalized or destroyed. The broken glass strewn all over the streets gave the pogrom its name: The Night of Broken Glass.

The pogroms on *Kristallnacht* were carried out in broad daylight, for the entire world to see. The condemnation by some leaders would convince the Nazis of the need to pursue their goal more covertly in the future, which is why nobody knew about the Wannsee Conference until much later. History only knows of its existence because one of the thirty copies (marked number 16 of 30) believed to have been distributed to the participants, was found in the files of the German Foreign Office in 1947, by American war crimes investigators.

The failure of the international community to take any action undoubtedly led Hitler to conclude that his assumption about the global contempt for the Jews was correct, and that no country would oppose his aim, which he made explicit in January 1939: "If international finance Jewry within Europe and abroad should succeed once more in plunging the peoples into a world war, then the consequence will be not the Bolshevization of the world, and therewith, a victory of Jewry, but on the contrary, the destruction of the Jewish race in Europe."

World War II began on September 1, 1939, with the German invasion of Poland. Shortly afterward, Heinrich Himmler, the head of the Gestapo and the SS, created special mobile killing units within the SS, the *Einsatzgruppen*, responsible for liquidating all political enemies of the Reich. They were placed under the command of his deputy, Reinhard Heydrich. On September 21, 1939, Heydrich sent a secret memo to the chiefs of the *Einsatzgruppen*. It euphemistically refers to the "final aim" of the Nazis, which he says would take some time, and details to the stages necessary for fulfilling it in the short-term.

The "first prerequisite," which Heydrich said should "be carried out with all speed," was the "concentration of the Jews from the countryside into the larger cities." If an explanation for this action was needed, he wrote, they were to say, "that Jews have most influentially participated in guerrilla attacks and plundering actions." Foreshadowing future plans, Heydrich said to create "as few concentration points as possible...so as to facilitate subsequent measures," and to choose locations along railroad lines.

Heydrich also gave instructions for the creation of Jewish councils, the notorious *Judenrats*, that would face the moral and ethical qualm of whether to collaborate with the Nazis in the hope of saving some Jewish lives, or resisting. The decision to create what Heydrich referred to in the memo as "Councils of Jewish Elders" (*Jüdische Ältestenräte*) was part of the scheme to force Jews to participate in their own destruction.

Heydrich's memo was specific about the composition of these councils. They were to be comprised of up to twenty-four male Jews who were "influential personalities and rabbis," and given full responsibility "for the exact punctual execution of all directives issued or yet to be issued." He added, that the councils were "to be warned of the severest measures" if they disobeyed. One of the roles these councils would play was also hinted at in the memo's instruction that the elders be "informed of the dates and deadlines for departure, departure facilities, and finally departure routes. They are then to be made personally responsible for the departure of the Jews from the countryside." The memo makes no mention of where the Jews might be deported.

Two years later, the implementation of the radical solution to the Jewish question to accomplish the "final aim" began when the *Einsatzgruppen* were assigned to kill Jews during the invasion of the Soviet Union, in June 1941. Ultimately, these mobile killing units would murder an estimated 1.4 million Jews.

The Nazis had experimented with gassing prisoners at Chełmno, a camp thirty miles northwest of Łódź. Prisoners there were forced into vans with tubes directing the carbon monoxide from the exhaust pipe, into the cabin, where they were trapped. In less than three years, these vans were used to kill and dispose of the bodies of more than 150,000 people.

This approach was deemed too slow and cumbersome, and there remained the problem of burying the bodies. The next stage in the genocide was tested on September 3, 1941, when six hundred Soviet prisoners of war, and 260 ill or weak prisoners at a concentration camp in Poland, known as Auschwitz, were herded into an experimental gas chamber. The Germans filled the room with crystalline hydrogen cyanide gas, an insecticide with the commercial name Zyklon B. The test was "successful," and the gas chamber was used for mass murder, starting in January 1942.

Thus, the extermination of the Jews was already in full swing when Heydrich invited fourteen high-ranking Nazi Party and government officials to the SS-owned villa we had come to visit. Later, the meeting became known as the Wannsee Conference.

Heydrich ran the meeting. He was chief of the Reich Main Security Office and Deputy Reich Protector of Bohemia and Moravia. He was assassinated by Czech partisans in Prague, in 1942. Also present was State Secretary Roland Freisler of the Reich Ministry of Justice and President of the People's Court, who was killed in an air raid in Berlin, on February 3, 1945. Rudolf Lange was an SS and police official who commanded a division of the *Einsatzgruppen,* and was either killed in action by the Soviets, or committed suicide at Poznań, Poland, on or around February 23, 1945. Heinrich Müller was head of the Gestapo. He was last seen in Hitler's bunker on May 1, 1945, and is the most senior Nazi who was never captured or confirmed to have died. Also present were Adolf Eichmann, a senior group leader of the SS, who was convicted of war crimes in Israel after one of the most sensational and consequential trials in history, and executed on June 1, 1962.

Only three of the fifteen participants were executed for their crimes after the war, despite the evidence that showed they had, over cognac, after a nice breakfast, spent ninety minutes discussing the SS plan to kill all the Jews of Europe. Heydrich wanted to assert SS responsibility for the "Final Solution," and to stress the importance of the various government bodies coordinating their actions to accomplish their goal quickly and efficiently. Eichmann, Heydrich's subordinate, recorded the minutes, which were subsequently edited by Heydrich, who substituted euphemisms for references to actions planned against the Jews.

We do not know everything that was said, since Eichmann's notes were not verbatim, but the euphemisms, such as the "new possibilities in the East," and "the Final Solution of the European Jewish Question," make clear the roles the various departments would play in transporting Jews from occupied territories to extermination camps in Poland. The scope of the Nazis' vision is evident from a table listing eleven million Jews, by country, who were subject to the "Final Solution." What is striking is that this list includes several countries, some neutral during the war, not usually associated with the Holocaust, such as England, Ireland, Sweden, Switzerland, and Turkey. One imagines they formed part of the German "living space" (*Lebensraum*) that was to be cleared of Jews "in a legal manner."

According to the "Wannsee Protocol," as the minutes are known, the Nazis had succeeded in causing 537,000 Jews to emigrate from Germany between January 1, 1933, and March 15, 1939. Wealthy Jews and Jewish organizations, it noted, had financed the emigration. The focus of Nazi operations was changing, however, from encouraging emigration to deportation: "The evacuated Jews will first be taken, group by group, to so-called transit ghettos, in order to be transported further east from there."

There was some concern for the impact of deporting Jews on the Reich economy. "Secretary of State Neumann stated that Jews employed in essential war industries could not be evacuated for the present, as long as no replacements were available."

The minutes make sickening reading; the plan for the Jews is explicit, and the attitude is unmistakable. "Jews fit to work will work their way eastwards constructing roads. Doubtless the large majority will be eliminated by natural causes. Any final remnant that survives will doubtless consist of the most resistant elements. They will have to be dealt with appropriately, because otherwise, by natural selection, they would form the germ cell of a new Jewish revival."

One of the remarkable aspects of the meeting, and of the Holocaust in general, is the absence of any evidence that Hitler ordered the murder of the Jews. The assumption of the attendees was that Heydrich was operating under the explicit orders of the Führer, but no such orders have ever been found. According to Yad Vashem, the World Holocaust Remembrance Center in Jerusalem, they may have been given orally, or passed through an intermediary. We only have documentation that Heydrich was acting under the authorization of Himmler. As brazen and wicked as his plan was, Hitler took extraordinary steps to make sure that no written orders from him as to the annihilation of European Jewry would exist. There are public speeches he gave, promising to destroy European Jewry, with "the prophecy" of January 30, 1939 in which he said, "If international finance Jewry inside and outside Europe should succeed in plunging the nations once more into a world war, the result will be not the Bolshevization of the earth and thereby the victory of Jewry, but the annihilation of the Jewish race in Europe"—being the most famous. But no written orders have ever been found, which shows you how far Hitler went to suppress evidence of war crimes. This would be a feature of nearly all Nazis, especially in the final days of the war, doing their utmost to conceal the scope of the genocide and their involvement.

I brought my family into the conference room at Wannsee, and stood at the table where Heydrich gave his briefing. I read from facsimiles of the minutes. I was already familiar with their contents, but reading them still aroused a combination of astonishment and rage at the audacity of the Nazis' plan for such evil on such a large scale. At no time did anyone present raise any objection to a scheme for exterminating an entire people. They did not bother to debate the policy. They were only there to discuss the details of its enactment. The Holocaust was an extraordinary crime carried out primarily by ordinary men. These were some of the most powerful ministers in the German government, some from sophisticated and highly educated backgrounds. They were not monsters or people with histories of mental illness. They were just doing their jobs.

What is crazy about the Wannsee Conference is that by 1942, Germany was already fighting a war against every significant power on earth, and yet they spent the day discussing how to deploy their scarce resources to conduct a continent-wide genocide of the Jews. To see a dramatic reenactment of the conference, I recommend the excellent film *Conspiracy*, starring Kenneth Branagh, that aired on HBO.

According to *Encyclopedia Judaica*, some scholars see Wannsee primarily as symbolic because the decision to kill the Jews of Europe had already been made. Some historians believe the timing of the meeting was related to some concern in Berlin, over the news that German Jews had been killed during mass shootings in the Soviet Union, in November 1941. They argue the meeting in Wannsee was partly aimed at getting the participants' approval for murdering all Jews, including German nationals. During the meeting, the group discussed, for example, whether certain Jews should be exempt, such as decorated veterans from World War I, and *Mischlings*—people with both Aryan and Jewish ancestry. It was decided that no Jew would be exempt. "Never before," as it says at the United States Holocaust

Memorial Museum, "had a modern state committed itself to the murder of an entire people."

It is, perhaps, not surprising that it took a long time for the German government to make the Wannsee mansion a museum. After the war, the building was used for a few years as a college, and then later became a youth hostel and place for local school children to play during their summer vacation. It was not until 1965 that a Polish Jewish historian named Joseph Wulf began a public campaign urging the government to create an international Holocaust document center at the mansion.

A survivor of Auschwitz, Wulf moved to Berlin in 1952. He had promised himself if he survived the war that he would dedicate his life to exposing the Nazis' crimes. But he died a disappointed man in his efforts to establish a Documentation Center at Wannsee. "I have published 18 books about the Third Reich," he wrote to his son, "and they have had no effect. You can document everything to death for the Germans. There is a democratic regime in Bonn. Yet the mass murderers walk around free, live in their little houses, and grow flowers." Wulf committed suicide on October 10, 1974, by jumping from the fifth-floor window of his Berlin apartment.

"As long as the generation that had been active during the Nazi period were still in positions of power, they were reluctant to create memorials to what were either their own crimes, or the crimes of their peers," said Stefanie Fischer, a postgraduate researcher on anti-Semitism, at Berlin's Humboldt University.

It was 1986 before the Mayor of Berlin, Eberhard Diepgen, announced a plan to create a memorial at Wannsee. Diepgen had been shocked when he learned about the Wannsee Protocol as a student in the 1950s. "There have been many cases of government-sponsored mass murder," said Diepgen, "but that a highly modern state, working with such brutal success, killed all the members of a race that it could capture, including mothers, children, and old people—that is unique and without any historical parallel."

It was a particularly fitting coda to the history of the Wannsee Conference when the staff at the Israeli embassy in Berlin held their weekly meeting in the same building on April 25, 2017—seventy-five years after the protocol for the Final Solution was completed.

It was also gratifying to see groups of schoolchildren touring the museum. Education is indispensable for preventing future genocides. "Let us not deceive ourselves about what we have done," said Rita Süssmuth, the president of the German Parliament, when the Wannsee house opened as a memorial. "Experience tells us that whatever we repress catches up with us. No one can flee from their history."

At the dedication, Heinz Galinski, an Auschwitz survivor and head of Germany's largest Jewish organization, stated: "In this house, on January 20, 1942, a barrier of civilization was broken and the abyss of barbarism was opened."

My children reacted with numbness to Wannsee. It was all too much to absorb. How could civilized men have sat around a conference table by a picturesque lake, and planned the gassing of 1.5 million children? The kids walked around the villa with their explanatory headsets on, trying to absorb the trauma. They had not slept an entire night on the plane. But now they were wide awake. Calmly and perfunctorily, they asked me questions: "Where did Heydrich sit at the table? When they walked in, where was the food situated? Did they pop grapes in their mouths as they discussed the gassing of the six million?"

The banality of my children's response was at once troubling, and perhaps, appropriate. Wasn't that the real shocker of the Wannsee conference? The utter ordinariness of it all? A bunch of boring bureaucrats, headed by the third-most evil man that ever lived, gathered over alcohol to discuss the most efficient way to carry out a continent-wide genocide.

But then, disgust registered on my children's faces as a group of German teenagers came through with a guide who was lecturing to them in German. I could see the distaste in their eyes, almost as though they regarded this group as partially culpable for all that had happened. The last thing my kids wanted was to hear German spoken in this sacred space. It seemed like a desecration. Yosef especially had a visceral reaction to seeing the German guide saunter through the villa, his students following in his wake.

I pulled my kids aside. "Today's Germans are not responsible for the Holocaust," I said. "We don't believe in vertical accountability, where the sins of the parents get passed onto the children. We believe only in horizontal accountability, where those who were alive and allowed this, and voted Hitler into office by democratic means, and those who carried out his genocide, are culpable. It's actually a beautiful thing to see that Germany brings its high school students here so that they can know what their parents and grandparents were part of. We should applaud all efforts Germany makes today to educate about the Holocaust." It surprised me, but my kids accepted my words and reacted differently afterward, warming to the presence of our German acquaintances.

Shaina, who had learned about the Wannsee Conference at her University course, asked the most questions and joined me in explaining much of the material to her siblings. Baba walked around in a fog. I could see that this was the beginning of a disillusionment with God and religious belief that would only increase over the course of our trip. "The scope of what happened is unimaginable. It's sickening," she told me. "It's disgusting." And while she did not yet say it out loud, I could tell she was wondering, "What are we doing here, and why did you bring me?"

CHAPTER 3

BERLIN: NAVEL OF THE NAZI WORLD

The Israeli at Tegel Airport wasn't kidding when he told us to take off our *yarmulkes*. Less than a year later, in April 2018, two young men wearing *yarmulkes* were attacked in an upscale neighborhood in the German capital. One victim was a twenty-one-year-old Israeli Arab who said he wore the *yarmulke* to show solidarity with his Jewish friends. A video of the assault showed a young man whipping him with a belt while shouting, "Yahudi!"—*Jew*, in Arabic.

Following the attack, one of Germany's Jewish leaders, Josef Schuster, said he would advise people visiting big cities against wearing *yarmulkes*. Other Jewish leaders were angered by his suggestion. I was with them. I was determined to walk as a Jew in Germany, and I was not about to give in to threats from anti-Semites. I was taught by my teacher and mentor, the Lubavitcher Rebbe, Rabbi Menachem Mendel Schneerson, to be a proud Jew and never hide my identity. My boys and I never removed our *yarmulkes* throughout our journey, even in cities where anti-Semitism was on the upswing. Fortunately, aside from some menacing stares, some of which got downright creepy, we never had any violence.

A week after the 2018 assault, more than two thousand Germans of various faiths put on *yarmulkes* and marched in Berlin and other cities around Germany, to protest the attack and show solidarity with German Jews.

This is the good news-bad news story of modern Germany. The country has done a great deal to educate people about its dark history through compulsory study of the Holocaust in schools, and dozens of memorials, museums, and other forms of documentation. Moreover, they have instituted legislation aimed at preventing a resurgence of Nazism; the display of Nazi iconography is forbidden. But it cannot be denied that neo-

Nazis and anti-Semitism are present in Germany, expressed in the rise of far-right political parties and in the antipathy toward Jews shown by some misguided Muslim immigrants.

My kids were immediately uncomfortable with being in Berlin. Yosef especially expressed displeasure. He and I clashed on the issue. "This place is disgusting," he told me. "They hate Jews here. They murdered us. And they haven't changed. Look at the way they look at us."

I understood, but rejected his outrage. "They put a Holocaust memorial right in middle of Berlin, at the seat of government. They're trying to come to terms with their past. It's a different generation. They didn't commit the Holocaust."

But Yosef would have none of it. "They hate Israel. They always criticize Israel, and don't give a damn about the Palestinians who blew up Jews. And Jews get attacked here all the time. They're afraid to even wear *yarmulkes*. Because they all know that they hate us here."

I strongly disagreed. His position—understandable perhaps for a teenager trying to process the unimaginable slaughter of his people in the lifetime of his grandparents—contradicted my core belief that every person should be judged by their own actions amid a wholesale rejection of collective punishment. The problem was, it seemed, that the evidence was on his side. Everywhere we looked around Berlin, there were monuments to the brutality of the German people against the Jews—from the former headquarters of the Gestapo and SS, to the former site of the Reich Chancellery, from which Hitler conducted the war and the Holocaust. And this is not to mention the two-thousand-year history of Jews being persecuted and slaughtered in Europe, and Germany in particular, especially during the crusades. Still, I insisted to Yosef that we as a family reject collective punishment and vertical accountability.

Jews have been persecuted in Berlin since they came in the 13th century to escape the Crusaders in southern Germany. In 1349, the Jews were accused of starting the Black Plague, and were expelled, returned, and sent away again at different times, until 1571, when they were banned for nearly a century. Jews slowly began to return in 1663. The first synagogue, known later as the Old Synagogue, was built in 1714, and the community established a cemetery, a *mikveh* (ritual bath), and a hospital. Jews became successful merchants and bankers, but, as everywhere else in Europe, faced a variety of restrictions and were heavily taxed.

Philosopher and scholar Moses Mendelssohn arrived in Berlin in 1743, and urged Jews to integrate into secular society. He also helped establish the *Jüdische Freischule* (Jewish Free School), which combined religious learning with a general education. Berlin subsequently became the center of the *Haskalah*, or Jewish enlightenment, during which many Jews assimilated. Jews were allowed to become Prussian citizens in 1815, and were technically given full equality in 1850, although they continued to endure bigotry and discrimination from their Christian neighbors. By this time, ninety-five hundred Jews lived in Berlin.

A major schism in the Jewish community of Berlin, and later the rest of the Diaspora, occurred with the founding of the Society for Reform in Judaism, in 1845, and the opening of a Reform temple in 1854. The Reform movement broke with many traditions of Orthodox Judaism, including holding services in German that featured an organ and a choir. Many Jews assimilated, which made it easier for them to become members of the social and economic elite.

By 1900, more than 110,000 Jews lived in Berlin, representing about 5 percent of the total population. Several new synagogues and other communal institutions were established, and many Jews became active in the Zionist movement. After World War I, Jews in Berlin enjoyed a golden age and became prominent in a range of professions. It was also a time of great creativity, as musicians, artists, and writers flourished. Meanwhile, the German economy deteriorated because of, among other factors, reparations payments required under the 1919 Treaty of Versailles. The government printed money to make the payments and to repay the country's war debt, but this led to hyperinflation, which made goods unaffordable. The US stock market crash and worldwide depression exacerbated the hardships in Germany as millions of people lost their jobs and major banks collapsed.

Hitler and his National Socialist German Workers Party (NSDAP— Nazi) exploited the misfortune of the people and promised to establish a strong central government that would ensure law and order, strengthen the economy, increase *Lebensraum* (living space) for Germanic peoples, and forge a society based on Aryan superiority and racial purity. In 1932, the NSDAP became the largest party in the Reichstag, holding 230 seats after winning 37.4 percent of the popular vote, and Hitler became chancellor on January 30, 1933.

A month later, the Reichstag building was set afire. A Dutch communist named Marinus van der Lubbe took the rap, but many people think the Nazis did it. Using the threat of a communist uprising as a pretext, Hitler rounded up members of the Communist Party and announced the Reichstag Fire Decree, which rescinded most German civil liberties, including rights of assembly and freedom of the press. This was followed by passage of the Enabling Act in March 1933, which enabled Hitler to create laws without the consent of the president or the Reichstag. He then purged the entire leadership of the storm troopers he had created as his personal guard in the 1920s, out of fear that they might challenge his leadership. During the Night of the Long Knives, which took place from June 30 to July 2, 1934, many senior officers, including Nazi leader Ernst Röhm—one of Hitler's earliest supporters—were shot.

On August 2, 1934, President Paul von Hindenburg died, and Hitler became Führer und Reichskanzler (leader and chancellor), making him the absolute ruler of Germany. All political parties other than the Nazi Party were outlawed. Germany withdrew from the League of Nations, and the swastika became the national flag.

I took my children around Berlin, teaching this history and showing them the major historical sites. They need to understand how a civilized society—perhaps the most developed in all of Europe—descended into unmatched barbarity in the space of a decade. We visited the site of the Reichstag, where Hitler gave so many of his infamous speeches, including the one referenced above, where on January 30, 1939, he basically stated, before the world, that he intended to annihilate the Jews of Europe:

> I have very often in my lifetime been a prophet and have been mostly derided. At the time of my struggle for power, it was in the first instance the Jewish people who only greeted with laughter my prophecies that I would someday take over the leadership of the state and of the entire people of Germany and then, among other things, also bring the Jewish problem to its solution. I believe that this hollow laughter of Jewry in Germany has already stuck in its throat. I want today to be a prophet again: if international finance Jewry inside and outside Europe should succeed in plung-ing the nations once more into a world war, the result will be not

the Bolshevization of the earth and thereby the victory of Jewry, but the annihilation of the Jewish race in Europe.

We visited the site of the Kroll Opera House, bombed to smithereens by the allies, but not before Hitler gave some of his most incendiary speeches rousing Germany to war. And we visited the headquarters of the Gestapo and SS, from which so much of the Holocaust was carried out.

The persecution of Jews began right away with the firing of Jewish civil servants, except those who had served in the military in World War I. On April 1, 1933, a boycott was declared against Jewish stores and businesses. That May, books written by Jews, and other authors considered subversive, were publicly burned in front of the opera house. Among the books added to the pyre were those by Albert Einstein, Franz Kafka, Sigmund Freud, Thomas Mann, Helen Keller, H.G. Wells, Margaret Sanger, and Marcel Proust. German Jewish writer Heinrich Heine wrote in his 1821 play, *Almansor*: "Where they burn books, they will, in the end, burn human beings too." The line is now engraved at the site of the book burning.

The site of the burnings, known as Bebelplatz, particularly moved our children. We got there late at night. A young German man stopped us and asked if we were Jewish.

"Whatever gave you that idea?" Yosef replied, sarcastically, as we were bedecked in *yarmulkes* and *tzitzis*.

The young man was warm and friendly, and started giving us ideas of other places we could visit that commemorate the crimes of the Third Reich. "You see, Yosef," I said, "there is a whole generation that wants to take responsibility and remember."

"He's a very nice guy, Tatty. But he's only one person."

The Nuremberg Laws, adopted on September 15, 1935, deprived Jews of German citizenship, prohibited Jewish households from having German maids under the age of forty-five, prohibited any non-Jewish German from marrying a Jew, and outlawed sexual relations between Jews and Germans. These measures were adopted to dehumanize the Jews and convince the rest of the German public that Jews were "parasites" who threatened the racial purity of the country and needed to be exterminated. Anyone who disagreed could be arrested and sent to the newly created Dachau concentration camp for political prisoners in Munich.

The mistreatment of Jews did not escalate into statewide violence until the evening of November 9, 1938—*Kristallnacht*, a coordinated nationwide pogrom that convinced any doubters that Hitler meant business. Assimilation was no shield against persecution. Even decorated veterans of World War I were dragged from their homes, beaten, humiliated, and arrested.

The Fasanenstrasse Synagogue was also destroyed. It had opened in 1914, in the presence of government, military, and city representatives. There was a procession of the Torah scrolls, and the ceremonial lighting of the eternal light. The rabbi said that the light of the lamp, like the love of fatherland of the Jewish community, would never be extinguished. The New Synagogue was also set ablaze, but was saved by a police officer, Wilhelm Krützfeld, who convinced the fire department to put out the fire because the building was an officially protected monument.

Kristallnacht occurred in plain sight and was covered by the media. World leaders could not feign ignorance, and yet President Roosevelt said and did nothing for nearly a week, before recalling the American ambassador from Berlin and declaring, "The news of the past few days from Germany has deeply shocked public opinion in the U.S....I myself could scarcely believe such things could happen in a 20th century civilization."

British Prime Minister Neville Chamberlain even allowed himself a little antisemitic reflection: "No doubt Jews aren't a lovable people; I don't care about them myself—but that is not sufficient to explain the pogrom."

Hitler took note of the world's inaction—it must have looked to him like no one cared enough about the Jews to challenge him. Three days after *Kristallnacht*, Hermann Göring convened a meeting of the Nazi leadership and announced, "Today's meeting is of a decisive nature. I have received a letter written on the Füehrer's orders requesting that the Jewish question be now, once and for all, coordinated and solved one way or another." On January 21, 1939, Hitler told the Czech foreign minister, "We are going to destroy the Jews."

Kristallnacht was meant to encourage the Jews to leave Germany. Seeing the writing on the wall, thousands emigrated, resulting in the Jewish population of Berlin dwindling to seventy-five thousand by the end of the year, less than half of what it had been before the Nazis. Many remained, believing they had survived the worst. No doubt, later they wished they had taken the hint. By 1941, most of the city was off limits to Jews. In October, the first one thousand Berlin Jews were transported to the Łódź Ghetto in Poland.

The next year, Alois Brunner, an SS officer and representative of Adolf Eichmann, was put in charge of the deportations, and he did his job with extraordinary efficiency, rounding up Jews in broad daylight and pressuring community leaders to identify victims for him. According to the Museum of Tolerance, "Brunner threatened to shoot one Jewish leader for every Jew absent from collection centers: when 20 Jews escaped, he took 20 officials, shot eight, and sent their families the ashes before deporting them." Ultimately, more than sixty thousand Jews were deported from Berlin: more than ten thousand to the ghettos in eastern Europe, about fifteen thousand to Theresienstadt, and more than thirty-five thousand to the extermination camps in Poland. On June 16, 1943, they declared the city *judenrein*, cleansed of Jews.

Alois Brunner, who went on to deport Jews from Austria (47,000), Greece (44,000), France (23,500), and Slovakia (14,000), escaped first to Egypt, and later to Syria, where he served for a time as an advisor to the secret police teaching them Nazi interrogation methods. The French government tried him in absentia and sentenced him to death, but Syria refused to extradite him. In a 1987 interview, he told the *Chicago Sun Times*: "The Jews deserved to die. I have no regrets. If I had the chance, I would do it again."

The Mossad sent him letter bombs on two occasions, which caused him to lose an eye and four fingers. He reportedly lived his last years under virtual house arrest in a basement in Damascus. It was rumored that he died in 2010, and finally his death was confirmed by the Simon Wiesenthal Center in December 2014, by which time he would have been 102 years old.

When the shattered capital was divided by the Allies into four zones, and Germany divided for forty years, most Jews settled in West Germany, but few survivors returned to their homes. In 1957, the West Berlin city government agreed to build a Jewish cultural center at the site of the Fasanenstrasse Synagogue, but Jewish life was moribund.

When the Berlin Wall fell in 1989, like the rest of the country, the Jewish community was unified. The city was also flooded by Jewish immigrants from the former Soviet Union. It provoked a crisis in German-Israel relations. Israel hoped that most of these Jews would make *aliyah*. However, many preferred to stay in Germany, where they thought economic opportunities would be better. The German government insisted the Jews should have a choice. Others argued that Germany had no obligation to allow them to stay since, as Jews, they had the right to automatic citizenship in Israel, and thus, were not really refugees. Still, the vast majority of the roughly fifty thousand members of the Jewish Community in Berlin speak Russian.

The presence of a large Jewish community in Germany baffled my kids, especially Baba and Yosef. "Who the hell would want to live here?" Yosef said. "I can't believe they can be in Israel, but they choose to come back to this giant Jewish cemetery of Germany." But our son Mendy had studied as a Rabbinical student emissary in Frankfurt for two years, sent there by the Chabad movement to help reinvigorate Jewish life in Germany. And he had felt accomplished in his work, and believed that the Jewish communities of Europe and Germany in particular were important.

"Hitler wanted to make Germany *judenrein*," I told my kids. "So why should we help him?" This provoked Baba's ire. "You mean to tell me, we have a choice between living in Israel versus being stuck here among all these people who murdered us, and you think Jews should live here?"

I replied, "Israel is the eternal Jewish homeland. But do you really want Europe cleaned out of Jews? Isn't Judaism a global religion? Aren't we meant to have global influence?"

"Yes," Baba said, "but that influence comes from the light we project from Israel."

The perception that conditions for Jews had improved in Germany, combined with the strength of the economy, led more Jews to settle in Berlin. Combined with the influx of Soviet Jews, the community began to grow. In 1999, the German government provided funding to train rabbis and cantors, and the first seminary since the Holocaust was established at the University of Potsdam's Abraham Geiger College. After the first three rabbis were ordained in 2006, German Chancellor Angela Merkel said the event was "special because many did not believe that after the Holocaust Jewish life would flourish in Germany." Today, three additional rabbinical seminaries are active in Berlin.

Prior to the war, Berlin had more than one hundred houses of prayer. Today, there are thirteen active synagogues, only four of which existed before the war. Four synagogues are museums, including the New Synagogue, which was constructed in 1866 and destroyed during *Kristallnacht*. It was renovated and serves as a cultural center and museum of Berlin Jewish history.

Berlin also has Jewish preschools and a high school. We stumbled across it by accident and were struck by the high level of security, with guards, a wall, and surveillance cameras. In 2003, the first Jewish-oriented college was opened by New York-based Touro College. There are also several kosher restaurants. In the past, I stayed at the Crown Plaza Hotel, which offered kosher meals and went out of its way to accommodate observant Jewish travelers. You can also walk along streets named after famous Jews such as Moses Mendelssohn, Baruch Spinoza, Rosa Luxemburg, Heinrich Heine, and Gustav Mahler.

The oldest Jewish cemetery in Berlin, on Grosse Hamburger Strasse, was in use between 1672 and 1827. Moses Mendelssohn is buried here. During the war, the Nazis destroyed the cemetery as part of a campaign to erase the Jewish dead, along with the living. German authorities after the war put up a symbolic tombstone in honor of Mendelssohn. I took my children there, and we found it to be an eerie place, nearly empty except for smashed tombstones glued together by post-Holocaust conservationists, and the one standing tombstone of Mendelssohn, replaced after the war. My kids were happy to visit, feeling they were honoring the memory of the dead after the desecration of the SS.

Only fifteen markers remain, most set against a wall. The graves themselves are gone, and the words on the tombstones have faded, and some are illegible. The emptiness of the cemetery is just what the Nazis wanted to achieve. Today, it is a publicly designated green zone. We tried to also visit the Weissensee Cemetery, which is the largest Jewish cemetery in Europe, with more than 115,000 graves, but it was closed when we arrived. I was surprised to see how important it was to my kids to still gather a glimpse of it, as they sought to climb parts of the walls.

This would begin a pattern that distinguished our trip. As much as my kids hated visiting the extermination camps, like Treblinka, where the Jews were turned into ash, they felt special about visiting actual cemeteries where the Jewish dead were properly interred and remembered. Death is death. Murder is murder. That is abominable enough. But cremation makes it that much more impossible to stomach. Cremation is not, and never has been, a Jewish thing. The ancient Romans cremated. The Jews buried. And the Christians, based on the Jewish teachings, did likewise, which is why you have the famous catacombs of Rome, and other areas, where Christians were buried in multiple layers to accommodate their large numbers.

For decades, Germans tried to forget and conceal their past, but that has changed. Public schools are required to teach about the Holocaust and bring schoolchildren to visit the former concentration camps. Reparation payments were made to victims, and laws were enacted to make it a crime to deny the Holocaust or to display Nazi symbols.

In 2005, Berlin opened a Holocaust memorial and museum near the Brandenburg Gate, just a block from Hitler's bunker, and within sight of the Reichstag. The Memorial to the Murdered Jews of Europe consists of 2,711 slabs of gray concrete of varying height, some rising as high as thirteen feet, representing the coffins of those individuals murdered in Nazi concentration camps. Some critics dislike that it does not say who killed the Jews, and that it does not have names or dates. *Tablet's* reviewer was so appalled, the title of the article was "Blow Up the Memorial to the Murdered Jews of Europe." I agree that the monument is inadequate, but the same would be true of any monument. No stone marker or museum can ever replace six million souls. Anything the Germans do will be inadequate. Still, I thought the monument's location—right at the locus of German government power— impressive, and that it was located near the Bundestag at the very heart of the German federal government was an important reminder to Germans that the Holocaust was carried out by their elected government, and with the full participation of the people. I pointed out this proximity to my children amid their protests that it was still inadequate.

Under the memorial is a small, but powerful, museum that provides a concise history of the Holocaust. Even my skeptical children were impressed with the power of the small museum. One picture in particular left us numb. It was of a little girl, about five years of age, who had just stepped off the train in Auschwitz. It was bitterly cold around her, and she had no shoes. Yet she was playing with something in her hands, oblivious to the horror that surrounded her. No doubt she was dead less than an hour after the picture was taken, her lungs filled with poison gas. As a father, my compassion went out to this Jewish girl, and I thought of the magnitude of her parents' pain, unable to protect her little feet from the frost, unable to fill her tiny stomach with any kind of food, and unable to protect her from the monsters they knew would devour her in so short a time.

I hated those who had tortured that little girl. I hated them with every fiber of my being. I felt a mixture of sadness and anger, rage at the very people who had put up the memorial to take a measure of responsibility for the actions of an earlier generation. My children shared this reaction of revulsion and pity. Of all the experiences that made them shudder through our painful Holocaust holiday, it was the plight of the children that affected them the most.

Outside Germany, the memorials say German Nazis, or make reference to German Fascism. The better ones identify the victims as Jews. In Germany, they refer to *Nazis* as if someone came from planet Nazi and imposed their will on the German people and then left. Or as some inexplicable collective madness that afflicted their grandfathers. Just to be clear: It was the Germans who comprised the Nazi Party and its apparatus that perpetrated the Holocaust. It was the German people, who in their tens of millions, served, as Jonah Goldhagen so eloquently put it in his book of the same name, as "Hitler's Willing Executioners."

Still, I believe that we do not visit the sins of the fathers upon the sons. Only the people at the time were responsible.

Berlin has many Holocaust memorials. Track 17 in the Wilmersdorf district commemorates the more than fifty thousand Jews deported from Grunewald Station. Beside the tracks, there are plaques listing every transport between 1941 and 1945, the number of people, and their destination. Bebelplatz, as I mentioned above, is the site of the May 10, 1933, book burnings. A monument at Rosenstrasse 2/4 pays tribute to the protests of non-Jewish women whose Jewish husbands were taken away. The Deserted Room at Koppenplatz contains an overturned bronze chair to remember those Jews taken on *Kristallnacht*. At Grosse Hamburger Strasse 15/16, the Missing House—an empty space between two buildings—lists the names of former residents of the house (some of whom were Jews) that stood there before being destroyed in the war. Even the Israeli Embassy has a memorial—six stone pillars at the entrance to symbolize the six million Jews murdered in the Holocaust. I wished we'd had the time to visit all of these sites.

We also visited the Topography of Terror Museum, where the SS and Gestapo headquarters stood before they were destroyed by Allied bombing. Outside, across the street, there is an exhibit showing the chronological progression of repression. You can see prison cells. You can still see bullet holes in the building nearby, which is now an art gallery. It is hard to imagine the fear people must have felt walking through this neighborhood full of black uniformed men going about their dark business, the nexus of the entire Nazi terror apparatus.

At the site of the 1936 Berlin Olympics, a stadium built in the grand imperial Roman style, by his favorite architect, Albert Speer, Hitler had a great propaganda triumph. Everyone knew about the persecution of the Jews, but no one boycotted the Olympics, supposedly separate and immune from politics. Some Americans protested—the governors of New York (Al Smith) and Massachusetts (James Curley)—and advocated boycotting the Olympics because of the Nazis' anti-Christian policies rather than their persecution of the Jews. President Roosevelt was warned that the Nazis would exploit the Olympics for propaganda, but left the decision of whether to participate to the chairman of the US Olympic Committee, Avery Brundage, who argued that politics had no place in sport, and said there was a "Jewish-Communist conspiracy" to keep the United States out of the Games.

The 1936 Games are remembered for the performance of Jesse Owens, whose victories were seen as a rebuke of Hitler's claims of Aryan supremacy. I regaled my children with tales of Owens's exceptionalism at the Olympics, and how his triumph laid waste to Hitler's claims of a white-Aryan master race. Indeed, when we would later visit the Smithsonian National Museum of Africa-American history in Washington, I was in awe to see the actual cleats worn by Owens at his Olympic triumph where he won four gold medals. My children have borne witness to how much of my career I have spent building bridges between the Jewish and African-American communities, including appointing a young Rhodes scholar named Cory Booker as my Oxford University L'Chaim Society president, in 1992. Today, he is our Senator from New Jersey.

Less well-known is that African-American athletes won fourteen medals, nearly one-fourth of the fifty-six medals the United States took home. One myth that emerged later was that Hitler had refused to shake Owens's hand because he was Black. But Hitler had been advised to either congratulate all or none of the winners, and had decided before Owens competed not to congratulate anyone.

After the Games, journalist William Shirer wrote: "I'm afraid the Nazis have succeeded with their propaganda. First, the Nazis have run the Games on a lavish scale never before experienced, and this has appealed to the athletes. Second, the Nazis have put up a very good front for the general visitors, especially the big businessmen."

The persecution of the Jews was suspended for the period of the Olympics. But William E. Dodd, the US ambassador to Germany, reported that Jews awaited "with fear and trembling" the end of the Olympic truce. Indeed, as soon as the athletes, dignitaries, and visitors left, the persecution of the Jews resumed and intensified.

During our tour, we also literally stumbled on one of the ways the Germans have memorialized the victims of the Holocaust. Throughout Germany there are small bronze plaques, *Stolpersteine* (stumbling blocks), embedded in the sidewalks and streets outside the last-known residences of individuals who perished at the hands of the Nazis. We randomly came across some on the street. Paid for by the city, each is carved and engraved by hand, by German artist Gunter Demnig. They all begin with the words, "Here lived…" and relate the names and stories of the victims.

The first *Stolpersteine* was placed in 1996. Since then, more than five thousand have been placed throughout the capital. The stones can be found in 916 places in Germany, but not in Munich, where, as Marjorie Ingall noted in *Tablet*, the leader of the Jewish community, a Holocaust survivor named Charlotte Knobloch, argued that allowing people to walk on the names of the murdered would be an insult. Still, more than sixty-three thousand have been planted in more than 1,100 locations in seventeen European countries. My children and I found the stones to be moving, their striking bronze color making them particularly visible. A few months after our visit to Berlin, a dozen stones were stolen. I don't know if the thieves were ever found, but donors stepped forward to pay to replace them. Around six hundred stones have been stolen since the project began.

One site the Germans destroyed to prevent it from becoming a place of neo-Nazi veneration was Hitler's bunker in the garden of the Reich Chancellery, where he and his mistress, Eva Braun, killed themselves as the Soviet tanks rumbled through the streets. The remains of the Chancellery itself, after being bombed into near oblivion by the Allies, were torn down in 1949. All that remains is a parking lot in a serene residential neighborhood, with an information board to remind you that in this thriving center of European civilization, with its prosperous and educated populace, they once went crazy and killed everyone who looked like us.

The final resting place of Hitler's charred body remains a mystery. Norman Stone, Oxford's late Regius Professor of History who wrote the introduction to my book *Moses of Oxford*, told me that he was invited to inspect the Soviet archives on Hitler, and discovered they had Hitler's jaw, which he held in his hand. Stone says Stalin ordered his troops to make sure Hitler was dead, and to take his remains. Since his body was too badly burned to be recognizable, he was identified by his dental records, apparently with the help of his dentist. The jaw was taken by the Soviet secret police.

Even people who know all about the war and the Holocaust are fascinated by its relics. This morbid curiosity is creepy, but understandable. What is not understandable is the continuing fascination and sympathy for the Nazi ideology. In Germany, it is banned. In America, the First Amendment gives neo-Nazis the freedom to say and do what they want, as long as they don't engage in violence. Once the internet became a public tool, they exploited it to spread their hate worldwide. The country that did the most to wipe out the evil of Nazism is becoming—at least, to some degree—an incubator for a global network of white supremacists, neo-Nazis, and Hitler admirers.

Notwithstanding laws intended to prevent a Nazi revival, neo-Nazis remain active throughout Germany. A few weeks after we left Berlin, five hundred neo-Nazis held a march commemorating the death of former Hitler deputy Rudolf Hess. Police shut down the march and arrested forty people. Some residents and activists also confronted the Nazis to block the march. A survey of German Jews in *Die Welt* the week before reported that 60 percent have thought about emigrating because they no longer feel safe; 75 percent saw anti-Semitism as a major problem, and have little hope for the future; and 29 percent said they have been harassed or offended for being Jewish. The German government's anti-Semitism representative, Felix Klein, warned them not to wear a *kippah* "at every time and place in Germany…My opinion on the matter has changed following the ongoing brutalization in German society."

The attitude of Jews in Berlin was perhaps best expressed by Rabbi Daniel Alter, who was attacked in front of his seven-year-old daughter as he prepared for the Jewish High Holy Days, in 2012. Mike Ross of the *Boston Globe* asked him if Jews will ever feel at home in Germany. "My suitcase is definitely unpacked," he replied, "but I know where it is."

In Berlin alone, there were 947 anti-Semitic incidents in 2017. Anti-Semitism, Charlotte Knobloch told me, is "in the heart of German society."

She described a climate of "aggressive anti-Semitism," including physical attacks, which "has been strengthened from the right and left and in the Muslim community."

It would be wrong to suggest that anti-Semitism is purely a European phenomenon that grew out of Christian doctrine. It is also a problem throughout the Muslim world, where the words of the Koran have been used to promote Jew-hatred. For example, the Koran says: "They [the Children of Israel] were consigned to humiliation and wretchedness. They brought the wrath of God upon themselves, and this because they used to deny God's signs and kill His Prophets unjustly and because they disobeyed and were transgressors" (Sura 2:61). According to the Koran, the Jews try to introduce corruption (5:64); have always been disobedient (5:78); and are enemies of Allah, the Prophet, and the angels (2:97–98). Jews are also compared to apes and pigs (5:60).

To be sure, these are selective quotes from the Koran, and the case could also be made that Jews, for centuries, fared far better under Muslim rule than Christian. But these beliefs about the inferiority of the Jews, especially as they are promoted by radicals and extremists, is one important reason why the possibility of peace between Israel and its surrounding Muslim nations can prove so difficult. The demonization of Jews often leads to violence.

Much of the increase in anti-Semitism in Germany is attributed to the large influx of Muslim immigrants, "bringing a different type of anti-Semitism into the country," Chancellor Angela Merkel told Israeli TV. The government's position against anti-Semitism is clear—it pays millions every year to Holocaust survivors and the state of Israel. But Merkel is wrong to blame immigrants for the upsurge in violence. In the first half of 2018, wherein anti-Semitic crimes increased by 10 percent in Germany, the vast majority were committed by right-wing extremists; that is, native Germans. A German intelligence report found that 126,000 Germans had extreme political views in 2017, an increase of 9 percent. The report also categorized twenty-four thousand people as right-wing extremists, though only six hundred as neo-Nazis.

I remembered coming to speak in Dresden a few years earlier, at a national Jewish Shabbat retreat that happened the same weekend there was to be a right-wing, fascist-style demonstration with participants from all over Germany. We were at a hotel resort a few miles from the city center, so we were in no immediate danger. But the police were so worried about harm coming to any Jewish guest that they stationed a large number of police to protect us. It was unforgettable.

The official attitude of the government is obviously not shared by all citizens. Some struggle to come to terms with their past, especially as their excuses are exploded by historical revelations. It is no longer possible for them to claim to have been unaware of Hitler's genocidal intentions and his implementation of the Final Solution. The German press and indeed the world press covered the imposition of the Nuremberg Laws, the pogroms on *Kristallnacht*, and Hitler's speech expressing his goal of exterminating the Jews.

In a diary called *My Opposition*, which came to light only in 2011, Friedrich Kellner of Berlin writes of how he was appalled by the Nazis' scapegoating of the Jews. He believed it was the type of diversionary tactic used throughout the ages by rulers seeking to hide their guilt. "The entire action against the Jews was no different from throwing down a piece of meat for the beasts" wrote Kellner. "This cruel, despicable, and sadistic treatment against the Jews that has lasted now several years—with its final goal of extermination—is the biggest stain on the honor of Germany.... They will never be able to erase these crimes." In another entry, Kellner correctly predicted: "when the retribution comes, the innocent will have to suffer along with them."

Kellner also learned about the deportation and mistreatment of Jews outside Germany. "A solider on leave here said he personally witnessed a terrible atrocity in the occupied part of Poland," wrote Kellner in 1941. "He watched as naked Jewish men and women were placed in front of a long deep ditch, and upon the order of the SS, were shot by Ukrainians in the back of their heads, and they fell into the ditch. Then the ditch was filled in as screams kept coming from it."

As a Jew visiting Germany, I have very strong emotions that I cannot shake: Is this really the place from which the world's greatest evil spread in the lifetime of many of the people still known to me? Could any people so advanced and civilized have concealed in them an inner beast waiting to break free at the first demagogic moment? Did Jews suffer and die on the very boulevards that I now stroll as a tourist? And is it right that I feel a certain distance from the innocent Germans that now surround me?

I conveyed my deep discomfort to my kids, even as I continued to emphasize that I did not hold today's Germans accountable for the Holocaust. But my protests increasingly fell on deaf ears as they continued to absorb the full horrors of the anti-Jewish genocide, committed in the midst of a supposedly enlightened society.

"How can you defend this?" Baba asked me. "Don't you realize what it would have taken for six million Jews to be murdered, how many people had to have participated to make it possible? These are the parents and grandparents of the people we're meeting now." I understood my children's emotions. For Jews, going to Germany is a real challenge. Going to Germany and focusing almost exclusively on places of Holocaust memory is excruciating.

It was at that point I understood that the German and Jewish people were forever locked in what Martin Luther King Jr. called a "single garment of destiny." Today's Germans feel self-conscious around Jews because of the enormous guilt this generation feels about what their parents and grandparents perpetrated. Jews have conflicting emotions of anger for what happened, and remorse for implicating, ever so slightly, a generation of Germans who, for the most part, want to make things better. After all, they are not the ones who perpetrated the Holocaust. As the prophet Ezekiel (18:20) says, "The one who sins is the one who will die. The child will not share the guilt of the parent, nor will the parent share the guilt of the child. The righteousness of the righteous will be credited to them, and the wickedness of the wicked will be charged against them."

But in a larger sense, Jews and Germans are connected by something far deeper and more mystical, two vexing and insoluble questions that tug at their basic humanity. For the Germans, the question is, *How could we have done this? How could we have hated so deeply as to have become so unquenchably bloodthirsty?*

For the Jews, the question is equally unanswerable: *How could God have allowed this? Where was He when it happened? And how could human beings have perpetrated a slaughter so unimaginable?*

The only theological response to the Holocaust is to challenge God, to show righteous indignation toward God, and to rise to our Hebraic calling of being *Israelites*, people who wrestle with God.

I am a religious Jew. I would never advocate severing our relationship with God over the Holocaust, but believe we must strengthen it by being more honest and not ignoring what happened on God's watch. Our intimate relationship with God requires honesty, forthrightness, and humility.

And so two nations—oppressor and oppressed, perpetrator and victim—remain forever connected by a cosmic question mark hoisted above their very existence.

CHAPTER 4

SACHSENHAUSEN: THE CONCENTRATION CAMP NEXT DOOR

On June 27, we left Berlin and drove until we came to a country road roughly a half-hour outside the city, that leads to the Sachsenhausen concentration camp. Terrible things happened along this way: We stopped by a sign that read *TODESMARSCH, April 1945*, with a map and a drawing of prisoners in blue-striped shirts with triangles on their breasts. This was the route of the death march from Sachsenhausen, to move the prisoners further into the center of Germany after the camp was evacuated as the Red Army approached from the East. Many people died in their tracks here, where today there is a bike trail where cyclists can enjoy a pleasant ride.

My children and I love cycling, and often do long rides. We discussed how bizarre it would be to ride this path, knowing the horrors it had witnessed. Was it right to turn it into a recreational path?

It was a beautiful sunny day, and the yahrzeit (annual memorial) of the Lubavitcher Rebbe, Rabbi Menachem Schneerson, my spiritual mentor, whose inspiration and global vision for disseminating Judaism and universal values was pivotal in my becoming a rabbi. On this day, even as we got our first look at the machinery of murder, we remembered the Rebbe's dream of a world without suffering and death. We have to reach for that ideal, however impossible it may seem. Faith means we can perfect the world little by little until Moshiach (the Messiah) comes, and we can all be reunited with the Rebbe.

I was pleased to see the German government saw fit to place markers like this to acknowledge these terrible episodes of Nazi cruelty. I'm not sure how many people know these markers exist, or bother to stop, like we did. I would have found them more helpful if they had English translations, but the markers are there to remind German people of their history. The prisoners were emaciated and riddled with disease. They had been brought to Sachsenhausen to die, and the Germans were making sure they did, even as they were about to lose the war.

When we arrived in Oranienburg, the site of the Sachsenhausen camp, we were struck again by the beauty and tranquility of the neighborhood. As we were filming a Facebook Live video, Shaina said, "It's so peaceful here."

That's the thing about concentration and extermination camps, I told her. It's the same way at Auschwitz. Complete silence. Utter serenity. Like a graveyard. You are there to try to understand what took place, and put yourself in the shoes of the Jews imprisoned here, but the echo of the horror is faint in this beautiful, tranquil place. And you feel guilty enjoying the tranquility and beauty.

Many visitors to Berlin are unaware there is a concentration camp nearby, but there's no way you can miss Sachsenhausen if you go to Oranienberg. The camp's guard towers face a street of houses. Sometimes you hear stories that the Germans did not know about the Final Solution and what was being done to the Jews. This is a bald-faced lie. Prison camps were typically located in towns and villages, impossible to ignore. The smell of starvation and death must have wafted across the street, and the ashes from the crematoria fell like snowflakes on people's heads.

We arrived at 8:30 p.m., too late to enter the camp. We saw the entrance gate with the sign that told that cruel lie—*Arbeit Macht Frei*—Work Sets You Free. The next thing we saw was the sign for a café. It weirded me out to think of eating dinner at a concentration camp. I'm not knocking it, because I understand the need for tourism at these places, and travelers have needs. I would much rather there be concession stands and have tourists come, than remove them and have nobody visit. Still, it is disconcerting.

Since we could not go inside, we had to content ourselves with looking at photos and captions on the outer walls of the prison. Had we gone in, we could have seen the roll call area, the site of the gallows, the jail, some of the barracks, and the crematorium.

Sachsenhausen was completed in 1938, by slave laborers from smaller camps in the area, many of whom died during construction from starvation, disease, or the actions of the SS guards. Sachsenhausen ultimately had forty-four subcamps. The scope of the continent-wide system of camps, ghettos, and killing centers was immense. Each of the twenty-three main camps had subcamps—nearly nine hundred in total, some with euphemistic names, such as *care facilities for foreign children*, where pregnant prisoners were sent for forced abortions. As the Germans conquered country after country, the need for more camps grew. Researchers have discovered that the number of camps was an astonishing 42,500, including 30,000 slave labor camps, 1,150 Jewish ghettos, 980 concentration camps, 1,000 POW camps, 500 brothels, and thousands of others. Sachsenhausen was just one of nearly 3,000 camps in the Berlin area alone.

The original prisons were called *concentration camps*, an anodyne phrase that suggested those incarcerated there were merely to be physically concentrated in one location. Jews were not the first to be sent to the camps. They were initially used for political opponents, such as Communists, as well as people considered deviants, such as homosexuals. Very few people survived imprisonment in these facilities. An estimated fifteen to twenty million Europeans died in the various camps and ghettos.

Sachsenhausen was completed just before *Kristallnacht*. In November 1938, six thousand Jews were sent to Sachsenhausen, and several hundred were killed there. Following the invasion of Poland, thousands of Polish-Jewish prisoners were sent to the camp. Before the end of the year, the number more than doubled from five thousand to nearly twelve thousand. Many died during a typhus epidemic when the SS refused to provide the prisoners any medical care. The number of dead from shootings, hangings, malnutrition, disease, and other causes increased to the point where a crematorium needed to be built in April 1940.

Sachsenhausen was primarily a labor camp rather than an extermination center. Prisoners were forced to work in SS workshops for German companies, such as the aircraft manufacturer Heinkel, which used six or eight thousand of them to work on the He 177 bomber. German reports said the "prisoners are working without fault," but the crash of some of these aircraft led to suspicions that the prisoners had sabotaged them. The prisoners who were unable to work had to stand at attention for the entire work day.

Later in the war, the Nazis also engaged in a cash counterfeiting scheme to undermine the British and American economies. Operation Bernhard involved 140 Jewish craftsmen found among prisoners at different camps, who were sent to Sachsenhausen to forge American and British currency under the supervision of SS Sturmbannführer Bernhard Krüger. The dollars were never perfected, but the Germans introduced fake British £5, £10, £20, and £50 notes into circulation in 1943, and the Bank of England never found them. *The Counterfeiters*, an Austrian-German film about the operation, won the 2007 Academy Award for Best Foreign Language Film.

An electric fence ran along the inside of the camp. Anyone who came too close to the fence would be shot by the guards. Prisoners caught trying to escape would be hanged in front of their comrades.

The Nazis' idea of a joke was to name the area for executing inmates, *Station Z*. They found it amusing that the entrance to the camp was through Building A, and the exit for those executed was through Station Z. The SS invited high-ranking Nazi officials to witness the efficiency of their new killing center on May 29, 1942, and shot ninety-six Jews execution-style. Less than a year later, a gas chamber was added to Station Z.

By mid-January 1945, more than sixty-five thousand prisoners, including more than thirteen thousand women, were imprisoned at Sachsenhausen. In the early years of the war, most of the Jewish prisoners were sent to camps in the East, and in October 1942, all the remaining Jews were sent to Auschwitz. The camp was repopulated with Jews in the spring of 1944, when Hungarian and Polish Jews were transferred from ghettos and camps to Sachsenhausen to meet the demand for slave labor. Approximately eleven thousand were in the camp at the beginning of 1945.

As the Red Army approached Berlin in the spring of 1945, the SS ordered thirty-three thousand inmates on April 20–21, to start marching northeast. Thousands died along the way, either from natural causes (if you can call death after the ravages of prison camp life natural), or from being shot by their guards. Soldiers from the Red Army and Polish Infantry entered Sachsenhausen on April 22, 1945, and found three thousand emaciated survivors, nearly half of them women. Sadly, as occurred following the liberation of other camps, many of these people were in such horrible condition that they died soon after finally tasting freedom.

Altogether, approximately two hundred thousand people passed through Sachsenhausen between 1938 and 1945. Some one hundred thousand inmates died there from exhaustion, disease, malnutrition, abuse, or execution.

In late 1945, a Soviet military tribunal tried and convicted sixteen Sachsenhausen camp functionaries.

After the war, the Soviets used part of the camp to incarcerate Nazis and political prisoners. Over the course of five years, sixty thousand people, including six thousand German officers, were interned in the camp. At least twelve thousand died of malnutrition and disease by the time the camp closed in 1950. In 1990, mass graves were discovered from the Soviet era, and a separate museum was opened to document the period.

The remaining buildings from the Sachsenhausen camp were preserved as part of a national memorial inaugurated in 1961, by the East German government. As in other camps located in the Soviet bloc, the Communists downplayed the murder and deportation of Jews. Their motives? Hard to say. But they undoubtedly included a wish to minimize sympathy for the Jewish people, and by extension the State of Israel, which the Soviets treated as a mortal enemy, backing the Arabs instead. They also wanted to pretend that Hitler's principal war was against Russia and communism, and that the Soviet Union was the primary victim of Hitler's atrocities. The murder of six million Jews did not fit their narrative. The historical record was corrected much later, after German unification.

Throughout our trip, I was particularly interested in learning what happened to the companies that collaborated with the Nazis. In the case of Sachsenhausen, I wanted to find out if the Heinkel aircraft company survived. The founder, Ernst Heinrich Heinkel, was tried for war crimes and apparently acquitted because of his wartime opposition to Hitler. Germany was prohibited from manufacturing aircraft by the Allies, so Heinkel started a new company in 1950, to build bicycles, motorcycles, and a minicar. The company later built aircraft for the West German Air Force, and ultimately became part of the European Aeronautic Defense and Space Company known today as Airbus, the European multinational corporation that produces civil and military aircraft. Although the Heinkel company is mentioned on the Airbus website's timeline of aeronautical history, I did not find any reference to its wartime activities.

German industries who exploited slave labor during the war got a pass from the highest court in West Germany. One of Heinkel's slaves, Edmund Bartl, a political prisoner at Sachsenhausen, claimed he was beaten, suffered from thirst and hunger, and became nearly blind from sparks from the welding machine he was forced to operate without safety goggles. In 1959, after Heinkel's death, Bartl sought compensation from the company, in a German court, for his pain and suffering and denial of wages. He won a limited judgement in a lower court, and then the appellate court expanded the ruling to grant him greater compensation. German industry was frightened that all the surviving slave laborers would come after them and put them out of business. Fortunately for them, the Supreme Court dismissed Bartl's claims on the grounds that he had filed his claim too late. "The German judges," wrote Benjamin Ferencz, the chief prosecutor for the US at the Einsatzgruppen war crimes trial, "had succumbed to the temptation to temper justice not with mercy but with expediency." To add insult to injury, Bartl was ruined financially and had to pay court and attorney fees for both sides.

The visit to Sachsenhausen was the family's first glimpse of the Nazi prison and extermination system. We saw it from afar, beyond the walls, and did not see the barracks or the crematorium, and it did not have a particularly dramatic impact on any of us. The kids understood that horrible things had happened here, close to the Nazi center of power. But Sachsenhausen lacks the infamy of some of its sister camps. It certainly did not prepare us for what we would see later.

CHAPTER 5

DRESDEN: ALLIED WAR CRIMES OR DIVINE JUSTICE?

It was another nice day on June 28, when we took the two-hour drive from Berlin to Dresden, a beautiful city along the Elbe River that was destroyed in the war and rebuilt to resemble the pre-war city known as the *Jewel Box,* for its Baroque and rococo facades. Walking the clean streets and admiring the architecture, you would have no idea that in the spring of 1945, there was nothing but rubble where we were standing. The beauty is an illusion, like Disneyland. It is all rebuilt, having been flattened by British and American bombers.

I had explained beforehand that we were stopping in Dresden because it had been firebombed by the Allies, and was the site of a massacre of German civilians that raised profound ethical questions. To his dying day, Churchill refused to apologize for Dresden, believing that total war and the bombing of German cities was essential to breaking the enemy's will to fight. But was there also a motivation of vengeance for the nightly bombing of London during the Blitz? And if there was, could it be forgiven? How would my children feel when they heard that approximately twenty-five thousand German civilians died in the bombing. Would they feel that, having brought Hitler to power and supported his war, they deserved it? Or would they feel that civilians are never legitimate targets, and that Dresden was a war crime as grave as the Holocaust itself?

That said, few people know about the Jews of Dresden, or what happened to them during the war. In some ways, their history illustrates the peculiar persistence of Jews in the face of continued repression.

The Jewish community of Dresden is old, dating to the mid-12th century. The record is unclear, but it appears the entire population was wiped out or expelled in 1349, because there is no reference again to a Jewish community until 1375. The massacre occurred when Jews were falsely accused of spreading the plague by deliberately poisoning wells. According to *Encyclopedia Judaica,* the Jews were expelled again in 1430, and did not return until the early 18th century. The community grew as Eastern European Jews moved to the city after World War I, and at least six thousand Jews lived in Dresden in 1925.

On *Kristallnacht,* 151 Jews were arrested and shipped to Buchenwald. The city synagogue, which had been designed by the same architect as the city's magnificent opera house, was one of more than seventeen hundred throughout Germany destroyed by the Nazis on *Kristallnacht.* Nearly two-thirds of the Jewish population of roughly seven thousand escaped before the Final Solution, but few of the Jews who were deported from Dresden survived. A handful escaped the final scheduled deportation, thanks to the Allied bombing of Dresden. Only forty-one remained at the end of the war.

After the war, as they had many times in the past, a small number of Jews returned to Dresden. In 1950, a new synagogue was opened. It was not until the fall of the Berlin Wall and the immigration of Jews from the Soviet Union that the population began to grow again. In 2002, the synagogue destroyed on *Kristallnacht* was redesigned and reopened on its original site, with the Star of David from the original synagogue above the new building's entrance.

The Allies did not bomb Dresden, or anything else, to save the Jews. They did it to break the will of the German people to fight. In early 1945, the Germans were in retreat, but still showed no signs of surrender. The Allies were already bombing German cities when the most destructive attack of all was launched against Dresden, on February 13. At the Yalta conference, Stalin had pushed for more Allied air raids against German cities that were ferrying troops to the Eastern front, and Dresden was a rail center that had yet to be bombed. The city, famed for its Baroque beauty, had been spared thus far. It was crowded with refugees and virtually defenseless after its anti-aircraft guns were sent to the western front.

More than twelve hundred British and American bombers took part in the two-day raid, which created a firestorm that burned for a week and turned the city center to ashes. Thousands were believed buried under the rubble of collapsed buildings, or incinerated by the fires. No one knows exactly how many died in Dresden. The official death toll is estimated to be up to twenty-five thousand. But some, less credible, estimates go beyond one hundred thousand. Afterward, the Germans forced Allied POWs to dig out the bodies at Dresden. One of them was the novelist Kurt Vonnegut, who was forever haunted by his experience; it appears in his work again and again.

It is an interesting philosophical, legal, and moral question as to whether the bombing of Dresden should be regarded as a war crime. The political answer is that the victors make the rules, and the powerful can get away with actions that weaker nations cannot. Allied leaders believed that shortening the war by breaking the German people's will to fight would ultimately save lives on their side. That was certainly Harry Truman's calculation when he ordered that atomic bombs be dropped on Hiroshima and Nagasaki, and refused to ever apologize, believing, to the last, that he had saved at least a million American servicemen who would have been killed invading the Japanese mainland. While the Japanese memorials mourn the loss of life, they do not condemn the United States.

Dresden was not the only target of the Allies' strategic bombing campaign. At least fifty thousand people died in Hamburg and Berlin, twenty thousand in Cologne, fifteen thousand in Magdeburg, four thousand in Würzburg, and eighty-seven thousand in the towns of the Ruhr. Altogether, six hundred thousand civilians, many of whom were women and children, were killed, and eight hundred thousand were injured. These are just figures for Germany, which ignore the tens of thousands who died instantly after the United States dropped atomic bombs on Hiroshima and Nagasaki, or the tens of thousands who died in conventional bombing runs on cities like Tokyo.

So should moral armies bomb civilians? Certainly, when it comes to Israel, which always makes every effort to lessen civilian casualties—even putting their own soldiers and pilots in severe jeopardy to protect civilian life—the world has a double standard. Every time Israel is involved in a conflict, the government is accused of using disproportionate force. Military force is a blunt object. What is the correct, proportionate use of military force?

Since the stated goal of Hamas and Hezbollah is the destruction of Israel, isn't the appropriate response the destruction of both organizations?

Wouldn't random missile strikes on Lebanese and Palestinian cities be proportionate to the indiscriminate Hamas and Hezbollah rocket attacks on Northern and Southern Israel? Even so, Israel stays its hand.

Dresden shows that the Allies were willing to do almost anything to win the war. Israel would not and could not ever do what the Allies did at Dresden. It is not just that Israel is held to a higher standard and is routinely pilloried by the UN and various human rights organizations, regardless of its intentions or efforts to avoid civilian casualties. Rather, it's because conducting an all-out, merciless war is contrary to the value Judaism places on human life.

What would I have done if I were the president of the United States, or prime minister of Britain, in 1945?

I asked my kids, "What would you have done? Knowing that about ten thousand Jews were being gassed every day for four years, would you have bombed the German cities to get them to stop?"

These questions haunted us throughout our trip. Would I have ordered the use of the atomic bomb, or the firebombing of Dresden, if I thought that it would end the war sooner and save countless lives? Would I have done so, knowing it could hasten the end of the war and stop the Holocaust?

For my children, the thought of Germans paying a price for the Holocaust was compelling. Why *should* they just get away with it?

"Tatty," Yosef, Shaina, and Baba told me, "if people are not punished for the worst crime in the history of the world, if they are left to live their lives in peace while Jewish children are turned into ash, then it will just happen again."

CHAPTER 6

PRAGUE: HITLER'S FAILED MUSEUM

Prague is one of the most beautiful cities in Europe, with a long and colorful Jewish history dating to the year 970. My kids were relieved to be in this great city, largely preserved from destruction during the war—home of Kafka, site of famed Jewish synagogues and cemeteries, and a city of startling beauty. After visiting concentration camps and sites of mass bombings, they were now walking gleefully through the streets of Prague, with the carnival atmosphere of fellow tourists. They couldn't believe that we were suddenly in a tourist hub. They were also happy to be in a place where we had family history. My wife Debbie's mother was born in Prague in 1946, just one year after the war, one of the first children of Holocaust survivors.

At the same time, I began to witness a growing awareness in my children that was unpleasant to behold. They were becoming conscious that they are part of a tragic people. Other people could come to Europe to see the sights, buy roast chestnuts in the winter and ice cream in the summer. Jews come to Europe and have to confront that two generations ago, and for two thousand years before that, we were slaughtered en masse throughout the continent. We travel from cemetery to cemetery, memorial to memorial. No wonder so many Jews choose to assimilate and become invisible. Who would want to live with so much pain? Who would want to be a living target? Wasn't it easier just to disappear?

But my kids, raised in a committed and observant Jewish home, had no such choice. They could not disappear. They could only choose not to visit Europe. Not to go to these horrible places where, beneath the carnival-like atmosphere, lay rivers of blood. And I could sense their growing resentment that I had brought them here.

Today, Prague is more like a museum of Jewish life, as it was before World War II. This was Hitler's intention. He wanted the people of the Third Reich to see what the Jewish people he made extinct had left behind. Prague was to be a museum of a lost race, an extinguished ethnicity, so it was no small satisfaction to bring my Jewish family here as testament to the indestructibility of the Jewish people.

As was the case throughout Europe, the suffering of the Jews in Prague did not begin or end with Hitler. The Jews were persecuted by the Crusaders toward the end of the 12th century. In 1142, parts of the Jewish quarter, as well as the oldest synagogue, were burned down. In 1179, the Church instructed Christians to avoid touching Jews who were confined to a ghetto that was locked at night. In 1215, the Fourth Lateran Council required Jews to wear distinctive clothes, prohibited them from holding public office, and limited the amount they could charge for interest on loans.

The situation improved in the mid-13th century when King Přemysl Otakar II granted Jews religious freedom and allowed them some autonomy, while also granting them protection. A synagogue, The Altneuschul (Old New Synagogue), opened around 1270, and is the oldest preserved synagogue in Europe, and in my opinion, the most wondrous.

During Easter 1389, Jews were accused of desecrating the Host. In the Catholic faith, the wine and wafers consumed during the mass are considered the blood and flesh of Christ, transubstantiated through the ceremony. So if you harm the cracker, you are brutalizing the actual body of Jesus. Catholics used to accuse Jews of breaking into churches and abusing the wafer to torture Jesus. Don't laugh—thousands of Jews have been murdered throughout history over this absurd libel. In this case, the clergy incited a pogrom, the Jewish quarter was razed to the ground, and most of the three thousand Jews living in Prague were killed. One survivor, Rabbi Avigdor Kara, wrote an elegy describing the attack that is read every year in Prague, on Yom Kippur.

Over the next two centuries, Jews returned to Prague, and they found themselves forced to seek protection from different groups vying for power. Unsure of which group would dominate, their allegiances shifted between the nobility and the bourgeoisie of the city.

The Jewish community experienced a growth spurt in the 16th century, and Jews were allowed to acquire land adjacent to the ghetto. During the reign of Ferdinand I, Jews were briefly expelled twice from the city. The community grew to around seven thousand and flourished after his death under the more tolerant rule of the Hapsburg's Maximilian II (1564–1576) and Rudolf II (1576–1612), as mathematicians, astronomers, geographers, historians, philosophers, and artists were drawn to Prague.

The city also became a center for Jewish mysticism, in part because of the work of Rabbi Judah Loew ben Bezalel (1525–1609), also known as the Maharal. The Maharal was a great Talmudic scholar, but was also known for his secular knowledge of mathematics, astronomy, and other sciences. He was a friend of the astronomers Tycho Brahe and Johannes Kepler, who introduced him to Emperor Rudolph II. According to Jewish folklore, Rabbi Loew created the Golem, an artificial man made out of clay from the banks of the Vltava River, whom he brought to life through magical Kabbalistic formulas in order to protect the Jews.

By the late 17th century, despite a plague outbreak, a devastating fire, and a series of persecutions, the Jewish population had grown to 11,600, making Prague one of the largest Jewish communities in Europe. A census in 1729 found that Jews were artisans, tailors, shoemakers, hatters, goldsmiths, butchers, barber-surgeons, and musicians.

This golden age ended during the reign of the avowed anti-Semite Empress Maria Theresa, who expelled the Jews in 1745. They were allowed to return by her son Emperor Joseph II, who issued the Edict of Toleration in October 1781, and allowed Jews to participate in trade, commerce, agriculture, and the arts.

By 1848, the Jewish population had nearly grown back to its pre-expulsion size, and Prague was once again one of the largest Jewish communities in Europe. That year, Jews were granted equal rights under the first Austrian Constitution, and were no longer forced to live in ghettos. They were subsequently allowed to own property, and the community moved from the original part of town into a more modern residential and commercial quarter.

Jews became caught up in the culture war between those Czechs who wanted to preserve their culture and language, and those who wanted to adopt the German language. One of those who became prominent in German literature was Franz Kafka. Jews also became increasingly active in Zionism by the end of the century. In 1933, Prague hosted the

Eighteenth Zionist Congress. Jews also became active in national politics, forming a Jewish party that was represented in the parliament after World War I. By 1930, 356,830 persons in the Czechoslovak Republic identified themselves as Jews.

The beginning of the end for most of Prague's Jews was September 30, 1938, when the Munich Agreement was signed and the fate of Czechoslovakia handed over to Adolf Hitler. On March 15, 1939, the entire country was occupied by German forces, with the western region of the country called the Protectorate of Bohemia and Moravia. Adolf Eichmann established a branch of the Central Office for Jewish Emigration to encourage Jews to leave the country. And thousands did, including approximately nineteen thousand who escaped to Palestine. When the war began, more than ninety-two thousand Jews lived in Prague, almost 20 percent of the city's population. Less than one-third survived the war.

One man was prescient about the future of Czech Jewry after Munich. Nicholas Winton, a British stockbroker, anticipated the German occupation of Bohemia and Moravia, and was shocked by the violence against the Jewish community in Germany and Austria during *Kristallnacht*. After learning of the *Kindertransport*, the rescue effort launched in Britain to rescue German and Austrian Jewish children, Winton decided to organize his own rescue operation for children in Czechoslovakia. In March 1939, he created a Children's Section under the British Committee for Refugees from Czechoslovakia in Prague, and let it be known that he could provide safe haven for Jewish children. He also raised money to fund the operation in London, and sought out British families for foster homes. Remarkably, he did this all in his spare time, after working in his regular job at a stock exchange.

The operation got underway just in time, with the first transport leaving Prague by plane for London on March 14, 1939, the day before the Germans occupied the Czech lands. Winton managed to get seven additional groups of children out on trains that took them to ships crossing the English Channel to Britain. The operation ended when the war started. The last transport left Prague on August 2, 1939. It is believed that Winton saved 669 children, but his efforts were not revealed until 1988. He was later named a Righteous Person by Yad Vashem, made an honorary citizen of Prague, and knighted by Queen Elizabeth.

Unfortunately, it was not possible to save most of the Jews of Prague. The Nazis expelled Jews from most professions, associations, and organizations, and required them to wear the yellow Star of David. The man put in charge of suppressing resistance to Nazi occupation in the area was Reinhard Heydrich, head of the Reich Main Security Office, who would chair the Wannsee Conference. On May 27, 1942, he was assassinated.

There is a thrilling movie called *Anthropoid,* about the plan to kill Heydrich. Operation Anthropoid was planned by the Czechoslovak government-in-exile in London, with the help of the Special Operations Executive, the British espionage agency, and carried out to demonstrate that senior Nazis were not beyond the reach of Allied forces, and that Czechs were prepared to resist the Germans. Heydrich was chosen as the target because of his high position and reputation for cruelty and ruthlessness. He was just thirty-eight when he died. And yet, by that age, he had become a monster. He was cold as ice, seemingly bereft of even a semblance of human compassion. Hitler described him as "the man with the iron heart."

Jozef Gabčík and Jan Kubiš were chosen from among the exiled Czech soldiers based in Britain to go to Prague, where they met with other members of the resistance. The assassination attempt took place as Heydrich made his daily commute from his home to Prague Castle. Gabčík stepped in front of Heydrich's Mercedes convertible and tried to open fire with his Sten submachine gun, but it jammed and Heydrich shot at Gabčík. Kubiš threw a grenade at the Mercedes that fell short. Gabčík and Kubiš were convinced their mission had failed, and fled to a safe house. They did not know that shrapnel from the grenade blew through the car, causing some of the material from the seat to become lodged in Heydrich's body. As it decomposed, the material slowly poisoned him. He suffered an agonizing death over the course of nearly nine days.

It was difficult to find the place where Heydrich was assassinated because the streets have completely changed since the war. For example, the tram is gone. You have to look at old photos. A stone monument was erected in the approximate spot where he was killed, and there is a small display explaining what happened, along with an outstanding and moving sculpture of the three parachutists with their arms out wide in a circle. It's not easy to find, but if you're careful, you can view it from the highway that passes nearby.

Just a few days before we arrived in Prague, the city marked the 75th anniversary of the murder of the men who killed Heydrich. The Czech assassins are considered heroes, and when we arrived, wreaths and flowers were still outside the church where they were murdered. I always come to pay my respects. Can you imagine the courage it takes to parachute into a country and kill the number three man in the Nazi hierarchy? It is unfortunate their names are not familiar to Americans, because they were two of the greatest heroes of the 20th century. Most Nazis got away with their crimes—Hitler, Himmler, Goebbels, and Göring all took the coward's way out by committing suicide.

As we spent a beautiful night walking across the Charles Bridge, Dovid Chaim asked me why the Czech paratroopers, sanctioned by the Czech government-in-exile, killed Heydrich if they knew the Nazis would retaliate, and whether I thought assassinating him was worth the cost. Some people opposed the operation because of the likely reprisals.

I replied that it was absolutely worth the risk. Hitler was murdering millions all over Europe, anyway. It was important to kill a senior Nazi to make the rest of the leadership fearful, and to demonstrate that they would have to pay for their crimes. It was also crucial to show the terrified citizens of Europe living under brutal Nazi occupation that the leadership were mere mortals who could, and should, be killed. It's a shame that more Nazi leaders were not eliminated.

At this point, the children began to show signs of emotional and moral fatigue. My nineteen-year-old daughter, Baba, witnessing the all-encompassing carnage of the Holocaust, had been questioning the existence and goodness of God. Yosef, then only sixteen, was complaining about how hard he was found it visiting these places. I wanted to show the kids that there was some palpable divine justice, and that some of the villains did pay for their crimes.

The Allies were never able to kill Hitler. The closest anyone got was on July 20, 1944, after Colonel Claus von Stauffenberg placed a briefcase carrying a bomb, under the conference table, during a meeting at the Wolf's Lair field headquarters in Poland. Which, years later, I would visit. When one of Hitler's generals tried to get closer to the map on the table, he inadvertently kicked the briefcase under a thick pedestal that muffled the blast. Instead of killing Hitler, he was only wounded, a fluke that cost countless more lives.

I sympathize with my daughter's feelings when I contemplate the small things that God could have done to save the Jews of Europe. "Yes, Baba," I said, "if God had allowed von Stauffenberg to kill Hitler—if the general did not move the briefcase perhaps six inches—history would have been radically different. With Hitler dead, Germany might not have continued the war. The machinery of death in the extermination camps might have stopped. It might have saved perhaps a million more Jews."

"Then why didn't He do it?" she said. "Where was He when all this happened? How could He have silently watched all this tragedy? And does He still deserve our love and devotion if He was a silent witness?"

"God seemed to be hiding throughout the Holocaust," I told her. "I agree there is no excuse."

"Then why are we still religious? Why don't we abandon Him the way He abandoned us?"

There was no good answer. I could only look at her in silence.

The assassination of Heydrich showed, however infinitesimally, that evil could be punished, that a basic order to the universe still existed, and that God was watching. But why didn't He do so much more?

Remembering Heydrich's murder raised the question of why greater efforts were not made to assassinate Hitler. Was it because he was out of reach? I would have thought Heydrich, too, would have been out of reach, given his high position in the Third Reich. Nevertheless, the partisans succeeded in killing him. Moreover, the Czech government-in-exile in London ordered his assassination, knowing there would be reprisals.

In response to the assassination, more than thirteen thousand Czechs were arrested, and as many as five thousand people were murdered. The Gestapo believed the assassins were hiding in the village of Lidice, and the Nazis entered the town on June 9, 1942, and killed 199 men. They deported 195 women to Ravensbrück concentration camp, and took ninety-five children prisoner—eighty-one of whom were later killed in gas vans at the Chełmno extermination camp (eight were adopted by German families). The Czech village of Ležáky was also destroyed because a radio transmitter belonging to the underground was found there. I would later visit Lidice, and found the memorials there to be unbelievably moving. I cannot describe the feeling I got when seeing teddy bears being left by modern visitors mourning the children murdered decades earlier.

The Germans were still unable to find the assassins, however, and issued an ultimatum that they would execute more people if the killers were not found by June 18, 1942. Gabčík and Kubiš initially hid with two Prague families, and later took refuge in Karel Boromejsky Church. In exchange for a reward, one of the members of the underground, Karel Čurda, turned himself in to the Gestapo and disclosed the names of the people who helped the assassins. The Nazis subsequently raided the home of the Moravecs, one of the families Gabčík and Kubiš hid with. The matriarch, Marie Moravec, asked to go to the bathroom and killed herself by biting into a cyanide capsule. Her husband, and seventeen-year-old son, Ata, were taken into custody. Ata was tortured and shown his mother's severed head in a fish tank, and warned that if he did not cooperate, his father would be killed. Ata revealed the assassins' hiding place. A few months later, he and his father, his fiancée, her mother, and her brother were executed at Mauthausen.

Waffen-SS troops laid siege to the church where Gabčík and Kubiš and other members of the underground were hiding. Armed only with pistols, the Czechs had managed to hold off the larger, well-armed German forces and inflict a number of casualties. Kubiš, Adolf Opálka, and Jaroslav Švarc were killed after a two-hour gun battle. Gabčík, Josef Valčík, Josef Bublík, and Jan Hrubý committed suicide in the crypt after the Nazis tried to flood it.

I consider Gabčík and Kubiš—who today are lionized as two of the greatest Czechs of the war—to be heroes of all mankind. My children were in awe of the Czech paratroopers, and adopted them as heroes. They were inspired to find that the killer Heydrich had met such a gruesome end. They wanted to know every last detail of the operation, and of their last hours fighting the SS who had come to kill them. It gave them hope that at least someone—*someone*—had paid for their role in the Holocaust.

Funeral ceremonies were held for Heydrich in Prague and Berlin. Hitler attended the latter and placed the German Order and Blood Order medals on the funeral pillow. Karel Čurda, the man who betrayed his comrades, was tried, convicted, and hanged for high treason, in 1947.

The assassination of Heydrich did not slow or stop the Nazi commitment to the Final Solution. In 1941, the Nazis established a ghetto in Theresienstadt (Terezín), about thirty-seven miles outside Prague, which served as an SS-run transit camp for Jews being deported to extermination camps. It was also used by the Nazis for propaganda purposes, as a "model Jewish settlement," to show the world how well it was treating the Jews under their "care."

Heydrich had informed his comrades during the Wannsee Conference that Theresienstadt would be used for certain categories of Jews; in particular, elderly Jews and veterans. To the extent that they publicly talked about the fate of the Jews at all, the Nazis maintained that German Jews were being resettled in the East to work. Since elderly Jews could not be expected to work, the Nazis said they were sent to the "spa town" of Theresienstadt to retire. Heydrich believed the ghetto offered a "practical solution" to "eliminate at one stroke the many interventions [on behalf of these Jews]." According to the US Holocaust Memorial Museum, after Heydrich's death, "prominent Jews, especially artists, musicians, and other cultural figures whose disappearance in a killing center might provoke inquiry from their communities, or even from abroad" were also directed to Theresienstadt.

Eichmann informed Jewish leaders from Berlin, Vienna, and Prague (or more accurately, the heads of Nazi-run organizations designed to assist with the deportation of Jews from those areas) of his plans during a meeting in the Reich Security Main Office, on May 29, 1942. He said, "...the total evacuation of the Jews was planned from the *Altreich* [Germany before 1938], the *Ostmark* [Austria], and the Protectorate." All Czechs living in Theresienstadt were required to move by May 31, 1942, to make room for the Jews who would be forced to move there. Eichmann said, "Jews under 65 years old would emigrate to the East, and those over 65, as well as some groups of those under 65, such as men seriously disabled in the War, and those who received medals in the World War, etc., would be sent to Theresienstadt for permanent residence." The Jewish leaders were told the money to maintain Theresienstadt would come from the Jewish community organizations in Berlin, Vienna, and Prague.

It is hard to imagine now, what it must have been like for the Jews of Czechoslovakia, who were told to pack no more than two suitcases and to report to the train station, where they were transported to a spot just outside of Prague. They walked about two miles, not knowing where they were going. When they entered the gate with the ominous *Arbeit Macht Frei* sign, the Germans confiscated their valuables. I communicated all this to our children to make the experience more vivid.

As in other ghettos, the Nazis appointed a *Judenrat* to manage the lives of the Jews in Theresienstadt. Jacob Edelstein was appointed head of the council. Like other Jewish leaders, he hoped that if he made the people in his care indispensable to the war effort, he could stave off their deportation. Jews worked inside the ghetto, in the kitchen and various workshops. Some Jews were forced to do more arduous work outside the camp, on construction projects, and in the Kladno mines. Edelstein was also responsible for municipal services, providing education and organizing cultural activities. Jews inside the ghetto managed to create a remarkable cultural life, with lectures, concerts, and theater performances. Artists made drawings and paintings portraying life in the ghetto, many of which were hidden, and discovered after the war. Jews were also permitted to continue their religious practices.

Despite his best efforts, Edelstein could do little to help his people survive the overcrowded, unsanitary conditions, disease, and lack of food. Half the ghetto's population, nearly sixteen thousand people, died in 1942 alone, forcing the Nazis to build a crematorium to dispose of the large number of bodies. Jews were constantly moved in and out of Theresienstadt. By mid-1942, most of the Czechs had been deported, and the majority of the ghetto was German and Austrian Jews. In September 1942, the hybrid concentration camp and ghetto reached its peak capacity of roughly sixty thousand, but more than forty-two thousand were deported to Auschwitz that year.

In January 1943, Eichmann appointed Paul Eppstein of Berlin and Rabbi Benjamin Murmelstein of Vienna to join Edelstein in running the council to keep the Jewish leadership divided and passive. Like other *Judenrat* leaders, they were put in the agonizing position of playing God. Whenever they were asked to determine who would be deported, they were deciding who would live—at least for the short-term—and who would die. The Germans always held out the hope that if the Jews cooperated, they could survive. They went to great lengths to deceive them. To convince elderly German Jews they were going to a retirement community in Prague, for example, they were offered home-purchase contracts, or asked for deposits for room and board.

In August 1943, following the destruction of the Białystok Ghetto, several thousand Jews were discovered hiding. The adults were shot in front of the children. Afterward, 1,260 children under fourteen were transferred to Theresienstadt, where they were isolated from other ghetto residents, along with a small group of people assigned to care for them—one of whom was Ottilie Kafka, Franz Kafka's sister. On October 5, 1943, the children and their fifty-three caregivers were deported to Auschwitz, where they all perished.

As we went about our travels, I understood that anything to do with the experiences of children during the Holocaust was an opportunity to help my own kids connect more deeply with the tragedy and horror of it all. It was for this reason that director Steven Spielberg picked out one doomed Jewish child to show in a red raincoat, in his black and white documentary-style film *Schindler's List*. The murder of six million Jews is incomprehensible. The numbers are just too large to process. But the death of one innocent child is a tragedy that we can all identify with.

One of the few places that protected the Jews was Denmark. Nevertheless, the Germans managed to capture 476 Jews, and sent them to Theresienstadt, where they lived in a separate compound. Demonstrating how it was possible to get the Germans to bend if a government had the will to challenge them, the Danish authorities pressured the Nazis to allow them to provide supplies to the prisoners and to allow Danish Red Cross representatives to visit the ghetto. Consequently, only one of the Danish Jews was deported, and fifty-two died in the camp. Four hundred twenty-three survived the war.

This was encouraging to my children. It helped them to know that despite the bottomless capacity for evil exposed by the Holocaust, there were also points of light that showed mankind's capacity for good. But a few minutes later, they would have to dismiss these inspirational stories as they confronted evermore gruesome events. Amid the all-consuming carnage, the points of light came to be seen as too little, too late.

The Nazis saw the Jews as non-humans. However, apparently, they thought people would be curious about them after they were gone. The Nazis planned to build a Central Museum of the Extinguished Jewish Race, where presumably citizens of the Reich would come to see what was left of the human equivalent of the Dodo bird. In Prague, they needed fifty-four warehouses to store it all, along with religious and ritual items from the surrounding Jewish communities. Today, much of that collection is in the Jewish Museum of Prague.

When reports about the death camps began to emerge at the end of 1943, the Nazis decided to allow the Danish and International Red Cross (IRC) to visit Theresienstadt to prove that they were not mistreating the Jewish population. To reduce overcrowding before their guests arrived, the SS deported more than 7,500 to Auschwitz. The remaining Jews were instructed on how to behave, and the Nazis created a kind of movie set to deceive their visitors. The Nazis began a beautification project. Flowers were planted throughout the ghetto, and fake stores, a coffee house, a bank, a school, and kindergartens were created for the occasion.

The delegation of two members of the IRC, and one Dane, arrived on June 23, 1944, accompanied by Theresienstadt commandant SS First Lieutenant Karl Rahm, and one of his deputies. The entire visit was planned meticulously. The inspectors spent only about six hours in the camp, ninety minutes of which was spent eating lunch. During the guided tour, they witnessed a soccer game in the camp square, with a cheering crowd. The Nazis had selected prisoners who knew how to play, and planned for one team to score a goal while the visitors were watching. They were also treated to a performance of a children's opera performed in a community hall built for the occasion. Children were given cots to take naps, and fed bread and butter. Most had never seen butter before. The Nazis built toy rocking horses and swing sets for them to play on for the benefit of the IRC.

A few weeks later, all the children would be gone, murdered in the gas chambers of Auschwitz-Birkenau. This was chilling to contemporary American Jewish children raised in comfort and security. My kids could scarcely believe it.

The visitors left impressed with the conditions of the ghetto, and unaware of its real purpose or typical circumstances. Afterward, the Nazis produced a propaganda film about the new life of the Jews, under the auspices of the Third Reich. A Jewish director, Kurt Gerron, was forced to make the film, showing men and women working contentedly on farms and in factories, making pottery and sculptures, seamstresses and tailors at work, children playing, sporting events, and concerts. Yellow stars are visible on their clothing, but people are smiling and seemingly happy, with no guards in sight. The film was intended to counter reports about the persecution of Jews, but it was only shown a handful of times before the war ended. After completing the film, Gerron, who had been told that he would be spared, and most of the other Jews involved behind and in front of the camera, were sent to Auschwitz-Birkenau.

One remarkable story, captured in the film *Defiant Requiem*, involves thirty-six-year-old Czech conductor Rafael Schächter. He discovered a piano in a basement in the ghetto, and began to recruit vocalists to perform Verdi's Requiem. He put on sixteen performances for the prisoners, with as many as 150 singers. His chorus was repeatedly deported, and had to be reconstituted several times. The last performance was in front of the Nazis and Red Cross visitors. Survivors said the performances gave them hope at a time of hopelessness. The performance in front of the Nazis was also seen by the participants as an act of defiance. Conductor Murry Sidlin, who now conducts the Requiem to tell Schächter's story, said he "learned that the requiem was a code. It talks about the end of the world and what happens to those who commit evil. Even as they were facing their own destruction, the Jews in that choir were telling the Nazis how the Third Reich was doomed." Schächter, along with his chorus, was deported to Auschwitz. He survived the camp, and three others, but died on a death march shortly before the end of the war.

My kids asked me why no one shouted to the Red Cross, or somehow communicated to them that everything they were seeing was a sham. If they had looked beyond the façade of buildings, they would have seen the truth about the ghetto. I explained that it is hard to place yourself in the shoes of people who lived in such complete terror. We cannot judge the inaction of Jews who knew that the moment they opened their mouths, they and their children would be murdered.

As in other ghettos, the members of the *Judenrat* could not save themselves, let alone their community. In December 1943, Jacob Edelstein was deported to Auschwitz, and later shot. Paul Eppstein was shot by the SS for an alleged escape attempt, in September 1944, on the eve of the last wave of deportations to Auschwitz. Rabbi Benjamin Murmelstein remained with Leo Baeck as his deputy to run the council. Murmelstein was feared and reviled by fellow prisoners for his assistance to the Nazis. Like other *Judenrat* members, Murmelstein claimed he was doing what he could to prevent the immediate execution of the Jews. Fellow prisoners accused him of accepting bribes to exempt certain people from being sent to Auschwitz, which meant others would have to be sent in their place. His behavior earned him the nickname *Murmelschwein*.

Murmelstein was the only head of a major *Judenrat* to survive the war. He was accused of collaboration by the Czech government, released, and then emigrated to Rome, where he was shunned by the Jewish community. In 1961, he published a memoir of his wartime experiences, *Terezin: Il ghetto-modello di Eichmann*, which failed to rehabilitate his reputation. When he died, he was buried away from his wife, in a corner of the cemetery, and his son was not allowed to recite the Kaddish over his grave.

In 1975, Murmelstein was interviewed by *Shoah* film director, Claude Lanzmann, and those conversations became the basis for his 2013 documentary, *The Last of the Unjust.*

I find Murmelstein's behavior reprehensible. Nevertheless, I cannot judge him. He is right when he told Lanzmann, "An Elder of the Jews can be condemned. In fact, he must be condemned. But he can't be judged, because one cannot take his place."

This question of Jewish collaboration became the subject of fierce debates throughout the trip. My daughter Shaina, who had just completed her Holocaust course at George Washington University, was adamant that we had no right to judge the collaborators. We could label their actions evil, while still withholding judgment on their character.

"We don't know, Tatty, what we would have done, confronted with the same experience."

But Yosef would have none of it. "They worked with the Nazis to kill Jews, while saving themselves. Why didn't they fight back? It's disgusting."

I said to him, "But you're not looking at this as parents. The Nazis told them that if they didn't collaborate, the first to be murdered would be their own kids. Perhaps when you, God willing, one day become a father, you might see things differently. That's why we can't judge."

As Germany's fortunes turned, Himmler and others decided to use prisoners at Theresienstadt as a bargaining chip in negotiations with the western powers. He and other SS leaders agreed to release twelve hundred Theresienstadt prisoners, in exchange for five million Swiss francs put up by Jewish organizations in an escrowed account in Switzerland. The twelve hundred reached freedom in Switzerland on February 5, 1945. Two months later, the Swedish Red Cross were allowed to transport the surviving Danish Jews to Denmark.

The IRC visited the camp again on April 6 and April 21, 1945, before taking over its administration on May 2. The commandant, and the rest of the SS, fled on May 5 and 6, just ahead of the arrival of Soviet troops, which entered the camp on May 9. The liberators found approximately thirty thousand survivors.

SS Lieutenant Karl Rahm, and the original commandant, Siegfried Seidl, were tried by the Czechs after the war. Both were convicted and executed. Anton Burger, who had replaced Seidl, was sentenced to death as well, but escaped to West Germany and lived in Essen under a false name until his death in 1991. More than one hundred Czechs had served as guards at the camp. Their commander, Theodor Janeček, died in prison awaiting trial in 1946. And his successor, Miroslaus Hasenkopf, was found guilty of treason, sentenced to fifteen years, and died in prison in 1951.

After World War II, 10,338 Jews settled in Prague. When the Communists took over the country in 1948, Jews were again persecuted, and restrictions placed on the practice of Judaism. Roughly half the community immigrated to Israel, Western Europe, or America. As a reaction to the Six-Day War, in 1967, Czechoslovakia severed diplomatic relations with Israel. This was followed a year later by the Soviet occupation of Czechoslovakia, which prompted more Jews to flee the country, leaving roughly two thousand.

Today, Prague is again a thriving center of culture. The collapse of the Soviet Union in November 1989, created the opportunity for a revival of Jewish life in Prague. Some property was returned to the Jewish community, and a number of institutions were re-established. Today, Prague has about sixteen hundred Jewish citizens, and many younger Czechs have a renewed interest in Judaism. The community has a Jewish kindergarten, an elementary school, a high school, two retirement homes, and two kosher restaurants. Four of the old synagogues—the Altneuschul (Old New Synagogue), High, Jerusalem, and Spanish—hold services. They survived because the Nazis used them to store Jewish objects and art. The Altneuschul is the oldest functioning synagogue in Europe, and the most famous. Services have been held there for roughly seven hundred years, interrupted only by the Nazi occupation. This was the Maharal's synagogue, and legend has it, the clay he used for the Golem is stored in its attic, which is off-limits to visitors. In 2017, the Old New Synagogue acquired two new Torah scrolls, the first such acquisition since the 1930s.

The Spanish Synagogue is also interesting because it was built in 1868, on the site of the original synagogue—the 12th century Altschul—with an interior filled with Moorish and Islamic designs, and art inspired by the Alhambra in Granada. During the Holocaust, it was used to store Torah curtains. Today, it is the headquarters of the Jewish Museum.

Many Jewish historical sites are in the area of the original Jewish ghetto of Josefov, including the Jewish Town Hall, which was built in the 16th century, and now houses the offices of the Federation of Jewish Communities in the Czech Republic. The Town Hall has a clock with two faces—one with Roman numerals, and the other with Hebrew letters. The city's Jewish

Museum has thousands of artifacts, documents, and religious articles. It also has materials from Theresienstadt, including a collection of drawings made by children in the ghetto.

While we were in Prague, I also wanted to focus on Franz Kafka. I wanted my children to know about how rich Jewish life was before the Holocaust, and also how conflicted it was. During his life, Jews were transitioning between being attached to their tradition, and abandoning it while still retaining their core identity. The esteem in which Kafka is held by the Czechs is reflected by the life-sized bust of the author erected at his birthplace. The house in which he was born is now a museum honoring his life and work. Kafka is not buried in the old cemetery of Prague. His tomb is in a newer one that opened in 1890. Nearby, is a memorial to his three sisters, who were murdered by the Nazis.

Kafka was a member of the Pinkas Synagogue, which was built around 1492. The names of 77,297 Jews who died in the Holocaust were written on the walls after the war, but erased by the Communists. They were later restored.

Prague's Jewish cemetery is the oldest and most famous in Europe, dating to the 15th century, and has tombs layered on top of each other because there was not enough space for all two hundred thousand bodies it received over the years. While Jewish cemeteries are usually on the outskirts of cities, this one is just outside the Pinkas and Klausen Synagogues. You can see how old the cemetery is from the erasure of the letters on the gravestones. The Maharal is buried there, in perhaps the most famous Jewish tomb in Europe; it is a pilgrimage site for Jews from around the world. The Czech government issued a stamp and a commemorative coin in 2009, to mark the 400th anniversary of the Maharal's death, and his statue now stands outside New City Hall.

The cemetery is cited in *The Protocols of the Elders of Zion,* as the site of the meeting of Jewish elders, something I only found out after we returned from our trip.

One of the more peculiar sites in Prague is the sculpture of Jesus on the cross, with a banner written in gold Hebrew letters on the Charles Bridge. The Hebrew was added in 1696, after an anti-Semitic incident involving a Jew named Elias Backhoffen. At the time, Jews had to wear a special conical-shaped hat, and he became the target of abuse while walking from the Jewish ghetto. According to the legend, Elias became so angry that he spit near the statue of Jesus on the bridge, and was then chased back to the ghetto by a Christian mob angered by his desecration of the statue.

The Jews locked the ghetto walls to protect him. A deal was hammered out between the Jewish community and Christian authorities that Backhoffen would pay to engrave on the statue, "Holy, Holy, Holy, the Lord of Hosts" in gold-plated Hebrew letters. It was a sacrilege for the Jews to have this reference to God hung around the neck of the statue of Christ. For centuries, people passed the sculpture without having any idea of its origins. It was not until 2000, that the city installed bronze tablets next to the statue, explaining in Czech, English, and Hebrew the inscription's origin and its intended purpose to insult the Jewish community.

Unlike many of the places we visited in Eastern Europe, the Czech Republic has not seen a dramatic upsurge in anti-Semitism. According to the Anti-Defamation League, it has one of the lowest levels of anti-Semitism in Europe. In 2000, Holocaust denial was outlawed, and public denial, questioning, and approval of, or attempts to justify the Nazi genocide, could result in a prison sentence of six months to three years.

I urged my kids to think about the victims—all the great Jewish sages that made the Prague Jewish community so famous, and the writers, musicians, and other artists who perished in Terezín and other camps. Who knows the contributions they might have made to Torah study and the arts had they just lived? And what about the fifteen thousand children who never grew to adulthood?

The Jewish people were entrusted with the Torah and a code of law whose foundation is the Ten Commandments. We are obligated to speak out. We cannot be bystanders. Elie Wiesel famously said, "Indifference, to me, is the epitome of all evil."

We must stop genocide, whether it occurs in Auschwitz, Treblinka, Majdanek, and Bergen-Belsen, or today in Syria, Sudan, or Myanmar. We *are* our brothers' keepers. The Torah is not just a holy book, it is a holy obligation. It represents a sacred commitment on the part of humanity to worship God and uphold the values we have been taught. We must honor the memory of all the victims of the Holocaust, and of all genocides that have stained the earth with the blood of innocents.

CHAPTER 7

KRAKOW: A JEWISH FESTIVAL WITHOUT JEWS

We had a long drive on June 30, from Bratislava, the capital of Slovakia—which we visited briefly—to Krakow, and were in a rush to make it in time for Shabbos, which fortunately begins late in northern latitudes in the summer. We got there with fifteen minutes to spare, at 9:15 p.m., and went to the Jewish Community Center, which hosted 650 people for dinner. I was told this was the largest Shabbat dinner in Poland since the Holocaust. Of course, there is an extremely small number of Jews in Poland today, and about 90 percent of attendees were not Jewish. But they are Polish non-Jewish lovers of the Jewish people, a living refutation of the widely held Jewish notion that Polish people are all bad. There is a fascinating revival among Polish people who want to learn about all things Jewish.

For the last twenty-seven years, Kazimierz, the ancient Jewish neighborhood of Krakow, has hosted a Jewish cultural festival of music, dance, film, lectures, and theater. Attending the festival was one of the reasons we came to Krakow, and in typical Boteach family fashion, we drove against the clock to make it on time.

I was invited to give a talk at the JCC as part of the festival, and I considered it one of the most important speeches of my life, although there were only one hundred people in the room. My children were all there and knew the importance I accorded it, given that it would be attended by survivors of the Holocaust. I was speaking about my books, *Wrestling with the Divine* and *The Fed-Up Man of Faith: Challenging God in the Face of Suffering and Tragedy*. It was especially poignant because I was addressing the Holocaust in a city whose Jewish community was almost annihilated, just forty miles from Auschwitz. I have given speeches on the topic of "Where is God when the righteous suffer?" in several places across the world. But to do so in Krakow, with Holocaust survivors in the audience, was a humbling experience.

I spoke with one survivor who grew up in Krakow, and now lives in Hawaii. He goes back to Poland in the summer, and gives tours of the Jewish sites in Krakow. He's a super-cool guy with a ponytail and a larger-than-life personality. I believe he's eighty-four or eighty-six now, and was thirteen when he was sent to Auschwitz. I met him through my friend, Professor Jonathan Weber.

I was intimidated by his presence at my speech. I felt that speaking about the Holocaust and theodicy was one thing. But doing it in the presence of someone who went through it at Auschwitz, just one hour's drive away, was a bit of a *chutzpah*. After all, what authority did I have?

He cried throughout my speech. I saw the three or four inflection points when he really connected with what I was saying. I said the only response to the Holocaust was to challenge and wrestle with God in righteous indignation.

I am a religious Jew. I would never advocate severing our relationship with God over the Holocaust, but believe we must strengthen it by being more honest and not ignoring what happened on His watch. Our intimate relationship with God requires honesty, forthrightness, and humility. When I finished, this incredible Hawaiian Holocaust survivor, who had cried throughout my talk, stood up in front everyone and gave me a big hug. It was validation like I have seldom felt before. My children all congregated around him and hugged him. They were in awe of his presence, and sat enraptured as he went to a corner of the room and shared his story with them.

Krakow is the second largest, and one of the oldest cities, in Poland. A Baroque city, and easily Poland's most beautiful, it was largely spared bombing by the Nazis during the war. It has also long served as one of the leading centers of Polish academic, cultural, and artistic life. Krakow was likewise a key center of Jewish learning, and the site of Poland's first yeshiva. Several notable rabbis taught there, including Rabbi Moses ben Isserles, known as the *Rema*, who became celebrated throughout the Jewish world for his commentary on the *Code of Jewish Law* (the *Shulkhan Arukh*).

Jews arrived in Krakow in the late 13th century, and a Jewish street, Judengasse—St. Anne Street today—was mentioned in 1304. Before the end of the 14th century, Jews had built a synagogue, *mikveh*, cemetery, and other communal buildings, and were afforded the right to engage in trade and moneylending. Because of the Christian prohibition on usury, Christians could not lend out money at interest, which inhibited the development of productive industries on any scale. Jews throughout Europe stepped into the vacuum and became moneylenders, which later led to their prominence in the banking industry.

Relations between Jews and non-Jews were strained, in part, because of economic competition. Blood libels and pogroms were recorded in 1407, 1423, and 1457. In 1495, Jews were expelled from Krakow to nearby Kazimierz. That town swelled with immigrants, and had a Jewish population of more than two thousand by the 16th century. Kazimierz also had six synagogues, and was the city where the first Hebrew books were published in Poland.

Krakow was a hotbed of religious fervor among Christians, who often engaged in persecution of their Jewish neighbors. The city was home to a university whose students, prompted by the anti-Semitic teachings of their professors, would periodically attack Jews. In 1631, a Jew was tried for ritual murder, and in 1635, Jews were accused of Host desecration. In 1663, a Jewish doctor accused of blasphemy was burned at the stake. Violence against Jews was common in the 17th century, and during a two-year period, when the Swedish Army occupied the city, the Jewish quarter was pillaged by Swedish and Polish soldiers. When the Swedes left, Jews were somehow accused of treason and collaborating with the enemy.

The bubonic plague killed one thousand Jews in Kazimierz, in 1677. Afterwards, Jews became subject to a variety of anti-Jewish restrictions. Nevertheless, they became successful traders, goldsmiths, and silversmiths. Their plight worsened, however, when the Senate of Poland prohibited Jewish commerce in Krakow, in 1761.

Violence against Jews escalated again during the Confederation of the Bar battles, from 1768–72, when Russians, and the confederates, demanded that Jews provide them with food, housing for soldiers, and help in spying on their enemies. Many Jews were lynched during this period.

In 1795, Krakow was annexed by Austria, and in 1799, all Jewish businesses were ordered out of the city. After the Krakow Republic was formed between 1815–1846, Jews were permitted to reside in the Jewish section of Kazimierz, and assimilated Jews were allowed to live in the Christian sections. A Jewish elementary school was opened in 1830, and in

1844, the first Reform synagogue was founded. Hasidism also flourished, and intercommunal tensions grew.

In 1846, Krakow became part of Austria once again. Jews stayed in Kazimierz until 1868, when the Kazimierz and Krakow communities merged. A network of Jewish schools was established, and Jews were active participants in the city's cultural life. Jews also became active in the Zionist movement. By the turn of the century, 25,670 Jews lived in Krakow—about 28 percent of the total population.

The First World War, part of which was conducted on Polish soil between Germany and Russia, naturally preoccupied the Poles. And after that, they were engaged in a war of survival against the nascent Soviet Union, which would have taken over the country had Marshal Józef Piłsudski not won the Battle of Warsaw in 1920. Wartime in Poland is always pogrom time, especially around Easter, and there were two bad ones in April 1918, and June 1919. Nevertheless, the Jewish population more than doubled to fifty-six thousand by 1931—with Jews represented in a wide range of professional and commercial fields. A reflection of the assimilationist trend was the tendency of Krakow's Jews to speak Polish rather than Yiddish.

At the start of World War II, sixty thousand Jews lived in Krakow—one-fourth of the city's population. The Nazis took over the city on September 6, 1939, and the city became part of the German zone of occupation known as the General Government. Hitler placed Hans Frank in charge of the area, and Frank set up his headquarters in the Wawel Castle in Krakow. When he took power, the area under his control contained 2.5 million to 3.5 million Jews.

"We must annihilate the Jews wherever we find them," Frank said, in 1941. And by January 25, 1944, Frank estimated that there were only 103,000 Jews left. He was captured by US troops on May 3, 1945, and tried and found guilty of crimes against humanity during the Nuremberg trials. The court found that, "Frank was a willing and knowing participant in the use of terrorism in Poland; in the economic exploitation of Poland in a way which led to the death by starvation of a large number of people; in the deportation to Germany as slave laborers of over a million Poles, and in a program involving the murder of at least three million Jews."

Frank was sentenced to death and hanged at Nuremberg Prison on October 16, 1946. US Army journalist Joseph Kingsbury-Smith witnessed the execution, and wrote, "He was the only one of the condemned to enter the chamber with a smile on his countenance. And although nervous and swallowing frequently, this man, who was converted to Roman Catholicism after his arrest, gave the appearance of being relieved at the prospect of atoning for his evil deeds."

In March 1941, a ghetto was built for Krakow's Jews. Able-bodied Jews were forced to work in factories inside and outside the ghetto. They worked in textile, munitions, and brickwork factories, as well as construction projects, such as building or repairing bridges and rail tracks. One of the factories that employed Jews was German Enamel Products (Deutsche Emalwarenfabrik) owned by Oskar Schindler. A better-known company that employed slave labor was Siemens, the company that laid the first transatlantic cable, and today is a successful diversified German corporation which runs ads on American TV.

Siemens kept its war-era archives secret for decades. It was only in 2011, that the company began to allow access to some of the documents. To its credit, the company website does acknowledge that at least eighty thousand workers were forced to work for Siemens. The company claimed it had to meet the Nazis' production goals, and rationalizes the decision of Carl Friedrich von Siemens, head of the company from 1933 to 1941, to cooperate with the Nazis. The company says he was "a staunch advocate of democracy," who "detested the Nazi dictatorship," but he acted in the interests of "the company's well-being and continued existence."

According to Professor Jonathan Wiesen, the company's board wrote reports after the war to "deny war crime allegations being leveled against it by the Allied powers and to remind the public of the significant role that the company would play in the reconstruction of Germany." The company actually claimed to be "worker friendly." Besides slave labor, Siemens also supplied X-ray machines used in medical experiments at Auschwitz.

To give one indication of the company's post-war insensitivity, Siemens introduced vacuum cleaners in Germany, using the name *Zyklon* (cyclone, in German). In 2001, the company planned to register the trademark Zyklon in the United States for a range of products, including gas ovens. Jewish groups were outraged, and Siemens was forced to issue an apology, and withdrew its application.

The first deportations from Krakow began in June 1942, when five thousand Jews were sent to the Belzec extermination camp. On October 28, 1942, the Germans deported nearly half of the remaining Jews in the ghetto, approximately six thousand, to Belzec. During the deportation operations, the SS and the police shot approximately six hundred Jews in the ghetto, half of them children—a terrible fact I shared with my kids.

Also in 1942, the SS built a slave labor camp in the suburb of Płaszów. Later, it became a concentration camp under the notoriously brutal commandant Amon Göth. Few people probably knew about Göth until they saw the frightening and largely historically accurate performance of Ralph Fiennes in *Schindler's List*, which earned the actor the Oscar for Best Supporting Actor.

Jews from the Płaszów labor camp were sent to work for Schindler, making munitions. However, he made sure that no functioning weapons were ever completed. Ultimately, Schindler saved 1,098 of his workers.

In October 1942, Himmler ordered the annihilation of the Jews of Krakow, and in March 1943, the Germans liquidated the Krakow ghetto, shooting approximately two thousand Jews, sending about two thousand others who were fit to work to Płaszów, and deporting the remaining three thousand to Auschwitz, most of whom were sent to the gas chambers.

Jews continued to be employed as slave laborers in Płaszów until the fall of 1943. From September until December, the SS and their collaborators murdered most of the prisoners. The exact number is unknown, but could have been as many as nine thousand. Those who were not shot were deported to Auschwitz, with the last group leaving on January 14, 1945. The Germans evacuated the city on the 17th, and two days later, Soviet forces entered Krakow.

Only two thousand Jews from Krakow survived the war. As in other parts of Poland, some Jews returned to their homes only to find their neighbors not pleased to see them. Approximately ten thousand Jews were living in Krakow between 1945 and 1946, during which time a series of pogroms drove most to leave. Today, approximately one thousand Jews live in Krakow.

While I wouldn't call it a resurgence, there has been a renewal of Jewish life in Krakow, even as Jewish numbers there remain relatively small. I have visited the community many times, and I find great comfort in its presence. A Jewish research institute was established at Jagiellonian University, and a Jewish Cultural Center was established in Kazimierz. In 2005, the Rabbi Moses Isserles Remuh Jewish Library, named for the famous 16th-century rabbi, opened in the city's Jewish youth club. That same year, the Shavei

Israel organization reported that it was dispatching Rabbi Avraham Flaks to become the city's first full-time rabbi since the Holocaust. Krakow now also has a flourishing Chabad house, domiciled in the 350-year-old Isaac synagogue, and run by Rabbi Eliezer Gurary.

We visited the Remuh Synagogue, which dates to the 16th century, and was also named for Rabbi Isserles. It is widely regarded as the second most famous synagogue in Europe, after the Altneuschul Shul of Prague. Rabbi Isserles wrote commentaries and additions to the *Code of Jewish Law* (the *Shulkhan Arukh*), written by Rabbi Yosef Karo for European Jews.

Shaina was particularly struck by the plaques on the wall in memory of the families lost in the war. "I remember one of the plaques said *Ferber family*," Shaina recalled, back home in New Jersey. "I remember it like it was yesterday. It was black with gold writing: Ferber family, eighty members lost. I remember thinking, *Wow, that's not just a family. That's generations.* That's why we are here. We are here for them, because who knows if there's a Ferber left?"

Baba did not like Krakow. She had come to Poland two months earlier with me, on the March of the Living, and swore she would never return to Poland. For her, it was like a giant Jewish cemetery. My friend Professor Jonathan Webber tried to shift the focus from the Holocaust to the positive aspects of Jewish life today in Poland, and to suggest that the Polish people have great love for the Jewish people. Baba said she was "not buying it." But Jonathan is devoted to Holocaust memory in Poland, and especially Galicia, where Krakow is located. He is a co-founder of the outstanding Galicia Jewish Museum, along with the late photojournalist, Chris Schwarz.

Jonathan showed us around and made the visit interesting, but Baba said she was uncomfortable every minute. "It was misery," she told me later. She felt guilty saying it, but she did not even enjoy going to the synagogue.

Baba had a strong reaction to our visit. She thought Krakow was a ghost town, and was enraged that the "Jewish festival" was held on Shabbat. She didn't think there was anything Jewish about it, and was offended that it was held where all the Jews used to live. She was also bothered by the Israeli restaurant in town, which had "Jewish foods," but was not kosher. For her, the town was "like a museum celebrating the life of Jewish dinosaurs that were now extinct." She said that, "Back in the 1930s, Jewish culture was alive, and the Jewish festival brought out the death of Judaism." She also felt like people were looking at our family as if we were from Jurassic Park.

"We were dressed like Jews," she said, "and I remember people looking at us like we were dinosaurs. They were shocked to see Jews at the Jewish festival." The festival is broadcast on Polish television, and the audience got to see the chief rabbi of Poland, Rabbi Michael Schudrich, say the Havdalah prayer—I was standing right next to him—that marks the distinction between the holy Sabbath and the mundane workweek.

Baba was so traumatized by all the death that surrounded us, and what she felt was the mockery of a destroyed Jewish life, that she wanted to leave the trip then and there. But she stayed for another three weeks.

I had a different reaction. I thought it was a remarkable opportunity to expose the Polish people to Jewish and Israeli culture. Where else is there a festival for a people that ceased to exist in a country?

The Jews, of course, did not simply cease to exist. They were annihilated. However, it was not the Poles who perpetrated the Holocaust, but the Nazis, and we dare not conflate the two. Yes, there were a great many Polish collaborators. But the Holocaust was carried out by the Germans once they had invaded Poland and crushed it.

On one hand, Poland represents tragedy—a cemetery of Jewish life. On the other hand, one can discern a clear resurgence of Jewish life. I disagreed profoundly with my daughter Baba, and this led to spirited discussions between us.

To be sure, there are many Jews around the world who agree with her. One of our closest family friends' mother is a Holocaust survivor from Poland, and has made her children and grandchildren promise her that they will never set foot there. I understand the sentiment. Her entire family was murdered. Still, I believe, like the Lubavitcher Rebbe, that there has to be Jewish life in Poland. And we have to reach out to non-Jewish Poles, especially those with an affinity for the Jewish people, like the thousands of attendees at the Krakow Jewish Culture Festival.

It was interesting to see how deeply Jewish life there can be felt. It was amazing, for example, to see non-Jews coming to the JCC to study Torah. I understand Baba's feeling, but Jewish life must be celebrated, even by those who are not Jewish, if only because there are, largely, almost no Jews.

Except for Baba, I think the rest of us found it a relaxing evening after all the horrific places we had been. It was a chance to enjoy music by world-class Israeli and Jewish performers, along with ten thousand people from all around Poland, and many more from Israel and Europe.

I wanted to enjoy the time with my family because I knew that our mood would darken in a few hours, when we drove to Auschwitz-Birkenau.

CHAPTER 8

AUSCHWITZ-BIRKENAU: WORDS FAIL

uschwitz is the single darkest place on earth, where civilized human beings reached unparalleled depths of cruelty and depravity. Horror and slasher films feature the most sadistic examples of torture and murder. And yet what happened at Auschwitz was infinitely more diabolical, sickening, and soul-destroying. The victims were not a handful of actors whose fates were meant to scare us. They were real human beings—1.2 million of them, including over a million Jews, murdered.

Baba may have put it best when she said "unbelievable" is such an overused word that it loses its meaning. But Auschwitz was truly unbelievable.

Auschwitz is the German name for the Polish town of Oświęcim, less than forty miles from Krakow. This location was chosen as the site of the death camp primarily because of its rail connections. On the way to the camp, we saw the rail lines—a spaghetti junction of tracks used by the Nazis to transport people to their deaths.

Debbie's relatives traversed these tracks and met their deaths at Auschwitz. That made the gruesome connection between the Jewish people and Auschwitz especially personal for Debbie, who was deeply traumatized by the visit. Our kids knew that members of their mother's family—their own relatives—were murdered here. But rather than making them wish to explore and understand the horrors perpetrated there more deeply, it repulsed them, and they visited begrudgingly and reluctantly. They were alienated by the pornography of violence that is often associated with visiting a death camp, and witnessing giant mounds of human ash. They felt it to be a desecration, but in the end, were persuaded by my argument that, to honor the six million, we had no choice but to visit the places they were murdered.

During the war, the area around the camp was cordoned off as a military zone because the Nazis did not want people to know what they were doing. But most were still aware if only because the stench of death and the flaky ash from cremated human flesh was everywhere. On our way to the camp, we drove through the village, past the Auschwitz cinema, the Auschwitz Kentucky Fried Chicken, and the Auschwitz shopping mall. I understand people live here, and I did not come to be critical, but it weirds you out to see all these conventional city features in such a horrifying place.

Auschwitz is the word that makes Jews shudder. It is the most horrible word in any language, summing up events so unspeakable in their monstrosity and their brutality that the human mind can't wrap itself around them. So when you take that word and you marry it to *KFC* or *cinema*, the incongruity is striking. That said, once the war ended, the Polish people had to go on with their lives. Still, I wonder whether the entire area around Auschwitz should have been cleared of residents and not been at all commercialized. That, perhaps, would have been more appropriate.

Before the war, Jews constituted roughly half the town's population. They were artisans and merchants. On January 25, 1940, the SS decided to build a concentration camp to confine enemies of the Nazi regime, provide a supply of forced laborers, and serve as a killing center. At first, most of the prisoners were Polish. But gradually, the percentage of Jews grew, and reached 60 percent by March 1943. Over the course of its nearly five-year history, approximately 1.3 million prisoners—among them, 1.1 million Jews—would pass through the gates bearing the promise *Arbeit Macht Frei*.

Sometime in 1941, Rudolf Höss, the commander of Auschwitz-Birkenau, was summoned to Berlin to meet with Heinrich Himmler. The head of the SS informed him that Hitler had issued an order to solve the Jewish Question for good. Himmler told him: "The existing extermination places in the East are unsuited to a large scale, long-term action. I have designated Auschwitz for this purpose."

One of the great mysteries of the war is why no evidence has ever been found of such an order from Hitler. No document has ever been produced with Hitler's signature. Nevertheless, secondhand references, such as this statement in Höss's autobiography, leave little doubt that Hitler ordered the murder of the Jews, and was aware that his wishes were being carried out.

Himmler visited Auschwitz in March 1941, and directed that it be enlarged to hold thirty thousand prisoners. He also ordered the construction of a second camp, with a capacity of one hundred thousand, to accommodate an expected influx of Soviet prisoners of war, and instructed Höss to supply ten thousand prisoners to construct a new I.G. Farben factory in nearby Dwory.

In October, work began on a new camp outside the village of Brzezinka, less than two miles from Auschwitz. This camp, known as Birkenau, or Auschwitz II, consisted of three hundred prison barracks, four gas chambers, and four crematoria designed by the firm Topf und Söhne (Topf & Sons). It was later divided into ten sections, including areas for women (twenty-seven thousand in 1944), men, Gypsies, and Jewish families deported from the Theresienstadt ghetto, separated by electrified barbed-wire fences patrolled by SS guards.

The Germans still needed workers to assist in the war effort. In the spring of 1941, German conglomerate I.G. Farben established a factory to manufacture synthetic rubber and fuels near the village of Monowice. A third camp—known as Buna, Monowitz, or Auschwitz III—was built to provide slave labor for the company from among its ten thousand prisoners. This was one of forty-four sub-camps that provided prisoners for various German industrial and armament plants, coal mines, stone quarries, fisheries, and farms. If prisoners became too weak or too sick to work, they were sent to Birkenau to be killed.

Auschwitz I is now a museum, and the exhibits are both instructional and gut-wrenching. We looked at pictures of people arriving at the camp with all the possessions the Nazis allowed them to take from their homes, usually no more than a suitcase. They dragged them across Europe, in stifling boxcars. I can't wrap my head around knowing that Germany actually did this. So how could anyone at that time have imagined what even now seems unimaginable?

It is particularly heartbreaking to see photographs of children. Many of them show the older siblings holding their baby brothers and sisters, and having no idea they will all soon be dead.

We always talk about the six million killed in the Holocaust, but that is just a number. It's too abstract. When you look at the pictures and see the rooms full of the hair, the luggage, and the shoes of the victims, the magnitude of the horror becomes real. Too real. Every pair of shoes and every suitcase represents a man, woman, or child who was murdered.

One room contains a mountain of hair cut from the women murdered in the gas chambers. The SS sold the hair for the German textile industry at a cost of fifty pfennigs (less than three dollars today) per kilogram. These monsters were making money off the hair of their victims. After the war, traces of hydrogen cyanide, the basic poisonous component of Zyklon B, were found when the hair was examined.

Another room is filled with luggage with people's names written on them. Yet another, with a mountain of shoes. Each pair of shoes once belonged to a person whose life was extinguished in a genocide.

The most important exhibit for me is the book with the names of the victims. There has been so much Holocaust denial, people saying it didn't happen. It is the lowest form of anti-Semitism to rob people of their dignity, even in death, by suggesting that they didn't die. But most of the names are in the museum. The very thickness of the registry is staggering. We were able to find the name of Debbie's great uncle, Zoltan Wiesner, who was murdered when he was a teenager. Finding the name of someone you know is moving and devastating.

It is also striking that all the killing took place virtually under the noses of the townspeople. Again, I don't begrudge people here who must get on with their lives. But one can see homes not far from where we were standing in the camp. We could also see people strolling through a park right behind the gas chamber.

On September 3, 1941, the SS tested Zyklon B as a killing agent for the first time, in the cellar of Block 11 at Auschwitz. The victims were sick prisoners and Soviet POWs. A larger permanent gas chamber was later built outside the compound, where prisoners lived. In the spring of 1942, two provisional gas chambers were constructed at Birkenau. Permanent ones were built in March and April 1943. The firm Tesch & Stabenow, known also as Testa, supplied the Zyklon B.

Only about 10 percent of the Jews arriving at Birkenau were registered, shaven, disinfected, and taken to real showers. These were directed to the barracks. The rest were sent directly to the gas chambers. Between January 1942 and March 1943, 175,000 Jews were gassed at Birkenau. To put that number in perspective, it would be like killing the entire population of Salt Lake City. The murders accelerated in 1944, when Hungary deported its Jews to Auschwitz. In just three months, beginning in May 1944, approximately 565,000 Hungarian Jews would be murdered. On one day alone—in August 1944—24,000 Jews were gassed at Auschwitz.

The Nazis went to great lengths to disguise their intent. Prisoners directed to the gas chambers passed neatly tended gardens. They entered dressing rooms and were told to hang their clothes on numbered pegs on the wall so they could find them after taking disinfecting showers. Signs written in different languages said, "Clean is Good," "Lice Can Kill," "Wash Yourself," and "To the Disinfection Area."

Approximately two thousand men, women, and children were then herded naked into what they thought was a large shower area. The doors were locked behind them, and soon the Zyklon B crystals were introduced, producing a toxic gas that filled the chamber. It took about twenty minutes for the poison—which had its warning odorant removed—to kill everyone inside. After ventilators were switched on to remove the fumes, the bodies were removed by Jewish prisoners known as Sonderkommando.

Some of us have seen Holocaust movies with scenes that take place in gas chambers. They sometimes capture the struggle inside, but none come even remotely close to depicting the horror of that experience. People did not just inhale the gas and go to sleep forever. I hesitate to offer a more graphic description, but people should know what it really was like. Filip Müller, a member of the Sonderkommando, described a gassing:

> Once the gas was poured in, it worked like this: it rose from the ground upwards. And in the terrible struggle that followed— because it was a struggle—the lights were switched off in the gas chambers. It was dark, no one could see, so the strongest people tried to climb higher. Because they probably realized that the higher they got, the more air there was. They could breathe better. That caused the struggle. Secondly, most people tried to push their way to the door. It was psychological—they knew where the door was, maybe they could force their way out. It was instinctive, a death struggle. Which is why children and weaker people, and the aged, always wound up at the bottom. The strongest were on top. Because in the death struggle, a father didn't realize his son lay beneath him.

When the doors of the gas chamber opened:

People fell out like blocks of stone, like rocks falling out of a truck. But near the Zyklon B gas, there was a void. There was no one where the gas crystals went in...Probably the victims realized that the gas worked strongest there. The people were battered—they struggled and fought in the darkness. They were covered in excrement, in blood, from ears and noses. One also sometimes saw that the people lying on the ground, because of the pressure of the others, were unrecognizable. Children had their skulls crushed. It was awful...There was everything in that struggle for life, that death struggle. It was terrible to see. [cite]

The SS could watch the scene inside through a spyhole in the door of the gas chamber. Auschwitz commandant Rudolf Höss used it on at least one occasion, and described what he saw:

Through the spyhole in the door, one could see how those persons standing nearest the shafts fell dead immediately. Nearly a third of the victims died instantaneously. The others began to huddle together, scream and gasp for air. Soon however, the screams turned into a death rattle, and a few minutes later all were lying down. By the time twenty minutes at the most had passed, no one was moving. [cite]

After the war, Höss recalled telling Adolf Eichmann of the shame he felt in being weak-kneed when hundreds of screaming, pleading children were pushed into the gas chambers. Eichmann replied to him "that it was especially the children who have to be killed first, because where was the logic in killing a generation of older people and leaving alive a generation of young people who can be possible avengers of their parents and can constitute a new biological cell for the reemerging of this people."

You might wonder why the prisoners failed to warn the incoming Jews of their fate. The truth is, it would have done no good. There was no escape. Müller recalled that one Sonderkommando did try to warn a woman who was married to one of his friends:

He came right out and told her, "You are going to be exterminated. In three hours, you'll be ashes." The woman believed him because she knew him. She ran all over and warned the other women, "We're going to be killed. We're going to be gassed." Mothers carrying their children on their shoulders did not want to hear that. They decided the woman was crazy. They chased her away. So she went to the men. To no avail. Not that they did not believe her. They'd heard rumors in the Białystok Ghetto, or in Grodno, and elsewhere. But who wanted to hear that?

The SS forced the woman to identify the Sonderkommando who told her. He was thrown alive into the oven.

The Sonderkommando would extract the gold teeth from the corpses and cut off the hair of the women. The victims' possessions, including those they had been forced to leave on the ramps when their boxcars arrived at the camp, were taken, sorted, and stored in barracks referred to as "Canada" (prisoners saw the country as a place of abundance) for later shipment to Germany.

The bodies were either buried in pits, or taken to the crematorium for incineration. The ashes were scattered into rivers, taken to a nearby village, thrown into fish ponds, and used to fertilize fields at camp farms. When some of the ovens malfunctioned, the corpses were burned outside on pyres.

The number of Sonderkommando varied with the numbers of prisoners sent to the gas chambers. When Hungarian Jews arrived for extermination, nearly one thousand prisoners were assigned to the Sonderkommando. In August 1944, 874 prisoners worked in two shifts in the four crematoria at Birkenau.

How could any Jew accept the job of herding their fellow Jews into gas chambers and putting their remains in crematoria? It was all part of the diabolical strategy of the Nazis to convince the Jews to collaborate in their own destruction. The Sonderkommando were given the choice of collaborating or becoming victims themselves.

A rabbi in one of the camps was asked by a Jew, whether it was permissible to help the Nazis to save themselves. The rabbi asked if his blood was redder than that of the other Jews. His position was that one Jew had no right to sacrifice the life of another. When faced with that choice, however, how many of us would be willing to give up our lives? It's easy to judge the *kapos* and the Sonderkommando. And those alive at the time have every right to judge. We who look in hindsight, however, have a more difficult time, not having been confronted with these life-and-death choices.

Not everyone gave in to their instinct for self-preservation. In July 1944, for example, 435 Greek Jews refused to work in the Sonderkommando and were immediately gassed. For the rest, though, it was just a matter of time. The Sonderkommando were always systematically killed and replaced so they could never tell anyone what they had witnessed.

In January 1942, Himmler told Richard Glücks, the Inspector of Concentration Camps, that one hundred thousand Jewish men, and fifty thousand Jewish women, would be deported from Germany to Auschwitz, as forced laborers. On February 15, the first Jews arrived at Auschwitz I. Beginning in March, transports began to bring Jews to Birkenau. When prisoners arrived, they went through the process of "Selection." Men and boys were directed to one line, and women and girls to another. Josef Mengele, the camp doctor, picked out prisoners for medical experiments. He and other SS physicians would look at each prisoner, and with a gesture, determine their fate, directing some to the right and others to the left. One direction led directly to the gas chambers, and the other to at least another day of life. The young and healthy prisoners were chosen to work in the camp, or at nearby munitions factories. Young children and their mothers, along with the old and infirm, were sent directly to the gas chambers.

Survivor Eva Mozes Kor described her arrival at Auschwitz in 1944: "Everything was going very fast. Yelling, crying, pushing; even dogs were barking. I had never experienced anything that fast or that crazy in my entire life." Her two older sisters and parents were taken directly to the gas chambers, while she and her ten-year-old twin sister were taken from their mother to be used as human guinea pigs for Mengele's experiments. "All I remember is her arms stretched out in despair as she was pulled away," Kor remembered. "I never even got to say goodbye."

Roughly two-thirds of new arrivals were sent directly to the gas chambers. Their names were never recorded, which is why it is impossible to know the exact number of victims. Those who passed the initial inspection enjoyed only a temporary reprieve. Many died from malnutrition, disease, and exhaustion due to the difficulty of the work and the poor conditions in the camp. Prisoners were crammed into barracks with three-tier wooden bunk beds and straw mattresses infested with vermin. The camp lacked sanitary facilities and was full of rats. Workers spent more than ten hours a day at their jobs. The SS ordered roll calls several times a day, and prisoners who were considered unfit to work were sent to Birkenau for gassing. Prisoners caught trying to escape, or suspected of helping with escapes, were hanged in public.

Of the approximately 1.3 million people sent to Auschwitz, 405,000 (half Jews, half other nationalities) were registered and tattooed with a serial number. Their body hair was shaven off, and their clothes taken and disinfected while they showered, and then they were given a striped uniform to wear.

Many people associate the Holocaust with images of people holding out their forearms to display tattoos. Auschwitz was the only place, however, where prisoners were tattooed. Originally, prisoners were identified by serial numbers written on their clothing. But when they died, they were separated from their belongings, and the Nazis had no way to identify the bodies. They introduced the tattoos to keep track of the fate of registered prisoners. Those sent directly to the gas chambers were not tattooed because the Nazis did not bother to register them. The SS also made exceptions for certain other groups of prisoners, such as non-Jews from Germany and Austria, who were "re-education" prisoners.

One of the many horrors of Auschwitz was the use of prisoners by Mengele, and other camp doctors, for medical experiments. Mengele was especially fascinated by dwarfs and twins, but everyone from infants to adults were used as guinea pigs. Many of the experiments resulted in the deaths of their subjects. Though, sometimes the patients would be intentionally killed so that autopsies could be performed.

The Nazis were interested in testing methods of sterilization in the hope of discovering a scientific means of wiping out non-Aryans through mass sterilization. Horst Schumann and Carl Clauberg—two names that might be less familiar than Mengele, but no less monstrous—used massive doses of radiation, and uterine injections, to sterilize Jewish prisoners.

Friedrich Entress, Helmuth Vetter, and Eduard Wirths were commissioned by the Bayer pharmaceutical company, one of the subsidiaries of I.G. Farben, to test new drugs on prisoners suffering from contagious diseases, some of whom were deliberately infected by the doctors. Another SS doctor, August Hirt, was given permission by Himmler to select prisoners from different backgrounds to be killed for a collection of skeletons he intended to use to demonstrate the superiority of the Nordic race. Of the 115 prisoners selected, taken to provide skeletal specimens, 109 were Jews.

I'm not sure it is possible to compare monsters, but Mengele would certainly rank among the worst. Beginning in 1944, he selected twins for experiments that allowed him to use one sibling as a control and the other as the guinea pig. "Three times a week, we were marched to Auschwitz to a big brick building, sort of like a big gymnasium," recalled Eva Kor. "They would keep us there for about six or eight hours at a time….We would have to sit naked in the large room where we first entered, and people in white jackets would observe us and write down notes. They also would study every part of our bodies. They would photograph, measure our heads and arms and bodies, and compare the measurements of one twin to another. The process seemed to go on and on." Still, she was aware that being a guinea pig was better than the alternative. "Being on Mengele's list was better than being on no list."

That list was no guarantee of survival. To the contrary, out of about three thousand children—1,500 sets of twins—only about two hundred survived. After conducting his measurements and experiments, Mengele ordered his patients killed by phenol injection so he could do a comparative analysis of their internal organs.

Less well-known than his horrific treatment of twins was Mengele's experiments at the "Gypsy Family Camp." In this lab, children suffering from noma, a type of gangrene that effects the mouth and genitals, which apparently was common in Roma (the preferred name for Gypsies), were killed so they could be autopsied, presumably in hope of finding a cure for the disease. The heads and organs of children were preserved and sent in jars to medical institutions for examination.

It is also important to note that the Roma were the only people beside the Jews that Hitler sought to exterminate. In January 1943, approximately twenty-three thousand Romani were deported to Auschwitz. Hitler would kill between 220,000 and 500,000 Romani, up to 50 percent of the nearly one million Roma living in Europe at the time.

The numbers of people imprisoned and murdered were staggering. By the end of 1943, nearly twenty thousand people were in Auschwitz I, almost fifty thousand in Auschwitz II, and fourteen thousand in Auschwitz III. That is the equivalent to exterminating the entire population of Camden, New Jersey. The numbers grew dramatically between May 15 and July 9, 1944, when 438,000 Hungarian Jews were transported on 147 trains to Birkenau. A special railroad spur was built into the camp to facilitate their handling. By the summer of 1944, all the other death camps were abandoned and only Auschwitz remained. From that point, until the camp was liberated on January 27, 1945, approximately 585,000 Jews were murdered.

Think about the Germans, often cultured, who carried out the daily task of murdering thousands of people. They did so amid the screams, the smells, and the horrific images of death. Then they would return to their families and listen to Mozart and read Goethe.

Think also about Dr. Nyiszli, who wrote a memoir of his collaboration with Mengele, called *Auschwitz: A Doctor's Eyewitness Account*. The famous Viennese psychoanalyst, Bruno Bettelheim, himself a camp survivor, observed that Nyiszli became a tool of the SS to stay alive. In the article, "Moral Dilemmas Faced by Jewish Doctors During the Holocaust," Michael Nevins relates that Bettelheim believed that Nyiszli rationalized his decision to collaborate with Mengele by focusing on his professionalism and ignoring how Mengele used his work. "He took pride in his professional skill irrespective of its moral implications." Bettelheim argued that the Jews, bludgeoned into submission through the unspeakable horrors of life under the Nazis, contributed to their own demise. According to Nevins, "Bettelheim suggested that this attitude, which enabled Dr. Nyiszli to volunteer his help to Mengele and the SS, only led to a moral inertia and physical passivity which made the Germans' job easier." In 1960 Bettelheim claimed of his fellow Jews that, "Like lemmings, [millions] marched themselves to their own death."

Bettelheim's insight is correct. The Nazis needed the compliance of the Jews themselves to achieve their objective. Needed them to walk on the trains under their own power. Dead people are heavy, and panicked crowds hard to manage, so the Jews had to be reassured, to an extent. The disbelief of citizens in a modern state that the new government really meant to murder them worked to the Nazis' advantage. Who, before the Holocaust, could have imagined a fate as gruesome as a gas chamber? A hatred this extreme and so destructive had no precedent in world history, and so people were slow to recognize it. When Jews heard rumors of the concentration and death camps, their response, before the truth seeped out, was disbelief, which the Nazis encouraged.

Debbie's sister-in-law's grandmother Alisa Herman, and her great-aunt Freda, were just eighteen- and nineteen-years-old when they arrived at Auschwitz and were met at the train by Mengele. When they first arrived on the second day of Shavuot, in 1944, he immediately sent their parents to the gas chambers. Afterward, they had to face selections, and were probably passed over because they got jobs working in the kitchens. They knew what it meant to be sent to the gas chambers, so they made a pact with each other that if the Germans tried to take them, they would run to the electric fence to end their lives rather than allow themselves to be gassed. These were the kinds of decisions prisoners made every day. Thank God they survived the camp and the subsequent death march.

I am always angered by the suggestion that Jews went like sheep to the slaughter. There was little that Jews deported to Auschwitz-Birkenau could have done. Most Jews were taken directly from trains to the gas chambers, with no idea of what fate awaited them, and no time to react if they had known. Still, even in Auschwitz, there were recorded assaults on Nazi guards, even at the entrance to the gas chambers.

Often, young people ask why Jews at camps that had thousands, sometimes tens of thousands, of prisoners, did not revolt against the relatively small number of guards.

The reality I discovered is that fighting back was next to impossible. People used to a halfway civilized existence are stunned by unconstrained violence and savagery. Most of the Jews were not soldiers trained to fight. They were ordinary men and women who were professionals, academics, shopkeepers, and business people. Many were too young or too old to fight. They were husbands, wives, and parents. How could they have fought against armed guards?

Even trained soldiers, such as the 350 American GIs sent to the Berga slave labor camp, did not challenge their guards. Like the Jews, they were in a weakened condition after riding in boxcars with no food, or suffering the deprivations of the camps for any length of time.

The camps were in locations where it was almost impossible to escape—in remote areas or cities filled with collaborators. Some managed to reach partisans or a safe haven. But most who did manage to get out of the camps were quickly found and executed. Attacking guards was likely a suicide mission, since the prisoner would either be shot in the course of the uprising, or afterward. Other Jews who did not participate in an escape or revolt would often be punished, so people who resisted had to consider the severe reprisals that would be sure to follow.

People wanted to believe they would survive, that when the train got where it was going they would be put to work or transferred to a better location. Why risk death through resistance when there was a chance of survival through cooperation?

The boldest example of resistance occurred in Birkenau, after prisoners learned that a group of Sonderkommando who were supposed to be transferred to the subcamp at Gliwice were instead murdered, and that another group was soon to be killed. Even before this revelation, prisoners had been preparing to revolt. They were aided by four brave women between the ages of eighteen and twenty-two—Ester Wajcblum, Regina Safirsztain, Ala Gertner, and Róża Robota.

Robota worked in the clothes depot. The others, in a nearby munitions factory. Together, they smuggled gunpowder to the men in Birkenau, sometimes using corpses sent to the Sonderkommando for disposal. The men used the gunpowder to make grenades. They also made and hid their own knives, hammers, and axes.

On October 7, 1944, at about 3:00 p.m., the Poles in Crematorium IV began the revolt. They were joined by the Sonderkommando of Crematorium II, who cut through the wires of the camp, allowing several hundred prisoners to escape. During the uprising, three guards were killed and twelve wounded.

The prisoners who escaped were caught and killed. Approximately 250 prisoners died during the battle, and 200 Sonderkommando were captured. Some were held for interrogation, and revealed the names of the women who had helped them. The rest were executed with single shots to the back of the head, and then disposed of by other Sonderkommando.

The women were tortured, but only told their inquisitors the names of dead Sonderkommando to protect those who may have survived. All four were publicly hanged on January 6, 1945, in the women's camp, just two weeks before Auschwitz was evacuated. Before her execution, Ester Wajcblum smuggled a message to a friend in the underground that said, "I know what is in store for me, but I go readily to the gallows. I only ask you to take care of my sister Hanka. Please don't leave her, so that I may die easier." She signed the letter, "Be strong and be brave."

The murder of Jews at Birkenau continued after the revolt, but Crematorium IV was never used again.

As Germany began to retreat, and Soviet forces advanced, Himmler ordered the destruction of the gas chambers and crematoria on November 25, 1944. The Sonderkommando dismantled the gas chambers and ovens in the crematoria. Crematoria II and III were blown up. On January 26, an SS squad blew up Crematorium V, the last of the crematoria.

On January 18, 1945, the SS forced approximately sixty thousand prisoners on a death march into what remained of the Third Reich. Keep in mind, this was in the middle of winter, and the men, women, and children were already emaciated and in ill health. Anyone who could not keep up was shot. An estimated fifteen thousand never completed the thirty- to thirty-five-mile trek to Wodzisław and Gliwice. The survivors were put on unheated freight trains and deported to concentration camps in Germany. One in four died en route.

When Soviet troops entered Auschwitz on January 27, 1945, they found approximately 7,500 half-dead prisoners, including about five hundred children under the age of fifteen. Many of the prisoners died after liberation. The liberators also discovered warehouses containing 836,525 items of women's clothing, 348,820 items of men's clothing, 43,525 pairs of shoes, 460 artificial limbs, seven tons of human hair, and thousands of toothbrushes, glasses, and other personal effects.

In less than five years, the Nazis killed an estimated 1.1 million Jews, seventy thousand Poles, twenty-five thousand Roma, and fifteen thousand Soviet prisoners of war, at the Auschwitz camps. Again, for perspective, that would be like exterminating the entire population of San Antonio, the ninth largest city in the United States. Only about two hundred thousand people imprisoned in the Auschwitz camps survived.

Between seven thousand and seventy-two hundred Germans and Poles served on the staff of Auschwitz at one time or another. No more than 15 percent faced justice. The Auschwitz camp commandant, Rudolf Höss, went into hiding in Germany, but was captured by the Allied military police in 1946, and handed over to the Polish authorities, who tried him and sentenced him to death. Fittingly, the monster was hanged on April

16, 1947, on gallows built close to his former villa near Crematorium I in Auschwitz.

In 1947, forty-one people were charged with crimes in a Polish court. Twenty-three were sentenced to death, including Höss's successor as commandant, Arthur Liebehenschel, and Dr. Maria Mandl, head of the women's camp, who was directly complicit in the murder of about five hundred thousand women. Dr. Johann Paul Kremer and Arthur Breitwieser had their sentences commuted to prison terms. The others were executed by hanging. Sixteen of the accused were given prison terms ranging from three years to life, and one person was acquitted. Other trials were held for at least 617 defendants, of whom thirty-four were sentenced to death.

Otto Moll, the man in charge of the crematoria, who supervised and participated in the shooting of prisoners and throwing them into the pyres, was transferred to a subcamp of Dachau after the evacuation of Auschwitz. He later led prisoners on a death march to the main camp. He was put on trial by an American military tribunal at Dachau, in November 1945, and convicted of war crimes. He was hanged on May 28, 1946.

German and Austrian courts did little to pursue criminals from Auschwitz until 1960. That year, the camp doctor Johann Kremer, who had been released from his Polish prison, was retried and sentenced to ten years imprisonment. However, the court counted his time in a Polish prison and released him. Carl Clauberg, the Auschwitz gynecologist, was sentenced to jail in Russia and later released. His retrial ended when he died in jail.

Another trial of twenty-two former SS officials and guards ended in 1965, with the conviction of eighteen men. Six of the accused were given life sentences, two were released because of ill health, and the rest received prison terms ranging from three and a quarter to fourteen years. Also, in 1965, an East German court convicted and executed another camp doctor, Horst Fischer, who, until then, had continued practicing medicine under his own name. Yet another doctor, Horst Schumann, who had carried out sterilization experiments at Auschwitz, found refuge in Ghana until 1966, when he was extradited to Germany. He was put on trial in 1970, but not convicted due to what they believed to be his deteriorating health. He was released from prison in 1972, but didn't die until 1983.

Trials were also held for men associated with I.G. Farben and Topf & Sons, for their roles in war crimes at Auschwitz. I.G Farben has one of the most despicable histories of any company now in existence. At one time, it was the largest company in Europe, and the largest chemical and pharmaceutical company in the world. Its scientists made several notable discoveries in chemistry and medicine, such as the first sulfa antibiotic. Two of its chemists won the Nobel Prize in 1931, and a third won the prize for physiology or medicine in 1939. During this time, the company became intimately involved with the Nazi Party, reportedly being the largest single contributor to the Nazi election campaign in 1933. Ironically, because of the Jewish background of some of its leaders and shareholders, far-right newspapers accused it of being an "international capitalist Jewish company."

Besides employing slave laborers, I.G. Farben held the patent for the pesticide Zyklon B, used to kill people in the gas chambers, which had been invented by the Nobel-Prize-winning Jewish German chemist Fritz Haber's research group at the Institute for Physical Chemistry and Electrochemistry. After the war, twenty-four directors of I.G. Farben were tried for war crimes, at Nuremberg, in 1947–48. In July 1948, thirteen were found guilty. They were sentenced to prison terms between one and eight years. Several of those convicted later became top executives in other companies, such as the Deutsche Bank and Bayer AG. And some of the people who were acquitted also became successful after the war.

The Soviet Union seized most of I.G. Farben's assets located in the Soviet occupation zone, as part of their reparation payments. In the western occupation zone, however, the company continued doing business. In 1951, the firm split into its original constituent companies, and today its successor companies include Agfa, BASF, Bayer, and Sanofi. While I.G. Farben still existed as a corporation, it tried to avoid paying compensation to survivors or their families, and was willing to consider payments to slave laborers from Auschwitz alone, and not from any other camps. It contributed about $300,000 to a foundation for former laborers of the Nazis regimes, before filing for insolvency in 2003. The remaining assets—totaling at more than $10 million—were sold to a private buyer.

According to the Bayer company website, the locations of the Lower Rhine consortium (or I.G. Farben, including Bayer) were among the sites of German industry that were considered "vital to the war." The company says that it needed to bring in "foreign and forced laborers from the occupied countries of Europe" when its employees were drafted. But says that "concentration camp prisoners were not employed in the Lower Rhine sites." As part of the I.G. Farben conglomerate that so enabled the Holocaust,

Bayer can hardly claim its hands are clean. Moreover, the company neither explains where the slave laborers came from, nor its commissioning of fatal medical experiments at Auschwitz.

The company and men responsible for designing the crematoria also have an interesting post-war history. Ludwig and Ernst Wolfgang Topf, the owners and managing directors of the firm Topf & Söhne (Topf & Sons), began supplying the SS with incineration ovens specially developed for the concentration camps by furnace construction engineer Kurt Prüfer, in 1939. Three years later, after the gassings began at Auschwitz, the company applied for a patent at the initiative of engineer Fritz Sander, for a "continuous-operation corpse incineration oven for mass use." After the ovens were dismantled at Auschwitz-Birkenau, the company used them to build new crematoria at Mauthausen.

Fearing arrest by the US Army after the camps were liberated, Ludwig Topf committed suicide on May 31, 1945. Ernst Wolfgang Topf fled to the Western occupied zones and was prevented from returning to his home in Erfurt, by the Soviets. Prüfer, Sander, and two other former employees of the company were arrested by the Soviets and sentenced to twenty-five years in a penal colony for assisting the SS in committing genocide.

In 1957, Reimund Schnabel's book *Macht Ohne Moral: Eine Dokumentation über die SS* (*Power without Morality: A Documentary Account of the SS*) was published with copies of two Topf & Sons documents providing evidence of the firm's dealings with the SS. Ernst Wolfgang Topf disputed the authenticity of the documents and insisted that "in our company, no one was guilty, either morally or objectively." According to the Society for the Promotion of the Topf & Sons Place of Remembrance, "for the remainder of his life he remained stubbornly convinced that the products of Topf & Sons had been misused in an unforeseeable manner, and clung to his concept of 'innocent ovens.'"

After the war, the company was nationalized by the East German government, and renamed Topfwerke Erfurt VEB. Except for the Topf brothers and the engineers serving penal sentences, the management remained the same as it was before 1945. Meanwhile, in 1951, Ernst Wolfgang Topf established a new company, J.A. Topf & Sons, which made crematory and refuse incineration ovens. The company went bankrupt in 1963. The Soviet company was privatized after the fall of the Soviet Union, and went bankrupt in 1996.

Justice was served in the case of the men responsible for supplying Zyklon B to the extermination camps. On September 3, 1945, the British arrested Bruno Tesch, director Karl Weinbacher, and employee Joachim Drosihn of the firm Tesch & Stabenow. They were charged with distributing the gas to concentration camps with the intent to kill humans. Tesch and Weinbacher were convicted and sentenced to death. They were executed on May 16, 1946. Drosihn was acquitted.

One man who never faced justice was Josef Mengele. When I was a boy, I remember hearing about the search for Mengele. The United States actually had Mengele in custody after the war, but did not know he was on a list of wanted war criminals, and released him. After hiding in Germany for nearly four years, he fled to Argentina. In 1959, West Germany issued a warrant for Mengele's arrest and requested his extradition. Following Israel's capture of Adolf Eichmann in Buenos Aires, Mengele moved to Paraguay before finally settling in Brazil. On February 7, 1979, he suffered a stroke while swimming, and drowned. He was buried in a suburb of São Paolo, under the name *Wolfgang Gerhard*. It is painful to think that "the angel of death" escaped justice.

One of the questions about the Holocaust that haunts Jews and historians is this: Why didn't the Allies bomb Auschwitz? It was a question my kids asked over and over again. We discussed the subject at length, and I explained to them that while Franklin Roosevelt remains one of the greatest men of the 20th century, his legacy will forever be marred because ,he did not bomb the gas chambers. He believed that the best way to stop the genocide was to win the war and that diverting any military resources from that goal was mistaken. But it is a hollow argument, as the United States bombed and raided far less consequential targets during the war, and had an obligation to undertake this most minimal of actions to stop the biggest genocide in history.

In September 1944, as news of mass deportations of Hungarian Jews began to reach the States, the Union of Orthodox Rabbis of the United States and Canada pleaded with the US War Refugee Board and War Department to bomb the railway lines headed to Auschwitz. Apologists for Roosevelt's inaction have offered a variety of excuses: the military could not carry out the mission; the Allies learned about the activities at Auschwitz too late to make a difference; prisoners would have been killed; it would have hurt the war effort. None of these excuses present a valid argument.

The Allies had information about the Nazi plan to exterminate the Jews as early as 1942. In June 1944, the United States received detailed information about the layout and operation of Auschwitz-Birkenau, from Rudolf Vrba and Alfred Wexler, two Jews who had escaped the camps that April. Even before that, historian Richard Breitman found that "there was enough generally accurate information about Auschwitz-Birkenau to preclude the argument that the Allies did not bomb the camp because they got the necessary information too late."

Both the British Secretary of State for Air, Sir Archibald Sinclair, and the US Assistant Secretary of War, John McCloy, argued that Auschwitz not be bombed. Stuart Erdheim notes, however, that bombing the camp would have been "no more complex than numerous other missions." Former US Senator George McGovern piloted a B-24 Liberator in December 1944, and his squadron bombed Nazi oil facilities less than five miles from Auschwitz. In 2005, McGovern said, "There is no question we should have attempted…to go after Auschwitz. There was a pretty good chance we could have blasted those rail lines off the face of the Earth, which would have interrupted the flow of people to those death chambers, and we had a pretty good chance of knocking out those gas ovens."

Erdheim concluded that Archibald and McCloy's assessment "appeared the most expedient way to implement the already established policy of not using the military to aid 'refugees.'" As to the concern with killing prisoners during a raid, the emphasis should have been placed on the far larger number of Jews who could have been saved.

Interestingly, the Jews in Palestine initially opposed bombing the camp. On June 11, 1944, the Jewish Agency in Jerusalem voted against requesting that Auschwitz be bombed because "it is forbidden for us to take responsibility for a bombing that could very well cause the death of even one Jew." At that time, they believed Auschwitz was a labor camp. A few weeks later, after receiving information that twelve thousand people arrived each day to be exterminated, Golda Meir, then a member of the executive committee of the Histadrut, along with her colleague, Heschel Frumkin, cabled their US representative, asking him to lobby the US government to bomb the railway and the camp itself.

Historian Mitchell Bard argues that "the focus on bombing Auschwitz may actually be misplaced, since that was just one of hundreds of concentration camps (albeit perhaps the worst). Many Jews could have been saved by bombing other camps as well. The Allies did bomb Buchenwald, for example, but not for the purpose of saving Jews."

Ultimately, David Wyman concluded in *The Abandonment of the Jews*, the failure to bomb the camp was a result of the Allies' indifference to the fate of the Jews. Roosevelt did save some Jews. But the numbers were relatively tiny, and it has permanently tarred his legacy. For example, he allowed about fifteen thousand German Jews already in the United States on visitors' visas to remain, and in 1940, sent a paltry list of two hundred names to the State Department, with instructions they be given emergency visas. He refused to lift immigration quotas, however, and opposed legislation proposed in 1939, months before the start of the war, that would have permitted twenty thousand Jewish children to enter the United States on an emergency basis. Politically, he was on solid ground, as polls showed near unanimous disapproval of the Nazis' treatment of Jews, but overwhelming opposition to admitting a large number of German Jews into the United States.

Debbie's sister-in-law says her grandmother remembers planes flying low over Auschwitz, and thinking, *Why are they not bombing the railway tracks?* She thought they were coming to bomb them. Imagine wanting to be bombed.

Elie Wiesel, a few years before he died, told me that of course the Allies should have bombed Auschwitz. It was necessary.

"But," I said, "you would have died."

"Yes, he said. "I would have died. But I would have died knowing there is justice in the world."

Auschwitz is holy ground because it is the largest Jewish cemetery in the world. We do not know for certain how many are buried there, because they were not given funerals, and their graves are not marked. On a daily basis, tens of thousands were turned to ashes in the crematoria as their remains floated up through the chimneys before being taken by the wind and scattered across the landscape.

For Baba, Auschwitz was chaotic. She felt like nothing was settled. "Chaos in my head. Chaos in my family. Chaos everywhere. It was really torturous," she said.

Debbie had a different reaction. She did not cry at Auschwitz, I think, because it was presented like a museum. Still, certain exhibits were powerful.

"The saddest thing I saw was the braids, the little girls' braids," she said, later. "Hundreds and hundreds. Piles of them." Debbie also found it heartbreaking to see the shoes and the suitcases and the graves.

Ironically, Auschwitz II Birkenau made a bigger impression on Debbie, even though it is mostly in ruins. "It was so big," she recalled. "It took us forever to get from one end to the other. It was so intricate and huge and massive. It just hit me—the scale, the number of people who died in a single day, the way Hitler industrialized murder. He perfected killing as many people as possible, as quickly as possible, and with such precision. This is the area where they go through the suitcases, and they go through the belongings, and they ship them off to Germany for the Germans. They got the victims to participate in their own demise. It's just horrifying." Debbie wondered why she wasn't crying at these sites of death and misery. "You can't," she decided, "because it's so cold and numbing." There were times she cried, but she said it was "when I thought of how we survived; we're strong and we exist."

You expect to see the personification of evil in some way. And there are the barbed wire and ruins of the crematoria. But otherwise, you see birds flying above serene fields of grass, all engulfed in an eerie silence, punctuated perhaps by the chirping of birds. It was a beautiful sunny afternoon. One would never know what happened here.

We walked the length of Birkenau. I hugged the Torah that I had brought with me—a special scroll dedicated to the memory of Elie Wiesel and the six million victims of the Holocaust—and held it to my chest as we traversed this empty shell of a horror movie set. But it was not pretend. It was the real place. It was redemptive to carry the Torah into Birkenau. My family's presence was evidence the Jewish people had survived this monstrous place, and all the others, and are now thriving across the world, and especially in Israel. The Torah is the symbol of the Jewish people, and the source of the laws and traditions on which our lives were built. It was my fervent prayer that the souls of the people who died here feel the sanctity of the Torah, that they know this Torah was written for them, and brought all the way from America to their final resting place, all so their memory will live forever.

I thought about this as we sweated on the hot, muggy day, trudging through the camp. Just as the thought of being warm and uncomfortable occurred to me, I felt flush with embarrassment. How could I even think of my minor discomfort in this place? On a day like today, half-starved, tortured men, women, and children—those who somehow avoided the selections that led directly to the gas chamber and the oblivion of the crematoria—staggering in the heat would have been thinking only about making it through another day.

It made me think more about the impact of the weather on prisoners' lives. The movies may sometimes show the conditions, but the focus is, understandably, on the cruelty of the Nazis. Even books rarely mention that prisoners were wearing those striped pajama uniforms in the rain, snow, and heat. They were not given freshly pressed uniforms each day. They wore the same clothes for days, weeks, months, and—if lucky enough to live that long—years. They had no winter boots for the snow, and were lucky to get sandals or clogs to protect their feet. They might shove paper inside their shoes to add some padding for warmth.

I visited Auschwitz during the winter of 2014, together with the Israeli Knesset, and it was hell on earth. The cold alone could kill you.

Given the combination of the weather, lack of food, unsanitary conditions in the camps, and brutally forced labor, it is a wonder that more people did not simply drop dead. I thought about how I occasionally get a cut, or injure a part of my body. Sometimes I just feel achy, or twist the wrong way and hurt my neck or back. A prisoner who sprained their ankle, or blew out their back, or had any injury that prevented them from working or standing outside in the cold or heat for roll call, would be sent immediately to the gas chambers.

Think also about how easy it was to contract diseases—everything from a cold to serious illnesses, such as typhus. The Nazis had no interest in making anyone better. The moment you became ill, your death warrant was signed, unless you were fortunate enough to recover quickly on your own.

Looking at my children plodding through the camp, with varying degrees of disillusionment and disgust, I also thought about the influence of age. Again, when you read about the Holocaust, books will talk about the number of kids or elderly who were murdered. They might mention that children and the elderly were typically sent directly to the gas chambers. However, what I found interesting was how great a role age played in a Jew's fate. I think sometimes about what I would have done if I lived in that time. But my choices would have been limited by many variables—where I lived, who my neighbors were, who controlled the area, and what skills I might have had. But age would have been among the most important.

It's easy for me to say that I would have resisted. But what if I had been a child at the time? Or elderly? If I was a healthy teenager, perhaps I could have survived by working, or joining a resistance movement. But if I was sickly, I would have been unfit. If I had been born with a disability, or developed even a minor mental illness with age, I might have been euthanized.

As those awful thoughts flowed through my mind, I tried to focus on each of my children and my wife. They were all God's gift, and I vowed to be sure to tell them each day that I love them, and to thank God that they are healthy and living safely today in Israel and America.

I snapped out of my reverie and continued to guide them through the camp. I told them about the arrival of the transports through the gates we passed through ourselves. The instant the boxcar doors opened, the Jews would face snarling dogs and SS guards with machine guns, screaming, "*Raus! Raus!*" (Out! Out!). The people emerged from boxcars filled with the corpses of those who didn't survive the trip, and were immediately subjected to this terror. They just hoped to stay alive and keep their family together. Fathers and mothers clung to their children. But soon they would be separated—men on one side, and women on the other.

I showed my family Crematorium V, situated all the way out in the woods, where the deeds could be concealed. A lot of tourists don't even know to visit. I then showed them Crematorium IV, located nearby. These were both industrial-grade killing machines. Even four crematoria working full time could not keep up with the number of bodies that needed to be burned. They had to lay them out in pyres. We stood by the pits where the SS disposed of the bodies. There is a marker with a Hebrew inscription: "In this place are scattered the ashes of men, women and children, which the Nazis murdered. May their memory be an eternal blessing."

Outside the remains of the crematoria are photographs taken by the Nazis, showing people waiting for their turn in the "showers" because the gas chambers were full. Can you imagine? The SS took pictures of people they were about to kill, who had no idea what was about to happen to them. As horrifying as the photos are, I am thankful the Nazis were so meticulous in documenting their activities. Otherwise, they would have succeeded in covering up their crimes when they destroyed the camp structures, making it easier for the Holocaust deniers to mask Nazi atrocities.

I showed my family Crematoria II and III, which were converted farmhouses. We walked the path of death. We finished as security guards were ushering people out. We were the last people in the camp, and we were davening the Jewish afternoon prayer as the sun was setting. It was a gorgeous sunset.

We felt ambivalent about praying at Auschwitz. Did this hell on earth deserve prayer? Did God deserve to be praised in this place he abandoned? Would God even hear us? As important as it is to preserve this place as a memorial and a place to educate future generations, I felt the urge to pray that this dreadful place would be swallowed by the earth, like Korach in the Torah. Then we thought of the victims and prayed for them and a better world.

Visiting Auschwitz had a different impact on Shaina than it did on the rest of us. It stimulated her to action. By coincidence, our visit occurred a few weeks after the revelation that Syria built a crematorium to dispose of the bodies of prisoners the Assad regime was executing.

"I saw that," she said, "and I broke down in tears. I couldn't stop crying. I was screaming, 'No one cares. No one cares!'" Later, she explained, "It hit me that before I went to Auschwitz, I would have seen that, and it would have troubled me, but I would not have cared enough to act. Once I left and I was back in my comfort zone of being home, but also having those memories in mind, I actually couldn't handle hearing that there was a Syrian crematorium, and that no one was doing anything. To me, it was an abomination that there should be crematoria again after what was done to the Jews seventy years ago. I spoke to my father, and he took out a full-page ad in the Washington Post. He didn't do it because of me, but he agreed it was important."

The World Values Network placed the ad in the *Washington Post*. It drew a comparison between the crematoria in Auschwitz in 1945, and what was found in Syria, where Assad has already murdered hundreds of thousands of people. The CIA identified a crematorium built by the Assad regime to dispose of the bodies. We urged President Trump not to repeat the mistake President Roosevelt made during World War II, and called on him to immediately bomb the crematorium in Syria.

Shaina also fought an internal battle with herself over how to behave. She said the craziest thing was that she was hungry. Starving. "I wanted to ignore it at first," she said, "because I wanted myself to feel pain. But I was so hungry, I ate before and after our visit. Seeing the camp did not make me lose my appetite. I remember struggling with myself because I was annoyed that I was eating in such a horrible place. But on the other hand, I thought I should intentionally eat here, because this is a place where my people were starved."

When I visit Auschwitz—and I have been there maybe ten times—I'm most disappointed in myself for feeling numb. I think, what is this void of humanity, this chasm of darkness? What rip in the fabric of the universe allows a place like this to exist? I can't make sense of it. I can't absorb it. I can't digest it. So you go numb. Walking along the path of death, the same road traveled by tens of thousands of Jews on their way to the gas chamber, I found myself reciting the psalm of David: The LORD is my shepherd; I shall not want…Yea, though I walk through the valley of the shadow of death, I will fear no evil, for Thou art with me…."

Perhaps the only good thing I can say about our visit to Auschwitz was that I fulfilled my daughter Cheftziba's wish not to come here on her birthday. Cheftziba was eight at the time, and would turn nine on July 3rd. It had been heartbreaking to hear her plea before we left New Jersey. So we went to Auschwitz on July 2nd, which happened to be the first secular *yahrzeit*, or anniversary of the passing, of Elie Wiesel, and was therefore extremely appropriate. Now, even though she would not spend her birthday in the death camp, we would go somewhere almost as bad—Łódź.

CHAPTER 9

ŁÓDŹ: GHETTO HORROR AND A JEWISH COLLABORATOR

After our despondent visit to Auschwitz, we had a two-and-a-half-hour drive to Łódź. We arrived at about 1:30 a.m., on July 3, and had to unpack and eat. We didn't get to sleep until about 3:30 a.m. We woke up the next morning to tour Łódź. For a change, we found kosher food at a communal kitchen that served Polish foods, like dumplings.

The city is impoverished, and the kids found it depressing. Baba had perhaps the best description of the experience, which Harry Potter fans can appreciate. "Łódź," she said, "has the power, like a dementor, to suck your soul out of you. It was hell on earth…."

OK, that's pretty harsh. But it's how she felt when she learned of the horrors the Jews suffered there.

Łódź is the third-largest city in Poland, eighty-five miles south of Warsaw. The Jewish presence in the city is more recent than in many of the other cities we visited. A handful of Jews first settled in Łódź in the late 1700s. They became factory owners, merchants, bankers, industrialists, and blue-collar workers as the city grew into an important industrial center under the Russians, who controlled it until the end of the First World War. This was some of the most fought-over ground in the world—the arena for combat between the German and Russian Empires, both of which persecuted the Jews.

Jews lived primarily in the Jewish quarter—Altstadt—but faced a variety of restrictions aimed at forcing them to assimilate in accordance with the tsar's policy at the time. They were not allowed to wear traditional Jewish garb, or send their children to Jewish schools. And they were expected to speak Polish, French, or German. Later, Jews were allowed to leave the Jewish quarter and settle wherever they wanted, after the tsar decreed they were free to settle in Polish cities.

Several synagogues were built in the late 19th century to accommodate the growing Jewish population. The first orthodox synagogue, the Alte Shul, or the Stara Synagogue, was constructed in 1860. The largest synagogue, the Great Synagogue of Łódź, a reform Shul, opened in 1883. The Synagoga, or Daytshe shul, built in 1888, was the first synagogue where the sermons were given in Polish instead of German.

By the end of the century, Łódź had a Jewish population of nearly one hundred thousand. The city continued to grow, with the population at the time of the First World War reaching five hundred thousand, including 170,000 Jews, most of whom were poor Orthodox followers of Hasidic rebbes. Some Jews were successful retailers who operated most of the city's factories. But most workers were Poles. Many Jews could only find work in sweatshops.

The Jewish community became more diverse when many Orthodox opponents of Hasidism arrived from Lithuania, Belarus, and Ukraine. Jews also became active in the labor and Zionist movements, which created tensions with industrialists and opponents of Zionism, such as the followers of the Gerer rebbe, who believed a Jewish State should not be created until the arrival of the Messiah. Though most Jews spoke Yiddish, they increasingly used Polish.

The YIVO Institute noted that "until the 1920s, Jewish education in Łódź was dominated by the traditional *heder*, although some yeshivas were established before 1914. Few girls in Łódź received formal Jewish education before World War I. In interwar Łódź, a majority of Jewish girls attended public elementary schools. In 1912, Markus (Mordekhai) Braude, preacher of the progressive Synagoga, founded the first Jewish gymnasium (secondary school) in the Russian Empire. It became a model for bilingual Polish–Hebrew secondary schools in interwar Poland, educating middle-class children in a Zionist spirit."

The Jewish community thrived with many charitable institutions, social clubs, newspapers, Zionist organizations, and literary and artistic activities. Jewish tradesmen engaged in tailoring, shoemaking, meat-cutting, printing, and paper workshops. The economy deteriorated, however, during World War I and the occupation of the city by Germany, which cut Łódź merchants off from their Russian markets. Many factories were destroyed during the fighting. After the war, the plight of the Jews worsened, especially with the onset of the Great Depression. Anti-Semitism also became a more serious problem, and organized attacks killed and injured Jews in 1933, 1934, and 1935.

The Germans captured and occupied Łódź on September 8, 1939. At the time, the Jewish community of 230,000 constituted roughly one-third of the city's population, and was the second largest in Europe, after Warsaw. As in other towns, the Nazis quickly instituted anti-Jewish measures. Jews were forced to wear yellow armbands (the Star of David badges were introduced on December 12), their bank accounts were frozen, possessions stolen, political and labor organizations disbanded, and had a curfew imposed. On September 14, Rosh Hashanah, the Nazis ordered Jewish businesses to stay open, and synagogues to close. Soon after, all but one of the synagogues were burned or demolished. Many prominent Jews, particularly political and social activists, were arrested, murdered, or sent to concentration camps.

Poles and Jews were deported to make room for ethnic Germans. During the first six months of the war, more than seventy-five thousand Jews left Łódź. Many fled to Warsaw and other parts of Poland, or areas occupied by the Soviet Union. On November 11, 1939, most of the members of the Council of Jewish Elders in the city were arrested, tortured, and shot.

On February 8, 1940, the remaining Jews were moved to a ghetto the Germans renamed Litzmannstadt (Litzmann's city) on November 7, in honor of a general who captured the city during World War I. The man placed in charge was thirty-eight-year-old Hans Biebow, a coffee trader from Bremen before the war—another example of an ordinary German turned monster. After the war, he went back to Bremen, until a survivor of the ghetto recognized him. He was extradited to Łódź, where he was tried and convicted of war crimes, in April 1947, and executed by hanging on June 23.

There was never any doubt about the purpose of the ghetto. Friedrich Übelhör, the German governor of the Kalisz-Łódź district, who ordered construction of the ghetto, said, on December 10, 1939: "The establishment of the ghetto is only a transitional measure. I reserve for myself the decision as to when and how the city of Łódź will be cleansed of Jews. The final aim must be to burn out entirely this pestilential boil."

In the course of herding tens of thousands of Jews into three poor neighborhoods of Łódź over the next several weeks, more than seven hundred people were murdered. On April 30, 1940, the ghetto was sealed from the rest of the world by a wooden fence surrounded by more barbed-wire fences. Streetcars for non-Jews passed through the ghetto, but were not allowed to stop inside it. As the YIVO Institute documented: "Unlike in Warsaw, there were few opportunities for smuggling, escaping, or maintaining contacts with the outside world. Whereas in Warsaw tens of thousands of Jews attempted to hide 'on the Aryan side,' only a handful of instances of such concealment are known in Łódź."

Initially, more than 160,000 people were crammed into an area of roughly 1.5 square miles. In October 1941, the Nazis planned to deport sixty thousand German Jews to Łódź, and Übelhör complained to Heydrich that the ghetto was already overcrowded. Heydrich made clear that he was unhappy with Übelhör's position, and ultimately it was agreed that twenty thousand Jews and five thousand Gypsies would be sent to Łódź and the rest to other ghettos.

The ghetto population still grew, as Jews deported from Vienna, Prague, Luxembourg, Germany, and other Polish towns were isolated in Łódź. By the summer of 1942, approximately two hundred thousand Jews were living in the ghetto, which consisted primarily of dilapidated houses without electricity, gas, water, or sewerage. That number decreased, however, as approximately forty-five thousand Jews died from disease and starvation.

The Nazis took all the Jews' valuables. The Jews would try to hide them. Apparently, some people tried to conceal them in cellars, but the Nazis dug them up. One man waiting for a smuggler saw a man and a woman burying their belongings in the cemetery.

Unlike Warsaw, there was no uprising in the Łódź Ghetto. There were some instances of resistance, mostly passive, with Jews forming secret yeshivas, political and social groups. Jews continued to observe rituals and practices of their faith, and did their best to create some semblance of normalcy in the ghetto. They would hold lectures and concerts, and engage in social activities.

Jutta Szmirgeld, age fourteen, described how important these activities were to maintaining her sanity:

It was forbidden to gather more than three or five people. It was punishable by death, but we were sometimes even fifteen teenagers....I never had such marvelous hours. I ran to my organization and there I forgot. I forgot my mother. I forgot my brother. It's not nice, but I really forgot. The life was different there. There, I saw the blue sky with stars. The sky of the land of Israel. [cite]

One of the most controversial Jewish figures during the Holocaust was Mordechai Chaim Rumkowski, a businessman and orphanage director who was sixty-two-years-old when the Nazis appointed him to head the *Judenrat,* on October 13, 1939. According to Jennifer Rosenberg, "No one really knows why the Nazis chose Rumkowski as the Älteste (Elder of the Jews) of Łódź. Was it because he seemed like he would help the Nazis achieve their aims by organizing the Jews and their property? Or did he just want them to think this so that he could try to save his people?"

Like members of other *Judenrats*, Rumkowski faced the impossible challenge of keeping himself and other Jews alive by appeasing the hate-crazed Germans who were determined to murder them all. Though he reported to Biebow, Rumkowski was responsible for the welfare of the ghetto residents. He set up the factories to employ Jews, hoping that the Germans would keep alive workers who were meeting their needs. The *Judenrat* organized public kitchens and allocated food. Rumkowski established forty-five religious, secular, and vocational schools, as well as a summer camp and orphanage. A Jewish police force was responsible for maintaining order, and the ghetto had its own court and prison system.

Rumkowski's picture appeared on ghetto currency. Referred to as "Rumkies," the notes were worthless outside the ghetto. He did this to try to prevent smuggling, by making it impossible for people to pay for goods outside the ghetto with regular currency. He also created a post office with stamps bearing his image. Rumkowski even performed marriages when the Nazis barred rabbis from conducting the ceremonies.

Rumkowski was a self-promoter who constantly tried to burnish his image as the ghetto's savior. The *Times of Israel* described a poster in which "Rumkowski is surrounded by grateful ghetto inhabitants raising their arms to hail him. In the background, the chairman's realm is depicted not as a dilapidated ghetto, but as a leafy, productive commune. The streets are devoid of beggars, and only the fecal workers hauling away people's waste are out roaming. Between the hovering Rumkowski and his idyllic domain, hospital workers transport a stretcher-bound woman, all while the chairman observes his handiwork."

Ghetto residents took out some of their anger and frustration on Rumkowski since they could do nothing to vent against the Nazis. At one point, workers went on strike and distributed leaflets that said: "Brothers and sisters! Turn out en masse to wipe out at long last, with joint and unified force, the terrible poverty and the barbaric behavior of the Kehilla [*Judenrat*] representatives toward the wretched, exhausted, starved public… The slogan: bread for all!!"

Most Jews over the age of fourteen worked ten to fourteen hours a day in a network of nearly one hundred factories built in the ghetto to produce items for the Germans, including uniforms and munitions for the German Army. These factories generated millions of dollars in profit for the Nazis. Initially, Rumkowski had proposed that workers be paid and given food, but the Nazis agreed only to provide them with meager rations. Most workers got watery soup once a day. Some received a loaf of bread meant to last five days, some vegetables, and ersatz coffee.

One young girl offered a sense of what it was like living under these conditions, in her diary: "I bought rotten and stinking beets from a woman, for 10 marks. We will cook half today and half tomorrow. Does this deserve to be called life?"

The winters in Poland can be frigid, and Jews in the ghetto did not have enough wood or coal to make fires to stay warm or cook food. Jews would desperately search for firewood and tear apart anything made of wood that could be used for fuel. No one was surprised at the decline in the Jewish birthrate. According to YIVO, about 3,100 Jewish children were born in Łódź every year prior to the war. A total of 2,326 were born during the five years Jews were confined to the ghetto.

Rumkowski had near total control over the ghetto population, and was reviled for his dictatorial manner. There were even rumors of him sexually molesting women and children, and using the threat of deportation to silence his victims. Since he was responsible for labor assignments, as well as food distribution, he had tremendous power. People who disagreed with him could end up being punished by the courts he set up, or deported. Ghetto residents were resentful that their health was deteriorating while

Rumkowski and other officials seemed well-fed. Rumkowski also carried on a somewhat normal life, even as he was helping the SS put together lists of Jews to deport. He became romantically involved with his legal advisor, Regina Weinberger, and married her.

Rumkowski's writings show that he thought he was doing the right thing by saving what he could. But ultimately, he was forced to choose who should be sent away. He complied with the orders from the Germans and chose fifty-five thousand people for deportation in the first five months of 1942. Although rumors swirled in the ghetto, no one knew the fate of the deportees in early 1942. Some believed they had been set free. In April, the Gestapo circulated a false report that Jews were being deported to a camp with "exemplary food" and opportunities for the fit to work.

Slowly, the noose tightened. The Nazis reduced the amount of food allowed into the ghetto, and then promised a meal to people who got on the transports. On September 1, 1942, German military trucks pulled up to the ghetto's hospitals, and SS troops came and took away the patients. The next day, Rumkowski was ordered to prepare twenty thousand people for deportation, including the sick, children under ten, and adults over sixty-five. On September 4, at 4:00 p.m., Rumkowski announced to the residents: "A grievous blow has struck the ghetto. They are asking us to give up the best we possess—the children and the elderly. I was unworthy of having a child of my own, so I gave the best years of my life to children. I've lived and breathed with children. I never imagined I would be forced to deliver this sacrifice to the altar with my own hands. In my old age, I must stretch out my hands and beg: Brothers and sisters! Hand them over to me! Fathers and mothers: Give me your children!"

The Jewish leader of the ghetto was actually commanding parents to hand over their very own children to be taken away to God knows where. It led to a wave of suicides the very next day, on the part of parents who refused to comply. Could a Jew have given that speech?

I had to find the exact place where Rumkowski delivered it to even believe it had occurred. We spent the afternoon searching for the place, based on wartime photographs. A guide we hired took us to where he claimed the place to be. When I tried and failed to match the photos, I knew he was wrong. So we searched ourselves, and after a few hours, found the exact spot—an empty alleyway with no marker that we could see. To my children, I read the text of the harrowing speech, from the spot where

Rumkowski delivered it. Three-quarters of a century later, it did not lose its horrible potency. It is one of the most abominable speeches ever delivered by a Jew, in history.

The following day, a curfew was imposed, and the SS, with the help of local police, Jewish ghetto police, and firemen who were promised their relations would be spared, searched for Jews to deport. More than five hundred Jews were murdered during the roundup of approximately fifteen thousand people, including six thousand children.

"I saw two wagons full of little children drive past the open gate," recalled Sara Plagier, age sixteen. "Many of the children were dressed in their holiday best, the little girls with colored ribbons in their hair. In spite of the soldiers in their midst, the children were shrieking at the top of their lungs. They were calling out for their mothers."

The deportation trains traveled thirty-seven miles northwest to the Chełmno killing center. In typically deceptive fashion, the Germans greeted the newcomers with promises of work, food, and a shower. After leaving their clothes behind for disinfection, the Jews were herded into trucks they believed were taking them to the showers. These were no ordinary trucks, however. These were mobile gas vans built so the engine exhaust would be directed into where the passengers were confined. The airtight doors were sealed, and the engine turned on, filling the van with carbon monoxide fumes. The drivers could hear the victims' screams.

It took roughly ten minutes to kill everyone inside. When the noise subsided, the van would drive to a disposal site. The Germans initially emptied the van's "cargo" into mass graves, but later burned the bodies in crematoria and scattered the ashes in the nearby fields. More than seventy-seven thousand Jews and five thousand Roma from the Łódź Ghetto were sent to Chełmno between December 1941 and July 1944.

Rumkowski was a sucker and a patsy. But what choice did he have? Refusal would not have saved anyone, since the Nazis would have either killed him, or found someone to take his place, or simply chosen who to deport themselves. How do we assess his culpability?

Maimonides wrote that if an enemy lays siege to your town, and you are told everyone will be spared if you turn over one person, you cannot send that person to the enemy. The honorable example is the chairman of the Warsaw *Judenrat*, Adam Czerniaków. He could not bring himself to sacrifice others, and took cyanide at his desk on the day the deportations were supposed to begin. He left a note, saying: "They demand me to kill children of my nation with my own hands. I have nothing to do but to die."

After the children and elderly, there were no more deportations from the Łódź Ghetto for nearly two years. One of those who remained behind noted that, "…here and there, there are some mothers weeping in a corner for a child or children shipped from the ghetto, but as a whole, the mood of the ghetto does not reflect last week's terrible ordeal." The writer found it "beyond comprehension" that people were more concerned with rations of food than the loss of loved ones. Perhaps that was because some of these people felt reassured by the postcards they received from people who had left the ghetto, which indicated they were doing well. The recipients could not have imagined that the Nazis had forced the senders to write these messages.

There were no deportations from September 1942 to the beginning of June 1944, and Rumkowski must have felt vindicated. Jews had mixed emotions, often based on the information available to them. Some, for example, believed they would be kept alive because they were needed for the German war effort. Indeed, they had produced consumer goods and arms that allowed the ghetto administration to make millions of dollars.

The news filtered into the ghetto that the Germans were retreating as the Soviets advanced, and some Jews dared to hope they would outlast the Nazis. One diarist wrote, on July 25, 1944, "One can feel the coming liberation in the air. The Russians have captured Lublin. In Germany, there was an attempt on Hitler's life…."

Unbeknownst to Rumkowski and the rest of the ghetto, however, the Nazis were liquidating all the other ghettos in Poland, and Łódź was the last one on the list. When the Soviet army started to close in on Łódź, the Nazis acted with dispatch. During the summer of 1944, they closed the factories and the institutions of the *Judenrat*. About three thousand Jews were told in June and July that they were being transferred to work camps in Germany. Rumkowski urged Jews to report for deportation, but many refused. In the end, there was "a shameful, shocking street scene [of] Jews hunting other Jews like game." [cite]

On August 15, Rumkowski issued another proclamation:

JEWS OF THE GHETTO,
COME TO YOUR SENSES!!!
VOLUNTEER FOR THE TRANSPORTS.

You will make your own departure easier.

ONLY THOSE WHO REPORT VOLUNTARILY HAVE THE
ASSURANCE THAT THEY WILL GO WITH THEIR FAMILIES
AND WILL BE ABLE TO TAKE ALONG LUGGAGE.

I advise you to report TONIGHT to the Central Prison or at the
assembly center on 3 Krawiecka Street.

Altogether, more than seventy-six thousand Jews were transferred to
Auschwitz-Birkenau, where most were sent directly to the gas chambers.

On August 30, 1944, Rumkowski and his family were deported. Biebow
gave him a letter commending his administrative ability in order to "protect"
him just before he disappeared. Nobody knows for sure what happened to
him. Some accounts suggest he was gassed. Others say he was killed by
prisoners who had been deported from Łódź, or by the Sonderkommando.

Yad Vashem notes that, "some historians view Rumkowski as a
collaborator and traitor. Others believe he made a serious, yet flawed,
attempt to rescue as many Jews as possible." Primo Levi, an Auschwitz
survivor, wrote in his book, *The Drowned and the Saved*, that if Rumkowski
had survived, "no tribunal would have absolved him, nor, certainly, can we
absolve him on the moral plane. But there are extenuating circumstances:
an infernal order such as National Socialism exercises a frightful power of
corruption against which it is difficult to guard oneself. To resist it requires
a truly solid moral armature, and the one available to Chaim Rumkowski…
was fragile."

Historian Richard Rubenstein is less sympathetic: "He had no concern
for the individual. To an extent apparently unsurpassed by any other Nazi-
appointed Jewish leader, he was the Führer of his tiny kingdom for much of
his reign, a role he appears at times to have savored."

I come down somewhere in the middle. We cannot judge him from
our current time and place. I did not stand in his shoes. I can only hope
that I would have behaved differently. But it is impossible to know what
any of us would have done under such impossible circumstances, and I
therefore reserve judgment. But judged by the people and victims of his

time, Rumkowski was an abominable collaborator who worked with the Nazis to exterminate the Jews in the tragic belief that he was saving them.

My kids had no sympathy for Rumkowski. His story and his memory sickened them.

Unlike other cities in Poland, the Jewish community made a remarkable comeback in Łódź, in part because Warsaw was in ruins. By 1946, approximately thirty thousand Jews had moved to Łódź, mostly survivors and people who had fled to the Soviet Union. After the Soviet takeover in 1950, most political and social institutions were closed, and half the Jewish population left for Israel. A second wave of immigration to Israel took place in 1956–57 around the time of the Hungarian uprising. Most of the remaining Jews left after an escalation in anti-Semitism following the Six-Day War, in 1967.

Today, Łódź is home to roughly seven hundred thousand people, only two thousand of whom are Jews. I was thrilled to meet the president and vice president of the Jewish community, who are doing a remarkable job of keeping Jewish life alive in Łódź. The city has a kosher restaurant, two synagogues, a rabbi, and a *mikveh*. One of the synagogues dates to the late 18th century, and survived the war because it was hidden in a corner of the ghetto. In 1968, the Communists closed the only Jewish school, and a new one was not opened until 2015.

Shaina found the city depressing, but was happy to find that Jews refused to leave. "We need to be everywhere," she said. And I agreed with her.

Today, there are plaques around the city with maps of the ghetto, and explanations of what took place. But the first monument was not erected until 1956. The stone obelisk located in the cemetery resembles a crematorium chimney. A menorah, the great symbol of Jewish life, and a broken tree, traditionally an image of death, are also a part of the design. The inscription in Polish, Hebrew, and Yiddish reads: "Innocent Jewish victims of Łódź…May they be forever remembered in our hearts."

In recent years, many historical markers have been affixed to buildings where important ghetto institutions were located. The city has also had a variety of exhibitions and events about the war. According to the leaders of the Jewish community, forty thousand Jews from around the world visit Łódź every year to learn about the city's history.

We walked past an imposing red brick Catholic church in Kościelny Square. The spires of St. Mary's Assumption's Church are familiar in pictures of the ghetto. Since there were no non-Jews in the ghetto, except Roma, the Nazis used it initially as a warehouse for property stolen from the Jews, and later, as a sorting plant for feathers and down.

Nearby is a major street with a tramline. During the war, Jews were not allowed on that street, so the Nazis constructed a bridge over the road for Jews to pass from one side of the ghetto to the other. Meanwhile, the non-Jewish residents of the city used the street as if nothing unusual were going on around them. They drove cars, rode bicycles and trams through the center of the ghetto. They could see the Jews around them, and the Jews could see their former neighbors going about their normal lives.

"Passing through that bridge was a significant effort, a physical one for some, a mental one for others," Arnold Mostowicz wrote in *With a Yellow Star and a Red Cross*. From the top of the bridge, "some tried to find the elements of city life, like traces of life in outer space; others would nostalgically recall their past normal lives in the far downtown skyline, a normalcy which was often grey, empty, dull, in which they had hardly ever lived happily, unaware of how many different natures happiness can have."

We went to the Radegast train station, for example, from where the Jews were deported. No trains run from there anymore. It was turned into a museum in 2002, with photographs and books with copies of the lists of people who were put on the transports. These lists compiled by Rumkowski and his minions contain the names, birth dates, places of origin, and dates they were deported. It was heartbreaking to see all the names, pages and pages of them. There is a memorial the length of one-and-a-half football fields that seems to go on and on with copies of pages from the deportation lists for each year displayed along the walls. On the ceiling is a train track, and the tunnel terminates in a room with an eternal flame and a chimney that is meant to represent a crematorium. On the walls are plaques engraved with the names of the places of origin of the victims.

One of the trains with three original boxcars was also preserved. I've never seen three boxcars together, and we were able to go inside. At Auschwitz, you can only see the outside of the boxcar. As we walked around the space which the Germans crammed to the limit with Jews, who had no food or water, and only buckets within which to relieve themselves, Baba was recording me on Facebook. In the background, you can hear her saying, over and over: "Oh, my God…Oh, my God…."

We went to the Łódź Cemetery. It is one of the largest Jewish cemeteries in Europe, covering nearly one hundred acres. Established in 1892, about 230,000 Jews are buried there. So many Jews went up the chimneys of the death camps' crematoria, were dumped in mass graves and ditches, or left by the side of roads and burned in pyres, I am not sure that people know that many victims of the Holocaust do have individual graves. In Łódź, there are approximately forty-five thousand of them, although few of their occupants are identified.

Unlike many cemeteries we saw in Eastern Europe, the Łódź cemetery is well-maintained. A foundation for its preservation was created in 1996, and Israeli volunteers come each year to help with the upkeep. Many graves are unmarked, but the Jewish community kept meticulous records of each plot. Israeli soldiers participate in a program in which they clean up the cemetery and place markers with the names and dates of the lives of victims. Over the years, memorial plaques have also been added to the wall near the entrance of the cemetery to honor the victims hastily buried there.

The cemetery is a peaceful place of proper burial, more uplifting than the city, which is the place that feels haunted.

There was nothing that felt redemptive in Łódź. Not even the way they made the monuments. The train station is all gray concrete. It's hard to look at. The communal institutions are poor, and the buildings in disrepair. We were able to buy kosher food, but the kids complained that it was tasteless, which is not a complaint so much as an observation about the extreme poverty of the modern Jewish community in Łódź. Throughout the city, you just feel tremendous despair. But that only made me admire the Jewish communal leaders even more, struggling as they are to uphold Jewish life in a city with few resources and the most terrible past.

Baba was particularly affected by Łódź. "I think that was the worst of the worst. It doesn't seem like it can get any worse, but it does," she said, when we returned. "It's this tiny community. It's horrible, so depressing. I don't see how any Jews live there."

Shaina says Jews have to be everywhere. Baba says Łódź is an accursed dump not fit for Jews. Who's right?

Baba also recalled visiting the place where the burial society, the Chevra Kadisha, prepared bodies for interment. The Chevra Kadisha still operates out of the same building used during the Holocaust. People in the 1940s were dying by the hundreds every day, and they were mostly ultra-Orthodox

Jews who had to be buried according to Jewish tradition, which includes a ritual washing of the body, known as the *taharah*.

"They had this horrible black washing board in the shape of a body. Then we saw the rolling board they used to bring the bodies from outside the cemetery, into the cemetery. It was so disgusting."

The cemetery was even more traumatic for Baba. As we walked among the graves, we came across many rusty metal plaques placed by the Israel Defense Force, with the dates of the births and deaths of victims. Some of them were young nineteen-year-old women, the same age as Baba.

Months later, Baba said she felt like she had lost her mind through visiting the horrible killing fields that consumed the Jews of Europe, and was losing her faith. "How can you still believe in God after seeing Łódź and all the other horrible places?" she asked herself.

She discovered her convictions were deeply rooted when she contemplated violating the Sabbath and eating non-kosher food. Even though the thought of doing so crossed her mind—almost in an attempt to punish God for the Holocaust—she could not bring herself to violate the commandments.

"I knew I was being mad at God, so I knew he was still around. I felt guilty because I was saying these painful things. I kept repeating to myself the Hebrew verse from Exodus (5:22–23) when Moses asks, 'Why, Lord, why have you brought trouble on this people? Is this why you sent me? Ever since I went to Pharaoh to speak in your name, he has brought trouble on this people, and you have not rescued your people at all.'"

Baba was distraught, and looked to the teachings of the Lubavitcher Rebbe for help resolving her feelings. There are more than fifty volumes of the Rebbe's correspondence, and according to an unofficial Chabad tradition, if you open one of these books randomly, you will find guidance. Baba opened a random letter of the Rebbe online that echoed the verse from Exodus in which Moses challenges God. In response to a question about understanding the Holocaust, the Rebbe said the only thing one can say when visiting these places is, "Why have you acted cruelly with this people?" Baba said she chanted that line over and over, and wanted to cry. "I didn't see anything beautiful in life anymore."

She found some solace from something else she read from the Rebbe. When he was asked how he could continue to believe in God after the Holocaust, he replied, "How can you believe in man?"

What he meant was that you cannot reject the idea of absolute morality and believe in only man-made rules, which are subjective, when man has proven that he cannot properly serve as the guardian of good and evil.

Throughout the trip, these questions haunted me. We visited Łódź on the third of July, which was Cheftziba's ninth birthday. Our youngest had asked us not to make her celebrate her birthday in Auschwitz. So we purposely visited Auschwitz the day before to comply with her wishes. Instead, she spent her birthday amid the horrors of Łódź, hardly much of a consolation, and hardly better. But this is the price we pay for being part of a people that experienced such horrors amid our commitment to always remember and never forget.

CHAPTER 10

TREBLINKA: THE GREAT DECEPTION

"It was hell, absolutely hell. A normal man cannot imagine how a living person could have lived through it—killers, natural-born killers, who without a trace of remorse, just murdered every little thing."

— Kalman Taigman,
Survivor of the Treblinka Uprising

We started out late-morning on July 4th, from our hotel in Warsaw, slowly weaving to the outskirts of the city and onto the open roads that would take us to our next stop about fifty miles northwest, near an old quarry known as Treblinka. I had never been to the site of the infamous extermination camp, and felt a sense of foreboding.

We saw signs on the highway for the city of Białystok. I realized then that I was heading along the path of the Warsaw-Białystok railway, the route the Jews of the Warsaw Ghetto had taken on their way to Treblinka.

I thought of those rail lines sending thousands of Jews to their deaths every week, trains carrying as many as seven thousand people packed in cattle cars with barely enough room to stand. Families and strangers huddled together with no food, water, or fresh air. I could not bear to imagine how those Jews must have felt, confined to boxcars designed for livestock, during the searing heat of the summer and freezing cold of winter. How could they avoid panicking as they hurtled down the tracks, unaware of their final destination or fate?

I felt sick and needed air. I rolled down the window and let my arm rest on the doorframe. Even driving at this speed, with the wind buffeting me, I could feel the slow burn of the summer sun.

I closed the window.

We reached the highway exit not long afterwards. This was where the Jews would have reached the Treblinka station on the main railway, before making a righthand turn down a new track that had previously been used to transport gravel. From there, it was just two and a half miles to the camp.

We reached the circular parking lot, and I pulled up to a clearing between the only two cars in the lot. Apparently, death camps get as many summertime visitors as one might expect—which is not many at all.

"What do you all notice is different about this camp?" I asked my kids.

"What do you mean? Where's the camp?" Dovid Chaim strained to see the view from his window, struggling to understand why I had asked about a camp, when all he could see was forest and fields.

"Exactly. Where's the camp?"

When we arrived, there was nothing there. Just a wide-open, thirty-acre clearing amid an otherwise untouched, densely wooded forest. The Nazis had destroyed every remnant of the camp. So it was left for me and the markers to explain to the family what had once stood on this killing field, and the horrors that took place there.

The passengers did not realize they had reached a dead end. The Nazis had perfectly crafted their arrival platform to mislead them as to just where their train cars had come to a halt. They thought they were stopping at a transit station on the way further east. A sign indicated the name of the station was *Ober Majdan*, a familiar landed estate not far from the camp. The walls of the station had train schedules, names of destinations, a clock, and a ticket window.

It was an elaborate hoax. The destinations were invented, the timetables irrelevant, and the clock had unmoving hands painted on a white, dangling clock face. The ticket booth was permanently closed.

This was such an eye-opener for me. This level of deception was inhuman. I don't know if there are words for that level of subterfuge. How sick do you have to be to concoct such a plan? And the Jews had no choice but to literally go along for the ride.

Thousands of Jews are estimated to have died aboard the trains. After their horrific journey, the Jews who survived must have been happy to get out of their crowded cattle cars and breathe fresh air. Most probably failed to notice the discrepancies of this makeshift station. If anything, many of them may have tragically felt a sense of hope.

Treblinka was the ideal location for the Nazi plan, conveniently located equidistant from the Warsaw and Białystok Ghettos, which held five hundred thousand and sixty thousand Jews, respectively. More important, it was about three miles from the main Warsaw-Białystok railway, which meant that it was secluded enough to muffle the sounds of murder and hide the Nazis' crimes.

The original camp, Treblinka I, built in November 1941, was a slave labor camp. It also served as a labor education camp for non-Jewish Poles. The extermination camp at Treblinka, known as Treblinka II, was built in April 1942, a little over a mile away. In fact, many Polish prisoners from the Treblinka labor camp were forced to build the death camp a half-hour's walk from where they slept. They were, however, a small part of the Treblinka workforce. The majority of those who built the extermination camp were Jews rounded up from the villages surrounding Treblinka.

As in the story of Masada, where Jewish slaves were compelled to build the ramp used by the Romans to destroy the Jewish fortress, Polish Jews were forced to build the structures used to murder their brethren. They had no choice. Lucjan Puchała, a Polish prisoner who had helped build the train tracks leading to the death camp, recalled how "the SS-men and Ukrainians supervising the work killed a few dozen people every day, so that when I looked from the place where I worked to the place where the Jews worked, the field was covered with corpses."

Puchała also had no idea of the camp's true purpose until later, when he overheard a conversation among the Germans. He was horrified at his unwitting participation.

Though the labor was carried out by Jewish and Polish prisoners, the entire project was overseen by two private German engineering firms: the Schönbronn Company of Leipzig, and the Warsaw branch of Schmidt-Münstermann, both commissioned by the Central Construction Agency of the Waffen-SS. German industry was complicit in the Holocaust: Siemens, Krupp, BMW—the list is as long as it is surprising. Here, we see respectable civilian German engineering firms were willing to lend their expertise to construct a camp to exterminate human beings. It is impossible that they should not have known what the gas chambers and crematoria were for.

Treblinka was built in conjunction with two other extermination camps at Sobibor and Belzec, all part of a Nazi initiative known as Aktion Reinhard, named for the assassinated Reinhard Heydrich, to systematically exterminate the Jews of occupied Poland. The new camps would be extermination camps. There would be no pretense of *Arbeit Macht Frei*. Nearly every person who arrived was immediately put to death. In just two years between 1941 and 1943, two million Jews would perish in these factories of death.

The first trainload of six thousand Jewish deportees from the Warsaw Ghetto arrived at Treblinka on July 23, 1942. In Treblinka's first two months of operation, between four and seven thousand Jews would be sent daily from Warsaw to Treblinka. According to official SS reports, by mid-September 1942—less than two months after the first transport arrived—256,000 Jews had been incinerated on site.

The camp's first commandant was Irmfried Eberl, a young doctor of psychiatry from Innsbruck, who distinguished himself as one of the earliest proponents and defenders of Hitler's T4 euthanasia program, which systematically killed Germans who were disabled and mentally ill. He was appointed the chief medical director of the killing centers at Brandenburg and Bernberg while still in his twenties, and was chosen to run Treblinka because of his already considerable experience in systematic murder.

Eberl, however, was overconfident in his ability to kill on the mass scale expected by his superiors. SS-Unterscharführer Willi Mentz, an SS officer at Treblinka, said Eberl "was very ambitious," and he "ordered more transports than could be 'processed' in the camp." Consequently, "trains had to wait outside the camp because the occupants of the previous transport had not yet all been killed," resulting in the death of many of the people stuck in the boxcars, whose bodies were piled up on the platform. The smell of the decomposing bodies reached towns as far as six miles away, jeopardizing operational secrecy and attracting the disapproval of the Nazi leadership. They were unhappy with his inability to process all the bodies of the people he was killing, and dismissed him for inefficiency. Captured in 1948, Eberl killed himself before trial.

Eberl was replaced by Franz Stangl, who had been running the death camp at Sobibor—a monster who could also make the trains run on time. In 1970, while serving a life sentence in prison, Stangl gave an interview describing in chilling detail his arrival at his new command at Treblinka:

We could smell it from kilometers away…as we drove into what was Treblinka station, there were hundreds of [corpses]—just lying there—they'd obviously been there for days, in the heat. In the station was a train full of Jews, some dead, some still alive…

What Stangl saw, however, was not just bodies, but the things they had left behind:

When I entered the camp and got out of the car on the square, I stepped knee-deep into money; I didn't know which way to turn, where to go. I waded in notes, currency, precious stones, jewelry, clothes. The smell was indescribable…

The most shocking part of Stangl's account, however, was what he saw just a few hundred feet away from the piles of lifeless bodies. Along the outer edges of the forest, and "all around the perimeter of the camp, there were tents and open fires with groups of Ukrainian guards and girls— whores from Warsaw, I found out later—weaving, drunk, dancing, singing, playing music…"

How these Ukrainian guards could dance in clear view of such a monstrous display of death is a mystery. What mental defect could explain such indifference to the most blatant desecration of human life? Stangl put an immediate stop to this offense to military order. Under his direction, Treblinka was an effective killing machine, with no dancing.

By the time the last trains arrived on August 21, 1943, approximately nine hundred thousand Jews were murdered at Treblinka. If you do the math, that's twenty-three hundred Jews killed every single day, day after day, for fifty-six weeks. In just thirteen months, more people were killed at Treblinka than in any other camp, besides Auschwitz.

The Nazis tried to hide what they had done at Treblinka. As the Red Army approached in August 1943, they had one final gassing, and then had the remaining Jewish prisoners take apart the camp—the barracks, the gas chambers, the crematoria—brick by brick. The Jews were then shot, and the Nazis took bulldozers to the blackened earth and planted saplings in the clearing. They even built an old-looking barn on the site of the death camp, leaving a Ukrainian man named Oswald Strebel to live there with his family, farming the cursed earth. He was given this new home on one condition:

if anyone were to ever ask how long he had been there, he was to answer that he and his forefathers had been farming that land for as long as they could remember.

Strebel abandoned the area in 1944, unable to find happiness farming one of the largest mass graves on earth. Once he was gone, looters descended upon the camp, looking for gold and other valuables that might have been left by the Jews on the way to their deaths. When they began to dig, they found the train depot with no departing passengers. That was how the world found out about Treblinka.

Franz Stangl made a good run from the hangman. He was sent to fight partisans in 1943, with the apparent expectation that he would not live to tell anyone what he had done in the camps. But he somehow survived, and was captured by American forces in Austria, in 1945. They nearly let him go, before they found out who he was. Before he could be tried, Stangl escaped from prison and fled to Syria with help from Bishop Alois Hudal, who helped established the "ratlines" that assisted Nazis seeking to escape from the Allies.

Nazi hunter Simon Wiesenthal tracked him down, tracing his progress from Syria in 1949, to Brazil in 1956. Wiesenthal did not find out where he was until 1964, when a former Gestapo officer informed him that Stangl was working as a mechanic for Volkswagen, in São Paulo, Brazil. Wiesenthal subsequently convinced the Austrian authorities to seek his extradition for his role in the Nazi euthanasia program and the Sobibor and Treblinka death camps.

Stangl was arrested by the Brazilian police on February 28, 1967. Poland and Germany also sought his extradition, and Stangl was ultimately sent to Germany, where he stood trial in 1970. He was sentenced to life imprisonment for his role in the murder of more than one million people, but lasted only seven months in a Düsseldorf prison before dying of heart failure. Stangl told an interviewer a day before his death that his conscience was clear, and that he "never intentionally hurt anyone."

All that is left of this hell on earth is a clearing in the forest we could see from the parking lot. The rail lines were gone, pulled up by the Nazis, along with the rest of the camp. But there was a subtly placed memorial in the shape of a train track. It was made of large stone slabs, each as wide as a railroad tie, lined up in a stonework lattice leading toward the large clearing where the camp once stood.

We walked along the railway and into the clearing. One of the first things I noticed was how small Treblinka seemed—at least in comparison to the other camps I had visited, which had shocked me with their apparent endlessness. Camps like Dachau and Auschwitz seemed like the setting to a nightmare, with shadowy structures sprawling infinitely in all directions, as if to deny all hope of escape. Treblinka, however, felt small—if only from its footprint.

We all knew why it felt that way. No Jew ever slept here overnight. Here, there was no opportunity to cling to life through work or cooperation; all but a handful of prisoners chosen for the Sonderkommando units were killed upon arrival. The Nazis had no need for parade grounds to hold roll calls, or areas for slave laborers to work, or even barracks to house prisoners.

We continued into the clearing. The forest was dense on all sides and cut evenly along the perimeter of the camp just beyond where barbed wire had confined the prisoners. The tree line was yet another enclosure, as sturdy and forbidding as a stone wall.

My daughter Shaina noticed this as well. "It's as if beyond the wooden fence and barbed wire, the forest was holding them in. The Jews must have felt so trapped. Everything about this place makes you feel trapped."

Baba joined in. "My God. I can't even think of what the Jews must have felt when they got here. Everywhere they looked, they were closed in. Literally, alone in this unnatural space in the middle of a forest so thick that—even if you did manage to escape—you would have nowhere to go."

She was right. Treblinka holds you with the grip of total seclusion.

I saw something else in the walls of the forest that surrounded the camp. In their abrupt, unnatural way, they reminded me of the walls of the Red Sea as they split during the Israelites' exodus from Egypt, allowing the Jews safe passage from the land of their enemies. At Treblinka, however, the message was the reverse. Here, it was man who had split the forest to deliver the Jews away from the safety of their God.

In the center of the clearing, there was a large monument. It was unlike any other I had ever seen. It was not geometrical or neatly arranged. Instead, it seemed chaotic. It consisted of massive slabs of rock, torn straight from the quarry that had once existed at Treblinka. They were rough, natural, and unsculpted, with harsh, protruding spines along their edges. It looked as though there was something trapped within each stone, trying desperately to escape—to *scream*. They were arranged without any sense of order, tossed about in what amounted to a massive circle. The memorial was meant to represent the innumerable headstones that should have been lining the fields in neatly set rows. To me, the scattered, jagged stones appeared as fragments of the victims' torn souls.

In the middle of this circle of stones was a tall rock structure, at the top of which one could make out a relief that depicted a crowd of skull-like heads waving disjointed hands toward the heavens, apparently begging for air. On the other side, there was a menorah, representing light, I imagine. I could not understand just how light figured into any of this.

As we walked back toward our car, I found myself detached and largely absent. No one seemed to notice, not even my nine-year-old daughter. She, and the rest of my family, felt the same way. We could barely look at one another, let alone conduct a conversation.

Throughout the visit, I had carried with me the special Sefer Torah that we had written in memory of Elie Wiesel and the six million victims of the Holocaust. I held on to it for dear life, as if it represented a powerful beacon of hope and light in an infinite chasm of evil and darkness. In every picture we took at Treblinka, you can see how tightly I was clinging to the Torah, its white mantle representing purity in a place of insufferable evil.

I saw a stone, strewn among the others, with the inscription *Janusz Korczak*. I had seen the memorial to this man in Warsaw just the day before. It depicted the elderly Korczak looking mournfully into the distance, his hands resting on the shoulders of the children who surrounded him.

Born Henryk Goldszmit, he had adopted the pseudonym Janusz Korczak to enter a literary competition, and subsequently became known for writing children's books and advocating for their rights. Though trained as a doctor, Korczak opened an orphanage for Jewish children in Warsaw. He designed the orphanage to operate as a "children's republic," complete with a parliament, court, and newspaper.

When the Nazis conquered Warsaw in the fall of 1939, they forced his orphanage to relocate into the ghetto. Korczak saw this as an opportunity to bring joy to the ghetto's Jewish residents, who were living in the most wretched misery. He had his children learn popular Polish plays, which they performed for their fellow Jews trapped in the squalor of the ghetto. By mid-1943, the Nazis began to prepare for the deportation of Warsaw's Jews to Treblinka. Many of the Germans had heard of Korczak, and, impressed by his work, wanted his life spared. On at least five occasions, he was given the opportunity to leave the ghetto, and likely would have survived the war. Korczak, however, refused to abandon the children that he cared for. He would be with them, he said, until the very end.

On August 5, 1942, the Jews were ordered to assemble at the train station in Warsaw. Korczak told the children to put on their finest set of clothes, and to choose their favorite toy to carry in a small blue satchel on the journey ahead. Together, they boarded the train.

Joshua Perle, an eyewitness, described the event:

Janusz Korczak was marching, his head bent forward, holding the hand of a child, without a hat, a leather belt around his waist, and wearing high boots. A few nurses were followed by two hundred children, dressed in clean and meticulously cared for clothes, as they were being carried to the altar…On all sides the children were surrounded by the German, Ukrainian, and this time also Jewish policeman. They whipped and fired shots at them…The very stones of the street wept at the sight of this procession.

Władysław Szpilman wrote in his book, *The Pianist,* how the children walked toward the trains in a "happy mood." Korczak had told them they ought to be cheerful, since they were headed for the country, where "at last they would be able to exchange the horrible suffocating city walls for meadows of flowers, streams where they could bathe, and woods full of berries and mushrooms." The meandering path they took to the trains is shown in the Warsaw Jewish Museum, and it seems they got lost a few times as they marched. If only they had never found their way. When they arrived at the train station, a popular legend goes, an SS officer recognized the man as the author of one his favorite children's books. He, too, offered to spare the life of the old writer. Korczak, again, refused.

Later that day, after the grueling train ride to Treblinka, he marched into the gas chamber, together with the two hundred young children who had trusted him with their lives, their love, and their faith.

I stared at the stone memorial. It was all I could do to keep from abandoning hope as I stood on the same spot where those children threw one last look toward their father and gleaned from his calm demeanor that one last bit of hope—just moments before they were taken away.

Cheftziba walked over and stood quietly next to me. She slowly mouthed the name of the Polish writer, syllable by syllable, being thrown off by the oddly placed Z's. "Oh, Janusz Korczak! From the orphanage!"

"That's right, Cheftziba. Remember?"

After a few moments, she looked up toward me, squinting in the sun.

I had bought Cheftziba one of his children's books that was translated into English, and she loved it.

"Is this where Janusz Korczak is buried?"

"Well, it might be, Cheftziba, but we don't know."

"Why don't we know where he's buried?"

I wondered, and not for the last time, if I had done the right thing by bringing my young children to this place of evil and death. How do you answer a question like that from a nine-year-old? Do you tell them that Janusz Korczak was incinerated into ash? That his remains were scattered by the wind, into the forest and beyond? How can I explain that a man who sacrificed his life to give comfort to his children is not actually buried *anywhere*? What do I say if she asks about the burial place of the two hundred children, all about her age, who came from his orphanage?

"Well, he's probably buried right here, Cheftziba. We don't know, because all that was left was his ashes. And they were scattered near here. That's probably why the stone was placed here."

She looked on silently, and I felt my eyes well up.

Dovid Chaim was just a few feet away. He was eleven. They were both the age of the children brought here with Korczak. I couldn't bear to think of it. How helpless children are at this age—unable to fight, unable to run. But beyond that, they could not comprehend their fate—too young to know evil. Innocent.

This would be the most difficult part of our trip. In the family conversations we had after our return home, all seemed to agree the day we visited Treblinka was our trip's inverted summit—the deepest depths to which we would plummet.

My daughter Baba was the first to say it. "Treblinka was the worst. I don't know why. It just hit me in a way no other place could. I almost feel bad saying that. I mean, I know more people were killed at Auschwitz, but Treblinka...it just felt...*darker*."

No one seemed to disagree.

I think one reason Treblinka had such a profound impact, is its isolation. At Auschwitz, you meet other Jews who are visiting, and feel a sense of camaraderie. But this is a haunted place in the middle of woods that much fewer people visit. The only comfort I found was in carrying the Elie Wiesel Torah, consecrated to the memory of the six million, with me. People would come up to kiss the Torah. Then this strange occurrence happened. Just when we were feeling really alone at the death camp, a bus suddenly turned up with Jewish pilgrims from New York. It was a blessing to suddenly run into a group of alumni from Yeshiva University, and meet the scholar who was leading them, Rabbi Herschel Schacter, the head of the Rabbinical Academy at Yeshiva University, and one of America's greatest Torah scholars. Our family took a picture with Rabbi Schachter.

I was not fully aware of the impact that Treblinka had on the children when we were there. Shaina said later that she had been really frustrated and angry with me. I asked her to get something from the car, and she ordinarily would not have thought twice about going, but everything was bothering her at that moment, and she did not want to walk alone to the parking lot.

"I remember feeling, when I walked," she recalled, after the trip, "how sickening it was to be in the middle of nowhere and see how the Nazis tried to keep it so secluded. Some of the camps were in the middle of cities, but this one was in the middle of nowhere. How did they even transport Jews here? I felt that frustration. I was an angry person in Treblinka. I remember walking in the big, open space with all the memorials and stones everywhere, and the first thing that hit me was that I didn't feel anything."

I also did not realize how profoundly Yosef was affected. But Shaina did. "I'm very close with Yosef and all my siblings. I'm the older sister, so I feel a certain responsibility. I saw him walking. I believe he was holding the Torah for my dad. He was looking down shaking his head. He came up to me and said, 'Shaina, I don't know what to think. I don't know what to think. I don't know what to think.' He was saying it in a broken, sad way. He wasn't crying, but he was confused, and you could tell he was in pain."

Shaina teared up at the memory. "As an older sister, it was devastating to see how this experience could break a sixteen-year-old. He was this young kid, so positive and happy, and he was confused and hurt. When he said that, it hit me that we were in the evilest place."

Shaina also had an interesting perspective that had not occurred to me. She said one thing that struck her was the thick trees circling the memorials that took away some of the emptiness. The forest had covered this entire area, but the Nazis had gone to great lengths to clear it to make room for their killing center.

"I remember thinking how the Nazis cleared this area," Shaina said, weeks later, from the comfort of our New Jersey home. "They wanted to kill Jews so much they had to clear this space, which was probably so difficult. Think about the manpower needed to take down that many trees. They made a perfect circle in the middle of nowhere just to exterminate Jews in secret. It was so incredibly evil to be able to think of something like that. These thick trees really stuck out. It's not like other parts of Poland and Europe, where trees are very separated. These were huge, towering trees bunched together."

The trees really spoke to Shaina in a way I had not considered. This is how she explained it:

As a Jew who grew up with Torah in our life, we always learn that one of the key things is that nature witnesses things. God says, a lot of times the mountains and the valley will be my witnesses for your relationship with me. I remember thinking, there's no evidence of what happened here. It's an empty space with just memorials. But there are trees. I felt like the trees witnessed everything, and they were still standing strong. Okay, they don't have life like human beings, and they are not animate, but they are the only things that witnessed the evil. The only thing that can remember, besides the survivors, are these trees. The forest is here forever. The trees saw what happened. I remember, that was very eerie. It sounds weird, but to me it was very real at the time. I just remember staring at the trees. Big, huge trees.

Shaina was also struck by what the Nazis did to hide the evidence of their crimes, and the magnitude of the deception. "They were in the middle of nowhere, but they had to take out the bodies and then burn them—the ones they had already buried. They didn't want the world to know what they were doing, and they got Jews to do this dirty work for them."

I was unaware that Shaina was having this internal monologue. I could see, however, the impact Treblinka and the other places of evil were having on Baba. She was only nineteen, but looked as if she had aged decades in just two weeks. She looked haggard and overwrought. My heart ached as I realized the terrible toll it was all taking on her.

As we piled into the car, I watched Baba rush to put her headphones in her ears and turn on her music. She leaned her head against the window and closed her eyes. I could tell from the quickness of her movements that she had been anxiously awaiting the opportunity to finally escape.

I understood. Taking my cue from her, I turned on the car radio, rolling the dice with whatever Polish radio had to offer. We drove off twice as fast as we had on the way in, submitting to the irrepressible urge to do what nine hundred thousand Jews tragically could not—escape.

CHAPTER 11

TYKOCIN: THE END OF THE SHTETL

A professional tour guide had told me about a town called Tykocin, which he said was the last shtetl. I had heard my whole life about shtetls, and was interested to see it. But if we changed our plans, we would get to Warsaw after the kosher restaurant where we planned to have dinner had closed. It's such a miracle to find kosher restaurants in Eastern Europe that there was no way we were giving up the opportunity. Everyone was hungry, but Shaina was insistent that we go to the shtetl.

"I said, 'I need to see Tykocin,'" she recalled, after the trip. "I remember saying, 'We have to go. It's worth it. Forget the rest. This is our opportunity to see a real shtetl.'"

Everyone agreed, so we took the hour-and-eight-minute drive to Tykocin. It was a gorgeous drive through the middle of nowhere, passing through little Polish villages with dilapidated wooden houses and fields. Poland is devout in its Catholicism, and there were crosses everywhere and little boxes with religious icons. Shaina said she felt like we were back in medieval times. A thousand years ago, the Crusaders had marched through Europe on their way to fight the infidels in the Holy Land, killing Jews as they went, with the sanction of the religious authorities.

Here, there were no trees. Just open fields. The Jews had nowhere to hide, not only for lack of hiding places, but for the attitude of the Poles in these little Catholic villages. I told her that these were little close-minded towns that probably never saw a Jew before, so when they heard about Jews being exterminated, and a Jew wanted to hide, they would not help them. In fact, the Germans had encouraged the Poles to loot Jewish property in Tykocin.

Like most people, the image I had in mind was of Anatevka, from the film *Fiddler on the Roof*. As we drove into the small town, across the bridge that spans the Narew River, we felt like we were indeed traveling back in time, to the days when Jews lived in small towns like this. The first thing we saw were a lot of wooden houses. One of them had a big Jewish star on it, carved in the wood. Shaina said she thought, "Wow, this is a Jewish village."

An empty Jewish village. There was no one around—eerie. We walked along the cobblestone streets and came upon a massive building that was the central synagogue. They have an exhibit outside—Maintaining the Memory—with pictures of the Jews who had lived there, and information about the history of Jewish life in the town.

Tykocin was regarded as one of the most important Jewish centers in Poland in the 17th and 18th centuries, second only to Krakow. In the early days, Jews were involved in the trade of salt, spices, and textiles. It also became a center for Talmudic study, and many famous rabbis lived in the city.

The Baroque-style synagogue was built in 1642, in place of an older wooden building. It was the second biggest synagogue (after Krakow) in Poland at the time. It has been preserved and renovated, and is now a Jewish museum. Inside are beautiful murals, illustrations of plants and animals, and pages from the daily prayer book, which apparently were done by an artist, rather than a Hebrew scholar, because they contain some spelling errors. The synagogue was sufficiently impressive to be voted one of the "new seven wonders" of Poland, in a contest sponsored by the Polish edition of *National Geographic Traveler* magazine. That's remarkable, considering Tykocin is not a major tourist attraction. In fact, the forty thousand visitors each year are primarily Israelis and other Jews.

In later years, the community was involved in the production and sale of beer and vodka, the meat trade, tanning, and the leasing of property. Under Russian rule, Jews were engaged in the timber trade. In the mid-19th century, nearly thirty-five hundred Jews lived in Tykocin, comprising 70 percent of the population. The decline of the economy led many Jews to immigrate to North America. *Fiddler on the Roof* ends with Tevye saying he is taking his family to America.

At the end of the 19th century, and beginning of the 20th, Zionism became popular among Jews in Tykocin, and people began to emigrate to Palestine. Those who remained in the town engaged in various crafts, and owned mills, breweries, a tallit factory, and a paintbrush factory. Approximately two thousand Jews, roughly 44 percent of the population, lived in Tykocin at the time of the Nazi invasion. Some Jews escaped to North America and Palestine. When the Germans turned the city over to the Soviets in 1939, as part of the agreement to split Poland between them, Jewish refugees from German-occupied areas were allowed into the city.

In June 1941, Hitler betrayed Stalin and invaded the Soviet Union. The Wehrmacht rolled east over the Polish plain, and the Germans returned to Tykocin. On August 25, the Jews were ordered to gather in the market for resettlement in a ghetto in Czerwony, but they got no farther than the Lupochowa Forest, where they were shot by the *Einsatzgruppen* and buried in pits that had been prepared in advance. It is believed that fourteen hundred people were killed that day. Their names are on a plaque on the western wall of the synagogue in Tykocin.

We wanted to visit the Lupochowa Forest to see where the Jews were murdered, but it was already dark and we had to resume our journey. Looking it up online, however, I saw that there is a marker that says, in Hebrew and Polish: "Mass Grave of the Victims of the Shoah in Tykocin." There are also three pits surrounded by a fence, with a large stone inscribed in Polish: "Here lie 3000 Polish citizens brutally murdered in the years 1941–1943 by the Hitlerite thugs. Honor their memory."

I personally would not have used the word *thugs*. It is far too mild.

The commander of the *Einsatzgruppen* was SS-Obersturmführer Hermann Schaper. His unit was probably also responsible for massacres in Łomża, Radziłów, and Jedwabne. He was investigated for war crimes in 1964, but there was insufficient evidence to prosecute him, despite witnesses positively identifying him as the perpetrator in a number of massacres. The case was reopened in 1974, and in 1976, a German court found him guilty of murdering Poles and Jews. Justice delayed is often justice denied: Schaper was sentenced to just six years imprisonment, and was released early for medical reasons. He died of old age, in his nineties.

After the war, a handful of survivors returned to Tykocin, but they were attacked by Polish nationalists, and subsequently immigrated to Palestine.

There was a display for the Righteous Among the Nations, indicating that at least two Poles in Tykocin took action to save the Jews. Jan and Władysława Smółko were recognized by Yad Vashem in 1984, for taking in two brothers, Michael and Menachem Turek, who had been smuggled out of the Białystok Ghetto. The Smółkos provided them with Aryan documents, and supported them financially for about a year and a half, until the city was liberated. After the war, one brother moved to Israel, and the other to Australia. "In risking their lives to save the Turek brothers," Yad Vashem recognized that "the Smółkos were guided by humanitarian and patriotic motives, which overrode considerations of personal safety or economic hardship."

On the one hand, I can't help but think how grateful I am that there were people like the Smółkos. While on the other hand, it horrifies me that so few people were willing to follow their conscience and act morally to save the lives of others. If every Pole had the same courage as the Smółkos, if only a larger fraction of the population had followed their example, many more could have been saved.

Dovid was also especially affected by the story of Tykocin. Before coming on the trip, he said he knew the Holocaust was horrible. But he could not imagine how unbelievable it was for everyone in a shtetl to be shot; for people to be shot in a forest before an open grave; or worse, to be forced to dig *their own* graves, as so many of the Einsatzgruppen had done in other locations, knowing they were about to be killed; and for an entire community to be wiped out in a second. We all felt the horror and anger of being unable to so much as comprehend the human capacity to conduct such evil.

Next door to the synagogue is a hotel—Villa Regent. The name of the hotel is written in Hebrew, the logo has a menorah, and signs on the front of the building read "Restaurant" and "Rooms," in Hebrew, to identify these amenities to the target demographic. The hotel restaurant—Tejsza—was new and beautiful. It advertises itself as a Jewish restaurant, but it is non-kosher, and Jewish foods cost more than the typical inexpensive Polish dishes. The tables had candlesticks, a menorah, and wooden dolls dressed like Hasidim. A shtreimel—the fur hat worn by Hasidic Jews—hung in a corner, and Hasidic music played in the background.

Shaina was furious about the restaurant selling tchotchkes, especially the little wooden dolls she thought were supposed to be rabbis. She didn't think it was respectful in a place where all the rabbis were exterminated.

"They were trying to make it very touristy, like it was once a Jewish town," she recalled, "so they had little wooden rabbis, like puppets."

Shaina was so upset that even though she had to use the restroom, she refused to go inside.

We did not go to the town cemetery, which dates to 1522, and is one of the oldest in Poland. We were told it has been neglected by the town, and some of the gravestones with Hebrew, rather than Polish, inscriptions are covered by the uncut grass. Many are no longer standing, and one visitor said there was cow dung everywhere because the locals use this "empty lot" to graze their animals. Since no Jews have lived in the town for decades, the last burial took place in the 1930s.

As we left town, we passed a huge church, which was also indicative of a shtetl. Typically, the Jews lived on one side of town, with a synagogue as the dominant feature, while the Christians lived at the other end, near a church.

Shaina said later that the town had a display with "biographies of the Jews who lived there, and the pictures and the descriptions were exactly like the ones in my storybooks." She recalled one about "the righteous guy who owned a supermarket, but he gave all his money to the poor people." The stories reminded her of ones she had grown up hearing, which made them real. "I saw pictures of these people. But no one was there. So that really depressed me. I was angry. Whenever I get upset, I go to my dad and start questioning. Why aren't we reclaiming things like that? I was really down because we got there, and it's like a real shtetl, but no one was there. It was like a ghost town. It hurt because all the stories I grew up with about the shtetl were fun, illuminating, happy, and about Judaism flourishing. Then you get there and you're like, where are all these people? Oh, they were taken to a forest and shot by the *Einsatzgruppen*. They were all killed in one hour."

A lot of people asked me why I was going to Poland, especially Polish Jews who vowed never to visit their homeland after surviving the Holocaust. One Polish Jew, a prominent philanthropist, told me she was utterly disgusted by Poland. She would never visit Poland, even on the March of the Living, and would not speak the language.

As someone who did not have to endure what she did, I cannot question her judgment. Nevertheless, I have a different view. We can never forget what happened. We have to always remember the martyrs. We have to understand the history. For someone like me, who is devoted to combating genocide, and educating myself and others about genocide, I must know how this happened. The Germans were fighting a world war, and they still took the time and devoted untold resources to kill everyone in this tiny town of no strategic value.

As Shaina said: "I remember thinking, *Wow, all these happy moments came to an end, and I'm standing here at that end.* It was really hard because you heard all these stories about the shtetls, and those Jews don't exist anymore."

And that is how we spent July 4, 2017. On America's Independence Day, we visited a town where not only Jewish independence, but all Jewish life, was brought to an end. The only bright spot was knowing we were citizens of a nation that stands for freedom. The United States did not stand by and do nothing, as so many countries would later do, while genocides were committed in places such as Rwanda and Cambodia. If the United States had not entered the war and defeated Hitler, the Jewish people today might be an extinct footnote of history. The possibility is too horrible to contemplate.

CHAPTER 12

LOMZA: THE SEARCH FOR MY ROOTS

I wanted to visit the place where my grandfather was born, so we traveled to his hometown of Lomza, a tranquil country town only an hour away from the death vortex of Treblinka. Lomza was situated along the bank of the Narew River, which also flows through Tykocin. We stood on a hill overlooking the river valley, and felt glad knowing that my grandfather had grown up in such a gorgeous place.

Beyond the river, however, the town was incredibly depressing. I never thought of myself as Polish, but this was the place that gave me my Polish-Jewish roots, and it felt dispiriting. Maybe it was nicer when my grandpa lived there, but much of the town was destroyed in the war that swept back and forth across Poland. What is left has the bleak communist repressive feel of many towns in Eastern Europe once under Soviet control. Everything that was built since the war is ugly. Fortunately, my grandfather left around 1905, and eventually brought his entire family over to join him in America. Had he not done so, they would have been murdered.

My children saw that visiting Lomza was different for me. When I visited the other horrible places of Jewish memory and genocide, I was mourning for my people. Here, I was mourning for my actual family. Yes, my grandfather and his family had gotten out. But how many cousins and other relatives had been murdered by the Nazis who made Lomza *judenrein*?

Like so many Polish towns, Lomza has a long Jewish history that ends in tragedy. It began in the 14th century when Jews who engaged in various crafts, and the trade of timber, salt, and raw materials, settled here. Jews were persecuted at various times as control of the city passed from one sovereign to another. By the second half of the 19th century, Jews accounted for nearly half the population. In 1851, the great and central Beit Midrash was built for prayer and study. According to the YIVO Institute for Jewish Research, the first Lithuanian-styled yeshiva in Poland was founded in Lomza, in 1883. That same year, a cemetery and a Chevra Kadisha (Burial Society) were also established.

At the end of the 19th century, and during the early part of the 20th, Zionism took hold in the city, and local branches of the religious and revisionist Zionist movements opened. The community of roughly nine thousand was a cultural center with nine newspapers, a theater group, and a sports association.

In 1920, during the Russo-Polish War, many Jews joined the Polish Army. At one point, the Bolsheviks conquered Lomza. But it was recaptured by the Poles. The Polish general who led the counterattack suspected the Jews of being collaborators with the Russians, and imprisoned some, and forced others to clean up the city and rebuild the Narew bridges blown up by the Russians.

The situation for Jews deteriorated in the 1930s, with the worldwide Great Depression and the coming to power of Hitler in Germany. Opportunities for Jews were restricted. Limitations were placed on other trades and businesses, often with the intent of giving the work done by Jews to Christians. In 1936, sanitation inspectors closed every Jewish bakery because they did not satisfy the city's hygienic requirements. The same year, spurred by Christian clergy, Polish youngsters blocked the entrances to Jewish shops to prevent Christians from entering. Violence against Jews led the community to organize self-defense teams to protect the synagogue and Jewish shops. Riots erupted during the summer of 1937, with Polish students from the elementary school attacking kids at the Jewish elementary school with knives. The following March, the cemetery was vandalized.

When the war started, Lomza was bombed on September 7, 1939, killing more than a thousand people, including many Jews. Three days later, the German Army entered the city and occupied it for eighteen days. During that time, they abused the Jews—for example, beating congregants and desecrating Torah scrolls during Jewish religious services. All able men were rounded up and sent to a prison camp in Germany.

The Soviets came next on September 28, 1939, and confiscated the property of wealthy residents. Jews were arrested, and many drafted into the Soviet army. As a precaution, the historic yeshiva was transferred to Vilna.

Less than two years later, the Germans were back. Some Jews apparently escaped with the retreating Soviets. On July 4, 1941, exactly seventy-six years before we arrived, the Nazi persecution of the Jews began. Jewish property was confiscated, and as occurred elsewhere, the Nazis humiliated Jews in the streets—cutting men's beards and indiscriminately beating them. Jews were required to wear yellow badges on the front and back of their shirts or jackets, and to work. Periodically, the Nazis would round up groups of Jews and take them to the Galczyn Forest and shoot them. It is estimated that two thousand Jews were murdered in the forest during the Nazi occupation.

In mid-July 1941, a *Judenrat* was established, headed by Mendel Mushinski, a Jewish refugee from Germany. On August 12, all the Jews were moved to a ghetto in the market area of the city. The exact number is uncertain, but the estimates range from ten thousand to eighteen thousand. The Jews were forced to build their own workshops, with tools and materials they had to supply, to help the German war effort by making ammunition, soap, boots, and other goods. Some Jews were forced to work outside the ghetto, in a quarry, or paving roads. On August 16, the Jews were assembled, and the *Judenrat* was given a list of about two hundred names to call out. Those who came forward were taken to the forest and shot.

As in other ghettos, Jews organized a welfare system that provided food, care for children and the elderly, and a hospital. The conditions deteriorated, and diseases, such as dysentery and typhus, spread through the ghetto, killing an unknown number of people. The Germans had put barbed wire around the ghetto, with a sign on the gate that said, in German and Polish: DANGER DISEASE. It is not clear whether this was a warning about actual sickness in the ghetto, or an indication of the German view of Jews as diseased parasites.

The situation grew worse as Jews from surrounding towns were brought to Lomza, causing severe overcrowding. The *Judenrat* asked for the ghetto to be expanded, but the Nazis had a different solution to overcrowding—they took another two thousand Jews to the forest and executed them.

At one point, thirty Jews apparently escaped, and the furious Nazis ordered the *Judenrat* to turn over forty Jews and two members of the council. It is not clear if their lives were threatened if they did not comply, but that was the case elsewhere. According to Yad Vashem, the *Judenrat* "handed over to them all the mentally ill, along with some cripples and old people," and two members of the *Judenrat*. All forty Jews were murdered in the forest.

On November 1, 1942, the *Judenrat* was given four hours to evacuate the ghetto. Thousands of Jews had already been executed, or died from the conditions in the ghetto. On the eve of the liquidation of the ghetto, the director of the hospital committed suicide. Most of the remaining Jews—between eight thousand and ten thousand—were transferred to a transit camp before being deported to Auschwitz, in January 1943.

After learning the terrible history of Lomza, all I could think was *God bless America*. The United States took my grandfather in when he was a teenager, around the turn of the 19th century. He labored and brought his family over, one by one, and eventually fought in World War I as an American soldier in France.

Though my grandfather died when I was young, I remember him well. After my mother moved us to Miami Beach from Los Angeles, when my parents divorced, my grandparents lived right near our school, and I used to visit my grandfather almost every day. I knew he was from Poland, but he rarely talked about Lomza. I loved my grandfather, Frank Paul, very much, but he was already elderly and sick when I was a boy. He died a month before my bar mitzvah, forty years ago. He was about eighty years old. I say *about*, because the records of Jews who were born in Poland before the turn of the century are not entirely accurate. I miss him very much.

I was glad to have the opportunity to visit his birthplace, because this was probably the closest to my roots I will ever get. My father was born in Iran and left there when he was a teenager. I never visited where he was born, because as an American, and especially as a Jew, this would almost certainly be a one-way trip.

Maybe it's easier to go back to places if your relatives, as far as you know, missed the Holocaust. What happened in Lomza was typical of the way the thing went in small towns all over Europe.

I hoped to find the house where my grandfather was born, but I never did. There's little left of this town because so much was destroyed. There were few people on the street, and they didn't appear friendly—maybe because we didn't speak the same language.

Looking at a large map of the city, I could see the Jewish cemetery where I'm sure relatives on my maternal side must be buried. But, as the day was slipping away, I could not try to find their graves. We looked for Jewish sites, but all were destroyed by the Nazis. The synagogue was razed by the Germans early in the war, and as much as we tried, we could not find the place where it stood. Although, I was told it is marked by a memorial plaque with an inscription in Polish and Hebrew, that reads:

> From July 1941 to November 1942, in the streets: Dworna—now 22—go Lipca, Senatorska, Woziwodzka, Zielona, Żydowska—now Zatylna, and Rybaki—the Nazis set up a ghetto, where they exterminated 9,000 Poles of Jewish ethnicity. 3,500 of them were shot in the woods near the villages of Giełczyn and Sławiec. The German occupiers established 15 ghettos in the towns of Łomża region. The tragic fate of around 40,000 people living in them led to the extermination camp in Treblinka. May the memory of them and of those who were helping them in those terrible days last.

God bless the people of Poland and Lomza. I was privileged and gratified to visit the city of my grandfather's birth. But I love America, and I could not be more grateful to the United States for giving my grandfather the gift of life. On this 4th of July 2017, I have never felt more grateful to be an American.

CHAPTER 13

WARSAW: THE JEWS FIGHT BACK

arsaw, a modern European city that was our base of operations for the Polish leg of the trip, is the epicenter of the Holocaust. The city was utterly destroyed in the war as the Nazis and the Polish resistance had it out, and then the Russians swept in. Most of the Jews were already dead, killed in the camps or the ghetto by the time it was razed.

Three million Jews once lived in Poland, fully half the population of modern Israel. Today, there are more ghosts than people. Only nine Jewish communities survive in a country that once boasted more than twelve hundred. In Poland, anyway, Hitler succeeded in his goal of a *judenrein* Europe.

Jews settled in Warsaw during the 15th century, and built a synagogue and a cemetery. But they were intermittently persecuted and driven out of the city entirely, from 1527 to 1768. They settled on the outskirts of Warsaw, but the Christian merchants still kept them out of the city. The situation of the Jews in Warsaw did not improve until the partition of Poland in 1795, when it came under the authority of the Kingdom of Prussia, which was more lax in its regulation of their activities. Jews were merchants and traders, tailors, hatters, and furriers. As in many places in Europe, one profession where Jews became prominent was moneylending—a business often forced on them because of restrictions on owning land. By 1810, the Jewish population had grown from less than eight thousand at the turn of the century, to 14,600 in 1810—about 18 percent of the population.

In 1809, a Jewish quarter was established in the city. Only Jewish bankers, merchants, manufacturers, army suppliers, and doctors were allowed to live there, and only if they agreed to wear European-style clothing and send their children to non-Jewish schools.

In 1815, Warsaw became the capital of the Kingdom of Poland, under the Russian tsar, and the Jewish population grew exponentially from 15,600 in 1816, to 72,800 in 1864. Though the city was one-third Jewish, limitations continued to be placed on the Jews, including the denial of citizenship. Alexander II appointed a Pole to govern Warsaw, who eliminated discriminatory taxes, allowed Jews to settle anywhere in the city, and removed bans on holding office and practicing certain trades.

By this time, most Jews were Hasidic and Yiddish-speaking, though a small number associated with the Enlightenment Movement and established a German Synagogue, in 1802. As the YIVO Institute noted: "This was not a 'reform' synagogue of the type then developing in Germany, but the arrangements for worship had a number of modern features, including a sermon, initially given in German, and from the late 1850s, in Polish."

The largest synagogue in Warsaw was the Great Synagogue in Tłomackie Square, which was built in 1878. It held Reform services in Polish for as many as twenty-four hundred people. The complex had a large hall, meeting rooms, an archive, a library, and a school.

Jews were often caught in the vortex of Polish politics, and had to decide whether to join uprisings against the tsar. Some did. But others were wary; the Russians ruthlessly suppressed any opposition to tsarist rule. Warsaw prospered, and the Jewish population grew dramatically as Jews fled pogroms in Russia, and 150,000 emigrated from places such as Lithuania, Belorussia, and the Ukraine. By 1914, 337,000 Jews lived in the city, nearly 40 percent of the total population. Though a growing number assimilated, the community remained overwhelmingly Orthodox and Yiddish-speaking. The city had roughly three hundred synagogues, most of which were Hasidic. During this period, Yiddish literature flourished, thanks in large measure to the work of author and playwright I.L. Peretz.

Many Jews became active in Zionist groups, while those who belonged to the socialist Bund opposed Zionism and the revival of Hebrew. Orthodox Jewish groups also clashed with the Zionists. When World War I began, most Jews sided with the Germans because they believed their lives would be better with less persecution, provoking the animosity of the Russians and Polish nationalists. During the German occupation, from August 1915 until November 1918, the lives of Jews improved, as did relations between Jews and Poles. Everyone began to suffer, however, following the war and the onset of the Great Depression. Approximately forty thousand Jews immigrated to Palestine in the 1920s, in large measure because of excessive taxes and other discriminatory measures imposed on them by Prime Minister Władysław Grabski.

In the mid-1930s, under the influence of events in Germany, anti-Jewish violence accompanied a boycott of Jewish businesses and other discriminatory measures. "The air in Poland is permeated with anti-Semitic hatred," wrote Boris Smolar, who reported from Warsaw for the Jewish Telegraphic Agency, on August 7, 1934. "It is openly stimulated by the strong Polish political party, the National Democratic party, commonly called the 'Endeks'…[whose] propaganda campaign hints of possible pogroms, both in the press and in the open, at secret meetings and at public gatherings…."

That year, Poland signed a non-aggression pact with Germany, and anti-Semitism became more overt, with Jews sometimes attacked, or even killed, on the streets. In addition to taxing the Jews, several restrictive measures were adopted, such as limiting the percentage of Jews in university courses, and segregating them from their classmates. Cardinal August Hlond accused Jews in 1936, of fighting against the Catholic Church, spreading pornography, engaging in various criminal activities, including "white slavery," and being in "the vanguard of atheism, Bolshevism and revolution." Hlond was canonized in 1992, and named Venerable in May 2018, after Pope Francis approved a decree recognizing his "heroic virtues."

Despite the persecution, Warsaw's Jewish population continued to surge, reaching 375,000 in 1939, making it the largest Jewish community in Europe.

In September 1939, Warsaw was bombarded by German forces, and surrendered on September 29. Polish civilians, viewed by Nazis as subhuman, were used as slave laborers, interned in camps, and expelled and executed. The Nazis sought to destroy Polish culture and national identity, and that was just the Poles. The Jews were in for it even worse. As in Germany, they were systematically removed from society: they couldn't teach school, practice medicine, possess cash, own a radio or a telephone, travel by train, or mail a letter abroad. They were subject to a curfew, had to wear a star on their coats, and all the Jewish schools and synagogues were closed.

Chaim Kaplan, an educator and diarist of the Holocaust, wrote, in his diary: "The gigantic catastrophe which has descended on Polish Jewry has no parallel, even in the darkest periods of Jewish history."

As early as February 1940, the Nazis raised the idea of creating a Jewish quarter in Warsaw, according to Waldemar Schön, Head of the Department of Resettlement in the Warsaw District. Initially, he said objections were raised because it would disrupt the economy, and that because "about 80 percent of all the skilled labor was Jewish, it was indispensable and could not be shut away." This concern faded in succeeding weeks, and the decision was made to go ahead with establishing a ghetto to protect the German Army and population from the Jews, "carriers of the bacteria of epidemics." Jews also needed to be separated, Schön said, because "Jewish thinking and action had up to now dominated the population of the eastern lands." He added: "The beneficial effects of the elimination of Jewish influence can now already be seen. If the German task of reconstruction is to be successful at all, then the freedom of Jewry to act in the area must be ended."

In April 1940, the Nazis began to erect ten-foot-high walls topped with barbed wire to create a ghetto for the Jewish population. More than one hundred thousand non-Jewish Poles were ordered to leave the area, and 138,000 Jews to move in. Schön commented that it was surprising the resettlement which took less than six weeks and succeeded "without any blood being shed, and with the aid of police pressure only in the final stage." The Nazis were aided by the *Judenrat* and the Polish mayor.

On November 16, 1940, the Nazis searched the city and caught 11,130 Jews who were forcibly taken to the ghetto. In addition, 1,170 food stores and 2,600 other stores owned by Jews were sealed by the police. The same day, the ghetto was sealed. Ultimately, as many as a half-million Jews would be confined to a 1.3-square-mile area, with an average of seven people to a room. On November 19, all Jewish property found outside the ghetto walls was confiscated. The ghetto was turned into a city within a city. As in other ghettos, the Germans established a *Judenrat* under the leadership of an assimilated Jewish engineer named Adam Czerniaków.

The *Judenrat* established schools, hospitals, orphanages, recreation facilities, prayer rooms, and an orchestra, hoping they could ensure the survival of the community by cooperating with the Germans. They also engendered animosity from their fellow Jews, who accused them of collaboration, favoritism in who they chose for labor assignments, and selfishness. Chaim Kaplan, a teacher before the war, wrote:

"the *Judenrat*, in the language of the Occupying Power—is an abomination in the eyes of the Warsaw Community. When the Council is so much as mentioned, everyone's blood begins to boil. If it were not for fear of the authorities, there would be bloodshed.... According to rumor, the President [Czerniakow] is a decent man. But the people around him are the dregs of humanity....known as scoundrels and corrupt persons, who did not avoid ugly dealings even in the period before the war. The Community has become for them a milk-cow and an unending opportunity to take bribes, to rob the poor and crush the oppressed."

The *Judenrat* was instructed to give preference to productive members of the ghetto. Independently, the Jewish Self-Help Organization assisted the more vulnerable Jews, such as orphans and other children, and set up three hundred soup kitchens. Food was rationed by the Germans, and was below subsistence levels, providing less than 10 percent of the normal daily required calories.

One key to survival was smuggling. Children as young as five or six would be sent in and out of the ghetto. Women, often disguised as Aryans, smuggled food and medicine. The Nazis were less likely to suspect women because of their sexist view, which made it easier for females to pass through checkpoints and roadblocks. "These heroic girls are in mortal danger every day," ghetto chronicler Emanuel Ringelblum wrote, in May 1942. "Without a murmur, without a moment of hesitation, they accept and carry out the most dangerous missions. Nothing stands in their way."

The Germans shot most of the smugglers they caught, including the children. Nevertheless, the smuggling never stopped.

Without these courageous Jews, the situation inside the ghetto would have been even worse. Still, between 1940 and mid-1942, eighty-three thousand Jews died of starvation and disease. Indeed, one of the most harrowing experiences I have ever had of the Holocaust was holding in my very hands, at the Jewish Historical Institute of Warsaw, where the Ringelblum archive is kept, the actual death certificates of Jews who died in Warsaw during these years where the cause of death was listed as "Starvation." The Germans forced families to pay for their burial. If they did not have the money, the bodies were left to pile up in the streets. The Ringelblum archive includes video of the emaciated bodies of children being pushed aside by pedestrians in the ghetto so they could walk by.

Despite the hardships, few Jews committed suicide. Chaim Kaplan explained why:

> "Logically, we are obliged to die. According to the laws of nature, our end is destruction and total annihilation....But even this time we did not comply with the laws of nature. There is within us some hidden power, mysterious and secret, which keeps us going, keeps us alive, despite the natural law. If we cannot live on what is permitted, we live on what is forbidden. That is no disgrace for us...The Jews of Poland—oppressed and broken, shamed and debased, still love life, and do not wish to leave this world before their time. Say what you like, the will to live amidst terrible suffering is the manifestation of some hidden power whose nature we do not yet know."

The Germans began mass deportations to the new Treblinka death camp, in July 1942. After almost three long years of trying to maintain the ghetto and keep the Jewish population alive, Czerniaków was faced with the same dilemma presented to Rumkowski in Łódź: the Nazis demanded that he identify several thousand Jews each day for deportation, including children. By this time, he knew they were being sent to their deaths. The deportees were to take enough food for three days, about thirty pounds of baggage, and their valuables. Czerniaków wrote, in his diary: "Sturmbannführer Hoefle called me into the office and informed me that my wife was free at the moment, but if the deportation failed she would be the first to be shot as a hostage."

Czerniaków pleaded for the exemption of orphans, but the request was denied. He could see the writing on the wall. To his fellow Jewish Council members, Czerniaków wrote: "I can no longer bear all this. My act will prove to everyone what is the right thing to do." The desk where he took his life with a cyanide capsule is now in the Polin Museum of the History of Polish Jews in Warsaw.

Chaim Kaplan, who had been so critical of Czerniaków, saw him in a different light after his suicide: "His end proves conclusively that he worked and strove for the good of his people, though not everything that was done in his name was praiseworthy. Czerniakow earned immortality in a single instant."

Between July 22 and September 21, 1942, Yom Kippur, about 265,000 Jews were sent for extermination in Treblinka, from the Umschlagplatz, a train station at the edge of the ghetto. Jews were packed in locked boxcars. The Nazis offered people who voluntarily reported to the station, bread and jam. But that did not work, so the Germans began to raid houses. According to Yad Vashem, "City blocks would be closed off, and the Jewish Police would remove the buildings' residents to the streets. The Germans would carry out a selection while Polish or Ukrainian policemen would search in the abandoned homes for Jews in hiding. Many Jews who hid in the buildings or tried to escape the selection on the street were murdered on the spot. Most of the Jews who underwent the selection were chosen for deportation and sent to the Umschlagplatz."

Additional deportations were carried out in the following months. Over the course of these *aktions* (actions), more than ten thousand additional Jews died or were shot, twelve thousand were sent to slave labor camps, and twenty thousand sought refuge on the Aryan side. The Nazis thought they had left about thirty-five thousand Jews in the ghetto, but another twenty thousand were in hiding.

After the deportations began, the Jewish Combat Organization (Żydowska *Organizacja Bojowa*—ŻOB) was created under the leadership of twenty-three-year-old Mordecai Anielewicz. The group had roughly five hundred members, and managed to make contact with the Polish underground and smuggle some pistols and explosives into the ghetto. Another organization, the Jewish Military Union (Żydowski Związek *Wojskowy*—ŻZW), was established by a group of about 250 Revisionist Zionists (more militant Jews who believed in fighting for independence in Palestine) who maintained a tunnel to the Aryan part of the city.

Paweł Frenkel, the leader of the ŻZW, told a meeting of the Jewish military fighters that they would fight and die, but they would not be forgotten: "Of course we will fight with guns in our hands, and most of us will fall. But we will live on in the lives and hearts of future generations and in the pages of their history….We will die before our time, but we are not doomed. We will be alive for as long as Jewish history lives!"

After a respite in deportations, the Nazis launched a large-scale action on January 18, 1943, aimed at transferring thousands of Jews to slave labor camps. By this time, the Jews had learned that earlier transports had gone to Treblinka, and Treblinka was an extermination camp. The resistance groups feared that was the real destination, and decided to fight. Using the limited arms smuggled into the ghetto, the ŻOB and ŻZW engaged the small SS and police units sent to carry out the operation. They had joined a group of people being marched to the Umschlagplatz, and at a prearranged signal, opened fire on the guards. Jews scattered during the battle. Most of the Jewish fighters were killed, but the Nazis had been so surprised by the resistance, they withdrew on January 21, after sending away only about five thousand Jews.

The underground organizations believed they had stopped the deportations, but were realistic enough to realize it was only temporary. According to Yad Vashem, "They knew that they would have to fight to their last man, and their goal was not survival, but 'resistance for resistance's sake.'"

The Jews in the ghetto had shown they would not go like sheep to slaughter. The members of the resistance groups subsequently prepared bunkers, trained new recruits, and smuggled additional weapons into the ghetto in anticipation of the Germans' return. The ŻOB managed to increase its strength to more than 750 fighters, but obtained only nine rifles, fifty-nine pistols, Molotov cocktails, and a couple grenades. The underground called on the people to fight, rather than allow the Germans to deport them:

> Jews of Warsaw, the hour is drawing near. You must be prepared to resist. Not a single Jew should go to the railroad cars. Those who are unable to put up active resistance should resist passively and should go into hiding....Our slogan must be: 'All are ready to die as human beings.'

The Germans had also learned the lesson that the Warsaw Jews were prepared to fight. Himmler subsequently sacked the chief of the SS and the police, and gave Jürgen Stroop, an experienced SS officer, responsibility for liquidating the ghetto. On February 16, 1943, Himmler gave the order to "achieve the disappearance from sight of the living-space for 500,000 *Untermenschen* (sub-humans) that have existed up to now....and reduce the size of this city of millions—Warsaw—which has always been a center of corruption and revolt."

German forces arrived at the gates of the ghetto, on April 19, 1943, the eve of Passover. They found the streets deserted. Jewish defenders opened fire on the approaching troops, killed twelve, and forced them to withdraw. The SS came back with a Wehrmacht detachment and other reinforcements, which ringed the ghetto with flame-throwers, artillery, and tanks. The Nazis set up loudspeakers, calling on the Jews to surrender. Some women, the elderly, and young children came out, but most of the population remained in their hiding places.

The Nazis were not used to fighting a guerrilla war, and ultimately decided to burn down the buildings to force the Jews into the open. An anonymous woman's diary described the scene:

> I go out into the street, [it is] burning! Everything around is on fire. [Whole] streets!....Apartments are burning, workshops, warehouses, stores, and entire buildings. The entire ghetto is a sea of flames. There is a strong wind, which blows out sparks from the burning houses to the ones which do not burn yet. The fire immediately destroys everything. A stunning sight. The fire expands so [fast?] that people don't have time to flee the houses, and perish inside in a tragic manner....The ghetto walls are completely surrounded, no one can enter or leave. [The] clothes are burning on people's bodies. Screams of pain and crying, houses and bunkers are burning, everything, everything is in flames.

On May 8, the command bunker of the ŻOB at 18 Mila Street was captured. Mordechai Anielewicz either died from poison gas, or committed suicide to avoid being taken prisoner. Most of the civilians surrendered, but about one hundred fighters died. In his final letter, Anielewicz wrote to his comrade Yitzhak Zuckerman:

> Peace be with you, my dear friend. Who knows whether we shall meet again? My life's dream has now been realized: Jewish self-defense in the ghetto is now an accomplished fact....I have been witness to the magnificent, heroic struggle of the Jewish fighters.

At one point, two young Jews appeared on the roof of a building in Muranowski Square. While bullets flew around them, they raised the blue and white Zionist flag with a Star of David in the middle—what is now the

Israeli flag—in one more act of defiance. I have gone to that exact location to close my eyes and see how a group of starving, barely-clad Jews flew the Israeli flag over the Warsaw Ghetto as the SS closed in for the final assault.

By May 16, the fighting was over, and Stroop announced that "the Jewish quarter of Warsaw no longer exists." He said his forces had captured 56,065 Jews, and announced that he was going to blow up the Great Synagogue on Tlomackie Street, outside the ghetto, and therefore still standing, as a symbol of victory.

Altogether, an estimated, three hundred Germans were killed; seven thousand Jews died fighting, or perished in the fires, or were shot on the street. Approximately seven thousand ghetto survivors were sent to Treblinka. Most of the remaining forty-two thousand were sent to the slave labor camps at Poniatowa and Trawniki, and to the Majdanek death camp. A handful of survivors escaped to the Aryan side, where members of the underground continued to help Jews hide and escape.

The uprising was remarkable. A handful of mostly unarmed Jews fought two thousand German troops for thirty-five days. It was the first popular uprising against the Nazis, and damaged their prestige while inspiring Jews and others to resist them. Even Minister of Propaganda Joseph Goebbels expressed grudging respect for the Jews during the fighting:

> "The only thing noteworthy is exceptionally sharp fighting in Warsaw between our Police, and in part even the Wehrmacht, and the Jewish rebels. The Jews have actually succeeded in putting the ghetto in a condition to defend itself. Some very hard battles are taking place there, which have gone so far that the Jewish top leadership publishes daily military reports. Of course, this jest will probably not last long. But it shows what one can expect of the Jews if they have arms."

So much of what the Nazis did to the Jews went unreported in the West. But the Warsaw Ghetto Uprising made the front page of *The New York Times,* on April 22, 1943. An Associated Press story from Sweden the previous day reported that a Polish radio station had broadcast a message before going off the air: "The last 35,000 Jews in the ghetto at Warsaw have been condemned to execution. Warsaw again is echoing to musketry volleys. The people are murdered. Women and children defend themselves with their naked arms. Save us." A *Times* editorial on the one-year anniversary of the uprising expressed "profound respect for those brave men, women, and children who, almost barehanded, fought the tanks and the guns of the Nazi beast through thirty-five days of horror, and died rather than yield....What is important is that they, the most helpless and hopeless of Hitler's victims, defied the tyrant's wrath and set for the rest of us an example of courage that history can scarcely match."

Some of the surviving Jewish fighters joined the Polish underground, which launched another uprising on August 1, 1944, to liberate the city. They expected the Soviet Army to back them. But though they were nearing the city, they did not. Stalin feared a resurgent Polish nation that would come to life after the war, so he stopped his army on the other side of the Vistula, and watched as the Poles were slaughtered. The Germans again crushed the rebellion and destroyed the city center and 95 percent of Warsaw. Thousands of captured Poles were sent to concentration camps, and 166,000 were killed, including as many as seventeen thousand Jews who either fought in the battle, or were found hiding in the city. When the city stadium was built years later, the bones of one hundred thousand people were found in a mass grave, and reburied in the city cemetery.

Much of what we know of life in the ghetto was discovered in the Oneg Shabbat (Sabbath pleasure) Archive. Emanuel Ringelblum, a historian, doctor, and author, organized a group that secretly compiled information about Polish towns, conditions in the ghetto, and the resistance movement. They also documented the deportation and extermination of Polish Jewry. According to Ringelblum, "Everyone wrote—journalists, authors, teachers, social activists, young people, even children." The materials were hidden in three milk cans. One was found in 1946, and a second in 1950, but the third is still missing.

When the Soviets finally liberated Warsaw, fewer than 175,000 people were left, less than 6 percent of the pre-war population. Approximately 11,500 of them were Jews.

After the war, roughly ten thousand Jews returned to Warsaw. A Jewish Historical Institute and Social and Cultural Society were established as Jews tried to rebuild their community, which had been all but wiped out. Many Poles were not welcoming. They were unwilling to admit their complicity in the destruction of the Jewish community, and in some places, reacted with paroxysms of violence, most notably in Kielce.

On July 1, 1946, Polish soldiers, policemen, and civilians attacked the Jews, killing forty-two and injuring forty others, all on the pretext of a blood libel. It may be hard to believe, but in the year 1946, Jews were still being murdered over the false belief that they murder Christian children to use their blood in their Passover matzos. The museum curator at Kielce—which I had visited one year, after my visit with my children to Poland—a courageous Polish Catholic devoted to the memory of the murdered Jews, had tears in his eyes as he showed me the shoes of a baby who had been murdered in the pogrom.

Life for the Jews of Warsaw did not improve under Communist rule. Many Jews emigrated in the first two decades after the war because of anti-Semitism and Communist persecution. The situation became acute in 1968, when the Communist leadership started a particularly vicious anti-Semitic and anti-Zionist campaign that included stripping thousands of Jews of their jobs and property. About twenty thousand were expelled, or chose to leave, while being forced to give up their citizenship.

After the collapse of Communism in 1989, a more vigorous effort was made to revive the community. Before the war, Warsaw had the second largest Jewish community in the world. Today, Warsaw's population is nearly 1.8 million. No more than five thousand are Jews. The city does have six operating synagogues, a Jewish elementary school and kindergarten, a sports club, a Yiddish theater, a JCC, Jewish periodicals, a kosher cafeteria, and a kosher restaurant. The Jewish Community Center has about four hundred members, and on Sundays, hosts a Boker Tov (Good Morning) event for people to come for Middle Eastern food and other activities. The community is led by the Chief Rabbi of Poland, my good friend and a devoted servant of the Jewish people, Rabbi Michael Schudrich.

Only a small piece remains of the ghetto walls, which were about eleven miles long. A small monument marks the spot where the Jewish fighters built their command bunker on 18 Mila Street. Leon Uris wrote a novel about the uprising, titled *Mila 18*. The first time I came to Warsaw looking for the bunker, the cab driver took me to a house with that number because all the homes in the ghetto were destroyed, and new housing with similar numbers was rebuilt here. A confused woman answered the door of her modern home, and I understood I was in the wrong place. The exact location of the bunker is unknown, so the monument is approximately where it stood.

A littler further down the street is the place where Anielewicz, and more than one hundred other fighters, are buried under rubble from the original street. A memorial stone reads: "Grave of the fighters of the Warsaw Ghetto Uprising built from the rubble of Mila Street, one of the liveliest streets of pre-war Jewish Warsaw. These ruins of the bunker at 18 Mila Street are the place of rest of the commanders and fighters of the Jewish Combat Organization, as well as some civilians. Among them lies Mordechai Anielewicz, the Commander in Chief." In Israel, Kibbutz Yad Mordechai was named in memory of Anielewicz, and a monument is erected in his memory, at its entrance.

Near Mila 18 is a plaque, installed only in 2012, honoring the leader of the ŻZW, Paweł Frenkel. Sadly, his role in the uprising was largely ignored for political reasons—the ŻZW was related to the right-wing Betar group, while Anielewicz's fighters were associated with Hashomer Hatzair, which the ruling party in Israel, up until the 1970s, more closely identified with—until former Israeli defense minister Moshe Arens publicized the ŻZW's contribution to the fighting. According to Arens, the group's performance was denigrated because "Anielewicz's people viewed them as fascists and refused to work in cooperation with them." The more influential Labor Zionists, in what was then Palestine, wrote much of the history of the period and tended to overstate the actions of its followers in Europe, and minimize those associated with their rivals from the Revisionist movement. As a leader of Betar, which inspired the ŻZW, Arens wanted to give Paweł and his comrades their due.

No doubt there is some truth to Arens' argument. But that does not change my conviction that Mordechai Anielewicz is one of the greatest Jewish heroes who ever lived, and I was moved to tears to have the honor of visiting his birth home in the Polish city of Wyszków, near Warsaw, about a year before the publication of this book. Accompanying me on that trip was the son of another great Jewish commander, former Israeli Prime Minister Yitzhak Rabin, Yuval Rabin.

My family and I walked along a street named after Shmuel Zygielbojm, a Jewish member of the Polish government-in-exile. A monument to him explains that he killed himself in London, on May 12, 1943, to protest the inaction of the Allies. Unlike most other instances where Jews were being murdered, the whole world knew what was happening in Warsaw and still did nothing to come to the aid of the valiant Jews fighting for their lives.

In a letter to Władysław Raczkiewicz, the president of the Polish government in exile, Zygielbojm wrote:

The responsibility for the crime of murdering all the Jewish population in Poland falls, in the first instance, on the perpetrators, but indirectly it also burdens the whole of humanity, upon the peoples and governments of the Allied states that, so far, have made no effort towards a concrete action to put a stop to this crime…

I cannot remain silent. I cannot live while the remnants of the Jewish people in Poland, whose representative I am, are being exterminated. My comrades in the Warsaw Ghetto perished with their weapons in their hands in their last heroic battle. It was not my destiny to die as they did, together with them. But I belong to them and in their mass graves.

By my death I wish to make the strongest possible protest against the passivity with which the world is looking on and permitting the extermination of the Jewish people. I know how little human life is worth today, but as I was unable to do anything during my life, perhaps by my death I shall help to break down the indifference of those who have the possibility now, at the last moment, to save those Polish Jews still alive, from certain annihilation.

It is an unbelievably stirring, powerful suicide note, and my children were moved to tears to read it. They could not believe the courage of a man who would lay down his life simply to draw attention to the annihilation of his fellow Jews.

We also walked along what used to be the main street in the Jewish part of Warsaw. An exhibit has been installed with photos and descriptions of Jewish life before and during the war. We also walked past the restored Nożyk Synagogue—the only synagogue to survive the war, because the Nazis used it as a stable. Today, it is the synagogue headquarters of Rabbi Schudrich, the chief rabbi.

In 2014, the Polin Museum of the History of Polish Jews opened on the grounds of the ghetto. It is one of the finest Jewish museums in the world. Additionally, in Warsaw you will find the Jewish Historical Institute, which now includes a library of sixty thousand volumes, and Ringelblum's Underground Archives. The librarian was kind enough to show us some of the documents.

I didn't realize the extent of the archive. It was amazing to see, for example, the original pages clerks filled out to register each resident of the ghetto. These are important because they have names and photos to provide a record for Jews today who are looking for information about their families, or making restitution claims for money and property. We also saw registration forms for the survivors created just after the war. Another document listed Jews who were liberated from concentration camps and sent to Sweden. We were especially moved by the examples we were shown from the collection of ten thousand death cards filled out by Jewish doctors in the ghetto. Many were damaged by fire and have burn marks, but they are still legible, listing the causes of death as starvation, bombing, and cancer.

At the Jewish museum, I also read some of the most haunting words I have ever seen. They were from the testimonial of a Sonderkommando, found hidden at Auschwitz, who was describing the look on the faces of the Jews as they entered the gas chambers:

> Fear permeated everyone to the marrow...those people locked inside...they tore their hair out, realizing that they had been so naive as to allow themselves to be led here, within these locked doors. Their voices rising to the heaven gave vent to their spirit in the only way they could; they let out their last great scream of protest against this greatest of all injustices meted out against the entirely innocent.

The look he perceived was not only one of fear and terror, but also one of a startling realization of the Nazis forcing and cajoling the Jews to collude in their deaths. The Jews had been murdered amid the hope that some might survive—that a fate as gruesome as a gas chamber was an impossibility. But it was all a grotesque fabrication. The Germans' intention was the destruction of all the Jews of Europe, even if today we can scarcely believe it.

The museum is one of the many positive examples of how Poland is confronting its past. The preservation of the death camps is also an important contribution to educating people about the Holocaust. When I first started visiting Poland nearly thirty years ago, and traveled to Auschwitz with my friend, Professor Jonathan Weber, most of the explanatory signs spoke of millions of "victims" of the Nazis. Today, it says *Jews*, who were more than 90 percent of the Holocaust's victims.

I do think they could do more to commemorate and educate about the Warsaw Ghetto Uprising. The world Jewish community, and humanity at large, should be grateful for the work of the Polish government in preserving Holocaust sites. But more can still be done, especially to highlight armed Jewish revolts that took place against the Nazis.

Poland is the only major country in Europe that has not passed legislation for the restitution of property seized by the Nazis or nationalized by the Communists. This is an issue that should and must be addressed. In 1997, Poland did adopt a law for the restitution of communal-owned property, but most of the claims have not been resolved.

In another positive development, the Polish government pledged $28 million in 2017, toward restoration of the Jewish cemetery, founded in 1799, and nearly destroyed by the Nazis. Approximately 250,000 people are buried in the cemetery, including those who were murdered in the ghetto. A memorial to Jewish martyrs, along with a sculpture of Janusz Korczak, was erected in the cemetery. Although Jewish law normally does not permit the burial of someone who committed suicide, inside a Jewish cemetery, Adam Czerniaków's family received special dispensation to inter his body with the other Jews from the ghetto. In any event, today this law is not applied, as the Orthodox rabbinate now defines suicide as being caused by mental illness. We do not want to inflict further suffering on the family of the deceased, nor blight the memory of the departed.

More depressing are the mass graves in Warsaw. The extreme unevenness of the earth is a harrowing sight when you realize what caused it: not all the victims were cremated, and their bodies decomposed over time, creating these large indentations in the ground.

We visited the monument at the Umschlagplatz, which is white stone with a black stripe, representing the colors of a traditional tallit. Erected in 1988, it resembles an open freight car and bears the first names of four hundred Jews, each commemorating one thousand victims. Also etched on the wall are the words, "Along this path of suffering and death over 300,000 Jews were driven in 1942–1943 from the Warsaw ghetto to the gas chambers of the Nazi extermination camps." A dark brown stone arch on top of the monument has images of trees, symbolizing a shattered forest and the destruction of the Jewish people.

At the Umschlagplatz, Baba said to me, "Why did you bring me here? There is a limit to how much horror we can absorb." She was overwhelmed by the tragedy, and had a difficult time believing in a God that allowed the Holocaust to happen. Later, Baba said, "The Umschlagplatz will haunt me for the rest of my life."

Baba was not the only member of the family uncomfortable in Poland. "I didn't feel like they hate us, or they're showing us anti-Semitism," Debbie recalled, after the trip. "I just felt like they don't care for us. It may not be their fault. But I got the feeling that they are indifferent to the level of suffering our people endured on their soil. They don't really understand what a Jew is."

Debbie and I disagreed on this issue, and her opinion would change with time. We would later become acquainted with Polish Prime Minister Mateusz Morawiecki, who visited our home in the United States, and whose home I visited in Warsaw, and I was impressed with his government's commitment to Jewish memory and the preservation of the camps. I would likewise become acquainted with other Polish government officials, especially those serving at the Consulate in New York, and can personally attest to how seriously they take Poland's commitment to Holocaust memory and building bridges with the Jewish community.

Aside from those working for, or affiliated with Chabad, Jews who live in Europe hide their Jewishness. Debbie wanted to see more overt displays of Jewishness in Poland. "So even if you meet a Jew," she said, "you don't know he or she is a Jew. It's only when you see Shmuley with his beard and his *yarmulke*, and he's loud and he's very proud. He's totally out there as a Jew. Everybody knows us. I see people's reaction to a *yarmulke* and a beard. But I don't know what they're thinking. Are they thinking, *Oh, Jewish, Israel, Palestinian.* I don't know. Maybe they were thinking: *These people were here seventy years ago, and we thought Hitler wiped them out, but this one got away.* Or are they thinking, I'm so happy that the Jewish people are returning to Poland, and that Hitler's vision for their destruction has been defeated. I would like to believe the latter, and we met enough Polish men and women who were extremely kind to us and went out of their way to welcome us, to justify that conclusion."

Shaina had a different reaction. She said she was never afraid in Poland because she was raised to be a proud Jew. "If anything, I felt pride when they stared at us," she said, after the trip. "For me it was like, we look like history, but we're here. This is what a Jew looks like." She didn't find it condescending. "If anything, it gave me Jewish pride that we're walking through the streets and it's freaking people out. Seventy years ago, we would have been sent, God forbid, who knows where. To be able to walk freely, I felt a sense of pride." Shaina said she did not feel the same anger toward the Poles that Baba felt, and understood that it was not the Poles who perpetrated the Holocaust, even as many aided and abetted the Nazis in their program of murder, and others were indifferent to the suffering of their neighbors, or took the opportunity to rob them. Baba also understood this. But the long history of anti-Semitism in Poland was, for her, hard to get past.

CHAPTER 14

BIAŁYSTOK: BURNED ALIVE
IN THE SYNAGOGUE

At the other end of the Treblinka railroad is Białystok. Much of the city was razed by Allied bombing, and by then, the Jews were already dead. There's nothing left of them but a monument where they were burned alive in their synagogue.

Białystok was a center of Jewish learning, labor activism, and Zionism. Jews first came to the town in 1588, and by the late 19th century made up more than 75 percent of the town's population. In 1913, a third synagogue was constructed. Jews became involved in the textile industry and owned nearly all the mills, shops, and factories. Jews also became active in the Bund, a Jewish workers movement that staged a strike in Białystok in 1882. By the end of the century, Jews had joined the socialist revolutionary fervor of the time, as well as the growing interest in returning to the Jewish homeland, the Land of Israel. Białystok became a center for Hibbat Zion, an organization that advocated a revival of Jewish life in what was then Palestine.

Białystok had long been an important religious center where many well-known rabbis and scholars lived. The Great Synagogue was an enormous building with a tall dome and spire. At the beginning of the 20th century, Jews became targets of a series of pogroms in which hundreds were killed and wounded and raped and robbed and beaten, just like in *Fiddler on the Roof*. The tsar's soldiers, as well as local Christians, attacked Jews, and many decided it was time to emigrate to North America. A pillar in the Bagnowka Jewish Cemetery memorializes the victims: "…the inhabitants of this city fell upon our brothers, the sons of Israel, plundering at noontime and plundering houses and possessions, and they murdered about 80 men and women and children."

The situation for Jews and other residents of the city worsened during World War I, when fighting between the Russian and German armies destroyed much of the city and killed about six thousand Jews. The city's population fell from seventy thousand to less than forty thousand. The Jewish community never completely recovered from the war, and its economic situation worsened when Jewish businesses were boycotted in 1937.

Still, when World War II began, fifty thousand Jews lived in Białystok, comprising nearly half the population. On September 15, 1939, the Germans took control of the city, but transferred it to the Soviets just a week later, as part of their agreement to divide Poland. Tens of thousands of refugees from German-occupied areas poured in. The Soviets shut down Jewish businesses and declared many Jewish activities illegal.

The Germans returned less than two years later, on their way to fight the Soviets. On June 27, 1941, a date that would become known as "Red Friday," the *Einsatzgruppen* (the SS's mobile killing unit) herded Jews into the great synagogue. The exact number is unknown, but estimates range from seven hundred to two thousand. The doors were locked and a grenade was tossed in to set the building on fire. Soldiers stood outside, listening to the screams of the people burning alive, until most of the synagogue and all the Jews were reduced to ash. Later, the *Einsatzgruppen* took four thousand more Jews into an open field and executed them.

In Białystok, we did not know where to find any of the handful of remaining Jews, so we had to find a non-Jew who could give us directions to the synagogue. We went to a few bars that were still open and asked where to find it. No one knew. Or at least, could not communicate to us that they did, since we don't speak Polish and could not find anyone who spoke English. We finally asked a policeman who, amazingly, answered us in a few words of Hebrew.

Apparently, he had trained with some Israeli police who had come to Poland for a week. You can imagine how pleasantly surprised we were to find a police officer so late at night, in middle of a town where so many Jews had been murdered, who evinced such an immediate and deep-seated affinity with the Jewish people. He could not have been nicer, and he took us to the exact place where the synagogue once stood, right in the center of the city. There is a black slab monument with a menorah on top. A photograph taken in 1922, of the Great Synagogue, is attached, along with a bronze plaque of the synagogue, and a sign posted in 1995, written in Hebrew, English, and Polish, that says: OUR SPLENDID SANCTUARY FELL VICTIM TO THE FLAMES ON JUNE 27, 1941. 2,000 JEWS WERE BURNT ALIVE IN IT BY THE GERMAN NAZI MURDERERS.

On the ground, cobblestones form a Star of David. On top of the stones is a memorial made of the twisted steel from the melted synagogue dome. Together, our family stood on this hallowed ground and recited psalms, and I found solace holding the Elie Wiesel Torah.

Immediately after Red Friday, the surviving Jews were restricted to a ghetto that was divided into two parts separated by the Biała River. The Germans created a *Judenrat* with Efraim Barasz as its chairman. As in other ghettos, it was given the unconscionable task of choosing which Jews should fill the Nazis' quotas for work and deportation. Jews were forced to work in factories to manufacture textiles and weapons for the German war effort.

As in all ghettos, conditions were overcrowded, with little food or water. The Jews suffered from malnutrition and disease, but did their best to keep each other alive. They established schools, soup kitchens, hospitals, and a police force.

They did not know it, but their situation was hopeless. During one week in February 1943, two thousand Jews were shot, and ten thousand deported to Treblinka, where all perished. Like other *Judenrat* leaders, Barasz believed, or perhaps let himself believe, that the Nazis would be satisfied each time they deported or killed a group of ghetto residents. Maybe the idea that the Nazis were determined to exterminate every Jew was too big to get your head around. Nobody knew the full scope of the Final Solution until after the war. It's difficult to process information as true that is beyond belief. It's a classic case of cognitive dissonance, where the mind simply cannot acknowledge something too terrible to accept.

And it was not just incomprehensible to the Jews. In *Beyond Belief,* Emory University scholar Deborah Lipstadt explains how the international press had cognitive dissonance as well. Atrocity stories had little credibility because of all the phony reports and propaganda of World War I. Everybody knew German soldiers didn't really eat babies in Belgium. Vague government reports about the overall casualties, without distinctions, obscured the fact that the Jews had been targeted for annihilation.

Lipstadt writes:

Both the means of murder—gas—and the size of the victim population—many millions—reinforced the natural barriers of incredulity. In a certain respect these were healthy doubts—the mind's rebellion against believing that human beings were capable of sinking to such levels of depravity—but they made it easier for the perpetrators to camouflage their plans.

Hard-boiled newspaper editors, accustomed to stories of gangland violence and political corruption, were skeptical of reports of unbelievable atrocities received from their correspondents. And when they did publish them, they were typically buried in the back of the paper. But the reports did appear in the national press. "25,000 Jews Seized in Southern France," reported the *New York Times,* on August 28, 1942. "35,000 Jews Executed in Five Polish Towns," said the *New York Herald Tribune,* on March 21, 1943.

In *Forgotten Victims: The Abandonment of Americans in Hitler's Camps,* Mitchell Bard shows that the US government knew what was happening, as did the press and the International Committee of the Red Cross (ICRC), whose mission it was to report on conditions in prison camps and to provide relief. After the war, head of the information department, Roger Du Pasquier, would admit that making a fuss about the camps "would have made it impossible for [the Red Cross] to continue its activity on behalf of millions of military captives."

Bard doesn't buy this explanation. "The organization's options were limited by the Nazis, but the idea that the Red Cross therefore had no moral responsibility to speak out on behalf of concentration camp inmates because it threatened the good work it was able to do for POWs is, in retrospect, obscene."

The behavior of the world's governments, the pope, the press, and the ICRC in the 1940s, all make Edmund Burke's words echo in my ears: "The only thing necessary for the triumph of evil is for good men to do nothing."

The end of the Białystok Ghetto did not occur without a heroic example of doomed Jewish resistance. Two underground groups in the ghetto united in July 1943, under the command of Mordechai Tannenbaum and Daniel Moskowicz. Tannenbaum had been sent to Białystok by the Jewish Combat Organization in Warsaw. The underground was assisted by Barasz, and apparently was also able to smuggle in some weapons and supplies from resistance groups outside the city. Besides planning to fight the Nazis, the underground gathered documents and smuggled them out of the ghetto and hid them on the Polish side of the city so there would be a record of the community and its fate (the archive was found after the war, and most of the documents are now in Yad Vashem in Jerusalem).

When the Nazis ordered the final liquidation of the ghetto, in August 1943, the thirty thousand remaining Jews were surrounded by German troops and Ukrainian collaborators. The three hundred to five hundred Jews in the underground had few weapons—mostly pistols and Molotov cocktails—and no chance of stopping the soldiers from entering and clearing the ghetto. But they hoped to make it possible for some people to escape, especially fighters who could join the partisans hiding in the forest.

The revolt began on August 16, and the underground held off approximately three thousand German troops for almost a week. The Nazis sent tanks and armored cars into the ghetto and killed hundreds of fighters each day. The Germans discovered seventy-two in a bunker, and killed all but one. When the last stronghold was about to be breached, Tannenbaum and Moskowicz committed suicide.

According to the US Holocaust Memorial Museum, Chaika Grossman was sent by the Jewish underground in the Vilna Ghetto, to her hometown of Białystok, where she posed as a Polish Christian so she could operate on the Aryan side of the city. She helped smuggle weapons into the ghetto, and fought with the resistance. About 150 Jews managed to escape and join the partisans with her help. Grossman was active in the resistance throughout the war. She survived and moved to Israel, where she served in the Knesset.

In the article, "Armed Resistance in the Krakow and Białystok Ghettos," Sheryl Silver Ochayon says fighters in Białystok were inspired by those in Warsaw, but did not have the support of the population. Also, the Germans had learned a lesson from the earlier battle, and in Białystok, it was their forces that surprised the Jews.

Why didn't more Jews resist? There are examples of brave men and women who fought against all odds to help their fellow Jews. Still, why didn't thousands more Jews in the ghetto join the fight? They had no weapons, but couldn't they have overwhelmed the smaller number of soldiers? Why didn't they answer the underground's call to revolt? Making the Germans pay a price, as they did in Warsaw, also had the benefit of demonstrating to the Nazis that the Jews were not what they considered *Untermenschen* (inferior people). Didn't they know by now that they were doomed either way?

The Warsaw Ghetto fighters did resist once they understood that they were all to be murdered. With almost no food or weapons, they realized they had no choice but to fight back. They held out for twenty-eight days against German heavy artillery, and then, like the Masada fighters before them, who preferred death to torture and lifelong slavery, many fighters of the ghetto took their own lives.

Zivia Lubetkin, another leader of the underground in the Warsaw ghetto, said the fighters understood they had no chance of defeating the Germans in battle, but still believed they would win: "…despite our meager force, we knew that eventually we would get the better of them, we, the weak, with our belief in justice, in humanity, and in a system so vastly different from the one in which they gloried."

I've also come to understand the conventional notion of resistance is too narrow. It is not just about fighting back in a literal sense. The Majdanek museum has an interesting take on this, noting that *resistance* can take different forms. For example, some prisoners resisted by secretly performing their religious rites, and concealing devotional items. Others engaged in artistic endeavors, pursued educational activities, or participated in collective singing. Prisoners were also involved in activities that I would more commonly associate with resistance, such as establishing contacts with underground organizations outside Majdanek, smuggling illegal correspondence, and attempting to escape. Even the more benign acts of resistance could be punished by torture or death.

Resistance can also be spiritual, and take the form of sanctifying God's name. Jews have an obligation to live, but many fought, knowing they were going to die and became martyrs. Throughout Jewish history, we had to make peace with the idea of martyrdom, because we were displaced, weak, and vulnerable. And we have always been ready to give up our lives for God's glory. But Judaism has never reveled in martyrdom. We are a religion of life. We believe in living for the Torah, not dying for it, unless there is no choice but to make the ultimate sacrifice.

As for the six million Jews who were martyred in the Holocaust, they are the holiest among us. We dare never to judge how they responded to the Nazi German onslaught against them. They were Jews of tremendous courage, subject to the most inhumane deprivations and barbarity. I agree with Holocaust survivor Viktor Frankl's observation that "no man should judge unless he asks himself in absolute honesty whether in a similar situation, he might not have done the same."

None of us has ever faced what they confronted. So we bow our heads in silent resignation, to their sacred memory.

Like many Jews, I was raised as a boy, hearing that the Jews of the Holocaust had gone to their deaths "like sheep to the slaughter." The term was designed to convey the mass killing of innocents. But it was only when I grew older that I realized it was a horrible pejorative which really conveyed that the Jews refused to fight back and defend themselves. Using the term was a double insult to the martyred six million, conveying a false cowardice, as well as blaming the victims for their own massacre. I have never used the phrase *like sheep to the slaughter* since.

Who are we to judge six million Jews who, attacked by the most powerful army Europe ever saw, gave themselves hope that being "deported to the East" meant a life that might spare their children from starvation and death? Who are we to judge parents who knew that, were they to fight back, the first who would die would be their babies?

During the Eichmann trial in Israel, prosecutor Gideon Hausner asked Yitzhak Zuckerman, one of the leaders of the ŻOB during the Warsaw uprising, why more Jews didn't revolt. He said:

> It is an error to think that only the Warsaw Ghetto fought and rebelled. In several places the last of the Jews tried to revolt. I cannot accept the idea that my comrades in Czestochowa, who had less arms, less Jews, less fighters, and they fell upon the Germans with their fingernails and fought until the last moment—I cannot accept the idea that they did not fight. I am convinced that they put into this struggle of theirs not less than we in Warsaw, even though they did not achieve the same effect.

It took only three days for the Białystok Ghetto to be completely emptied. Most of the Jews were deported to the death camp at Treblinka. Those fit to work were sent to Majdanek, where most later were transported to camps at Poniatowa, Bliżyn, or Auschwitz.

Most of the two thousand Jews left in the ghetto by the time of the final deportation—among them, Barasz—were sent to Majdanek. Among them were a handful of Jews who managed to survive by hiding on the Polish side of the city, as did sixty Jews who joined the partisans. It is believed that only two hundred Jews from Białystok survived the camps. The city was liberated by Soviet troops in August 1944.

After the war, 1,110 Jews returned, but it was still dangerous. Polish bandits removed Jews from trains, robbed, and even killed them. A courageous group of survivors tried to rebuild the community. Yedidia Hamburg, a member of the post-war Jewish Reconstruction Committee, said they located Jewish children who had been taken in by Christian families, and tried to bring them "back under Jewish influence."

The difficulty of life in Białystok, and the allure of Palestine and other countries, led many of the survivors to immigrate. By the end of 1948, only 520 Jews remained. Today, nearly seventy years later, out of a population of three hundred thousand, there are only five. The city is virtually *judenrein*. In this town, Hitler accomplished his goal of eradicating the Jews.

I looked for the cemetery, and I found a young Pole who pointed to a city park and said that was the Jewish cemetery. Then he looked me right in the eye and said, "I'm sorry." He regretted that they had turned the cemetery into a park where people strolled around, and dogs urinated.

"Thank you for saying that," I replied, as my children looked on, not knowing how to react. On the one hand they were grateful that a Polish citizen had expressed his regrets for the transformation of a Jewish cemetery into a recreational space. On the other, they wondered why Białystok had not corrected this affront.

In the park, once the Bema Cemetery, there is a large stone area where a Jewish Star made of green shrubs sits on cobblestones as a memorial to the dead. A sign nearby has a photo of the cemetery with the date 1840. The local municipality was going to allow the construction of a building on the site, and Lucja (Lucy) Lisowska, one of the last living Białystok Jews, fought the city and convinced them not to further desecrate the cemetery.

We did not know there was another cemetery known as the Bagnowka Cemetery, which did survive the war. The Nazis knocked down and damaged many of the forty thousand headstones in an effort to erase the remaining traces of the Jewish community, prior to fleeing in advance of the Russian push to the West.

According to Dr. Szymon Datner, a survivor from Białystok, on the second anniversary of the ghetto's liquidation, August 16, 1945, a monument was dedicated at the Bagnowka Cemetery. An inscription in

Yiddish was written on a black stone obelisk beneath a Jewish star, that read: "In memory of the sixty-thousand Jewish people of the Białystok Ghetto, murdered by the Germans, dedicated by a handful of surviving Jews. August 16, 1943–August 16, 1945. May they rest in peace." They added, "The people of Israel live."

In 1971, the local authorities decided to close the ghetto cemetery. They removed the Ghetto Uprising Heroes Monument, and the bodies of 230 Jews buried—some while still alive—in a rubbish heap, and mass graves were exhumed and reburied in the Jewish cemeteries. The area is now a public square. In 1993, on the 50th anniversary of the outbreak of the Białystok Ghetto Uprising, a restored obelisk was placed, commemorating the uprising. A plaque reads: "In this place the ashes of about 3,500 Jews, exterminated by the Nazis and killed during the Uprising in the Białystok Ghetto in August 1943, have been committed."

For years, the Bagnowka Cemetery was unattended and became overgrown and vandalized. Lucy took it upon herself to preserve the cemetery, and arranged to have an opening in the cemetery wall closed to keep out partygoers and vandals. She subsequently helped convince the mayor of Białystok to construct a wall to separate the Jewish cemetery from the adjoining Catholic cemetery. There is currently a restoration project being carried out by volunteers, which has reset and repaired hundreds of gravestones. Josh Degen, one of the organizers, explained why it is so important: "It will right a wrong inflicted on humanity by the Nazis. The memory of every grave we restored lives in all of us."

Three synagogues survived. The Cytron Synagogue, a small prayer house from the 1930s, served as a Jewish Community Center and funeral home after the war, and is now used as an art gallery. A second, the Shmuel Synagogue, was named after the city's most famous rabbi, Samuel Mohilewer. Built in the Moorish style, the synagogue was burned down by the Nazis and reconstructed after the war. Today, it is used as a training center for the police. The third, the Piaskower Synagogue, was rebuilt and houses a foundation named after Lazarus Ludwik Zamenhof, a Białystok-born optician who invented the Esperanto language.

I knew going to these places would be depressing, especially in Poland, where you go to one town after another and learn about massacres of Jews. But you must affirm life. That's why I wanted to bring the Elie Wiesel

Torah. By bringing the Torah—which to us Jews is the tree of life—I wanted to bring holiness to these places, and inspire our children to do likewise.

As it turned out, bringing a Torah on the trip was also nerve-wracking. It is a tremendous responsibility to keep a Torah—the holiest article in all of Judaism—safe, and to make sure it (God forbid) not be desecrated in any way. There are many laws in Judaism governing the treatment of a Torah scroll. Always, a member of the family was assigned guard duty to protect the Torah. My kids joked about my love affair with the Torah. They said it was my new baby because of the way I carried it with me everywhere in its special protective covering.

The Torah got me through a difficult day, on July 4, from Treblinka to Tykocin to *judenrein* Białystok. The enormity of the Holocaust oppressed me—the scale of the barbarity. But worse was the realization that in all these places where Jews were slaughtered, God was watching. God witnessed it all as it continued for years.

It was a long drive back to Warsaw. The kids were upset. They thought we were overdoing it, going to too many places, cramming in too much horrible stuff. Warsaw had a kosher restaurant, and we could have eaten like decent people, but everything was closed. Don't ever overestimate the importance of a good hot meal to children if you're dragging them on an extended trip, especially to places of unique suffering and misery. Going on an empty stomach makes the journey that much more miserable.

We called ahead and tried to get food delivered to the hotel. Not happening. So we missed dinner.

CHAPTER 15

LUBLIN: EUROPE'S GREATEST YESHIVA, VANISHED, AND A MOUND OF JEWISH BONES

n the picturesque town of Lublin, where are arrived on July 6, there remain only a handful of Jews. Lublin was once one the most important centers of Jewish life, commerce, culture, and scholarship in Europe, going all the way back to the 14th century. In 1515, the world's largest Talmudic school was established by Shalom Shachna, and the renown of its scholars was appreciated, even by the Polish kings, who granted sages of the yeshiva rights equal to those of scholars in Polish universities. They called it the "Jewish Oxford."

The kids were in a better mood today. Yes, we had to snack on potato chips and vegetables. But moving on to a new city, one they had heard of as a great place of Jewish learning, made them eager to discover its history.

In 1567, the Maharshal Shul was built. It was also during this active century of Jewish life that the Council of the Four Lands, the ruling political body for Jews in Poland and Lithuania, was headquartered in Lublin. By the beginning of the 17th century, approximately two thousand Jews lived in Lublin, but it wasn't what you would call a safe place. Jews were accused of blood libels (using the blood of non-Jews for making matzoh on Passover) and attacked. Cossacks burned down the Jewish quarter in 1655, and killed more than two thousand people. It took more than a century before the community recovered. By 1787, the Jewish district was rebuilt and had a population of thirty-five hundred.

During the late 18th century, Lublin became a center for Hasidism, best known as the home of Jacob Isaac ha-Hozeh, better known as the Seer of Lublin. While blind, it was said that he could see directly into people's souls. He died mysteriously, by falling out of his window.

Inter-religious tensions flared between the Hasidim and their opponents, known as Mitnagdim, and both groups maintained their own schools and synagogues. The Hasidim emphasized ecstatic and mystical devotion to God, and appealed to the less learned and the blue collar. The Mitnagdim emphasized scholarship, and looked down upon unlearned Jews, as peasants. Paradoxically, it was the Seer of Lublin who had one of the most profound quotations about belief: "Can He be God if He can only be worshipped in one way?"

Jews became increasingly prominent in business in the 19th century. A Jew owned the largest cigarette factory, and Jews owned 95 percent of businesses in the tanning industry. In 1877, the opening of a railway connecting Lublin with Warsaw contributed to an economic boom. A Jewish hospital opened in 1886, and a Hebrew school in 1897. As the 20th century began, the community was twenty-four thousand strong, nearly one-third of the population of Lublin. In addition to Yiddish newspapers, the first Jewish magazine was published, and a Jewish public library opened. Jews became active in the Zionist movement and the Bund, and various social, cultural, educational, and recreational institutions served the community.

Lublin had seven synagogues, and in 1930, Rabbi Meir Shapira founded the Yeshiva Chochmei Lublin (Jewish Rabbinical Academy). An estimated fifty thousand people came for the laying of the cornerstone, and ten thousand attended the opening. To become a student at the yeshiva, you had to memorize two hundred portfolios of the Talmud—about four hundred pages. It was a wonder for its time.

Shapira's legacy was his origination of the seven-year cycle of studying the Talmud, referred to as *Daf Yomi*. Shapira inspired Jews to study a folio (a two-sided page) each day, and if you do so, it is possible to read the entire 2,711 pages over the course of seven years. I had studied the cycle myself over a seven-year period, albeit haphazardly, and not understanding everything I studied. But at least I completed the cycle! And after being so incredibly inspired by the ninety thousand people I joined at Giants Stadium at the Meadowlands in New Jersey, for the 13th *Siyum Hashas,* on New Year's Day, 2020, I decided to start the seven-year cycle all over again, this time with Elisha Wiesel as my study partner.

Sadly, Rabbi Shapira became ill while traveling the world, raising money, and passed away at the young age of forty-six, before the first yeshiva class graduated. Ironically, his untimely death saved him from witnessing the ravages of the Holocaust, and perhaps God spared the saintly sage.

The Germans captured Lublin on September 18, 1939. They appointed a *Judenrat* and herded all the Jews of Lublin, plus refugees that had swelled the population to forty-five thousand, into two ghettos. In July 1941, SS Chief Heinrich Himmler came to Lublin and ordered the SS to build a concentration camp at Majdanek, just outside the town.

On March 16, 1942, deportations began. Those who were able to work for the Nazis were temporarily spared, but later killed in Lublin, or sent to Majdanek. A total of thirty thousand Jews were deported or murdered on the way in nearby forests. "The procedure is pretty barbaric," Reich Propaganda Minister Joseph Goebbels wrote in his diary, on March 27, 1942, "and is not to be described here more definitely. Not much will remain of the Jews." He remarked approvingly that the SS "is doing it with considerable circumspection and in a way that does not attract much attention…the ghettos that will be emptied in the cities of the General Government will now be re-filled with Jews thrown out of the Reich. The process is to be repeated from time to time."

Lublin was the first city in Poland liberated by the Russian Army, on July 24, 1944. Lublin served as a temporary Polish capital, too, until the liberation of Warsaw in January 1945. Many Jews who had escaped to the Soviet Union returned after the war, and about five thousand Jews resettled in Lublin. As in other cities in Poland, however, the prevailing anti-Semitism of Poles, combined with pogroms around the country, motivated most Jews to leave. A small community of about 450 remained until 1968, when an upsurge of anti-Semitism prompted about 120 to emigrate.

Today, the community is believed to number less than one hundred. Almost nothing remains of this once thriving center of Jewish life. A small synagogue is maintained on the second floor of the old Lublin Yeshiva building, with a display of some photos and documents. The main floor, as noted above, is now a high-end non-kosher restaurant. In the summer months, when there are many Orthodox Jewish tourists, a room in the basement is converted to a kosher restaurant, where our family was grateful to be fed, even though some of the kids had little appetite.

Shaina said she found it difficult to eat, even though she hadn't eaten all day, because she felt like crying and did not want anyone to see. "I was holding back my tears the entire time I was there."

When I was growing up, I heard so many stories about people who had lost their minds in the Holocaust, from grief. Wherever you travel around Poland, there's another sign about how many Jews were killed in that place. It beggars the imagination. We saw, for example, a plaque on the wall of the former Jewish orphanage, which indicates that this was the site where the Nazis murdered Jewish children on March 24, 1942. The people responsible for the children would not leave them, and perished.

Another characteristic Lublin shares with so many other Eastern European cities is that it is more a showplace for dead Jews, than modern Jewish life. There is a Holocaust memorial in the town square, and commemorative plaques at the base of the castle steps indicate where the Jewish quarter had once stood. The Jewish cemetery is the oldest in Poland, with gravestones dating to the 1500s. In addition to murdering the living Jews, the Nazis also targeted the dead, destroying tombstones and desecrating the cemetery in an effort to efface even their memory. The cemetery is a tourist attraction and a site of pilgrimage because the Seer of Lublin is buried there. A second cemetery, established in the 19th century, also damaged by the Nazis, is now being restored.

The whole family found Lublin depressing. Shaina was especially affected by the great yeshiva. "That was the place that had the biggest impact," she recalled, after the trip. "Earlier, we had visited a museum where the Lublin Yeshiva was located, that had a photo of the students. I remember thinking, *What happened to it?* Because I remember the picture was so beautiful, and there were so many students. These were European Jews, like shtetl Jews. It occurred to me, *You don't see them anymore.* Afterward, I became obsessed with the Lublin Yeshiva. I said to my father, 'We have to go to the Lublin Yeshiva,' and he said, 'I don't know if we're going to have time,' and I said, 'We have to. We have to see.'"

Shaina was appalled to discover it was now a hotel. There was a sign that said, "Scholars of Lublin," marking the site where thousands of students from all over Europe gathered to become scholars and to keep Judaism thriving. Shaina still had the image of the yeshiva in her mind, and instead all that remained was a hotel. She realized it would never be a yeshiva again.

"We walked inside, and people were asking for their room keys," Shaina recounted, later. "I just felt this was so odd. We went upstairs, and you see the rooms where they studied, and now they are hotel rooms. There was a synagogue, the original, and people still pray there, but you must pay for tickets, and they have to unlock the door because it's not open all the time. I recall thinking, *This place was once filled with students and prominent rabbis, but most of them were exterminated. This was European Jewry after they were exiled following the destruction of the Second Temple. They were teaching here at one point, and now it's empty.* And there were pictures all over the wall, of the students in the yeshiva. It broke my heart."

I shared Shaina's sense of heartbreak. After the war began, the books in the library were confiscated by the Nazis, and the students were deported to concentration camps. Shaina discovered that one student survived and moved to Israel, where he opened a yeshiva in Bnei Brak to continue the legacy of Rabbi Shapira.

"The reason it hurts me so much," Shaina said, "is that Hitler didn't just try to kill every Jew. He tried to kill a certain type of Jew. From 1939 to 1941, many of the secular Jews escaped because they knew Hitler was coming to power. They took trains, and they got out of Germany. By the time Hitler decided to systematically exterminate all the Jews, a certain type of Jew was left. To me, it was like this Jew barely exists anymore."

The Orthodox Jews, who were easy to identify, were all exterminated, and their way of life all but disappeared. Today, it survives in small pockets of Europe and certain places in Israel, such as Mea She'arim and Bnei Brak, where survivors of these communities settled after the war, and also in Brooklyn and New Jersey.

At one point, as we were walking through the town, we came upon a fountain with water coming out of the ground, and Dovid began tap dancing in the water. He had learned some moves from watching Michael Jackson. Some Israelis were staying in the hotel and were looking out the windows, staring at him. Shaina heard them say, "Is he wearing a *yarmulke*? Is he *dati* [observant]?"

"I got wet," Dovid explained, after the trip, "because we went to so many depressing places in one day. We went to Majdanek and the yeshiva. I felt like I had to let everything out. I just felt I had to dance."

"It was wonderful to see this young Jewish boy dancing where there was so much destruction," Baba recalled, after the trip. She was devastated by Lublin, that ghost town. It was a cumulation of her feelings of the trip to that point. She thought her love of God had diminished, and that the year she had just spent studying in Israel was wasted. God had fulfilled his promise to the Jewish people in Israel. How did God bear to watch the Holocaust as it happened?

It is a question that has bedeviled the Jewish people since the war, and tormented our family throughout the trip. For starters, let me say, there is no exoneration of God. Jewish tradition teaches us that it is not blasphemous to challenge, wrestle with, and beseech God. From the beginning of humankind, God established a moral code of good and evil. God told Adam and Eve that there are two trees—one you are allowed to take fruit from, and another that is forbidden to touch. There was no ambiguity. When Eve ate from the forbidden tree, humans lost that moral clarity. Good and evil are now intertwined, and we must sift through the chaos to restore this lucidity. God gave us commandments to teach us right from wrong—to uphold life and reject death. We naturally expect God to live up to those same principles.

That theology of defiance is what I taught my children. They saw it as incomplete, of course, but found comfort in our right to remain spiritually insolent amid our total devotion to God's commandments, and while embracing an observant Jewish life.

Cheftzibah and Dovid, ages eight and eleven, walk through the central Berlin memorial to the Holocaust, consisting of slabs that look like tombstones.

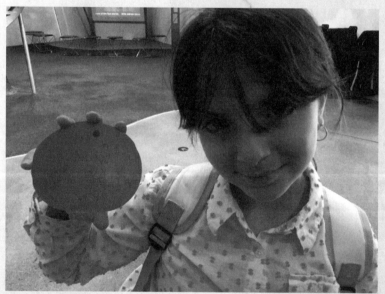

In Krakow, approximately forty miles from Auschwitz, Cheftzibah decides to write that "Mashiach," the messiah, should come now to bring the six million Jewish martyrs of the Holocaust back to us.

Rabbi Shmuley holding the Torah dedicated to the memory of Elie Wiesel, six million of the Holocaust, and the Tutsi of the Rwandan Genocide, outside the Remuh Synagogue in Krakow, Europe's second most famous surviving Shul.

Cheftzibah assists her mother in finding the name of Zoltan Wiesner, Debbie's great uncle who was murdered at twenty-two years of age in Auschwitz, and is found in the book of martyrs of the extermination camp.

Rabbi Shmuley and his children pray the afternoon Micha prayer at Auschwitz, as a glorious sunset falls on the darkest place on Earth.

Overcome by exposure to the horrors of the Birkenau crematorium, Rabbi Shmuley's daughter Shaina weeps in prayer.

Debbie and Cheftzibah exploring the box cars in Łódź, which took hundreds of thousands of Jews to their deaths in the crematorium.

Shmuley and Dovid are overwhelmed by the melted remnants of the Bialystok Great Synagogue where on June 27, 1941, approximately 2,000 Jews were burned alive by the Einsatzgruppen.

Cheftzibah peers at the memorial to Mordechai Anielewicz and the fighters of the Warsaw Ghetto, where on May 8, 1943, approximately 700 hundred killed themselves rather than being captured by the SS.

Rabbi Shmuley and his family tour the Auschwitz concentration camp holding the Torah dedicated to the martyred six million.

Amidst the desolation and bleakness of Birkenau, Dovid Chaim, age eleven, peers out at the vast emptiness.

Cheftzibah, age eight, walks through the Berlin Holocaust memorial designed to look like giant grave stones.

Rochel Leah seeks to decipher the ancient Jewish tombstones from the Jewish cemetery in Prague, Europe's most famous.

Rabbi Shmuley points out the bullet holes at the Orthodox Cathedral of Saints Cyril and Methodius in Prague where the three paratroopers, Jan Kubis, Jozef Gabcik, and Josef Valcik were murdered. This was two days after the 75th anniversary of their murder.

Dovid Chaim pulls his father towards the remnants of crematorium number 2 and 3 in the Birkenau concentration camp.

Rabbi Shmuley's family arrives under the infamous Arbeit Macht Frei sign in Auschwitz.

In a moment of spontaneous euphoria, Dovid Chaim rebelled against the constant grimness of the trip by dancing in the fountains of Lublin. Tens of spectators watched him, confused.

Rabbi Shmuley is struck by the utter horror of the shoes, bronze remnants of the Jewish children drowned by the Hungarian Arrow-Cross, Hitler's genocidal allies, in the Danube River.

Cheftzibah points to the shoes of Jewish children, drowned by the
Hungarian Arrow-Cross, the Hungarian equivalent of the SS.

Dovid Chaim ponders the story his father has just told him about Janusz Korczak, the
legendary head of the Warsaw Jewish orphanage, where in August 1942, Korczak led
around 200 children onto the box cars that would take them to their deaths at Treblinka.

Shaina is stunned by the sheer vastness of the Treblinka extermination camp.

Cheftzibah walks through the monuments to the murdered nearly one million Jews of Treblinka.

Rochel Leah and Cheftzibah rest after walking through the horrors of the Treblinka extermination camp.

The family walks through the retaining walls, which is all that remains of Hitler's Berghof Bavarian mountain retreat, where he spent one-third of the second World War, directing the Holocaust and the global conflict.

Cheftzibah stands outside the Majdanek extermination camp with its horrible mound of human ash and bones.

Shaina leans on the stone taken from the Mauthausen concentration camp, marking the spot where Adolf Hitler was born, in the city of Braunau am Inn, Austria. The children found visiting Hitler's birthplace eerie, haunting, and horrible.

The children explore the Prague Jewish cemetery, Europe's most famous, preserved by the Nazis as a "museum" to an extinct race.

Yisrael Zoltan Wiesner, Debbie's great-uncle, murdered in Auschwitz aged twenty-two. He was deported from Slovakia on April 2, 1943, and murdered at Auschwitz May 3, 1942.

Debbie stands with Rochel Leah (Baba) and Cheftziba outside the house that was once her great-grandparents' home in Kosice, Slovakia.

CHAPTER 16

MAJDANEK: THE NEIGHBORHOOD EXTERMINATION CAMP

Our last stop in Poland was the extermination camp of Majdanek. Majdanek, or little Majdan, was named after the Majdan Tatarski, a suburb of Lublin, where it was built by Order of SS Chief Heinrich Himmler, to house prisoners for slave labor. The camp opened in October 1941, and its first prisoners were Soviet POWs. On December 12, 1941, 150 Jews, seized off the streets of Lublin, became the first Jewish prisoners in Majdanek.

Majdanek was overrun so quickly by the Russians in 1944, that the Nazi guards could not destroy the camp and the evidence of their slaughter, as they did in other places like Treblinka. It is probably the best-preserved camp, with its crematoria and gas chambers intact—a standing rebuke to Holocaust denial.

Believe it or not, President Trump came to deliver a speech in Warsaw, on July 6th, and we got tickets. It was an amazing thing to behold. Amid our stark depression at the sites of Jewish annihilation, along came the American president to give a speech in the Polish capital—his first in Europe since becoming president. We were uplifted and inspired by this display of American power, knowing full well that it was the United States, and ironically, Russia, that had put an end to the Holocaust. But it also meant that we left for Majdanek late, at the conclusion of the speech, and arrived at the death camp late in the afternoon.

Holding the Elie Wiesel Torah close to my chest, I could not help thinking not only of the immorality of the Nazis, and the moral failure of the Poles, who, in the case of Majdanek, could see the barracks and the watchtowers and the mechanisms of death as they drove along the highway connecting Lublin, Zamość, and Chełm. Given the lengths to which the Nazis typically went to conceal their activities—building camps in isolated areas and closed military zones—it is astonishing to see an extermination camp that was so visible, just three miles from Lublin. They built it there like it was a normal thing; you can see the whole camp as you drive along. On one side, the camp and residences are separated by a street. On the other side, houses are literally abutting the camp. The people there were living so close that they surely witnessed some of the activities in the camp. They certainly smelled the burning bodies and saw the ashes and smoke rise from the crematoria. Today, you can see people walking their dogs within sight of the mounds of ashes of cremated Jews.

Majdanek was a place where Jews fit to work could avoid deportation to the main death camps. Thousands of Jews originally bound for Auschwitz and other camps were diverted to Majdanek to provide more workers. The respite was temporary, however, as those who became ill or unable to work were murdered. The Nazis did not even bother with the pretense that work would lead to freedom. There was no *Arbeit Macht Frei* sign on the gate. Conditions were primitive, with overcrowded barracks and no sewage system, as it was part of the plan for prisoners to die from starvation, disease, exhaustion, exposure, or mistreatment by the guards. Some prisoners transferred from other camps were killed upon arrival.

Many of the prisoners worked on construction inside the camp, or at tasks in the sewing shop, kitchens, storerooms, offices, infirmaries, and other facilities. Others were sent to work at manufacturing plants operated by the SS, making parts for Heinkel aircraft manufacturing company. According to the Majdanek museum, "…the worst assignments were those involving construction and earthworks, as these were continued regardless of the season or weather conditions. If there was not enough work to occupy all prisoners, nonsensical tasks were assigned involving e.g. carrying earth or stones from one place to another while running and being constantly abused by the guards."

In late 1942, gas chambers were built in Majdanek, and thousands of prisoners were killed, including many sent from Belzec after that camp was closed. Thousands of survivors of the Warsaw Ghetto Uprising were sent to Majdanek to become slave laborers. Though, many were killed as soon as they arrived. Bodies of the victims were initially buried in mass graves. Later, they were cremated, and the ashes were used as fertilizer.

Unlike other camps we visited, Majdanek did not have a railway depot, so prisoners were marched to the camp on foot through Lublin, from the railroad station several kilometers away. When they arrived, they were stripped of their personal belongings, and their hair was cut and sent out for use in "industrial production," after which, children and the elderly deemed unfit to work were sent to the gas chambers.

According to the camp museum:

Prisoners in the final stages of extreme emaciation or terminal stages of diseases were sent to special barracks known as Gammelblocks. There, deprived of food or any medical assistance, they were condemned to slow agony and death. Anyone still alive after several days inside would be taken to the gas chambers together with Jews deemed unfit for work.

In the fall of 1943, Himmler issued an order—Operation Harvest Festival (Erntefest)—to murder all the remaining Jews in the Lublin area, including the prisoners at Majdanek. Himmler was apparently afraid of the Jews revolting, after an uprising at Sobibor. On November 3, 1943, the Nazis killed eighteen thousand Jews in a single day, shot outside the camp fence, near the crematorium, and buried in giant pits. The Germans played dance music to drown out the sounds of the shooting and the wailing of the victims. According to the US Holocaust Memorial Museum, this was "the largest single-day, single-location massacre during the Holocaust." Altogether, approximately forty-two thousand Jews in different areas of Poland were killed by Operation Harvest Festival.

As Soviet troops approached in early 1944, the SS transferred thousands of prisoners from Majdanek, west to Auschwitz, Bergen-Belsen, Gross-Rosen, Ravensbrück, Natzweiler, and Płaszów, before abandoning the camp. On July 22, 1944, eight hundred prisoners were marched out of Majdanek and joined by two hundred people from the work camp on Lipowa Street. Those who could not keep up were shot. Some prisoners managed to escape, but 840 ultimately reached the last stop at Auschwitz. The Germans burned some of their documents and buildings, including the large crematorium. But the barracks and gas chambers were left standing.

Majdanek was the first major concentration camp to be liberated. By the time Soviet Forces arrived on July 23, fewer than five hundred prisoners remained. Approximately 150,000 people of fifty-four nationalities from twenty-eight countries passed through the camp. In less than three years, as many as 110,000—mostly Jews—were killed in Majdanek.

As was the case for most of the camps, few of the Nazis responsible for running Majdanek were tried for war crimes. Out of thirteen hundred perpetrators, only six SS men, including two *kapos*, were initially tried for their crimes, in late 1944. Four were sentenced to death. The other two committed suicide before they were sentenced.

Between 1946 and 1948, ninety-five more Nazis were tried. Seven were sentenced to death, and the rest were given jail sentences.

Decades later, sixteen defendants were tried in West Germany. In 1981, eight were found guilty. Two were released due to ill health. One died during the trial. Five were acquitted. One was sentenced to life imprisonment. And the remaining seven were sentenced to between three and twelve years in prison. "The ruling was widely criticized by prosecutors, politicians, and members of the general public," according to the Majdanek museum.

In October 2017, Germany charged a ninety-six-year-old former guard as an accessory to murder. He was twenty-two at the time he worked in Majdanek. The man, whose name was not released, was accused of participating in the Erntefest executions. The question arose, as it always does when an elderly Nazi is identified, whether someone that old should be tried. I believe General Dwight Eisenhower had the correct response following his visit to the liberated concentration camps. After referring to piles of bodies of people who had starved to death, burial pits, and other horrors he saw in the camps, Eisenhower said, "I think people ought to know about such things. It explains something of my attitude toward the German war criminal. I believe he must be punished, and I will hold out for that forever."

The German government decided in the 1960s, that there should be no statute of limitations for war crimes. And I agree that there can be no time limit on holding perpetrators responsible for genocide.

Interestingly, Majdanek became the first museum at a former concentration camp, in November 1944, before any of the other camps were liberated. During the Soviet occupation, all Polish citizens were required to go on government sponsored tours to the concentration camps, where they learned a propagandistic version of history, designed to provoke hatred toward the opponents of Communism.

Unfortunately, due to our arriving late at Majdanek, we did not have time to go through the museum. But I went back later on my own so as not to miss anything.

The camp warehouse contained eight hundred thousand pairs of shoes at the end of the war. These had been confiscated from prisoners sent to the Operation Reinhard camps at Treblinka, Belzec, and Sobibor. Some of the shoes were sent to Washington, DC, for a display at the United States Holocaust Memorial Museum.

It is also possible to visit the crematorium and see the ovens where the bodies of families were burned. One room contains a concrete dissection table, which was used to search bodies before cremation, for gold teeth and other valuables hidden in body cavities.

From the road, you can see the large, circular mausoleum that was built at the end of the path leading to the crematorium, which is now called the Road of Homage. An inscription on the dome of the building says, "Let our fate be a warning to you." Under the dome is what is perhaps the most gruesome of all exhibits in any of the concentration camps museums: a giant mound of bones, ash, and vertebrae of the victims, all mixed with earth. It is a sickening site that beggars description, and is almost impossible to process.

From the road, you can see a huge stone monument, the Memorial to Struggle and Martyrdom, which was erected in 1969. In 2003, an obelisk was erected at Majdanek, to the memory of Jewish victims of Erntefest. It is very different seeing Holocaust monuments in a place like Paris, which is beautiful, with lots of other things to see. In these places, there is nothing to distract from the Holocaust.

CHAPTER 17

SLOVAKIA: DEBBIE'S FAMILY STORY OF HORROR AND SURVIVAL

We left Lublin around 1:00 a.m., to reach Košice, once called the Paris of Slovakia, where Debbie's great-grandparents lived after the war, having barely survived life in nearby Michalovce, which was filled with horrible memories. It was a harrowing journey through the night, surrounded by dense fog, over narrow winding mountain roads, giant trucks coming at us from the other direction. But as the sun rose, we saw we were in beautiful mountain country. We reached Košice in the early morning.

We passed the café where her family had once sat, and saw the house where her grandparents lived. As we walked, I saw a vulnerability in my wife that I had never before witnessed.

I wanted to be protective and heal her pain, but moments like these only prove that sometimes, even in marriage, you just can't. I had let Debbie mourn, and shown as much support as I could. In Košice, she became our leader. In this chapter, she is our narrator. I'll let Debbie take it from here.

When I first mentioned Košice, Shmuley asked why I wanted to go, as he was concerned about the personal pain it would cause me. "There's nothing there anymore," he said. "There are no Jews there anymore. Thank God your family got out. Are you sure you want to go back?" He wanted to shield me from the trauma of seeing the place where my family had been subject to such extreme horror.

My grandmother never went back. She never *wanted to,* either. But I wanted to get a feel for something of her life before it was torn apart. I knew it would be emotionally excruciating. But I had to go.

We drove through the night. I was driving, which was difficult. The roads in Slovakia are horrible. But then we suddenly hit the outskirts of Košice. The sun was coming up. Fog and mist swayed everywhere around hills filled with grazing cows. It was the most beautiful setting—the backdrop for a moment I knew I'd never forget.

My grandmother Ica was born in Mikhalovce, about an hour from Košice, to Yehuda and Chaya Sara Wiesner. My grandmother had three sisters—Shari, Alice, and Edit—and two brothers, named Joseph and Zoltan. Another brother died at nine months, of diphtheria. Most of what I know about the family's history was from a memoir written by my great-aunt Shari, about life in Mikhalovce, a town of five thousand Orthodox and Hasidic Jews. There were five synagogues. The largest sat in the middle of the city, right outside the town hall. She said the town was so beautiful, happy, simple, and uncomplicated. She described how there was a mountain near their house, and they could see the counts and countesses going up on horses, toward a cemetery where all the families of the nobility were buried. It sounded so peaceful and idyllic.

My great-grandfather had a bakery with an oven so big that all the families in the town would put their *cholent* (a Jewish Shabbat stew) inside it to keep it warm on the Jewish Sabbath. He employed Jewish boys to help in the bakery. Girls from surrounding towns also came to work, and become apprentices in dress- and hat-making, or as nannies and housekeepers, so that the lady of the house could go and help her husband in the business. The reason many of these young people came into town was because they were the eldest of large families, and had to find work to help support the others.

The majority of the Jews in Mikhalovce came to my great-grandfather to buy bread, so he was often asked if he had any suitable young men working for him. Often, he helped match boys with orphaned girls who had no family to provide a dowry. My great-grandfather was a generous man, and when he heard that a poor family had a baby, he would say to his wife, "Serena, make honey *lekach* (cake). I will get a bottle of slivovitz, *eiche kichel* (egg crackers), and fish, and we are going to be the godparents of this baby." My aunt said this must have happened more than fifty times. Because he was such a charitable man who gave bread to everyone, he had many friends who looked out for him, which helps explain how he managed to survive.

My aunt remembered the family's last Passover Seder, in the spring of 1938. "We heard a big bang," she said, "and we all ran outside to see what had caused it. In the distance, we could hear artillery coming our way. The second part of the Seder passed very quickly."

In March 1939, German troops occupied Bohemia and established a protectorate in Slovakia, under the leadership of the nationalist Hlinka Party. By 1940, my aunt wrote, that Jews began to feel unwelcome in their own country. Jews could no longer go to school or travel long distances without a permit. Many Polish Jews fleeing the Germans came to hide in Mikhalovce, but it would not provide a haven for long. The Germans were clearly calling the shots. In hindsight, my aunt realized that the authorities had cleverly kept all the Jews together, only to make it easier to round them up later.

In 1941, my grandmother Ica married Joseph (Jozi) Valent. That year, all boys and unmarried men were taken to work in Nováky, Sered', and Vyhne. What they did not know was that they would be building camps for their own families.

The Hlinka officials soon began to use their authority to take advantage of the Jews. My aunt recalled a hardware store near my great-grandfather's bakery that was the largest establishment of its kind in Slovakia. The proprietor, Samuel Weizberger, was wealthy and owned acres of forests and vineyards. Some high official of the Hlinka Guard thought he would like to own a luxurious home, and decided to get rid of the head of this wealthy family. One afternoon, Shari was walking down the street near the store and the owner's residence, and saw two big Hlinka Guards in black shirts and highly polished boots, taking a protesting Samuel Weizberger away. They beat him until his face and clothes were covered in blood.

Shortly thereafter, a new law was enacted, barring Jews from being on the main street after curfew. All Jews were also required to wear a yellow band on their left arm. Non-Jews were forbidden to work for Jews.

When it snowed, the Guards ordered Jews to sweep the streets. This was another way the Jews were humiliated. Old, young, scholars, and professionals—the most highly respected and dignified people—were forced to shovel gravel and ice.

My great-grandfather had many powerful contacts. He knew people in the army, in jails, and in other administrative organizations. He always had informants, and they would warn him in advance of what the Guards were planning to do.

By 1942, my aunt said more than 80 percent of the people became Guards. As they grew, they looked for yet more ways to get rid of the Jews. Of course, the first step would be to take over more Jewish businesses. "Suddenly, when visiting shops," Shari said, "you would see strange faces serving, with the Jews now the employed help. A sign in the shop window would say the business was now owned by an Aryan."

Slowly but surely, all the Jewish businesses were confiscated. Our family's bakery was taken over by one of the workers. He was a baker, but he had no idea how to run a business.

On March 10, 1942, a new law stated that all unmarried women from the age of sixteen to forty-five were to register for work at a primary school. The whole city fell into turmoil. Many sympathetic young men married hastily to save girls' lives. The hospital was full of women who needed emergency treatment for appendicitis. None of them wanted to be sent away. That was just the first in a line of catastrophes for the helpless Jewish parents.

On March 18, 1942, a man named Pavel Collok came to the family's bakery and found my great-grandfather crying. "I have two daughters. and I would like to save them," he said. Mr. Collok put his hand in his pocket and took out a key, and said, "Send the girls to my place. But make sure they do not walk through the streets. Instruct them to come around the outskirts of the town."

My aunt Shari and her sister Alice got dressed, put on black stockings, kerchiefs, and glasses, and did as they were instructed. They knocked on the door where Collok lived, and an old lady opened it and told them to come in. They thought that when things calmed down, they would return home.

It did not work out that way. The Guards made plans for the deportation of boys sixteen to forty-five years of age. My aunt had two brothers, Joska and Zoli, who were that age. Joska was sent away to hide from the deportation. But Zoli was the younger and more delicate one. When my great-grandmother learned the Guards were coming to collect the boys, she went to bed, pretending to be sick, and hid Zoli under the quilt. When the Guards arrived and discovered Joska wasn't home, they began to search the house, and found Zoli in the bed.

My great-grandfather went to every official he knew, trying to bribe them into freeing Zoli. Finally, he got a document to get him released. But by the time Zoli's parents reached the railway station, it was too late. Zoli was already in a sealed wagon. When Zoli caught sight of his parents, he started to cry so loudly that his voice could be heard after the wagons started to leave. My great-grandparents mourned Zoli for the rest of their lives. He was just twenty-two years old. We would find his name in a register in Auschwitz, where he was murdered. He arrived at the extermination camp on April 17, 1942, and was murdered on May 3, 1942.

Meanwhile, my aunts Shari and Alice were hiding with the Collok family, with no knowledge of what was occurring in the outside world. By the end of March, my grandmother Ica and her husband decided to cross the border into Hungary. The family had connections with a neighboring peasant who helped a lot of Jews get across the border. Another relative wanted to join them as they crossed the border, and the three of them hid under a pile of straw in the peasant's wagon. When they were only a little over a mile from the border, a customs guard stopped the wagon and asked the peasant if he was smuggling Jews over the border. The peasant replied that he was taking straw home for his cows and horses. The customs officer took out his sword and started poking the straw to check if anyone was hidden. No one could ever imagine the fear and trauma these three people experienced as the sword came inches from their heads.

Ica and Jozi settled in Budapest. Jozi was an errand boy, and Ica worked in a chalk factory. They were living as Christians, and had the papers to prove it. They lived as an unmarried couple so they could obtain more ration coupons for food.

The people from Mikhalovce kept in touch with each other. Ica met a man in Budapest whose name was Ari Gottleib. Ari could tell that she was not from Budapest. She told him that she was only in Budapest six months, and came from Mikhalovce. He gave Ica a big hug and told the local baker to look after her because her father was also a baker who helped people when they were in trouble. From that day on, Ica and Jozi had enough bread to eat.

The first transport of families was on Shabbat, May 4, 1942. The Hlinka Guards, with the assistance of the *gendarmes*, announced on loudspeakers the day and hour the Jews had to be ready. The first to be called were the younger families, while the old and the infirm were left behind. My great-grandfather was lucky, because the government gave him an exception paper which protected children under twenty-one.

When the deportations began, my aunts remained in hiding in the Collok home. No one knew that they were hiding in the house, except Mr. Collok's wife and mother. At the first sign of danger, they went into the attic or basement. They wore slippers so no one could hear their footsteps.

The Guards would search from house to house, raiding local homes to see if they were hiding Jews. If Jews were found, the head of the house was considered a traitor, and in some cases, the entire house would be burned to the ground.

One day, the Guards went crazy, and the whole city was emptied. The rattle of boots and the barks of dogs tore through the city as the Guards searched its every street for any remaining Jews. The Colloks had a big trunk in the attic, and when the Guards got close, Alice and Shari were hidden in the trunk. Luckily, the dogs didn't take part in that search.

My aunts went home to their parents and younger sister Edit for a few weeks. Shari suddenly began to suffer terrible pain in her right leg. She ignored it for weeks, until she couldn't stand the pain anymore, and went to a doctor. He told her she had gotten arthritis from being cramped for hours in the trunk she was hiding in. He suggested that she go to the healing waters in Piešťany. However, Jews were forbidden to go there.

Shari's arthritis failed to improve, and the pain was unbearable. The doctor gave her some ointment, which didn't help, and she took hot baths and laid for days in bed. Finally, the doctor suggested that she lie on a blanket in the garden and let her mother collect bees to sting her. She spent twenty days in the garden, and on the last one, she had twenty bee stings. Her thigh was red and swollen, and she had to take hot baths to ease the pain. Strangely enough, this treatment cured her.

By early 1943, the Germans were preoccupied with their fight against the Russians, and the deportations would die down. This lull would not last long, however, as families, including those of powerful businesspeople, were rounded up in April. They were taken to work camps in Nováky, Sereď, and Vyhne. The camps in Slovakia were filling up quickly, and so the transports to Poland began.

My great-grandfather had to work in a demoted position. The *arizator*, the non-Jew who took over the business, made sure my great-grandfather knew his place. One day, the *arizator* had to leave the premises, and told another worker to watch the Jew to make sure he didn't steal bread. From that moment, my great-grandparents understood that their days were numbered.

By the end of 1943, the camps were full or overflowing, and some people tried to escape and join the partisans in the mountains. The Nováky, Sered´, and Vyhne camps were being emptied by the Guards because they needed more room for the next transport.

At the beginning of 1944, the situation in Hungary began to deteriorate. Young men were put into work camps, and the Slovak Jews thought it would be better to return to Slovakia. Many were caught at the border, however, and taken back to Hungary, where they were beaten and stripped of their belongings.

One day, a *gendarme* came to my great-grandfather's house and informed him that all the Jews of Mikhalovce were to be transported out of the city. He said, "I just want you to know that at four o'clock even, you will be taken."

On May 14, 1944, my family packed as much as they could carry, leaving most of their possessions behind, and boarded a train to Liptovský Svätý Mikuláš. Alice and Shari obtained new identity papers that identified them as Greek Orthodox. Shari had the new name of *Olga Stolarona*, and Alice was now *Anna Kostovcikona*. They went to work in a factory in Turcansky Svaty-Martin, and rented a room in a home that belonged to a Christian photographer named Etel Reiss and her Jewish husband, who they learned was hiding in her darkroom.

Mrs. Reiss left for a long-planned vacation, and shortly afterward, two Hlinka Guards appeared at the door. After examining Shari and Alice's papers, they searched the house and found Mr. Reiss and escorted him out of the house. My aunts learned later that Mrs. Reiss had informed the Hlinka Guards of her husband's whereabouts, and told them she wanted him removed from her home.

They found another place to live near the factory. They ate one meal a day—usually fruits and vegetables they bought at street stalls. With each passing day, they could hear the sound of artillery creeping closer. They kept their suitcases packed in case they'd have to flee the approaching fighting.

In August 1944, my aunts went to work, only to see half of the machinery and staff gone. They joined others in the town, by now all fleeing, and eventually made their way to the city of Banská Bystrica. After they arrived, they learned their brother-in-law Jozi, whom they had not seen for two-and-a-half years, lived in the city. Three weeks later, someone from Mikhalovce told them their parents and sisters had arrived in Banská Bystrica the night before, and were settled in a school. The family had a tearful reunion, and vowed to stay together from that point on.

In September 1944, after Yom Kippur, life became unbearable. The artillery was reaching the city, and the Gestapo's secret police seemed to be everywhere. The family decided to move closer to the mountains.

In the middle of October, my family left Banská Bystrica. Several weeks later, they settled in the village of Podkonice, where they discovered about one hundred Jewish families living on Christian papers. When they passed each other on the street, they would look at each other, but never acknowledged the relationship.

Knowing the risks, my great-grandfather decided that the family needed to split up. The first group was my great-grandparents and Edit. The second group was Jozi and Ica. And the third group was Alice and Shari. All of the remaining money and jewelry was split evenly.

My great-grandfather volunteered to work in a bakery so he could feed his family. Alice and Shari rented a room in an old lady's house. In exchange for board, they cleaned, did the washing, fed the cows and pigs, and helped her daughter with the household.

My great-grandfather carried two IDs. One identified him as a Jew, in case he would ever be questioned by the partisans who teemed in the local mountains. The other said he was a Christian, in case he'd ever be questioned by the Nazis. One day, a German patrol came into the room where my great-grandparents were living, and asked my great-grandfather for his papers. He gave them his Jewish ID by mistake. He started to plead that his wife was a very sick woman, and the reason they were living in the village was because they were afraid of the noise of the bombs. He had a sterling silver cigarette case with a ruby that he offered to the German, and said to him, "Young man, you must have a father, and I am sure that where he is in Germany, the bombs are also falling. I am a harmless old man."

The German said to keep the cigarette case. "I can take everything you have, even your life." He then told my great-grandfather, "Go with your family and hide, because I will leave you here, but the next patrol will come around and take you away." That was the day my family decided to build a bunker in the mountains. My great-grandfather worked in the bakery during the night. But during the day, he and Jozi went into the mountains to dig.

The Germans surrounded the village, and with a loudspeaker, announced that all men between the ages of twenty and thirty should register in the middle of the village. Jozi went to register, and returned home later, shaken. He said the men were put in a row, and the tenth man was shot. Jozi was number nine.

Many of the people hiding in the village moved into the mountains. Unfortunately, the village was full of spies for the Germans. The partisans would come out of the mountains for food supplies, and the next morning the German patrols would appear. On loudspeakers, they announced that all houses would be searched, and they would burn down those harboring partisans or Jews. Luckily, the house my aunts lived in was not searched.

During the first week of March 1945, my aunts went to work in the fields. One day, they returned to change their clothes, and heard a knock on the door. It was two men from the Gestapo, who said to collect their belongings and go with them. Somebody had informed on them.

The Gestapo ordered my aunts and other prisoners to march out of the city along the main road. They didn't know where they were going. Alice needed to go to the bathroom and didn't know what to do. Shari told her to go by the roadside. As she started to move, a German pointed his gun at her. She indicated that she needed to urinate, and was forced to do it in front of everybody.

The march ended back in Banská Bystrica. As they were standing in front of the jail, sirens went off. My aunt said she hoped a bomb would fall on them so their suffering and worries would be over forever. Fortunately, they were unhurt, and taken to the jail. They were put into a cell with two lesbians (arrested for indecency) by a warden who knew they were Jews, and intentionally separated them from the others. The next morning, the warden told them the SS needed help with cleaning and washing. He felt this would be better than staying locked up all day.

At 6:00 a.m. the next day, a Gestapo officer picked up my aunts. Shari worked in one bungalow, while her sister worked next door. They cleaned, washed, and ironed. As she worked, Shari could hear the Gestapo torturing prisoners. At 11:00 p.m., they were taken back to the prison.

Shari and Alice each had two dresses. Shari hid the $300 her father had given her, in the shoulder pad of one of the dresses. She would feel the pad to make sure the money was there whenever she wore the dress. One day, she wore her other dress, and when she returned to the cell, the other girls were gone, along with the money.

After five weeks in jail, she returned to her cell after work one evening, and was summoned by the Gestapo. A lieutenant started to question my aunt. He called her a Jewess and accused her of being a partisan. Shari said she was an orphan and was caught while fleeing the invading Russians. The officer left the room and apparently went next door to question her sister whom he thought was just a friend. When he returned, he told Shari her friend had given a different story.

My aunt described what happened next: I felt so sick with fear that I thought I would faint. All day, I was washing and ironing and could still smell the petrol on the driver's shirts and uniform. The lieutenant could see that I was unwell, and he told me to sit down. He asked if I had eaten. I said that I had eaten a piece of bread and had a coffee. The lieutenant rang another soldier and told him to bring me a coffee. When I got the cup of coffee, my hands were shaking, and he started to ask me questions again. I burst into tears. I grabbed my necklace, which had a big cross on it, and said, in a trembling voice, "Jesus Christ was sentenced, and so am I." The lieutenant just looked at me and called the other soldier to escort me back to my cell.

One night, the warden slipped Shari a piece of paper that warned her to leave the bungalow on Sunday at 10:00 a.m. He also gave her an address where they should go to hide. On the appointed day, Shari and Alice went to work as usual. They found the place smelled of beer and spirits from an all-night party. The soldiers were all fast asleep. Shari snuck into a room where their IDs were kept, and took them. She crept toward the door. It was one minute to ten when a Gestapo officer stopped her and asked where she was going. My aunt said she was going to church, and the officer let her pass. She met her sister outside, and they started to walk to their hiding place.

They were stopped twice by the Gestapo, who examined their IDs before letting them go. When they reached the address the warden had given them, they knocked on the door, and a gentleman answered and said, "Come in Wiesner girls. I was expecting you." When my aunt heard the name *Wiesner,* she felt like she would faint—it was the first time she had heard her real name in three years. The man was Mr. Spenik, and he was the cousin of Mr. Collok, who had saved them from deportation in 1942. Spenik told them he was also from Mikhalovce, and that his elderly mother and youngest brother were living with him. He said the Germans knew they were surrounded, but that did not stop the Gestapo from raiding homes and killing people.

Spenik took my aunts to the basement and directed them to the corner where a false wall was hidden behind a pile of firewood. This was to be their hiding place, which they shared with a Jewish boy who was already there. Whenever someone came for wood, they would tell my aunts what was going on in the city. Within a week, they learned the Soviets were preparing to take the city. The Gestapo went on one last killing rampage, leaving the streets and parks littered with dead bodies.

After a few more days, the shooting and screaming in the streets subsided, and my aunts were able to leave their basement hideout. My aunts were unaware that their family friend Mr. Kuna had gone to Mikhalovce beforehand to check if the Wiesner family had survived the war. He found my great-grandparents at home, heartbroken and in tears. They knew the Germans had captured my aunts, but didn't know if they had survived. Mr. Kuna said he was going west and would not return until he'd found their daughters.

One day, Mr. Kuna showed up and told my relieved aunts that their parents and family were home in Mikhalovce. He took them on a two-week journey, on wagons and trucks, all the way back to their home. They arrived in May 1945. Mr. Kuna went in and told my great-grandfather, "Mister Wiesner, I brought your two daughters home. But Shari is frightened to come because she lost the American dollars you gave to her for safekeeping."

The family was finally reunited. They were all crying and hugging each other. Mr. Kuna, however, had lost his entire family, so my great-grandfather invited him to stay as a guest for the next six months.

My family started to settle down and to pick up the pieces of their shattered lives. Then my great-grandfather started to complain that he was not feeling well. He told the doctor, "I just remember, that on one night, we could hear the Germans occupying the village. I was working in the bakery, and when I heard the shooting, I left the bakery and ran toward the mountains. Halfway up, I slipped on the ice and fell. I ignored the pain and continued to climb until I felt safe amongst the trees. I continued walking toward the bunker." The pain from this injury tormented him until his death.

My grandmother Ica was separated from her husband, Josef Valent, throughout the war. They ended up in work camps, and wouldn't find each other for a year. After the war, they met again and moved to Prague. There, my mother Eva was born in 1946.

In 1948, life in Czechoslovakia became precarious as the Communists took over the government. Jews began to make *aliyah* to Israel. My family heard that life in Israel was arduous, and people were trying to find relatives who could sponsor them in America, Canada, or Australia. My grandparents ultimately decided to move to Australia in 1950, which is where I was born. My great-grandfather Juda Wiesner stayed behind because he was too sick to leave. He moved from Mikhalovce to Košice, where he died and was buried in 1965.

When I first arrived in Košice, I felt thankful for my family's miraculous rescue from the Nazis. As I made my way through the city, however, I felt a searing awareness of the thousands of other families whose stories had ended not in reunion, but in death.

Jews had first appeared in Košice in the 15th century. When the city was annexed to Hungary in November 1938, the Jewish population was 11,420—about 15 percent of the total. An estimated 70 percent of Košices Jews were murdered in the Holocaust.

After the war, the town experienced a bit of a revival, although fewer than three thousand Jews lived in the city. Nearly half left for Israel after the state was founded.

According to the Slovak Jewish Heritage Center, there are about 280 Jews living in Košice. Amazingly, that makes Košice the second-largest Jewish community in Slovakia.

There's still a synagogue. We visited it and took pictures. Shmuley commented on how often we came across shuls in the middle of towns, which shows how central Jews were to these towns before they were wiped out. Four out of the five synagogues that operated here before the war survived. One is now used as a concert hall. The Star of David that once was part of its dome is now used as a Holocaust memorial in the Jewish cemetery. A second synagogue is a technical-lab building. The Orthodox synagogue on Puškinova Street, built in the 1930s, was recently restored. A bronze memorial plaque installed on the front of the synagogue in 1992 says that more than twelve thousand Jews of Košice were taken to concentration camps in 1944. There is also an Orthodox Jewish community compound, which serves as the center of Jewish communal life.

We were seeing places where the number of Jews was so high, and now they are just gone. It was so tragic. That was one thing about the whole trip—going to these towns where Jews no longer lived. People would see us walk by, and probably thought, *These were the people who used to live here, and they were all killed, and they are not here anymore. Look, there's one of them!*

…And that was how my wife, Debbie, experienced Košice. One of the most emotional moments of the visit occurred when we found the cemetery where her great-grandfather was buried. It was supposed to be open, but it had closed early.

Debbie is a by-the-book kind of person, and I have never seen her come close to breaking any rule. But she was desperate to see her great-grandfather's grave, and decided to climb over the gate, followed by some of our children. I watched in disbelief. Wow! I had never seen this side of my wife. Normally, I'd be the one scaling the fence, and she'd be the one telling me what a stupid idea it was. But there she was, indefatigable. Really, I was concerned for their safety, climbing a rickety fence that looked like it could collapse at any moment.

Soon, Debbie realized it was too dangerous, and gave up. But she was upset by her inability to place stones on the grave. As a husband, I felt I had failed her. I'm usually someone who can get things done, and if there is someone with whom I could have spoken, I'm sure I could have persuaded them to open the cemetery. But there was no one. No office. No phone number. No contact whatsoever.

I drove around the giant cemetery several times, prodding every possible entry point to see if we could enter. It was impossible. Debbie was sorely disappointed, as was I, feeling I had let her down.

Holocaust memory can bring spouses together. I wanted to do whatever I could to help connect my wife with her past. We pulled an all-nighter, driving on these crazy, terrible roads. We crossed the Polish and Slovakian mountains in the middle of the night to make it there. I don't even know if it was a responsible thing to do, but we were going to get there. Doing so made me feel much closer to Debbie. All my life, I have been devoted to Holocaust memory, and I was undertaking this trip for the memory of the six million martyrs of my people. But this particular leg was for Debbie. I was doing this for her because it was so meaningful, and so many of the stories she had told me about her family now came to life.

I hope, God willing, in the future, to take Debbie back to Slovakia, where we can complete our trip, and she can pray at the grave of her great-grandfather.

CHAPTER 18

BUDAPEST: A RIGHTEOUS GENTILE BECOMES THE JEWISH SAVIOR

fter the bleakness of Slovakia and its shattered remnant of Jewish life, we went to Budapest on May 8, a beautiful city bustling with vibrancy and Jewish renewal. The capital of Hungary has a colorful Jewish history dating back centuries. During the Holocaust, great deeds were done there to save many of the Jews.

Budapest straddles the beautiful blue Danube River, and is comprised of three areas: Buda, Pest, and Óbuda, or *Old Buda*. These independent towns were unified in 1873, when Budapest became the capital of Hungary. One source says that Jews lived in Buda as early as the third or fourth century, while another says a community was first established at the end of the eleventh. A synagogue was built as early as 1307. Though Jews were expelled from the city in 1348 and 1360, they later returned and became the most prominent community in Hungary.

When King Sigismund made Buda his home, he made the local Jews representatives for the entire country. After the king's reign, however, persecution of Jews intensified, as did violence against them.

When the Ottomans seized control of the city in 1541, many Jews fled Buda, while others were deported to other parts of the Ottoman Empire. Those who stayed were treated as second-class citizens and heavily taxed in accordance with Islamic law and practice. Nevertheless, their numbers grew, and they were allowed to engage in a variety of commercial and financial activities. When Austria invaded in the late 17th century, the Jews sided with the Turks—a sign of just how much the Jews suffered under Catholic Austria—and believed they might fare better under Islamic Ottoman rule.

But having picked the wrong side, they once again suffered the consequences. Roughly half of the one thousand Jews were killed, the Jewish quarter was plundered, and Torah scrolls were desecrated.

The Jews were expelled again from Buda in 1712, but allowed to return later by King Charles VI, who also granted some families exemptions from restrictions on their activities. This led to new violence against the community, but the emperor placed the Jews under his protection. Tranquility did not last long, as the virulently anti-Semitic Empress Maria Theresa again ordered the Jews out of Buda in 1746. The decree was reversed in 1783, by her son Emperor Joseph II.

The Jewish community in Pest was established around 1406. After the Austrians seized the city in 1686, Jews were barred from the living in the city. As in Buda, Emperor Joseph II lifted the ban, and the community slowly grew. Later, the Jews of Pest fought for Hungarian independence. In 1814, the first Jewish school opened in the city. By 1850, the city had perhaps as many as 15,700 Jews, many of whom were prosperous traders of grain, wool, and tobacco. The city also became a center of Jewish learning after a rabbinical seminary opened in 1877.

Jews first moved to Óbuda in the 15th century, but disappeared for the duration of Ottoman rule, and the community was not reestablished until 1712. This was a market town controlled by Count Peter Zichy, who extended his protection to the Jews in exchange for the payment of a tax. Óbuda was the site of the first secular Jewish school in Hungary, opened in 1784, and home to a small group of merchants and craftsman. A synagogue, which survived to the present, opened in 1820. By that time, thirty-five hundred Jews lived in Óbuda, nearly half the city's population. A flood in 1838, however, devastated the city, and most Jews ultimately moved to Pest.

Four years before the unification, the towns of Pest and Buda had a combined Jewish population of nearly forty-five thousand, roughly 16 percent of the Hungarian population, making it the fourth-largest Jewish city in the world. A Jewish hospital, and other institutions, opened in 1841. In 1850, the spectacular Dohány Street Synagogue was inaugurated. Designed in the Moorish style, it was the largest synagogue in Europe, and still today remains the second largest synagogue on earth. Orthodox Jews created their own institutions. The unique octagonal Rumbach Street synagogue was built in 1872, as was a school for boys in 1873; a secondary school four years later; and a hospital in 1920.

A schism in the community occurred in 1868, as the Orthodox objected to the development and popularity of a unique brand of Hungarian Judaism known as Neolog. This was a blend of Conservative and Reform Judaism, practiced by the majority of Hungarian Jews. They continued to use Hebrew in their prayers, but Hungarian for sermons. They built synagogues and adopted some of the trappings of Protestant churches, including the introduction of organs during services.

By 1900, Budapest had become the fastest-growing city in Europe, and the eighth largest. Jews remained active in commerce, and many got white-collar jobs as clerks, salesmen, accountants, and shippers. Very few Jewish children attended Jewish schools, and the community became increasingly assimilated. Jews largely abandoned the Yiddish language, for Hungarian.

Most institutions were run by the religious establishment, which oversaw 125 synagogues. Jews became more active in local politics following their emancipation in 1867. Several Jews held prominent positions. And one, Ferenc Heltai, served briefly as mayor of Budapest in 1913. After World War I, the Zionist movement became more active.

Jews faced discrimination in the economic sphere, and their opportunities in many fields were limited. Nevertheless, Jews were successful in entering professions where they had previously been barred.

The Jewish community enjoyed a growth spurt after the establishment of Budapest. In 1869, approximately forty-five thousand Jews lived in the city. By 1910, the number had grown to nearly 204,000. At its peak, Jews represented 25 percent of the city's population, before stagnating as the birthrate declined, conversions to Christianity increased, and Jews began to emigrate.

In 1930, the population was approximately the same as it had been two decades earlier. By the time World War II began, the community was still larger than most in Europe—approximately 185,000, roughly 16 percent of the population. This did not include another sixty-two thousand people who were considered Jews according to Hungary's Nuremberg-like laws, which were adopted in 1938. More Jews came in the first few years of the war to escape from Germany, Austria, and Slovakia.

For most of the war, Jews lived in relative peace and security in Budapest because Hungary's leaders viewed the Soviet Union as a greater threat, and sided with Germany. In 1939–1940, Jewish men were forced to work for the

Hungarian military, under harsh conditions that contributed to the death of at least twenty-seven thousand slave laborers prior to Germany's invasion.

In 1941, twenty thousand non-Hungarian Jews were sent by the Hungarian government, who were allies of Hitler, to German-occupied Ukraine, where they were murdered by the *Einsatzgruppen*. The following year, the Germans began to pressure Hungary to deport Hungarian Jews. But Prime Minister Miklós Kállay drew the line at handing over Hungarian citizens.

By the end of 1943, German defeats on the eastern front, which Hungarian troops had participated in, convinced the Hungarians that Germany would lose the war. Miklós Horthy, an admiral who was the regent and real power in Hungary, began to explore the possibility of an agreement with the Allies. To forestall further negotiations, however, the Germans entered Hungary on March 19, 1944. Horthy was allowed to remain in power, but Kállay was replaced with General Döme Sztójay, who was willing to accede to German requests for the deportation of Jews.

Those deportations began in April 1944, after the Hungarians began to concentrate the roughly five hundred thousand Jews living outside Budapest, in cities where they were isolated in ghettos. And thus began the fastest slaughter of human beings in the history of the world—a dark record to be superseded only in the Rwandan genocide fifty years later, which would see the slaughter of 880,000 Rwandan men, women, and children in just three months.

Even more efficiently than in Poland, these Hungarian Jewish ghettos were cleared out in days or weeks. SS Colonel Adolf Eichmann moved to Hungary and coordinated the deportation of the Jews with the Hungarian authorities. In less than two months, almost 440,000 Hungarian Jews were sent to Auschwitz-Birkenau.

After receiving a letter from Swedish King Gustav V, and a threat of post-war punishment from Western governments, Horthy halted the deportations on July 7. A train with sixteen hundred Jews was stopped at the border and sent back to Budapest, where almost all the remaining Jews of Hungary were now confined.

The respite was short, and the situation grew worse after Ferenc Szálasi and his fascist anti-Semitic Arrow Cross Party seized power from Horthy, with the approval of Germany, on October 15, 1944. Shortly thereafter,

Arrow Cross fanatics began to attack Jews in the street, and thousands were rounded up for deportation.

Roughly two hundred thousand Jews in Budapest were ordered to wear yellow badges. Eichmann appointed a *Judenrat*. Rather than concentrate the Jews in a ghetto, they were relocated to approximately two thousand homes spread around the city, marked with a Star of David. The Hungarians feared that if the Jews were all in one place, the Allies might only bomb areas outside the ghetto to spare the Jews. By scattering them, they hoped to use the Jews as human shields. The Allies bombed the entire city. Meanwhile, deportations resumed, and thousands of Jews from the Budapest suburbs were sent to Auschwitz.

On November 8, 1944, as many as eighty thousand Jews were sent on death marches to the Austrian border. Many were shot, or died of starvation, disease, exhaustion, or cold exposure. Those who survived were sent to concentration camps, or were forced to work on construction projects for the Nazis.

The same month, the Arrow Cross forced the remaining Jews into a ghetto in the neighborhood, relocating non-Jews elsewhere. In a decree issued on November 29, the government apologized for the inconvenience to non-Jewish residents:

> In this life-and-death struggle, which may decide the fate of the Hungarians for centuries to come, all of us must make sacrifices. The government is aware of the extraordinary difficulties that are bound to be experienced by the non-Jewish population scheduled for resettlement. With a firm belief in a better future, and as a pledge for victory, we must bear this sacrifice. I shall see to it that the resettled non-Jewish residents (owners, tenants, beneficiaries, Christian custodians or superintendents, etc.) shall receive apartments equivalent to those they were compelled to leave, on the Pest side of the city.

The Arrow Cross searched for Jews around the city. The spot where they shot an estimated twenty thousand Jews and threw them in the Danube is marked today by a powerful monument, made up of sixty pairs of shoes cast in iron—many with candles inside—on the banks of the Danube. The shoes were cast from shoes worn by Jews killed at Auschwitz.

In a twist of fate, in our visit to this moving monument, we were followed by Prime Minister Benjamin Netanyahu of Israel, who visited Hungary just a few days later.

Shaina was deeply affected by the shoes. "We were strolling along the beautiful Danube River, and I was shocked to suddenly see a memorial where kids were killed. I walked by myself, and I was staring at the shoes. Little size, big size, adult-size, children-size, beautiful shoes, boots. Some were flipped over. It was so real. That place had a huge effect on me because you understood that hundreds of people were shot in the water here, and all that remains of their existence are their shoes. When I got to the end of the long row of shoes, I burst into tears."

Soviet Forces reached Pest in January 1945, and liberated Buda on February 13. It took another two months to secure the rest of the country. About ninety-four thousand Jews remained in Budapest, another twenty thousand came out of hiding, and another twenty thousand returned from various camps.

What took the Germans three years to accomplish in Poland took just fifty-four days in Hungary. Approximately 600,000 of the 825,000 Jews living in Hungary in 1941, were murdered. Yad Vashem has an archive of 4.7 million names of Holocaust victims. But even after identifying 225,000 previously unknown victims, it still contains only about 80 percent of the names of Hungarian Jews who perished.

About 255,000 survived, largely because the Jews were not deported until late in the war, and the city was liberated before the Arrow Cross and the Nazis could finish their job. Another reason was the remarkable efforts of several righteous people who risked their lives to save as many Jews as possible.

The most famous rescuer of all was Raoul Wallenberg, one of the great righteous men of history. He came to Budapest as secretary of the Swedish Foreign Ministry, in July 1944, in coordination with the American War Refugee Board—set up by President Roosevelt, at the urging of Treasury Secretary Henry Morgenthau, after years of being accused of not doing enough to rescue European Jewry—charged with saving, at this late stage, as many as possible.

Wallenberg was a resourceful man with a pocket full of foreign money, and the protected status of a neutral diplomat. Sizing up the situation quickly, he saw he could play the Nazis, the Arrow Cross, and Hungarian government functionaries off one another. He rented a network of safe houses, and handed out a Swedish protective pass printed in yellow and blue, with the Three Crowns of Sweden in the middle. They looked authentic enough to the authorities, and though he was given permission to issue only a limited number of passes, he manufactured them by the thousands.

Valdemar Langlet, the head of the Red Cross in Hungary, acted as Wallenberg's agent before he arrived, renting big houses and putting up signs that identified them as a Swedish library or research institute. The buildings were used by Wallenberg and others involved in rescue, as hiding places for Jews. Wallenberg also took over thirty houses in Pest, hung a Swedish flag in front, and declared them Swedish territory, just as he operated the Swedish Legation as a safe house. An astonishing number of Jews—perhaps, as many as fifteen thousand—were sheltered in these houses. Diplomats from other countries followed his example and issued their own passes, and hid Jews in buildings under their protection.

Wallenberg was a man of enormous courage. At his own risk, he searched out Jews who were being deported. He would give them his passes, and when necessary, cajole or bribe the German and Hungarian guards to allow them to return with him to the city. He would intervene as Jews were being marched out of Budapest, handing out passes, food, and medicine. He even climbed on boxcars and stood on the train tracks to rescue Jews before they were taken away.

In the second week of January 1945, Wallenberg discovered that Eichmann planned to liquidate Budapest's largest ghetto. He had established a relationship—through bribes—with a member of the Arrow Cross named Pa'l Szalay. Wallenberg had Szalay tell General August Schmidthuber, commander-in-chief of the German troops in Hungary, that Wallenberg would make sure he was tried and hanged as a war criminal if he carried out the order to murder the Jews. The massacre was prevented. Schmidthuber was apparently killed in the subsequent fighting with the Soviet Army in Budapest. Szalay was luckier. Because of his cooperation with Wallenberg, he was given his freedom, while other Arrow Cross members were executed.

Wallenberg was last seen leaving the city on January 17, 1945, right after the Soviets liberated the city. Wallenberg and his driver stopped at the "Swedish houses" to say goodbye to his friends. He told one that he was not sure if he was going to be the Russians' guest, or their prisoner. They may have suspected he was an American agent, and they may have been right.

He subsequently disappeared, only to turn up dead in the KGB's notorious Lubyanka prison, on July 17, 1947, where they said he died of a heart attack.

Wallenberg's story is a rebuke to the notion that nothing could have been done to save the Jews during the war. In places like Hungary and Denmark, where people stood up to the Nazis, Jews were saved. In the countries where people were largely silent, such as Holland and Poland, 90 percent of the Jews were murdered.

Wallenberg is generally credited with saving as many as one hundred thousand Jews. The Hungarian examples were particularly noteworthy because of the number of people who were saved.

Another Swedish diplomat, Per Anger, arrived in Budapest in 1942, with responsibility for trade issues. He had already learned about the Nazi gas chambers in Poland, and was concerned when the Germans occupied the city in March of 1944, and began to persecute the Jews.

"The first days, we couldn't do so much," he told an interviewer. "I mean, we didn't know what was going to happen. We understood that now would be a hard time for the Jewish population, and it started just a few days later. So then we were forced to mobilize our powers. From that moment, everything that had to do with trade with Sweden, or other routine errands, were of course put aside, and we concentrated…the whole legation concentrated on one thing. To save…try to save human lives."

Before Wallenberg's arrival, Anger had begun to distribute provisional passports and special certificates to Jews. The Swedes insisted that the bearers of these documents be treated as Swedish citizens, and not be forced to wear the yellow star.

"Wallenberg, one day, was somewhere else," Anger recounts, in an article by David Metzler. "I went to a station from where a train with Jews was about to depart. There was no time to be diplomatic with the Germans. I explained that a terrible mistake had been done because they apparently were on their way to deport Jews with Swedish protective passes. If they weren't released immediately, I would see to it that [SS-Brigadenführer Edmund] Veesenmayer was notified. The German train commander didn't dare risking being reported to the feared Veesenmayer. I went in to the wagons to call for names, but only found two Jews with protective passes. With the help of the present Hungarian police officer, Batizfalvy, who in secrecy worked in cooperation with Raoul Wallenberg and me, I succeeded, in defiance of the SS commander's order, to leave the station with 150 Jews towards freedom, 148 of them without protective passes."

After the war, Anger remained in Sweden's diplomatic service. Like Wallenberg, he, too, was recognized by Yad Vashem as one of the Righteous among the Nations.

Another gentile who saved thousands of Jews was Carl Lutz, a Swiss diplomat. He was a vice-consul who represented the interests of several countries—including the United States and Great Britain—that had severed ties with Hungary. He worked closely with Zionist activists to forge documents to allow Jews to go to Palestine. In houses placed under his protection, Lutz sheltered three thousand Jews. All but six survived.

As the war turned against Germany, some Nazi officials began to explore the possibility of trading Jews for money or supplies to aid the war effort. Rudolf Kasztner was a Hungarian Jewish journalist and lawyer who established the Budapest Aid and Rescue Committee. He and another member of the committee, Joel Brand, were the instigators of talks with Eichmann, in an attempt to stop the deportations.

In the notorious "Blood for Goods" negotiations conducted with Brand, Eichmann essentially offered to sell one million Jews for ten thousand trucks and other goods needed by the Nazis. The Allies did not take the offer seriously, and did not want to negotiate with the Germans. The British considered it blackmail, and the Soviets feared they would be saddled with all the Jews, even though the deal was to send them to Spain. No one is sure why Eichmann made the offer, though one theory is he hoped to divide the Allies and persuade some of them to side with Germany against the Soviets. This was the last thing the Allies were interested in, as it was the Soviets who were bearing the brunt of the war, keeping German troops occupied in the East. Besides, by the time of these negotiations, there might not have been one million Jews left in Europe for Eichmann to sell.

Kasztner tried a more modest tack. He negotiated with Eichmann and Kurt Becher, who represented Himmler, and convinced the Nazis to allow a group of Jews to leave Budapest for a neutral country, in exchange for gold, diamonds, and cash. The Rescue Committee and the Central Council of Hungarian Jews prepared lists of passengers that included rabbis (notably, the Satmar rebbe, Joel Teitelbaum) community leaders, scientists, artists, journalists, Zionists, refugees from Poland and Slovakia, and members of Kasztner's family. The wealthiest 150 Jews paid $1,500 each to cover costs for themselves and others, including more than two hundred children. On June 30, 1944, thirty-five cattle cars carrying 1,685 Jews left Budapest for Switzerland.

John Merey was four years old when he, his parents, and eleven other members of the family boarded the train. He said they were met with three surprises. First, instead of a passenger train, they were loaded into cattle cars. Second, they thought they were being taken to Auschwitz, but it turned out they were going through a Slovakian town called Auspitz. Some passengers apparently left the train at some point, fearing they were headed for the death camp. The third surprise was that they were put through a delousing procedure when the train stopped in Linz. His mother remembered entering the shower room and not knowing whether gas or water would come out.

Nine days later, the Merey family and other passengers on the "Kasztner train" arrived in Bergen-Belsen. The name meant nothing to them, and they had no idea it was a concentration camp. Merey said their group was segregated and treated differently from other prisoners. They were not forced to work or wear uniforms. On August 18, 1944, more than three hundred of the Hungarian Jews were transported to Switzerland. Merey and his parents remained in Belsen and feared they would never get out. Months later, in December, the Mereys and 1,365 others from the Kasztner train were permitted to complete the journey to Switzerland.

Kasztner settled in Palestine after the war, and became active in politics and worked as a civil servant in the government. In 1953, Malchiel Gruenwald, who lost fifty-two relatives in Auschwitz, accused Kasztner of collaborating with the Nazis by failing to warn the Hungarian Jews that they were being sent to Auschwitz. When the Israeli government sued Gruenwald for libel, on behalf of Kasztner, the judge ruled in Gruenwald's favor, chastising Kasztner for having "sold his soul to the devil." Disgraced, Kasztner resigned from the government and became a recluse. In 1957, he was murdered by a former member of Lehi, a Jewish resistance movement that had militantly opposed the British occupation of Palestine. Almost one year later, Israel's Supreme Court overturned the main verdicts of collaboration, though they upheld the judge's charge that Kasztner had helped Kurt Becher escape punishment after the war by writing him a letter of recommendation.

When the war ended, there were still more than one hundred thousand Jews in Budapest, comprising 6.4 percent of the city's population.

Approximately a quarter of them left in 1956, when the Soviets crushed the Hungarian revolution. During the years of Communist rule, discussion of the Holocaust was taboo, but anti-Semitism was largely subdued. After the collapse of the Communist regime, the Holocaust became a topic of interest and scholarly research, and anti-Semitism also began to flourish.

The question of Hungarian guilt in the Holocaust is different from that of the Poles. Poland was an occupied country. Its government and intelligentsia were decapitated by the murder of hundreds of leading citizens, yet there were still many Polish partisans who resisted the Nazis. In Hungary, there was an intact government that collaborated with the Nazis and did their bidding: It was not the SS that killed Jews in Budapest. It was the Hungarians from the Arrow Cross.

Modern-day Budapest is once again a thriving center of Jewish life, with twenty-six shuls, as well as Jewish schools, hospices, a hospital, and kosher restaurants. Hungary has the third-largest Jewish population in Europe, after France and England. It was heartening to see robust Jewish life anywhere in Eastern Europe, after visiting so many places where there are only monuments to the vanished communities. We had an amazing Shabbos with many visiting Israelis at the Chabad house run by Rabbi Baruch Oberlander, a dedicated communal activist whom I had the privilege of going to yeshiva with in Jerusalem, in the mid-1980s, and who has been in Budapest for almost thirty years. The next morning, we went to pray at the beautiful Orthodox synagogue.

The Jewish part of Budapest is home to a vibrant club scene. Revelers from all over Europe were here to party, especially on Friday night, as we saw on our walk from our rented apartment to the Chabad house synagogue, where we enjoyed the most beautiful Sabbath celebrations. The sidewalk was packed with young clubgoers, and the line for one nightclub stretched right past the door of a *mikveh* (ritual bath). Debbie wondered how it would be walking through the club line, on the way to the ritual bath. It was weird for all of us, in the middle of a continent-wide trip to bear witness to the Holocaust, to suddenly come across thousands of clubbers and revelers.

Nothing remains of the Jewish ghetto in Budapest. The last section of the wall was destroyed in 2006, but a memorial wall was erected in the area, in 2008. Protestors who see it as an attempt by Hungary to minimize their complicity with Nazi atrocities tried to prevent the monument from being erected, and now use it as a gathering site for anti-government demonstrations.

At the center of Freedom Square is a statue to the Victims of the German Occupation, erected in 2014. The memorial does not mention the Jews, and some people believe it lumps together the Hungarian perpetrators and Jews they slaughtered. A bronze bust of Admiral Miklós Horthy, the leader who collaborated with Hitler, stands outside a church, and current president Viktor Orbán describes him as "a great statesman."

This is the Hungarian response to the Holocaust, in a nutshell, and some Hungarians at least are aware of the denial. "Many Hungarians, including Catholic priests, were all too willing accomplices in massacres and deportations. It's such a shame," Methodist pastor Gábor Iványi told the *Jerusalem Report.* "We've never really accounted for our unforgivable crimes against our Jewish compatriots. We can't keep lying to the world and ourselves about them."

The Holocaust museum was supposed to open in 2019, to commemorate the 75th anniversary of the deportation of the Hungarian Jews. There was controversy over plans to omit the role of Hungarians and their government in the genocide. "It is implied that Hungary was actually a nation of rescuers," said Robert Rozett, Director of the Yad Vashem Libraries. "This is a grave falsification of history."

There have been calls for the museum's content and Holocaust depiction to be put under the supervision of Yad Vashem or the US Holocaust Memorial Museum.

One of the most striking buildings in Budapest is the giant Dohány Street Synagogue, said to be the biggest in Europe and second largest in the world, seating up to three thousand people. It was built in 1859, right next to the boyhood home of Theodor Herzl, the founder of the Zionist movement. About 80 percent of Budapest's Jews are Neolog (most of the rest are Orthodox), and this is a Neolog synagogue. The building resembles a basilica, and has an organ. The ark contains twenty-five Torah scrolls recovered from other synagogues that were destroyed or looted.

One reason the synagogue survived is that it was used as a stable and radio tower by the Nazis. Eichmann had an office behind the rose window in the women's balcony. I'm not sure if the Nazis simply needed a place for their horses, or were intentionally desecrating the holy place—probably both—and they might have blown it up with the rest of the ghetto if not for the intervention of Wallenberg.

The Dohány is also the only synagogue in the world with a cemetery for the victims of the Holocaust in the courtyard. Christians bury their dead on church grounds, sometimes inside the church itself. But Jews typically bury their dead outside the city. A synagogue is a place of life, and Jews separate life and death. During the war, however, corpses were found in the streets of Budapest and brought to the synagogue, and buried in twenty-four mass graves in the garden that are covered with white mulberry trees and ivy. Families of the victims came later to put names on the graves, but it is unknown exactly who is buried where. A weeping willow tree made of granite and steel stands as a memorial to the victims.

Opposition to anti-Semitism is the official policy of Hungary's government. A few years ago, Prime Minister Viktor Orbán called the Holocaust "a national tragedy for Hungary," and admitted, "We were without love, and indifferent when we should have helped, and very many Hungarians chose bad instead of good, the shameful instead of the honorable."

Unfortunately, the government's official view is not shared by all Hungarians, and Hungarian Jews question Orbán's party's commitment to combating domestic anti-Semitism, which expresses itself in abuse and violence on a regular basis. Hostility toward Muslim immigrants is widespread, but the Muslims also hate Jews. According to Slómo Köves, who runs a Chabad outreach program, "Anti-Semitism can be a question of verbal abuse or physical safety." He told the *Jerusalem Report* that Hungarian anti-Semitism expressed itself primarily in verbal abuse, but militant Islam in Hungary can lead to verbal abuse as well as physical attacks against Jews.

Baba was having a difficult time in Budapest. Her uncle and aunt came from Australia to meet us there, and for the Sabbath we joined a large group of more than two hundred people at the local Chabad synagogue—many of them Israelis who had traveled for an international soccer tournament that featured Israel's national team. Everyone was having a nice time, but she was struggling with the feeling that her love of God was being diminished. She was furious at God. She felt like a year of her life at seminary in Israel, which is the natural course for young orthodox Jewish women after finishing high school, had been erased. Everything she had absorbed spiritually and intellectually from living in Jerusalem was lost.

"It's hard to believe God loves the Jewish people when you go to Poland or Hungary," she said, later. "This wasn't part of the deal for the Chosen People. I didn't sign up for this."

I understood how she was feeling. When you are in Israel, you see the Jewish people flourishing, and God's promise being fulfilled, and you love God. But here in Europe, we saw that God had seemingly broken his promises, that he was in hiding, nowhere to be seen. Baba said, "If we cannot bear to visit these places this many years later, how did God bear to watch it while it happened?"

I was heartbroken to see my daughter in such distress, and I wanted to lift her spirits. So we drove up to Buda castle on Saturday night, after the Sabbath, to see the lights of the city and the sparkling waters of the Danube. I thought Baba would love that. Instead, she didn't want to take pictures with the family. She was sullen and began to cry when I tried to comfort her.

"Why did you bring me here?" she said.

It was a question she had asked me many times before. I had largely refrained from answering it in the belief that, with time, she would come to see the importance of the trip on her own. But this time, I could tell she was saying it as a statement rather than a question. She did not want an answer. She was stating definitively that it was a mistake for her to be here, and that the longer she stayed, the more her despair would increase. The air was filled with tension as I felt a chasm open between me and my daughter, which I could not close.

Later, Baba recalled that moment. "I lost my temper. I was out of control. I said I just wasted a whole year of my life. I used such not nice language."

That's when Shaina jumped in. "We did not come to visit the concentration camps for God," she told Baba. "We came for the Jewish people who were murdered here, to remember them, to never forget. We did not come to be closer to God. Rather, we came *despite* what it does to our relationship with God. We did not come to be uplifted spiritually. We came prepared to be overwhelmed emotionally, even deadened, as we showed the six million that they are not, and never will be, forgotten. We came to bear witness, as Elie Wiesel used to say, for the six million, many of whom do not have relatives. We came *in spite* of God, not *for* God, so the victims know they will never be forgotten, and that people like us don't stop visiting because we can't handle it. You must commit yourself to that. They must be remembered. Our message is: We love you, we miss you, we mourn for you, we will never forget you. And we are there for your memory, now and forever."

The whole family had trouble in Budapest. My sister-in-law, Chana Raizel, who is married to Debbie's younger brother Yossi, was particularly upset by the shoe memorial, which leaves it for the visitor to infer the identity of the victims from the Hebrew writing on plaques on the ground, which are easy to miss.

"What stuck with me," Chana said, "was that my grandmother was taken to Auschwitz in 1944, with her sister and her parents. My great-grandparents were immediately taken to the gas chambers and the crematorium. My grandmother and her sister were walking around the next day, saying, 'Where's my mother? Where's my father?' Someone pointed to the chimneys and said, 'There's your mother.' So to see the shoes that could have been my great-grandmother's, my great-grandfather's is very emotional. Tourists don't necessarily know where these shoes are coming from, and I heard a tourist telling his wife, 'They shot some people, and they put them all together, and they bunched them, and they fell into this river.' I said, 'That's not correct. They did not bunch them together. They lined them up individually. Then they made them undress, because it was a harsh winter, and the killers needed everything.' This was in front of the parliament building, and everyone could see what was happening. There are homes across the street. The tourists didn't know who they were, and I held out my Magen David, and I said, 'They were Jews.' It's not represented enough. It's very hurtful, to say the least."

Statues can be controversial. In 2014, to commemorate the 70th anniversary of the German occupation of Hungary, the government erected a stone and bronze Memorial to the Victims of the German Occupation—a bronze statue of the Archangel Gabriel, representing "innocent Hungary," holding the sovereignty of Hungary in his hands, while a Nazi eagle with a talon stamped *1944,* descends on him as if to rip it from the people.

This monument, in one of the city's most famous parks, was so controversial it had to be erected under the cover of darkness. Jews saw the monument as an attempt to whitewash the history of Hungary's collaboration with the Nazis and the massacres perpetrated by the Arrow Cross. The Jewish community was outraged, and protested to Prime Minister Orbán, as did thirty members of the US Congress. Orbán's response was unapologetic. "The monument is not a Holocaust memorial," he said, "but a freedom fighting people's memorial of the pain of having its liberty crushed. This monument, paying tribute to the memory of the victims, reminds us all that the loss of our national sovereignty led to tragic consequences, claimed the lives of hundreds of thousands, and brought immense suffering upon further millions, the entire nation."

Survivors created their own memorial in front of the monument—placing stones, flowers, and photographs of victims. When a *Boston Globe* reporter visited in 2015, she saw a cracked mirror opposite the statue, "demanding that Hungary face itself." She found a note that said, "Say no to the falsification of history…the national memory poisoning, the state-level Hungarian Holocaust denial."

In the months before our visit, Chana Raizel said local Hungarians had desecrated the beautiful ad hoc memorial—taking down the items, trashing them, and chucking them in the garbage. "That's why," she said, "it's so important not to forget and to educate."

By the end of our time in Budapest, particularly after seeing Baba's reaction, I started to question my decision to make our trip so unremittingly intense. We really had few breaks from reliving the horrors that befell our people during the Holocaust. Debbie's brother Yossi was also doing a family trip with his children and his in-laws. They went to many of the same places we visited, but they did it much differently. They had a driver, and the itinerary was interspersed with more fun and entertaining activities—mixing concerts and touristy stops in between visiting the Holocaust sites.

In retrospect, if I could do one thing differently, perhaps I would have planned some entertaining detours in between all the horrible places we visited. I have no idea what fun there is to have in Warsaw. There was no time in our itinerary, and it just did not seem appropriate, given the purpose of our trip. I felt it would betray our total immersion into genocide memory. But perhaps I was asking too much of my children.

We have debated this issue countless times at our Shabbat table, over the past three years. My children think we overdid it. But I don't know if there is a *good* way to visit the killing fields of Europe.

CHAPTER 19

VIENNA: AUSTRIANS WELCOME THE NAZIS

O n our way to Vienna, we stopped at an outlet mall on the side of the highway. Even that was weird. But it did break things up to have a bit of retail therapy. It's amazing how little things like shopping for dumb stuff you don't need can improve everyone's mood. I bought a pair of shoes and a summer jacket. Debbie and the girls got dresses. Baba's mood brightened, as did everyone else's. Yes, it's a distraction. Yes, it's materialism. But a bit of it can lift the spirits, especially as our itinerary now called for a descent into the darkest parts of Austrian history.

Vienna is a beautiful city that, before 1938, was the capital of central Europe, the thriving capital of the liberal Hapsburg Empire, whose polyglot population mixed on mostly equal terms. It was the city of Freud and Wittgenstein, and Mahler and Klimt. Most people come for art, music, and beauty. But this was all lost on Family Boteach, amid our immersion in the horrors of the Holocaust.

It was here, in 1907, that young Adolf Hitler came, hoping to become a great artist. Twice rejected for admission to the Academy of Fine Arts, he became a resentful vagabond selling watercolors on the streets. The academy had its standards, and is not to be blamed. But it is one more of the vagaries of history that the decision of an admissions officer, or committee, contributed to the greatest crime in history. Just think if Hitler had been a slightly better painter, or even settled for becoming a professor of art history. He might never have moved to Germany, taken over its government, started a world war, and gotten millions of people killed. Hitler the failure roamed the streets of Vienna and fumed as he saw Jews who were prosperous and successful, respected in Viennese society.

We were here, at the scene of the crime, to see if we could find any clues to what made this man a monster, and what could have allowed him to plunge all of Europe, and much of the world, into the nightmare of the most destructive war in history. Why was he so obsessed with the Jews? What special kind of hatred could have led him to pursue them so murderously? What did he have to make the Germans love him so, even though he was nothing like the Aryan superman he told them they were?

"Face and head of inferior type, cross-breed; low receding forehead, ugly nose, broad cheekbones, little eyes, dark hair," was how Professor Max von Gruber of the University of Munich described his first impression of the man. Hitler did have blue eyes, but he stood just five-foot-nine-inches tall, and weighed about 170 pounds. In his own person, he was an ordinary man, not the blond superman he told the Germans they ought to be.

Historian Peter Hayes suggests the appeal of Nazi ideology was a "witches' brew of self-pity, entitlement, and aggression. It was also a form of magical thinking that promised to end all of Germans' post-war sufferings, the products of defeat and deceit, by banning their supposed ultimate cause, the Jews and their agents."

Here is an insight into how Hitler convinced "ordinary men" like himself to conduct an extermination campaign in which every norm of civilized behavior was tossed aside, and men, women, and children were subjected to mechanized butchery.

"The Holocaust was not mysterious and inscrutable," Hayes says, "it was the work of humans acting on familiar human weaknesses and motives: wounded pride, fear, self-righteousness, prejudice, and personal ambition being among the most obvious. Once persecution gathered momentum, however, it was unstoppable without the death of millions of people, the expenditure of vast sums of money, and the near-destruction of the European continent."

Hitler continues to horrify and fascinate because he defies analysis. I've probably read twenty biographies of the man, and all I have is clues that don't add up to a theory. Nothing we saw, from his birthplace to his childhood home; to Vienna, where he spent his formative years; to Munich, where he became involved in starting the Nazi Party; all across the trail of his crimes to Berlin, where he blew his brains out, could tell us what led him to become obsessed with the extermination of the Jewish people.

The first Jew mentioned by Viennese documents was called Shlom. He was installed as mint master by Duke Leopold V in 1194. Later, Shlom and his family were among the sixteen Jews murdered by crusaders. Still, the Jews went on living, and a synagogue was built approximately ten years later, which was one of the largest at the time, and a magnet for well-known rabbis of the era.

The Jewish community grew over the next three hundred years. As in most of Europe, Jews became moneylenders because they were barred from many trades and crafts. They were also prevented from owning real estate or engaging in farming.

In 1420, the Jews of Vienna were attacked for a blood libel, accused of desecrating the Host. A year later, Jews who refused baptism were burned alive. The remaining Jews of Vienna were subsequently banished by Duke Albrecht V, who confiscated their property and destroyed their synagogue. The stones from the synagogue were later used to build the University of Vienna, which contains a document that turns Jewish tragedy on its head as perhaps only the Austrians can: "In a miraculous manner the synagogue of the old laws was transformed into a virtuous place of learning devoted to the new laws."

The Hapsburg emperors who followed were more tolerant, and the Jews were allowed to return, and given protection in 1451. They established a Jewish quarter known as Leopoldstadt, in 1624. But Leopold I dissolved the ghetto in 1670. Jews were briefly expelled from the city, but were permitted to return in 1675, after paying the emperor and agreeing to accept a yearly tax.

Maria Theresa ruled Austria for forty years following the death of her father Charles VI in 1740. Her attitude toward Jews was reflected in her remark: "I know of no greater plague than this race, which on account of its deceit, usury, and avarice is driving my subjects into beggary. Therefore, as far as possible, the Jews are to be kept away and avoided." She imposed anti-Jewish laws and heavy taxes that made life difficult for Viennese Jews, but the situation improved when her son Joseph II came to power and issued the Edict of Tolerance, in 1781, which removed many of the restrictions.

The Jews were granted full citizenship in 1867, and Vienna became a magnet for Jews from other parts of the empire. The city's Jewish population grew from 6,200 in 1860, to 147,000 at the beginning of the 20th century. Vienna had a vibrant religious community with more than forty shuls, including two large synagogues. The Vienna Synagogue (*Stadttempel*) built in 1826, survived the war because it was constructed as part of a residential block; the Nazis could not burn the synagogue without also destroying the adjoining residences.

Vienna was a center of Hebrew publishing, and the *Haskalah* (Jewish enlightenment) movement. Theodor Herzl and Max Nordau invented Zionism. Jews moved into the mainstream of German culture, coming to prominence in business and the professions, and making significant contributions in the fields of psychology (Sigmund Freud and Alfred Adler), theology (Martin Buber), music (Gustav Mahler and Arnold Schönberg) and literature (Franz Kafka and Stefan Zweig).

I told my children these were things contemporary Jews can feel proud of. They needed to know that amid the horror of the end of European Jewry, we as a people had punched well above our weight in European history. But rather than making them feel better, it only exacerbated their feelings of despair: "You mean we contributed so much to European culture, and this is how they repaid us?"

After five centuries of Habsburg rule came to an end with the Great War, Vienna became the capital of the Republic of Austria, in 1918. No longer the capital of an empire, the city's economy shrank and its cultural importance dimmed. Roughly 170,000 Jews, and approximately 80,000 persons of mixed Jewish-Christian background, lived in Vienna in 1938, comprising more than 10 percent of the population as Austria fell under the influence of a newly aggressive Germany. Hitler summoned Austrian Chancellor Kurt von Schuschnigg to Berchtesgaden, in February 1938, and bullied him into accepting the absorption (the Anschluss) of Austria into Germany. Schuschnigg was forced to resign, but even his replacement as chancellor, by the Nazi sympathizer Arthur Seyss-Inquart, was not enough to save Austrian independence.

On March 12, 1938, German troops crossed the border without meeting any resistance. Nazi Germany incorporated the Austrian Republic in what became known as the *Anschluss* (union). Mussolini had given his prior approval to Hitler, and as Hitler predicted, the other European powers—France and Britain—were unwilling to take any action.

Marion Wiesel, wife of Elie Wiesel, recounted to me and my family, one Friday night at our home, how as a young girl of about eight, she remembers the German troops coming into Vienna. She witnessed the Anschluss.

We walked by the palace where Hitler made the announcement. Today, some Austrians make it sound like they were invaded. But if you look at the old photos of that day, you can see that the Viennese could not have been more excited. Church bells chimed to welcome Hitler, and the police apparently had a supply of red armbands ready for the occasion. The crowd was so raucous that Hitler stepped out on the balcony of the Imperial Hotel, where he was staying, and addressed the crowd:

> My German comrades, ladies and gentlemen! What you feel, I myself have experienced deeply in these five days. A great historic change has confronted our German Volk. But what you experience at this moment, the other whole German Volk also experiences with you: not the two million people in this city, but 65 million of our Volk in an empire! I am seized and moved by this historic change. And all of you live for this oath: whatever may come, no one will shatter and tear asunder the German Empire as it stands today!"

Amazingly, after he won the Noble Peace Prize in 1986, Elie Wiesel spoke from the exact same spot as Hitler, to a massive crowd, as his wife Marion related to us.

When the Nazis imposed the Nuremberg Race Laws, the Jews of Vienna quickly found out the meaninglessness of their previous status in society. In less than a year, many were fired from their jobs and stripped of their property. Some officials of the Jewish community were deported to Dachau.

This was the phase of encouraging the Jews to leave Austria. The Nazis would humiliate them by making them scrub the sidewalks and walls, and clean toilets. Jewish stores, synagogues, and schools were attacked. And on *Kristallnacht*, forty-nine synagogues were destroyed, and twenty-seven Jews were murdered in pogroms throughout the country. Approximately forty-six hundred Jews were sent to Dachau. Those who promised to emigrate immediately, leaving their property behind, were released. One survivor who fled the city at age fifteen, said, "The most terrible thing was not the way hundreds of thousands of Austrians celebrated Hitler's arrival, but the enthusiasm with which they dispossessed the Jews....We went from being people to non-persons overnight."

Many Jews sought to emigrate, but were required to pay an exit fee and register their immovable property, which the Nazis confiscated after they left. Reinhard Heydrich placed Adolf Eichmann in charge of the new Office for Jewish Emigration. Unlike most places occupied by the Germans, the Austrian Jews were largely successful in escaping. Nearly half of Austria's Jews had emigrated by May 17, 1939—thirty thousand to the US alone, and another twenty-eight managed to leave by the middle of 1942.

Emigration of Jews between the ages of eighteen to forty-five was outlawed on August 5, 1941, and deportations to extermination camps began on October 15. During the war, 47,555 Austrian Jews were sent to ghettos and detention camps in Poland and the Soviet Union. Many were murdered by local SS and police officials, or perished in the ghettos, of hunger and disease. By the end of 1944, fewer than six thousand Austrian Jews remained in Vienna, most partners in mixed marriages. When Soviet forces liberated Vienna on April 4, 1945, 150 Jews came out of hiding. Another 150 had survived working in the homes of SS leaders, or in warehouses for confiscated Jewish possessions. Of the more than sixty-five thousand Viennese Jews deported to concentration camps, only two thousand survived.

Today, the majority of Austria's nine thousand Jews live in Vienna. Most other cities have tiny communities with fewer than one hundred Jews. The Viennese community consists of Holocaust survivors and their children, returning Austrian expatriates, refugees from eastern Europe, and many Soviet and Iranian Jews.

The Jewish community (*Gemeinde*) funds a variety of Jewish institutions, including cemeteries, student organizations, and Zionist youth groups. Vienna has Jewish kindergartens and a primary school, as well as schools run by the ultra-Orthodox. In 2004, the first yeshiva built since World War II was inaugurated. Several Jewish journals and newspapers are published in the city, and Vienna hosts a Jewish sports club, a kosher supermarket, and kosher restaurants, butchers, and bakeries. After visiting so many cities where it was impossible to find kosher food, Vienna was like an oasis.

We stayed in a centrally located Airbnb apartment, where we could walk to all the historical sites. The kids were excited to be surrounded by real architectural beauty, and it was possible, for a brief while, for the marble white monuments of Vienna to cover over some of the darker history they hid, and which, for now, my kids did not necessarily want to see.

One remarkable footnote of history is that two of the giants of Jewish intellectual history, Sigmund Freud and Theodor Herzl, lived in Vienna at the same time and resided on the same street, just a few blocks from each other. Freud lived and worked at Number 19 Berggasse, from 1891 to 1938. And Herzl at Number 6, from 1896 to 1898. Yet they never met—at least, as far as we know.

Joseph Skibell noted in a *New York Times Magazine* article that Freud did "psychoanalyze Herzl's son, Hans, years later, diagnosing the suicidal youth as suffering, not surprisingly, from a profound Oedipal conflict." Hans killed himself in 1930, in Paris, following the funeral of his sister Paulina, who died of an apparent morphine overdose, and left a note saying he wanted himself and his sister to be buried with their father in Vienna. Theodor died in 1904, at age forty-four, and was buried in Vienna, but wrote in his will that he wanted his body, and those of his immediate relatives, moved to the Jewish State he hoped would one day be created.

In 1949, a year after Israel's independence, Herzl's body was transferred to Jerusalem and buried in what is now the Mount Herzl Cemetery, Israel's most prestigious military site of commemoration. We saw a video of the ceremony in the Jewish museum. The bodies of Herzl's parents and sister, as well as Hans and Pauline, were also eventually moved to Jerusalem. In 2007, Herzl's last descendant, his grandson, Stephen Theodore Norman, was also buried on Mount Herzl, sixty years after he, too, committed suicide. When you contemplate God's plan, you have to wonder why the Almighty took Zionism's greatest visionary so young, and each of his children in such tragic fashion.

Freud survived the war by escaping to London. Today, Freud's house in Vienna is a museum frequented by many tourists, and Herzl's home is not even marked with a plaque. Vienna's only tribute to Herzl is a square named in 2004, Theodor Herzl Platz. Given the outsize role Herzl played in Jewish history, it is strange he's not commemorated more in Vienna. He went to the University of Vienna and worked as a journalist here. This was the city where he wrote his famous book, *The Jewish State*, which became the foundation for political Zionism. Vienna is the site where arguably the seeds of the greatest tragedy in Jewish history were sown, as well as the Jewish people's greatest triumph.

We took a walking tour of the Jewish sites and Nazi sites in the city. The Viennese tour guide seemed very self-conscious as he pointed out places of Jewish memory and sites associated with the rise of Hitler and Nazism. He acted like he was doing something wrong. He asked all of us not to tweet about the tour, or post on social media, or even take pictures. When we passed the famous Vienna opera house, he didn't mention the fact that Hitler used to go there with his best friend and listen to the operas written by the rabidly anti-Semitic Richard Wagner. He didn't want to taint the opera house. Vienna does not want to be remembered as the city where Hitler hung out all those years as a vagabond, and maybe absorbed his Jew-hatred.

I guess there's discomfort among the Viennese about the Holocaust. There hasn't been a full accounting of their participation in it. Austria in general has done far less than Germany in reckoning with its past, treating Hitler as a German dictator, and overlooking how he was, in fact, an Austrian whose hatreds seemed to have been nursed in the anti-Semitic cauldron of Vienna at the turn of the 20th century. Of all the countries we visited, I felt that the Austrians have least confronted their past.

Officially, both Germany and Austria have banned the display of the swastika and Nazi memorabilia, and make efforts to prevent the glorification or resurrection of Nazism. When in 1986, Austrian President Kurt Waldheim was exposed as an officer for a German Army unit that engaged in brutal reprisals against Yugoslav partisans and civilians, and deported most of the Jewish population of Salonika, Greece, to the death camps in 1943, it was an international scandal. Waldheim implausibly claimed he did not know about any wartime atrocities, and an international commission of historians found "no proof" that Waldheim committed war crimes, but concluded he could be considered "an accomplice." Austrians could not avoid this confrontation with their history. The Austrian government issued a statement acknowledging its role in the crimes perpetrated by the Third Reich. Famed Nazi hunter Simon Wiesenthal also tried to educate his fellow Austrians and others about the Holocaust, and his Documentation Center in Vienna remains a clearinghouse for information pertaining to the Holocaust.

Vienna also has a Jewish square, *Judenplatz*, with a Jewish museum, offices for several Jewish organizations, and a Holocaust monument. The Memorial to Austrian Holocaust Victims, unveiled in 2000, is a concrete cube resembling a library of seven thousand volumes turned inside out. The base of the memorial has the names of the places where sixty-five thousand Austrian Jews were murdered by the Nazis. Today, Vienna has fifteen synagogues, but the only surviving synagogue from the pre-war era is the Vienna Synagogue (*Stadttempel*), which houses the community offices and chief rabbinate. Sadly, that synagogue has limited visiting hours, and must be guarded round-the-clock, because in 1981, two Palestinian terrorists attacked the Stadttempel, killing two people and wounding thirty attending a Bar Mitzvah.

We did not have any bad experiences during our visit to Vienna. In fact, Orthodox Jews in Vienna, unlike many other places in Europe, do not try to hide their identity, despite several disturbing developments, and an increase in anti-Semitic incidents in Austria. In 2012, for example, Vienna shockingly renamed part of the Ringstrasse boulevard that circles the inner city, after Karl Lueger, because of his role in modernizing the city, ignoring his rabid anti-Semitism. A poll taken in 2013 found that two out of five Austrians did not think things were all that bad under Hitler.

The rise to power of the anti-immigration and ultra-nationalist Freedom Party has alarmed the Jewish community. Riding the recent wave of anti-immigrant, anti-Islamization sentiment in Europe, the party received the second most votes in the 2017 election. The Jewish community hoped the governing coalition would not include the Freedom Party, but Austria's new Chancellor Sebastian Kurz awarded them six key cabinet posts. In his first post-election speech, Kurz sought to reassure Austrian Jewry, pledging to make "combating anti-Semitism in all its forms" a top priority. And Kurz is today viewed as a strong ally of the State of Israel.

Vienna is a beautiful city, and we were all happy we came, except Baba. "I love Vienna," she said, later, "but I can't enjoy it. I just feel depressed there. I feel like someone is stepping on me. I feel like I can't breathe. In Israel, there is a feeling of freedom and home and that easy way of breathing. It's the exact opposite in Europe."

I empathized with Baba, but I could not fully agree. Today's Europeans did not perpetrate the Holocaust. Today's Austrians are not the culprits. There has to be, I told her, some balance in fully acknowledging the depravity of their forebears, even as young Europeans today seek, we hope, to forge a new relationship with the Jewish people.

Many will not agree with me. Many will feel like Baba, that Europe's history is so steeped in Jewish blood that it will forever be seen by Jews first and foremost as a giant Jewish cemetery and death factory. But I, as a rabbi and Jewish activist, have to take a different approach, believing that we can rebuild new Jewish communities in Europe, while never overlooking or forgetting the horrible past.

CHAPTER 20

LINZ: HITLER GROWS UP AND RETURNS A CONQUERING HERO

We next followed the wide Danube, west to Linz, a Baroque city surrounded by hills that were verdant on this July day. It is also home to many tourist and cultural attractions, and the place to go for Linzer tortes. Although, regrettably, being Kosher, we did not partake. Composer Anton Bruckner and philosopher Ludwig Wittgenstein lived here. But after baked goods, Linz is most famous as the boyhood home of Adolf Hitler. He lived in the city from 1898 until 1907, when he left for Vienna.

I couldn't look at the place as if I were just an ordinary tourist. Knowing that he walked these streets, went to school and church, seeing that his parents are buried in the town cemetery, makes Hitler seem more real, more human. We stood in front of his nondescript house at Michaelsbergstraße 16, in the suburb of Leonding. The building was in disrepair for years. But in 2002, it was refurbished, and now serves as an office for the cemetery across the street. There is nothing to indicate a connection to Hitler.

How does a man become a monster? This was a question raised constantly with the kids. Are there any clues? Was it his upbringing? His environment? His genes?

Hitler's parents were not monsters. They were ordinary people, and there is nothing to indicate that they were responsible for his later beliefs. By all accounts, Hitler had a normal childhood in Linz. He had a stern father, whom he hated. But apparently, he loved his mother very much, and he had a positive relationship with the Jewish doctor who cared for her. In 1907, Hitler's mother, Klara, was diagnosed by her family physician, Dr. Eduard Bloch, with breast cancer, and died later that year. Hitler's family was poor and could not afford Bloch's fees, so he reduced them and would often not charge them at all. Hitler promised Bloch is "everlasting gratitude" for his service to his mother, and eve sent Bloch a postcard and handmade gifts.

When Hitler annexed Austria, he even asked about the welfare of Dr. Eduard Bloch, whom he called an "Edeljude"—a noble Jew. When the doctor's clinic was closed, Bloch wrote a letter to Hitler, asking for help, and he was subsequently protected by the Gestapo. Bloch emigrated in 1940, to New York, and wrote a sympathetic article about his experience with Hitler as a youth.

This is a bizarre story, and when I first heard about it, I found myself incredulous. Hitler was the most wicked, evil, man—veritably a human monster—that ever lived. And he hated the Jewish people with a ferocity that culminated in the greatest slaughter of human life in world history. And yet, a Jewish doctor was close to his family and worked to save his mother's life?

Indeed, the question of where and when Hitler began to exhibit strong, but especially lethal, anti-Semitism, is one that historians argue over till today. He does not seem to have exhibited virulent anti-Semitism before he entered politics. The officer who recommended him for his Iron Cross First Class in World War I was Jewish, and he seems to have had Jewish comrades and friends during the war.

How does a boy who grew up in a pretty little town full of civilized people—and who had a Jewish doctor who reduced his rates or did not even charge as he endeavored to save his mother—become a man who transports whole families to death camps where children are incinerated within an hour? He was not hatched by some devil. He didn't come from some evil planet. He was raised as an innocent child, like most children are. There is no evidence that he was the kind of kid to pull the wings off flies or bully other children. He started out like other kids, laughing, and playing ball.

Monsters are not born, they are created. They are made through their decisions, through horrible choices to become evil. Unlike Christianity, which maintains that everyone is born in sin, Judaism teaches that everyone is born innocent—neither good nor evil. It is our actions, in light of our knowledge of right and wrong, that determine whether we are good or bad.

Consider: if you were Hitler's babysitter when he was a child, would you have killed him? This is a mental game that people often play, but it's silly because Hitler the toddler was not Hitler the murderer. He was not the monster he would later become, as *a result of the choices* he made as an adult.

All the children had opinions on this question. Yosef thought Hitler had no reason to hate the Jews. He was simply a monster. And perhaps there is something utterly irrational in his hatred that can only be explained by something diabolically mystical.

But my daughter disagreed: "He wasn't like a dragon from the *Game of Thrones*. He did this as a human being."

Yosef's retort: "He's a monster. He killed millions of people, and he didn't care. He's not a person anymore."

I think they are both correct. Hitler, while undoubtedly a monster, was born human like every one of us. It was not his birth, but his choices and his actions that made him a fiend.

We went to see the graves of Hitler's parents. The headstone with the family name was removed in 2012, because it had become a pilgrimage site for neo-Nazis. I'm always of two minds whether they should destroy places such as the Führer's bunker, out of this concern for neo-Nazis. I tend to believe most sites associated with the war should be preserved for educational and historical purposes. Hitler's parents died when he was a youth. They had no responsibility for the actions of their son, and I see no reason to hate or punish them.

Still, it was eerie to be near their graves—a repulsive feeling of proximity to the source of so much evil. And stranger still to see the family house across the street, transformed into a child day care center with the children's toys and playthings outside. Imagine playing there and finding out later whose house it was. Unlike the gravesite, it never attracted Hitler fans. I think that it should be converted into a museum to educate people about Hitler's upbringing and his later atrocities.

Shaina asked me if Linz is tarnished because of its association with the Holocaust. I take my inspiration from Ezekiel 18:20, which says that you can't visit the sins of the fathers upon the sons: "The one who sins is the one who will die. The child will not share the guilt of the parent, nor will the parent share the guilt of the child. The righteousness of the righteous will be credited to them, and the wickedness of the wicked will be charged against them."

This is completely different from the Catholic concept of original sin. I don't believe in vertical accountability, but rather in horizontal accountability. People at the time allowed this to happen. The people who are the children are innocent.

So to make the residents of Linz today suffer because Hitler grew up here, or that their parents embraced him here, is unjust. They all know the worst person in the 20th century was born in their town; it is difficult for them to live it down.

I felt sympathy for the people in the tourist information center. They could see I was Jewish. I asked about places to go and did not expect anyone to say, "Oh, by the way, you may be interested in Hitler's historical sites." They're not going to say that. I understand that. And of course, they did not. I feel bad for the people in the city. When they see a guy in a *yarmulke,* like me, they know why I have come to the town. I don't fault them for it on an individual level. But collectively, as a city, they must acknowledge the historical connections, and my understanding is that they are increasingly doing so.

The city's tourism website, likewise, does not mention places to visit related to Hitler, but does provide a brief history of Hitler's connection to the city. In response to criticism, the city's director of public relations told the *Guardian,* in 2002, that Linz has been one of the few cities to confront its past. And this is true. In 1996, the town council decided to document the period before, during, and after the war. A number of publications were released on different aspects of that period, and abstracts of some of the findings appear on the city's website. Simon Wiesenthal founded the first Jewish Documentation Center in Linz in 1945 and was given an award by the city for his work in remembrance of victims of the war. Many streets have been renamed, some after resistance fighters and victims of the Nazis. At the school Hitler attended for two years, in Fischlham, southwest of Linz, a marker reads: "In Memoriam; Adolf Hitler learned to read and write here, 1895–1897; Not Heil—Unheil—He brought destruction and death to millions of people." On the other side is a piece of granite from Mauthausen.

On March 12, 1938, German troops marched triumphantly into Austria, and Hitler chose Linz, his adopted hometown, rather than Vienna or Salzburg, to declare the Greater Third Reich. There is no marker, as the Anschluss is not publicly celebrated in the new Austria. But we stood where it happened, below the half-oval, wrought-iron, rose-covered balcony of city hall, where Hitler was greeted by two hundred thousand cheering compatriots. "If Providence once called me forth from this town to be the leader of the Reich," he stated triumphantly, "it must in doing so have charged me with a mission, and that mission could only be to restore my dear homeland to the German Reich."

After his speech, the crowd broke into a chorus of "Deutschland Uber Alles," followed by the Horst Wessel song, the Nazi hymn to a deceased street thug. Hitler departed by automobile, toward Vienna, to chants of "*Sieg Heil, Seig Heil*." Windows of all Aryan homes in the square were illuminated, but Jewish homes remained in darkness.

It was a triumph for the former watercolorist. He saw that he could march his army into another country and be greeted with flowers, while his enemies did nothing. And he must have thought, *Wow! This is easier than I thought.*

Hitler thought to retire in Linz, and had a plan drawn for him by the best architects in Germany to turn Linz into an ideal city. He kept a model of it in the cellar of the Chancellery of the Reich, but the war interfered with his retirement. The only construction was devoted to the production of armaments and a bridge that still stands today, across the Danube. During the Allied occupation of the city from the end of the war, until 1955, the eastern side of the bridge was controlled by the Soviets, and the western end by the United States. Much of the city was heavily damaged by Allied air raids targeting the armaments industry in 1944–45.

Jews have lived in Linz since as early as 1304, but not many. The Jews were expelled from the city in 1421, and their synagogue was converted to a church. A new synagogue was not opened until 1877. The 1934 census counted only 671 Jews living in Linz. In May 1938, Jewish children were banned from public schools. Some Jews managed to leave for Palestine or other countries before *Kristallnacht,* on November 10, 1938, when the synagogue was burned down by the SS, and most of the sixty-five remaining Jews were arrested and ordered to leave within three days for Vienna. Perhaps a dozen Linz Jews are known to have survived the war.

At a dinner in 1941, Hitler was discussing the Jewish communities in Munich, Linz, and Vienna, and said "he was happy that Linz, at least, was already completely *judenfrei* (free of Jews)." According to Michael John's study of the city's Jewish population: "…although there are proven cases of individual help for persecuted Jews, there was no opposition worth mentioning to the anti-Jewish National Socialist policies."

While it is well-known that the Mauthausen concentration camp is located just outside the city, I was unaware that Linz was home to three additional smaller labor camps. The first camp, Linz I, held more than one thousand male prisoners, who were put to work processing the slag from the blast furnace at the Hermann Göring Reich Works, which split the profits from the enterprise with the SS. A second camp was created at Hitler's request, in 1944, to extend the air raid shelters in the city after the Allies began bombing Austria. And a third, Linz III, was opened later in 1944, to house slave laborers for the Eisenwerke Donau (Danube Iron Works) and the Linz steel industry. Once prisoners were unable to work, they were usually taken to Mauthausen and killed.

Approximately 7,500–8,000 prisoners were held in the three camps. According to Bertrand Perz, who wrote about the camps for the city's documentation project, eight hundred prisoners died in the three camps. He does not mention how many were Jews. It is unknown if any Jews survived in Linz II, but 299 Jews were listed as survivors of Linz I and III, which is nearly 8 percent of all survivors of those camps.

This history is important because so many people, mostly Jews, were enslaved by the Germans. According to Fritz Sauckel, the man responsible for manpower in Germany, of the five million foreign workers brought to Germany, only two hundred thousand came voluntarily. After the war, Sauckel denied that anyone was worked to death or mistreated. However, he was convicted of war crimes at Nuremberg, and executed by hanging, as were most of the SS men who ran the Linz labor camps.

The Linz I camp was badly damaged in an Allied air raid in July 1944, that killed 120 prisoners and had to be closed. I do not know if the raid purposely intended to strike the camp, but it is one of several examples of how the Allies could, and did, bomb camps, despite later claims that they could not do the same at Auschwitz. Around 1965, the association of French concentration camp survivors erected a memorial stone to the victims from Linz I and III, at a site near the grounds of Linz III. In 2001, the city of Linz created a Stone Field of Memory to the victims of Linz II, above a former air-raid shelter in the Linz botanical gardens. Today, there is also a museum, the Voestalpine Museum of Contemporary History, dedicated to the forced laborers.

After the war, Linz became a transit point for concentration camp survivors, many of whom left for Israel after the state was founded in 1948.

Four camps for Jewish Displaced Persons were apparently in the area until 1950. The census of 1954 found only fifty-four Jews living in Linz. The community grew slightly, and a new synagogue was built with cement walls and no windows, in 1968, on the site of the one destroyed in 1938. Today, there are approximately fifty Jews in Linz.

On July 13, we stood outside the Gasthof Wiesinger pub, in a suburb just outside the center of Linz, where Hitler's father died. He died of a heart attack, on a couch that's still there! Shortly afterward, his mother, Klara, also died, and Hitler was given an orphan stipend, which he used to move to Vienna.

I wondered if Hitler's father had lived, if he had remained under his father's influence, if he had not gone to Vienna, where the culture was permeated by anti-Semitism, would his life have taken a different direction? Would the world have been spared from his megalomania and his crimes? It is impossible to know.

I was again overcome by an eerie feeling. It was surreal to look at the couch and to know people were staring at us. The townspeople all knew why we were there, and were no doubt uncomfortable. But they cannot say anything, and also cannot deny their home's connection to Hitler.

CHAPTER 21

MAUTHAUSEN: THE QUARRY OF DEATH AND THE AMERICAN WHO SURVIVED

Some Europeans would have you believe the Holocaust was something carried out in secret—that Germans, Austrians, Poles had no idea what was happening to the Jews. An inspection of certain sites of mass murder will show that many of the Nazis' crimes were committed under the noses of non-Jews.

The Mauthausen concentration camp, where one hundred thousand people died and went up in smoke, is less than twenty miles from Linz. The camp is just on the outskirts of one of the quaintest towns you can visit in Europe, just an hour's walk from the train station, where the sign still says "Mauthausen." The townspeople had to know that atrocities were taking place from the transports, the rumors, the guards talking outside the camp, and the smell from the crematoria. A soccer field was located near the camp; thousands of Austrians came to cheer for the local team.

It must sound as outlandish to read as it is bizarre to write, how beautiful it is at Mauthausen. Not only is the town charming, the camp—not a summer camp, but an extermination camp—is located on a tranquil hill overlooking the Danube, with the Alpine foothills in the background. "It is unbelievable how beautiful it is," Shaina said.

On a summer day, the view was stunning, and I wondered if any of the half-starved, sick, and tortured prisoners would have noticed. Victor Frankl, in *Man's Search for Meaning*, wrote about being carried away by the beauty of mountains of Salzburg at sunset, while looking through the barred windows of a prison carriage taking him to a prison camp:

One evening, when we were already resting on the floor of our hut, dead tired, soup bowls in hand, a fellow prisoner rushed in and asked us to run out to the assembly grounds and see the wonderful sunset. Standing outside we saw sinister clouds glowing in the west and the whole sky alive with clouds of ever-changing shapes and colors, from steel blue to blood red. The desolate grey mud huts provided a sharp contrast, while the puddles on the muddy ground reflected the glowing sky. Then, after minutes of moving silence, one prisoner said to another, "How beautiful the world could be!"

How could Frankl and the other prisoners have seen beauty in those circumstances? How could such evil be perpetrated in a place of such beauty? How can you possibly make sense of this? All I could do to find comfort was to carry the Torah through the camp, to bring the Book of Life to this place of death.

Mauthausen was the central concentration camp in Austria, with another forty-nine prisons considered subcamps. Between its opening on August 8, 1938, and liberation on May 5, 1945, nearly two hundred thousand people were imprisoned in these camps. In the early years, most camp inmates were criminals, political prisoners, and Gypsies. Later, artists, intellectuals, and priests were incarcerated. Prisoners came from Poland, Czechoslovakia, the Netherlands, Yugoslavia, and the Soviet Union, and even Spain, after the Spanish Civil War. The first Jews arrived from the Netherlands in May 1941. From 1942 on, large numbers of Jews and political prisoners were deported from the occupied parts of Europe to Mauthausen, along with Soviet prisoners of war. Following the assassination of Reinhard Heydrich by Czech partisans in June 1942, most of the Czech prisoners were murdered. In May 1944, a number of Jews were sent from Auschwitz to Mauthausen, and more than three thousand died that year. Many Polish Jews were also sent to the camp after the Warsaw Ghetto Uprising was quelled. A larger number of Jews arrived in 1945, from Hungary. On May 3, 1945, a register showed a total of 64,800 men and 1,734 women at Mauthausen, including two US citizens.

Prisoners were housed in huts built to hold three hundred people, but double that number were crammed into them. The unsanitary conditions and minimal food rations led to epidemics of typhus and dysentery. Many prisoners were shot, and others were sent to gas chambers. Many were worked to death in the adjacent granite quarry where prisoners were forced to carry stones up 195 narrow, uneven steps, which came to be known as the *Todesstiege*, or Stairway of Death. Prisoners worked roughly eleven hours in summer, and nine in winter, breaking blocks of stone from the cliff by hand, or using explosives, and then carrying them out of the quarry while being whipped by Nazi overseers.

Some of these prisoners were Americans, captured GIs, as Mitchell Bard documents in his book, *Forgotten Victims: The Abandonment of Americans in Hitler's Camps.* In early September 1944, a group of American paratroopers was brought to Mauthausen. A former prisoner told war crimes investigators of one man forced to carry a 140-pound stone:

> He staggered and dropped it a number of times. He was bleeding and perspiring profusely. [SS Kommandoführer] Kisch screamed at him, and lashed him continually. At the top of the stairs, the man dropped the stone again, slumped on all fours as Kisch whipped him unmercifully. He waved his hand and said: "All right, all right," then staggered toward a barbed wire charged fence. By prearrangement with a sentry in a nearby tower, Kisch gave a sign and the sentry shot the American three times. He groped for the fence, straightened out as he hit it and died without a sound.

Another method used by the SS to murder their victims was to push them off the edge of the quarry cliff. Officially, these deaths were recorded by the Nazis as "suicide by jumping." But the SS called the Jews they killed this way, "parachutists."

In 1942, Heinrich Himmler ordered brothels to be created at several concentration camps to provide incentives for certain workers and prisoner functionaries. The SS recruited female prisoners from the Ravensbrück concentration camp and sent them as forced sex workers, to Mauthausen and Gusen. Many died after returning to Ravensbrück.

In 1943, Albert Speer, Reich Minister for Armaments and War Production, visited Mauthausen and demanded that prisoners be used to assist the war effort. The number of prisoners used for slave labor subsequently increased in various projects, including the production of parts for Messerschmitt fighter jets.

For me, one of the most sickening things about the Holocaust and its aftermath is how Speer came to be seen as "the good Nazi." Speer was sentenced at Nuremberg not to death, but to twenty years imprisonment. He claimed not to have known about the Holocaust. What utter balderdash. He was one of the Germany's most senior Nazis, and was Hitler's favorite, as well as his architect and armaments minister, credited with keeping the war effort going when production had severely decreased due to allied bombing. After the war, he published a bestselling book *Inside the Third Reich*. As to the Holocaust…no, he says, he didn't know. But he admits that perhaps he turned a blind eye because he didn't want to know. How virtuous! And how convenient.

Eventually, a letter would surface, wherein Speer admitted to knowing fully of Nazi plans to exterminate the Jews of Europe. That the world was taken in by Speer's lies is a disgrace. He was as evil as all his Nazi counterparts, and deserved the same death penalty that was given to Göring, Ribbentrop, Jodl, and others. Instead, he was released after twenty years at Spandau Prison in Germany, and became a millionaire from the profits of his book.

Prisoners who were unable to work were used in medical experiments, murdered by poison injection, gassed, and starved. Some were subjected to torture, such as being forced to stand in the courtyard in their underwear while guards hosed them down with freezing water. German doctors were very interested in hypothermia. Those unfit for any purpose were sent to the Hartheim killing facility near Linz, where the Nazi euthanasia program to murder the elderly, the mentally ill, incurably sick, and disabled was conducted.

Mitchell Bard interviewed US Navy Lieutenant Jack Taylor, who was given the assignment of helping to build a new crematorium. "We dawdled at our work to delay completion of the crematorium," Taylor said, "because we knew that the number of executions would double when cremation facilities were available." One morning, he was told by the *kapo* overseeing the project that if they did not finish it by the following day, the workers would be the first occupants of the new ovens. "Needless to say," recalled Taylor, "we finished the job in the allotted time." The next day, 367 prisoners from Czechoslovakia became the first to be reduced to ashes in the new ovens. An estimated four thousand people were gassed.

Because he was an American, prisoners trusted Taylor, and he collected testimony about the atrocities in the camp. I hesitate to write them down, but it is important for people to be aware of the depravity of the Nazis, which exceeded what Hollywood makes up for even the worst horror movies. According to Dr. Bard's book, Taylor learned prisoners had been executed by "gassing, shooting and hanging; clubbed with wooden or iron sticks, shovels pickaxes, or hammers; torn to pieces by dogs; were injected with chemicals; left naked in sub-zero weather after a hot shower; given scalding showers followed by whipping to break blisters and tear flesh away; mashed in a concrete mixer; drowned; forced over a 150 foot cliff; driven into the electric fence or guarded limits where they were shot; forced to drink a great quantity of water, then lie down and allow a guard to jump on their stomach; buried alive; had their eyes gouged out with a stick, had their teeth knocked out and genitals kicked and had a red hot poker shoved down their throat."

When rations in the camp were cut, Taylor said people in the hospital were cannibalizing their fellow prisoners after they died to keep from starving. He later learned he was supposed to be executed on April 28, 1945, but a friendly Czech destroyed the paperwork, so he was not included with the group from his barracks that was killed. Taylor later became a key witness in the war crimes trials.

During the first week of May 1945, the SS abandoned the camp. The gas chambers were still used to kill prisoners almost until the day they left. On May 5, US troops liberated more than eighty thousand men, women, and children from Mauthausen and its subcamps. When the Americans arrived, the camp was strewn with dead bodies. They found people so emaciated they looked like walking corpses, and tragically, many perished after liberation. It is estimated that of the two hundred thousand prisoners who entered the camp, as many as 119,000 would be murdered, including 38,120 Jews.

US troops captured the Mauthausen camp commandant, Franz Ziereis, on May 23, 1945, hiding in his hunting lodge on the Pyhrn Mountain in Upper Austria. He was shot three times in the stomach while trying to escape, and died in the hospital of his wounds after giving a deathbed confession to a former inmate of Mauthausen, Hans Maršálek. Former inmates took his corpse and hung it on the fence of the camp.

In 1946, sixty-one men responsible for Mauthausen were convicted of war crimes, and all but three sentenced to death. Forty-nine of the fifty-eight were executed. Another 306 people were charged in subsequent trials, thirty-seven of whom were executed. Most of the rest were given long prison sentences but were released early. The prosecutions went on for years: in the 1980s US federal civil courts stripped four former Mauthausen guards of their US citizenship.

Because of the proximity of the granite quarry, much of Mauthausen is made of stone, which gives it a feeling of greater permanence than the barbed wire of Auschwitz. The stone also provides material for dozens of memorials throughout the camp. Victims from thirty different countries met their end here. The first plaque was unveiled in 1948, by the Soviets to honor a general murdered in February 1945. More recent memorials were created to remember the Roma, Sinti, and others who perished. I found the hall of names of all the people who were murdered particularly moving.

Mauthausen is unusual because it has memorials erected by the families of victims. Inside the gas chamber, for example, there are plaques in memory of four of the prisoners who were gassed. The crematorium wall is also covered with memorial plaques.

Above the quarry is a stone in honor of the Jews commissioned by the Jewish Youth in Austria, which says in German that the Jews died here solely because they were Jews. In 1975, on the 30th anniversary of the liberation of Mauthausen, the cornerstone for a monument to the Jewish victims was finally laid. The monument itself is a large, abstract steel menorah constructed with six arms representing the six million Jews murdered in the Holocaust, and the seventh arm symbolizing the indestructible soul of the Jewish people. Beside the menorah, the Hebrew word *zachor* (remember) is sculpted in stainless steel.

Austria does not require Holocaust education in its schools, but individual Austrians, apparently, are taking it upon themselves to educate the next generation. I was pleasantly surprised to learn that many Austrian schoolchildren are brought by their teachers to Mauthausen. Europe is littered with these extermination camps, and they remain permanent monuments to inhumanity.

Wherever you go, whether it is skiing or hiking in the Austrian Alps, or floating on the beautiful Danube river, you must reckon with a place like Mauthausen that will scar the landscape forever. And so it should be, because you can't forget what happened. You can't pretend it didn't happen, and you cannot erase it.

CHAPTER 22

BRAUNAU AM INN: THE BIRTHPLACE OF HITLER

Hitler's birthplace was not on our itinerary, but it was only an hour from Linz, and I felt the need to go, despite a sense of foreboding. Knowing my kids would rebel, I only told them when we were on the way. They were not happy.

"Why take us to such a horrible place?"

This was the kind of tension that filled our Holocaust holiday, all throughout.

But go we did. I was committed to our confronting the full horror of what our people had experienced, notwithstanding the discomfort it would create. It seemed inconceivable that we could descend into the horrors of genocide memory hell without having the courage to confront the place where it had all begun.

We arrived in Braunau am Inn, a pretty, if unremarkable, town adjacent to the Inn River, which divides Austria from the German State of Bavaria. Braunau is located halfway between Linz and Munich, less than forty miles north of Salzburg. Even though Hitler was born in Austria, he fairly considered himself a German because it was only just across the river.

Being Chabad, you look at the world through a certain values perspective. The Rebbe always said that one person can change the world. That was his motto. Hitler was the ultimate example of one person changing the world for the worse. I wanted to go to the place where a normal baby was born, who nobody would have thought, as they changed his diaper and fed him, that he would go on to create the single most catastrophic event in world history. One man brought it about. Without him, it probably would not have happened. The Holocaust is inconceivable without Hitler. So how was a human like him possible?

I had to see the place.

It felt vile. I had an all-consuming feeling that I cannot fully put in words. There was a palpable sense of evil in the air. I had to walk around a little bit, and I did a quick Facebook Live.

When you grow up learning about Hitler and the Holocaust, places seem so far away, and the time seems so distant. I've studied about the Holocaust since I was a boy. As I discussed much earlier in the book, in my mind, the Holocaust was black and white. It was a crime so horrid that it could only have happened in the dark ages, a thousand years ago. But the Holocaust has *just* happened. People who saw it are still alive. They are not figures of history. They are our contemporaries. But the day is coming when all the participants—perpetrators and victims, alike—will be in their graves.

Now, walking down the street of this provincial town, on a beautiful summer day, I felt an excruciating sense of evil. I wanted to leave quickly. I tried to wrap my head around that the man responsible for the Holocaust was born right here. Although I knew there was no answer, I hoped somehow to find a clue in his hometown, to explain Hitler's motivations.

But it was just a normal town in Germany, on a normal day. You expect Hitler to be hatched in hell, expect him with claws and horns. But he was a baby born in this quiet town nestled on a picturesque river. There doesn't appear to be anything in the air or the water. The city is not evil. The people are not evil—although, maybe there remain some who participated in the Holocaust.

Shaina had a similar feeling. She said the city was beautiful and peaceful. "Just because someone that evil came from there," she said, "I didn't think it was fair to associate the people with that evil. I didn't feel like it was an evil place."

The residents are aware of their town's horrific claim to fame, but can do nothing about it. The town council in 2011, revoked any honors that may have been conferred on Hitler, despite the lack of any evidence that Hitler received any.

We walked down the street to where Hitler's family lived, and found a restaurant filled with diners right next door. Everyone was eating and laughing outdoors in the nice weather, with no apparent thought of the town's most infamous resident. I felt weird taking pictures there. I felt nauseated. Felt it was inappropriate to have a place of food and drink here. They should block off the whole street.

My children and I discussed the juxtaposition of a pleasant outdoor eatery in a place of such horror. Had they forgotten the past? Or worse, were they ignoring it?

The house itself is unremarkable. Hitler's parents were just passing through while Alois had a job as a customs official; they rented rooms to be close to the office. Adolf was born to Klara, Alois's third wife, on April 20, 1889, joining half-siblings Alois Jr. and Angela. Three years later, they moved when Alois was transferred to Passau.

You would not recognize the house if you did not know the address— Salzburger Vorstadt 15. There is no plaque or marker that says, *This is the building where Hitler was born.* In fact, there was nothing at the house until 1989—two weeks before the centenary of Hitler's birth—when the mayor, Gerhard Skiba, directed that a granite memorial stone be placed directly in front of the house, on public ground. His predecessor had wanted to put a tablet on the house, but the owner of the building, Gerlinde Pommer, objected because she said it violated her property rights, and feared it would make it a pilgrimage site for neo-Nazis, or target of anti-fascists.

Can't say that I blame her. And indeed, neo-Nazis and other admirers of Hitler rally outside the building every year on Hitler's birthday, attracting anti-fascist counter-protesters. Partly as a response, the Austrian government adopted a special law to expropriate the property from Pommer, in 2016, and is now considering demolishing the building. That recommendation has been controversial, and I agree with the opponents. I am utterly opposed to the building's demolition. It should be turned into a museum of the Holocaust.

Walking down the street of this provincial town, on a beautiful summer day, I could not wrap my head around that the man responsible for the Holocaust was born right here. There was an excruciating sense of evil.

Although I knew there was no answer, I hoped to somehow find a clue in his hometown to explain Hitler's motivations. How could he have caused so much suffering to so many? It wasn't just one person—it was the German people, it was the Austrian people, and all the people who participated. But Hitler was the leader who galvanized them all.

I kept asking myself, *How did this happen in a normal setting?* I wanted to find some toxic waste or radiation that might have altered Hitler's DNA in a way that would explain how this man became a monster, like Godzilla emerging in the movies, after some sort of nuclear accident.

Of course, we found nothing in the air or the water. Still, there's a part of you that wants to blame the city. But the city is not evil. The people are not evil—except the ones who participated in the Holocaust.

The only hint that Hitler was born in the building is that memorial stone. On one side, facing the building, is the German inscription from Mauthausen. On the other side, it says:

For Peace, Freedom and Democracy.
Never Again Fascism.
Millions of Dead Remind [us].

I found this message strange. What did it mean? Why is the emphasis on unnamed fascists, with no reference to Jews? Hitler was responsible for the death of millions of people, but there can be no question that his greatest crime was his genocide against the Jews.

I thought of better things the marker could say: *Our city repudiates the unspeakable evil he brought to the world, and we condemn the unfathomable darkness, and mourn the millions of innocent victims.*

As in other towns we visited, the residents all knew why we were there—an identifiable Jewish family, as we are—but nobody said anything to us. Not a lot of people in these places know much about Jews, other than that they were slaughtered here. And many young people do not even know that. They don't mean to look at us in a weird way, but they do because they don't see a lot of Orthodox Jews.

And the trend seems to be getting worse. With anti-Semitism on the rise across Europe, the Jewish presence will decline still further in Eastern and Central Europe, and even fewer Jews will be seen, leading to my great fear that Hitler will have his way, and Europe will ultimately be *judenrein*.

CHAPTER 23

LAKE KÖNIGSSEE AND THE BERGHOF: EXTRAORDINARY BEAUTY MASKING UNSPEAKABLE EVIL

Next, we drove to the beautiful Lake Königssee, in the Bavarian Alps, where Hitler's home movies show him with his mistress Eva Braun, and high-ranking Nazis, enjoying themselves in the lap of luxury while ten thousand Jews were being murdered every day in nightmare death camps. I wanted my children to see the juxtaposition.

The Bavarian Alps were Hitler's happy place. In 1925, after his release from Landsberg Prison, Hitler stayed in a cottage in Obersalzberg, a mountain retreat above the town of Berchtesgaden. During his time there, he finished dictating *Mein Kampf*. Later, using the money he earned from the book, he bought a larger chalet that was named the Berghof (mountain court). The home had a terrace with colorful umbrellas overlooking the mountain and lake, where Eva Braun would sun herself, often topless.

According to an article I read in the British magazine, *Homes and Gardens*, Hitler was "his own decorator, designer, and furnisher, as well as architect." Some of Hitler's watercolor sketches hung on the walls in guest bedrooms. We have Eva Braun to thank for our picture of what life was like at the Berghof. Braun was a photographer, and she took movies and photos while they were in the mountains. Movies show Hitler relaxing and playing with his German Shepherd, Blondi. These pictures only came to light after the war. Braun and Hitler only appeared in a news photograph once, when she sat next to him at the 1936 Olympics. The German people knew nothing about their relationship. Braun was also never allowed to be in the same room with Hitler during business or political discussions.

The Berghof was expanded into a sprawling complex after Hitler became chancellor of Germany. Many privately-owned homes and farms were leveled to construct a barracks for SS guards, an administration building, a hotel for visiting dignitaries, a greenhouse, and farm to produce vegetables for Hitler, who was a vegetarian. Other Nazi leaders, including Bormann, Albert Speer, and Herman Goring, built homes nearby. On an outcrop with a spectacular view of the lake and mountains above Obersalzberg, Bormann built a magnificent mountain home for the Führer that was named Kehlsteinhaus—the Eagles Nest.

It was important for my children to understand that Hitler spent roughly one-third of his time during the war, at his mountain redoubt. Even as the German people were being bombed to smithereens in their cities, and his armies were slowly annihilated, Hitler continued to enjoy the serene beauty of the Bavarian Alps. It was a German Camp David, where Hitler relaxed, carried out government business, and entertained dignitaries. Decisions about the lives of tens of millions of people were made here.

As the Allies closed in on Berlin in 1945, they wanted to make sure that Hitler could not continue to direct the war from the Eagle's Nest, and bombed it on April 25, 1945, which makes you wonder why they didn't do it sooner.

Four days after Hitler's suicide, retreating SS troops set fire to the villa in the mountains. After the war, fearing it would become a neo-Nazi shrine, the West German government demolished what remained of the SS barracks, the tea house, and the homes of Göring and Bormann. What a waste! Every structure directly associated with Hitler should be utilized—amid the legitimate fear of being becoming a shrine to neo-Nazis—as museums to educate the world about his atrocities, and to provide proof as to his crimes.

The US Army took over some of the buildings that survived the war, and used it for recreation facilities for soldiers stationed in Europe, until 1995, when they were returned it to the Germans. I remember visiting the Berghof area when it was still under American control. It had a large hotel, an Armed Forces Recreation Center for American soldiers, called The General Walker, and scores of American troops driving all over the mountain. I was thrilled to see them there. But the United States later returned the area to German control, and no American military personnel remain.

Today, the only thing left of Hitler's Berghof complex is a retaining wall. We saw a strange man who walked past us at the Berghof, picked up a brick right in front of us, and walked off with it as a souvenir. I'm pretty sure I caught the act and his face, on Facebook Live. I couldn't believe that he would want to have a piece of Hitler's home in his house. It made me want to vomit. It sickened my children. I suspect memento hunters come here all the time. It's hard to tell the admirers of Hitler, from the merely curious.

Three years earlier, Debbie and I were here, and actually saw candles in grooves of the retaining wall that we presumed were lit by neo-Nazis. I filmed that as well. It was vile to think of Hitler being memorialized in the way Jews remember their dead, with yahrzeit candles. Maybe that's an unfair interpretation of what we saw. Maybe it was for the victims of the Holocaust. But I don't think so.

To its credit, the German government built a Documentation Center in the Gästehaus Hoher Göll, the former guest house near the Berghof that was partially rebuilt to document the rise and fall of the Third Reich and the Holocaust. From the center, it is also possible to tour a complex of tunnels and bunkers the Nazis built. Other tunnels are accessible from the Hotel zum Turken, a charming alpine inn right next to the Berghof. I had visited the bunkers in the past, but my children had no desire to go inside them on this trip. The Berghof was just too closely associated with Hitler for them to feel any desire to explore its ruins.

The hotel also has an interesting history. The owner, Karl Schuster, did not support the Nazis, and one night in 1933, ordered a group of SS officers to leave the lounge. Bormann subsequently ordered Shuster to sell the hotel, and when he refused, Shuster was sent to Dachau. After three weeks of this special kind of pressure, Shuster agreed to sell the hotel, which became lodging for the SD and the SS. The hotel was damaged when the Allies bombed the Berghof, but restored afterward by Shuster's daughter. The family still owns the hotel.

The Bavarian Alps are stunning. And it was from this position of such awe-inspiring beauty that Hitler oversaw the greatest war and mass-murder the world has even known. While Eva Braun was swimming at the Konigsee, and Hitler was playing with his dog, Jews were being transported in boxcars to death camps, children dressed in rags were starving to death in ghettos, and his own soldiers were dying by the thousands in battle. The cult of the Führer who would sacrifice for his people was a total charade.

Such beauty, such infamy. The towns of Obersalzberg and Berchtesgaden can never escape that they were Hitler's homes, where he planned and conducted the Second World War and the Holocaust. I'm not making any judgments. I recognize these places all face a dilemma: Do they want the association with Hitler, or do they want it forgotten? They know they can't forget it. They have no right to forget it, and they don't want to be accused of forgetting it. They must find a balance, which, in my opinion, would involve placing historical signs on all the major places of interest, including relevant facts about the German genocide of the Jews, and the atrocities that were planned from these places.

CHAPTER 24

SALZBURG: THE SOUND OF MUSIC

alzburg, a Baroque town set amid the Alps, is the birthplace of Mozart, and the home of the von Trapp family, memorialized in the film *The Sound of Music*. I grew up singing the songs from *The Sound of Music*, and the town has created a tourist industry around the places where the movie was shot, with maps indicating the location of particular scenes. Though a different generation, the kids had also seen the movie, and were looking forward to this visit. Their interest only grew once they witnessed the architectural beauty of the city. We stopped there on our way to Munich to give everyone a break after so many depressing days in concentration camps and other awful places, and became ordinary frivolous tourists searching out sites from the movie.

Not so frivolous that we forgot about the Holocaust, however. The movie is all about running away from the Nazis, even though the von Trapps were Catholics and not Jews.

The *Sound of Music* is a story of the Anschluss. The hero is a Navy captain, "decorated for bravery in the Adriatic," who has the courage, unlike so many other Austrians, to stand up to the Nazis. Called up to serve in the German Navy, in 1938, he decides to flee his native country with his eight children and their lively governess, a former nun who has taught them all to sing. In real life, they got out just a day before Hitler closed the borders. The movie ending, where the family walks over the Alps to Switzerland, takes some poetic license, since the route over the mountains would actually have led to Germany.

I know it was schmaltzy, but we had to see the gazebo where one of the Trapp daughters, Liesl, meets her boyfriend Rolf, and sings, "Sixteen Going on Seventeen." I tortured my family and Facebook Live viewers with my own rendition. We found the actual gazebo in a beautiful park. We visited the house, now a hotel, where the movie was filmed, and the convent with the singing nuns, supposedly the oldest in the German-speaking world. We saw the cemetery where the family hides in the film, and the theater where they perform at the Salzburg Festival, which continues today.

In 2006, a controversial documentary came out that focused attention on the relationship between the music festival and the Nazis. Some of the film clips were apparently inaccurate, but it was true that Hitler once attended the festival, and that other German officers regularly attended. Arturo Toscanini led the festival orchestra until 1938, when he defected to the Boston Symphony Orchestra, taking with him his assistant Georg Solti. His successor, Wilhelm Furtwängler, strove, without success, to remain apolitical, even with Nazis in the audience. And after the war, the festival was led, for years, by the famous Salzburg-born conductor Herbert von Karajan.

A historian in the documentary calls von Karajan "a Nazi, a true believer," and critics accused him of joining the Nazi Party to advance his career, even as prominent Jewish conductors fled Europe. The president of the Salzburg Festival, Helga Rabl-Stadler, was interviewed in the film, and disturbingly remarked that there were "people around today who wish that Hitler and the Nazis were still here now."

Jews have lived in Salzburg since the middle of the 13th century. The first Jews either died of the Black Death, or were killed by Christians blaming the Jews for the plague in 1349. But by 1370, they were back, and a synagogue was established on what is now one of the main shopping streets in Salzburg. The street—Judengasse—was referred to as the "alley of the Jews." Our hotel was on this street, in what used to be a synagogue. It is a narrow street filled with small boutiques, with views of the mountains all round.

Salzburg's Jews engaged in the wine and grain trade, but were often restricted to moneylending. The lives of Jews were precarious for roughly four hundred years, from the 14th to the 18th centuries. They were heavily taxed, and liable to be murdered by their neighbors, or the state, for no good reason. In 1418, Jewish men were required to wear a pointed hat, and women a bell. According to one source, this was the only place Jewish women ever had to wear bells.

The townspeople found a new way to insult the Jews in 1486, when the city council commissioned a sculptor to carve a marble frieze of Jews sucking at the teats of a female pig—the Jews' Sow. The carving was installed on the town hall tower facing the synagogue. It was ordered taken down by either the archbishop or the emperor.

In 1498, six years after the Jews were expelled from Spain, Archbishop Leonhard von Keutschach barred them from Salzburg. He also ordered the sculpture to be returned to the town hall. It was later attached to an even larger clock tower built in the 17th century.

Not much had changed when Theodor Herzl spent time in Salzburg in 1885, and wrote a letter saying, "I spent some of the happiest hours of my life in Salzburg. I would gladly have stayed in that beautiful city, but as a Jew I would never have been able to gain a judicial position."

A century later, the city planned to put Herzl's flattering remarks about Salzburg on a plaque. But after much criticism, the plaque was inscribed with his full quote.

So it is perhaps not surprising that when the Germans arrived in Salzburg, they were met by cheering throngs waving flags emblazoned with swastikas. The Nazis destroyed the synagogue and Aryanized all Jewish property, forcing the Jews to sell their possessions for a fraction of their value. In the Residenzplatz of the old town, a plaque commemorates where the Nazis staged a massive book burning on April 30, 1938. By the end of the year, the Nazis declared the city was *judenrein*. Salzburg's Jewish community never recovered. The current Jewish population consists of only about one hundred people.

There used to be a Chabad house in Salzburg that was run by a roommate of mine from my Jerusalem Yeshiva days, but it relocated. This is one of those places where I believe it is important to support the existing Jewish community, as well as to encourage Jews to settle. My children ardently disagreed with me. Shaina, Baba, and Yosef all felt strongly that Jews should not be where they are not wanted. Europe's Jews should all move to Israel.

I take a different view. Judaism has an eternal homeland—Israel. But it is also a global religion with global influence, and I want to see diaspora Jewish communities flourishing around the world, including in Europe, and especially in Austria and Germany. It is also important because tourists come to visit these areas from all over the world, and Jews should have synagogues and facilities to accommodate prayer and community.

Salzburg has not come to terms with the role of its citizens in the Holocaust. There are several Stolpersteine set in the sidewalk in front of buildings that had housed Jews who perished in the Holocaust, as well as in front of the synagogue and cemetery. A memorial near the enchanting Mirabell Gardens is dedicated "to those who had been euthanized between 1941 and 1945," but it says nothing about the Holocaust. The choice of the world *euthanized* is also interesting. They were, of course, exterminated, not euthanized—a term that makes the mass murder of six million Jews sound like a humane way of putting them out of their misery.

Another monument dedicated to all Nazi victims is located behind the train station, which "acknowledges and regrets that National Socialist crimes were committed here and that citizens of this city were among those guilty of these crimes…Honoring the victims of yesterday means actively opposing all forms of fascism and struggling to protect human rights today." Not bad, but still it does not mention the Jews. Outrageous.

Not everyone shares the official regret, either. In 2016, the plaques dedicated to the resistance fighters in the cemetery were defaced with Hitler's name, the Stolpersteine were covered in black paint, and the Jewish stars on the gates to the temple were spray-painted yellow. The growing strength of the far right in the country was reflected in the recent election.

Austria is a beautiful place. But there is a serious reckoning that must be done in the country that gave birth to Adolf Hitler.

CHAPTER 25

MUNICH: WHERE HITLER ROSE AND THE FIRST CAMP WAS BUILT

I n Munich, we saw how unevenly Germany grapples with its history. Bavaria was Hitler's power base, where he started his political career, and his ideology had greater appeal here than anywhere else in Germany. The city is called München after some monks who lived there. Its history of persecuting Jews dates back centuries.

We drove to Munich via the Alps, and the city is situated not far from the glorious mountain beauty. But it harbors some dark secrets.

The earliest Jewish presence in Munich dates to the 13th century, when they apparently lived in their own quarter and had a synagogue, a ritual bath, and a hospital. As in other parts of Europe, Munich's Jews were periodically victims of blood libels. On October 12, 1285, following one of these accusations, 180 Jews sought refuge in the synagogue, which was burned down. The community was again wiped out during the Black Death, in 1348–49. It is unclear if the Jews died of the disease, were killed by neighbors who blamed them for the outbreak, or a combination of the two. As elsewhere, Jews were subject to legal restriction and extralegal attack. They were driven out by the local clergy in the 1400s, and didn't come back for three hundred years.

In 1805, a Regulation for Munich Jewry granted the Jews certain rights, and the population slowly began to grow and establish communal institutions. A Jewish school, a synagogue, and a cemetery were established over the next decade. A steady stream of immigrants from smaller communities in Germany, as well as Jews from Eastern Europe, swelled the population from less than one thousand in 1848, to about eleven thousand in 1910.

The future of the world was altered in 1919, when a thirty-year-old Austrian veteran of the Great War named Adolf Hitler, joined the German Workers' Party, becoming only its seventh active member. It was officially a socialist party, and its original stated covenant was firmly dedicated to socialist principles. But Hitler would purge both its socialist origins and agenda once he started gorging himself and the Nazi Party from the coffers of Germany's industrialist titans as they warmed to the would-be dictator. Two years later, he became chairman of what was now called the National Socialist German Workers' Party (*Nationalsozialistische Deutsche Arbeiterpartei,* or NSDAP). Hitler already was plotting to gain power, and created a personal army outfitted in brown uniforms. He also adopted an ancient religious emblem, the swastika, forever changing the world's image of what eastern religions used as a positive spiritual symbol.

Hitler believed Germany's leaders had betrayed their people by ending the war without having been defeated on the battlefield—the infamous *stabbed in the back* myth of Germany's defeat in World War I. He also thought the Versailles Treaty unfairly punished Germany, collapsing its economy through massive reparation payments. He found a lot of people to agree with him. He promised to restore the country's military strength to create a Greater Germany that would have space—*Lebensraum*—for the population to grow. Germany and surrounding countries needed to be purged of racially inferior and non-Aryan peoples, according to Hitler. In particular, he believed in the need to eliminate what he considered the malignant influence of the Jews. This was his program.

Hitler was a gifted and mesmerizing orator who could inspire a crowd. Although, at this point, he still had only about three thousand followers. Nevertheless, on November 8, 1923, he led his "army" to the Bürgerbräukeller—a beer hall in Bavaria, where local government leaders were holding a meeting. The Nazis captured the politicians, and Hitler fired a shot into the ceiling and jumped on a chair, yelling: "The national revolution has broken out!"

The so-called Beer Hall Putsch had been launched.

The following morning, Hitler and his associates marched toward the Bavarian War Ministry, where they were met by state police. There was an exchange of gunfire. Hermann Göring was wounded, and the man beside Hitler was killed as he pulled his leader to the ground. A total of sixteen Nazis died in the melee, and there was a spectacular twenty-four-day trial that made Hitler a national celebrity. Hitler was imprisoned in the Landsberg Prison, where, in the course of a five-year sentence, he wrote *Mein Kampf,* a manifesto where he laid out his plans, in surprising detail, which were ignored by just about everyone. Today, it is available in nearly every language, and can be purchased on Amazon, where I saw that 54 percent gave the hardcover edition five stars. It remains, in Mitchell Bard's phrase, "a bible for racists, anti-Semites, and sociopaths."

Later, when Hitler rose to power, he ordered the creation of a memorial to the "martyrs" of the Beer Hall Putsch, that was protected by an honor guard twenty-four hours a day, and he laid a wreath there once a year. Passersby, either on foot or bicycle, were required to salute the monument. In the Munich Documentation Center, there is a film taken by a tourist, showing people saluting as they went about their daily lives. Those who wanted to avoid this degrading ritual could go down a nearby alley referred to as "dodger's lane."

Hitler and his allies were released on December 20, 1924, after serving less than nine months of their sentences. Given his treasonous activity, one would have expected the government to deport Hitler—yet another decision that would have altered history. But instead, the trial judge said he should be allowed to remain, because Hitler "thinks and feels like a German."

Hitler learned his lesson from the failure of the Beer Hall Putsch, and began to organize his followers into a more conventional political party. In 1928, the Nazi Party participated for the first time in national elections, and won only 2 percent of the vote. Just four years later, Hitler won 37 percent. He had only become eligible for public office in February 1932, a month before the election, when he became a German citizen.

German President Paul von Hindenburg ran for re-election in 1932, to stop Hitler from coming to power. The great strategist of the war realized too late that he had underestimated the man he once called "the little corporal," and promised to put to work "licking stamps with my picture on them." Though Hitler came in second in the voting, the Nazis became the largest party in the Reichstag, and were supported by enough members of other anti-democratic parties to control a majority of its seats. Hindenburg was pressured to appoint Hitler as Chancellor of Germany, on January 30, 1933, and then died shortly thereafter, whereupon Hitler was appointed to a new office—Führer und Reichskanzler (Leader and Reich Chancellor)— effectively establishing himself as dictator.

We had brought the family to Munich because the kids had to bear witness to Ground Zero of Nazism, where Hitler rose to power in the beer halls, and hung out nearly every night in the city's restaurants and cafes. Munich is where Hitler built a following with his electrifying racist drivel, and where the Nazis found an eager audience for their anti-Semitic screeds.

The first concentration camp, Dachau, was erected on the site of an abandoned munitions factory about ten miles from Munich, in March 1933. The layout was designed by Theodor Eicke, who later became the chief inspector of all concentration camps, which he modeled after Dachau. It was surrounded by an electrified barbed-wire fence, a ditch, and a wall with seven guard towers. A metal gate at the entrance of the camp had the words *Arbeit Macht Frei* incorporated into the ironwork.

Dachau, the concentration camp and museum, was one of the first places we visited in Munich, and I described to my children how it was the place where the Nazi reign of terror began. We passed through the entrance with the chilling message over its gate—itself a product of forced labor. A communist prisoner named Karl Röder was forced to forge it. We considered the meaning of the slogan. Did they mean, *If you work, you will live?* Or that the potential to live would be realized through work? Why did Nazis choose this slogan?

Less well-known is the slogan on the roof of the museum, which once housed the laundry, kitchen, and showers. It says, "*Es gibt einen Weg zur Freiheit. Seine Meilensteine heißen: Gehorsam, Ehrlichkeit, Sauberkeit, Nüchternheit, Fleiß, Ordnung, Opfersinn, Wahrhaftigkeit, Liebe zum Vaterland.*" Which means, "There is one path to freedom. Its milestones are obedience, honesty, cleanliness, sobriety, hard work, discipline, sacrifice, truthfulness, love of the fatherland."

Just inside the gate is a plaque honoring the Americans who liberated the camp.

One of the crematoria is still standing. You can see its chimney. The cruelty of denying prisoners the dignity of a burial and last rites was part of the Nazi program of dehumanization. So many Jews literally went up in smoke and left their descendants with nowhere to go to grieve or pay their respects. I have heard of survivors who say the Kaddish all the time because they do not know the date their family members died.

We did not film inside the gas chamber or crematorium out of respect for the dead. An American congressman who wanted to document the brutality of the Nazis had filmed those areas and was criticized by the museum. Apparently, they thought it was disrespectful and inappropriate. I'm sure he meant no harm. The truth must be exposed, but we also must be sensitive. This is a place of unspeakable horror, and the sanctity of the lives lost cannot be compromised.

There are several memorials in the camp. The Jewish Memorial is made of black basalt lava, and slopes downward like a ramp. A menorah is above the building, and inside is an eternal light. The railing is meant to represent the barbed wire surrounding the camp. Chiseled over the entrance are words from Psalm 9: "Put them in fear, O Lord: that the nations may know themselves to be but men. Selah."

The International Monument is especially powerful and haunting. It is a dark bronze sculpture of skeletons hanging from barbed wire. On either side are concrete posts similar to those used to support the camp fence. Underneath are the dates of the camp's operation: 1933–1945.

The museum has excellent descriptions of the history of the camp and the Holocaust. I was particularly struck by the map of concentration camps. It showed the main extermination camps, but also many of the subcamps. People with some knowledge of the Holocaust have probably heard of the major camps—Auschwitz, Treblinka, Sobibor, Chełmno, Mauthausen, Theresienstadt, Bergen-Belsen, Sachsenhausen, Buchenwald—but have no idea that the Nazis built thousands of camps. Recent research has counted more than forty thousand—a staggering number.

One of the most horrifying exhibits is the film of the liberation of the camp (you can see it online in the Jewish Virtual Library). The footage shows what the Americans found when they arrived, including horrific images of corpses and survivors who were barely alive.

The most dispiriting part of the museum dealt with the aftermath of the war, and how almost no one was punished for the Nazis' crimes. At times, there were demands in Germany that people be punished, and there were the Nuremberg trials, and others that followed, for high-profile war criminals. But many others got away free.

Germans constantly used the excuse that "they were just following orders," but there seem to be few cases where the failure to carry out an order regarding the persecution of the Jews resulted in any punishment. Their orders were clear, and carried out to the letter. Take for example, Himmler's speech to senior SS officers in Poznań, on October 4, 1943. He spoke for three hours and devoted only about two minutes to the treatment of Jews, which he said should never be mentioned in public:

> Most of you here know what it means when 100 corpses lie next to each other, when there are 500 or when there are 1,000. To have endured this and at the same time to have remained a decent person—with exceptions due to human weaknesses—has made us tough, and is a glorious chapter that has not and will not be spoken of.

That silence applied especially to the women and children. Germany, Himmler said two days later, could "not allow the avengers of our sons and grandsons in the form of their children to grow up. The difficult decision had to be made to have this people disappear from the earth. For the organization which had to execute this task, it was the most difficult which we had ever had....The Jewish question in the countries that we occupy will be solved by the end of this year. Only remainders of odd Jews that managed to find hiding places will be left over.

On May 24, 1944, in another speech, Himmler said he wasn't such a bad guy:

> I believe, gentleman, that you know me well enough to know that I am not a bloodthirsty person; I am not a man who takes pleasure or joy when something rough must be done. However, on the other hand, I have such good nerves and such a developed sense of duty—I can say that much for myself—that when I recognize something as necessary I can implement it without compromise."

Hannah Arendt coined the term "banality of evil" to the describe the ability of the perpetrators to return to the routine of normal life after brutalizing and murdering their fellow human beings. This was a point I mentioned to my children. I told them that I never agreed with Arendt. People went along with Hitler because they had been marinating in anti-Semitism, and made the willful choice to cross over into evil. Yes, it seems inconceivable that any European leader would have said what George Washington did in his letter to the Touro Synagogue: that America would give "bigotry no sanction" and "persecution no assistance." I reject any notion of evil as "banal," even when routinized and carried out through bureaucratic structures. As Himmler himself tellingly averred, it is a conscious choice to eviscerate one's conscience, to suppress human emotion and empathy, and to embrace brutality.

Europe was rife with bigotry and persecution, and yet Europeans knew the difference between right and wrong. Looking at Eichmann, Arendt saw an ordinary man. Most of us, perpetrators and victims alike, are ordinary people. That's the meaning of the phrase. The perpetrators, unlike the victims, had a choice. We are all responsible for our choices.

Although many of the worst criminals escaped, took their own lives, or served short sentences, Peter Hayes reports, "European courts condemned and sentenced approximately 100,000 Germans and Austrians for criminality of one sort or another."

I was shocked to read this statistic, and not sure I believe it. If accurate, then at least some measure of justice was meted out to a far larger number of war criminals than I thought.

Today, most of the murderers are dead. But guards from Auschwitz, Buchenwald, Mauthausen, and Ravensbrück—all in their nineties—are still being prosecuted in Germany, for crimes they committed three-quarters of a century ago. They have escaped justice too long and may die before any court can try them. But still, their cases must go on. We have Simon Wiesenthal to thank for there being no statute of limitation in Germany for Holocaust crimes.

Many Nazis got away, whether through the Rat Lines to South America, or by explicit invitation by the Allied powers, who actively recruited former Nazis who could be used as spies against their enemies, and scientists who could aid their research efforts. Operation Paperclip brought approximately sixteen hundred Nazis to the United States, including prominent rocket scientists, such as Wernher von Braun, who is regarded as the father of both German and American rocket technology and space science.

The foremost leaders of the Third Reich escaped justice. Adolf Hitler, Heinrich Himmler, and Joseph Goebbels committed suicide. But twenty-two of the leaders of the Third Reich were tried at Nuremberg in 1945–1946, including Hitler deputy Hermann Göring, foreign minister Joachim von Ribbentrop, and Ernst Kaltenbrunner—Heydrich's successor—as head of the Gestapo. On October 1, 1946, the International Military Tribunal handed down its verdicts: eleven of the defendants were given the death penalty, three were acquitted, three were sentenced to life imprisonment, and four received sentences ranging from ten to twenty years. Göring was among those sentenced to death, but he committed suicide the night before his scheduled execution, probably with the assistance of an American soldier who secreted to him a dose of cyanide.

Aside from the Nuremberg trials, which were conducted by the occupying powers, many of the sentences were light. Many were even granted clemency. The West German government passed a law that all persons who did not qualify as major offenders would be allowed to return to the civil service. By the mid-1950s, the majority of the Nazi elite had been rehabilitated and were allowed to participate in the reconstruction of the country.

Gestapo official Wilhelm Harster, for example, was commander of the security police in the Netherlands. In 1949, he was convicted and sentenced to twelve years imprisonment for his role in the deportation and murder of Dutch Jews, but was released in 1953, and resumed his career in the administration of the Bavarian government before being forced into early retirement. In 1967, he was tried and sentenced to an additional fifteen years for the deportation of Jews to Auschwitz and Sobibor. He was given credit for time served, and pardoned in 1969.

I give the museum credit for taking this subject so seriously, because it's astonishing to see the degree to which the Nazis were rehabilitated, and how few were ever tried. At one point, Germany considered a law that would have made it impossible to try Nazi war criminals after 1965—an obscene attempt to let these murderers off the hook. Following protests, Germany ultimately decided there should be no time limit for prosecuting Germans accused of murder during the war.

We walked along the main path through Dachau, feeling surrounded by horror, even though most of the camp is now just an open area without structures. The road that connected the edge of the camp was only discovered in 2004. This was the route prisoners took when they were marched from the railway station to the camp.

I tried to describe for my children what it must have looked like: the people brought to Dachau in boxcars made for animals; crammed so tightly they could not lie down; given no food, water, or medication. They were dressed in whatever they had on when they were dragged from their homes, or ordered to report to the station in the heat of summer or cold of winter. I can't even imagine the smell of dead bodies or waste, overflowing the single bucket in each boxcar. These are horrors not captured when people talk abstractly about "the Holocaust" or the "six million" or try to depict them in a film. There is so much to contemplate. Where was God as this went on for years? Why didn't Hitler have one brain aneurysm, one stroke, one heart attack? It might not have changed everything, but his incapacitation would have saved countless lives.

The thing that's hardest to grasp is the inhumanity of man to his fellow man. Thinking about it all is emotionally excruciating and depressing.

It was nice, however, to see people of so many nationalities visiting Dachau to remember the victims. It is important for non-Jewish people to visit these sites.

Dachau was originally built to house political prisoners who opposed the Nazi regime—including Communists, Social Democrats and Christian clerics—and to scare the public into compliance. Later, Jews, Roma, Jehovah's Witnesses, gays, and others deemed enemies of the state, inferiors, or degenerates, were incarcerated. Prisoners were given striped uniforms, an identification number, and a color-coded triangle patch indicating their prisoner category (e.g., yellow for Jews, pink for homosexuals). Their heads were also shaved in order to dehumanize them, erase their identities, and reduce them from human beings to numbers.

The Jews were next. In April 1933, Hitler declared a national boycott of Jewish businesses, and non-Aryans were banned from a variety of professions. In 1935, the Nuremberg Laws were adopted, which deprived Jews of German citizenship, prohibited any non-Jewish German from marrying a Jew, and outlawed sexual relations between Jews and Germans. Jews had difficulty finding or holding jobs, were ostracized by their fellow Germans, and routinely harassed.

Many Jews left Germany, which, in retrospect, was the right move. But others, especially the more assimilated, felt they were part of the fabric of German society and would not be persecuted. They had a long history in the country, many had fought for it in the war, and they wanted to believe their fellow Germans would turn on Hitler and oust him from power. There was also the problem of having nowhere to go. Few countries, including the United States, wanted large numbers of Jewish immigrants. Even if they could find a country that would take them, they would have to be willing to leave virtually everything they owned behind as they were charged a tax of 90 percent of their wealth upon leaving the country.

The Nazi persecution did nothing but intensify, and many who did not emigrate came to wish that they had. Hitler ordered the destruction of the main synagogue in Munich, during the summer of 1938. This was followed by the pogrom on *Kristallnacht,* when two other synagogues were burned down, and ten thousand Jewish men were arrested and sent to Dachau. Most were freed within a few weeks or months in the hope that they would be encouraged to leave Germany. Many took the hint. Approximately forty-five hundred Jews who stayed were later deported, most to Theresienstadt.

Dachau prisoners were originally employed in the operation of the camp. They built roads, drained swamps, and worked in quarries. They were later forced to work in arms factories. More than thirty thousand prisoners from more than thirty subcamps of Dachau were used in slave labor. Following the Wannsee Conference and the adoption of the Final Solution, the deportation of Jews from Dachau to extermination camps in Poland began.

As at Auschwitz, German doctors performed gruesome medical experiments that did not comport with their Hippocratic Oath. Dr. Sigmund Rascher put prisoners in a decompression chamber to determine the maximum altitude from which crews of damaged aircraft could parachute to safety. Other prisoners were subjected to freezing temperatures so the Nazis could analyze hypothermia treatments. Professor Dr. Claus Schilling infected more than one thousand inmates with malaria to test medications. Prisoners were also poisoned, infected with tuberculosis, and cut for other experiments. They were forced to drink seawater to explore ways to make seawater potable. Many prisoners died, or were permanently crippled in these experiments.

As Allied forces closed in on Germany, the Germans forced more than seven thousand Dachau prisoners, mostly Jews, on a death march south from Dachau, to Tegernsee. Imagine being forced to walk for miles, after spending months or years in prison, with little food, wearing nothing but a tattered uniform and some form of inadequate footwear. Prodded along by Nazis, anyone who could not keep up would be shot. Many succumbed to starvation, cold, and exhaustion.

Three days later, the US Army arrived. General Dwight D. Eisenhower wrote: "Our forces liberated and mopped up the infamous concentration camp at Dachau. Approximately 32,000 prisoners were liberated; 300 SS camp guards were quickly neutralized."

There is a story about an American spitting in the face of the camp commandant when he came to surrender. Americans also liberated the survivors of the infamous death march.

There were some sixty thousand people still in the camp when the Americans arrived. Tragically, more than two thousand prisoners died after liberation because they were too far gone. The US Army brought Germans living around Dachau to witness the horror. They, of course, claimed to have had no idea what was going on.

During its years of operation, 1933–1945, more than 180,000 prisoners passed through Dachau. At least forty-three thousand died between January 1940 and May 1945. As in other camps, we will never know the true number of victims. More than one hundred members of the Dachau staff faced charges of war crimes related to atrocities committed in and around the camp. The main case tried at the end of 1945, involved forty-two Dachau officials, thirty-six of whom were sentenced to death, and the rest to various terms of imprisonment. Among those hanged in May 1946, were the commandant, Martin Weiss, and the camp doctor Karl Schilling.

Some prisoners and liberators took matters into their own hands rather than wait for any judicial proceedings. Prisoners turned on the guards after Dachau was liberated, reportedly beating several to death. The GIs were enraged by what they saw at Dachau, and witnesses claimed some of the SS soldiers were shot after they surrendered. Gen. George Patton ordered the charges dismissed.

There are two views of the justice of killing the perpetrators of the Holocaust. Given the number of SS members, and the larger number of war criminals, it was never reasonable to expect they would all be brought to trial. Indeed, one could argue that there might have been justice in shooting the SS, as it was a voluntary organization, with German soldiers choosing of their own volition to participate in the murderous group. Winston Churchill, in *The Hinge of Fate: The Second World War, Volume 4*, suggests that Stalin made this suggestion to him and Roosevelt at their meeting in Tehran in 1943.

Stalin was our host at dinner. The company was strictly limited – Stalin and Molotov, the President, Hopkins, Harriman, Clark Kerr, myself and Eden, and our interpreters. After the labours of the Conference, there was a good deal of gaiety, and many toasts were proposed.

Presently Elliott Roosevelt, who had flown out to join his father, appeared at the door, and somebody beckoned him to come in. He therefore took his seat at the table. He even intervened in the conversation, and has since given a highly coloured and extremely misleading account of what he heard.

Stalin, as Hopkins recounts, indulged in a great deal of "teasing" of me, which I did not at all resent until the Marshal entered in a genial manner upon a serious and even deadly aspect of the punishment to be inflicted upon the Germans.

The German General Staff, he said, must be liquidated. The whole force of Hitler's mighty armies depended upon about fifty thousand officers and technicians. If these were rounded up and shot at the end of the war, German military strength would be extirpated.

On this I thought it right to say: "The British Parliament and public will never tolerate mass executions. Even if in war passion they allowed them to begin, they would turn violently against those responsible after the first butchery had taken place. The Soviets must be under no delusion on this point."

Stalin however, perhaps only in mischief, pursued the subject. "Fifty thousand," he said, "must be shot." I was deeply angered. "I would rather," I said, "be taken out into the garden here and now and be shot myself than sully my own and my country's honour by such infamy."

At this point the President intervened. He had a compromise to propose. Not fifty thousand should be shot, but only forty-nine thousand. By this he hoped, no doubt, to reduce the whole matter to ridicule. Eden also made signs and gestures intended to reassure me that it was all a joke.

But now Elliott Roosevelt rose in his place at the end of the table and made a speech, saying how cordially he agreed with Marshal

Stalin's plan and how sure he was that the United States Army would support it.

At this intrusion I got up and left the table, walking off into the next room, which was in semi-darkness. I had not been there a minute before hands were clapped upon my shoulders from behind, and there was Stalin, with Molotov at his side, both grinning broadly, and eagerly declaring that they were only playing, and that nothing of a serious character had entered their heads.

Stalin has a very captivating manner when he chooses to use it, and I never saw him do so to such an extent as at this moment. Although I was not then, and am not now, fully convinced that all was chaff and there was no serious intent lurking behind, I consented to return, and the rest of the evening passed pleasantly."

I agree with Churchill that such an action would have been barbaric and contrary to all Jewish values which demands justice, not vengeance. But I would be lying if I did not admit to enjoying the Quentin Tarantino movie *Inglourious Basterds,* and the dramatic fantasy of vengeance exacted against the Nazis. Not all Nazi hunters were like Simon Wiesenthal, who brought them back for trial. Some Jewish British Army officers, and the Vilna Ghetto hero, Abba Kovner, did form groups that assassinated former Nazis. You can make a case that this would be warning to future murderers that they won't get away with it. Still, Jewish law and values would not allow it, insisting instead on the kind of noble justice that was carried out at Nuremberg through competent courts and jurists.

I discussed with my children these limited assassination efforts, and as you would imagine, surrounded by the horrors of what the Nazis has done to our people, they felt that there should have been more. More Nazis should have paid for their crimes. But I made the case to them that, as Wiesenthal often said, after the war, the Jews sought "justice, and not vengeance," making a powerful argument against extra-judicial killings, even of confirmed murderers.

This view is the one I wanted my children to embrace, however powerful their desire for vengeance after witnessing the killing fields of Europe. For the Germans, summary execution was a way of life and a way of war. But we Jews are not the Nazis. We pride ourselves on being fully human, with a deeply ingrained sense of justice. This was the view of the allied armies, and later, the State of Israel. That is why a trial was conducted for Adolph Eichmann when Israel could have simply assassinated him in Argentina. Today, Israel embraces a hybrid approach toward its enemies. It often brings terrorists for trial, but when that is not possible, the government sometimes orders that they be killed in order to stop them from murdering innocents.

In Munich, only 160 Jews survived the war. Following the war, roughly three thousand survivors returned to rebuild the community. Tens of thousands of Jews passed through the city on their way to Israel and other destinations. In the post-war years, anti-Semitic acts of desecration and vandalism still targeted the community's synagogue and cemetery. In 1970, the Jewish home for the aged was burned down; seven people died.

Between 1989 and 2004, the Jewish population more than doubled, primarily because of the influx of Jews from the former Soviet Union. In 2006, on the 68th anniversary of *Kristallnacht*, the Ohel Jakob Synagogue was dedicated. I have spoken there are as a scholar in residence on two occasions, and much enjoyed it. The rabbi of the community is a friend of mine. Today, Munich has six synagogues, a Jewish museum, and a community center with a kindergarten, an elementary school, a youth center, and a library.

In 2009, for the first time in seventy years, two Orthodox rabbis were ordained in Munich. It took decades, but the Jewish population finally is the size it was prior to the war, and Jewish life is once again thriving in Munich—albeit with Jews, for the most part, afraid to wear their *yarmulkes* in public.

We went to the Führer Building (Führerbau), where Hitler had his Munich offices. The Americans blew up a bunch of Nazi edifices, but they kept the Führer Building, which is now a music school. On my last visit, they let us go into Hitler's office, and there was a student practicing violin. I asked him what it was like playing violin in Hitler's office, where he signed the Munich Agreement with Chamberlain. The student honestly replied, "I don't feel anything."

I said, "Do you understand that for Jews it was very different?"

He replied, "I understand."

This time, we were not allowed into the school. I think it is outrageous that the Nazi headquarters is now a music school. It should be a museum telling the story of the Munich Agreement and Hitler's rise to power. It is also outrageous that visitors are not allowed in.

In the central square of Munich, the Marienplatz, there is a map and explanation of where the various Nazi buildings were. The Marienplatz, like most of Munich, was bombed to rubble, and after the war there was a debate over whether to rebuild the city as if it were brand new, or re-create its pre-war appearance. Frankfurt chose the modern approach, but Munich wanted the city to look like it did before the war.

One of the buildings that survived the war was Hitler's art gallery, which exhibited what the Nazis considered fine art, as opposed to degenerate art. The building was the first to be constructed in the distinctive grand style of Third Reich architecture that Hitler believed would impress visitors. In July 1939, a grand pageant celebrating two thousand years of German art was held here and attended by Hitler, Goebbels, Himmler, and Heydrich. After the war, the building served as a US officers' mess hall, before being turned over to the Bavarian government. Today, it is used for some temporary exhibitions, but is mostly empty.

In the heart of the old town, we visited a relatively new complex of Jewish buildings. One building, shaped like a cube, is now the main synagogue in Munich. The Chief Rabbi of Munich, who hosted me as a scholar-in-residence, took us inside the Ohel Jakob Synagogue to see the magnificent Torah scrolls that had been given to the Jewish community, and brought a sanctity to the revitalization of Jewish life. The synagogue is linked to the Jewish Community Center by a "corridor of remembrance" that commemorates the 4,587 Jewish citizens of Munich who were murdered by the Nazis. The complex also includes a great kosher restaurant. The large square in front of the synagogue and community center has displays about the community. It was nice to see Jewish life flourish in the city, and my children were soothed and impressed, especially with the outstanding kosher restaurant which specializes in excellent schnitzel.

One thing that I really wanted to see was the new Documentation Center. It is especially fitting that it was established in the Brown House, the building that had served as the first headquarters of the Nazi Party. I must give the city credit for creating this institution to expose the truth about Germany's wartime history so such evil never be tolerated again. The history of the Nazi Party is no longer the eight-hundred-pound gorilla nobody wants to talk about. The museum makes a powerful statement that

Munich will no longer hide its past, which has changed the environment to make Jews feel more comfortable visiting and living in the city.

At first, we were told the center was closed, and it looked like we would not get in. I showed the guards the museum website, which indicated they should be open on that particular Monday. They apologized, but repeated that they were closed.

I responded, "Your website says you're open. I traveled across Europe to get here. I came to Munich while the museum was under construction, and I've now returned with my family. All I ask is that you be fair and honor your word. It says in black and white that you're open today. I'm asking to go into this museum."

They called the chief curator, and I showed him the website, and he said, "If it says that it's open, it's open, and our staff will have to stay here while you visit."

So we were the only ones there. It was amazing. They did an incredible job of exposing Nazi atrocities, holding no evidence back. I find that the Germans do not whitewash anything in their museums, except their complicity in bringing Hitler to power, fighting for him, defending him, and that there were only two serious assassination attempts. They don't say any of that. They just act like the Nazis were an entirely separate group unrelated to the German people.

This was a point I made repeatedly to my children. Yes, the Germans take responsibility for the Holocaust, but only partially, insofar as they play a game of make-believe wherein the Nazis and the Germans were seemingly two different groups. When, in fact, Hitler was democratically elected, and never lost the support of the German people, until the very end.

Two years earlier, I had taken a tour of Munich with a courageous British guide who pulled no punches about German history. He took me to the first Nazi headquarters, which—believe it or not—is now an Apple store. The Bürgerbräukeller where the Putsch was made is no longer standing, but another Hofbräuhaus where Hitler delivered many of his speeches is a popular tourist attraction.

When we went, the place was packed with people enjoying the beer and the music. I'm not sure how many people enjoying the music and beer were aware of the historical role of the place in the establishment of the Nazi Party and Hitler's rise to prominence. We went upstairs to the festival hall, where on February 24, 1920, the Nazi Party platform was presented to a raucous crowd of two thousand people. There is no identifying marker, so you wouldn't know unless you knew. But this was where the fundamental principles of Nazi ideology were announced: "A member of the race can only be one who is of German blood, without consideration of creed. Consequently, no Jew can be a member of the race."

Downstairs, about one hundred middle-aged Germans danced to folk music and drank beer in giant Steins. It was utterly ordinary, on the site of such enormity. It was like the nondescript building in Braunau am Inn, where Hitler was born. Like the little nondescript villa on a lake, where the Wannsee Conference was held. Like a patch of forest that saw the horrors of Treblinka.

Interestingly, Munich rejected the installation of Stolpersteine plaques to honor Holocaust victims. Charlotte Knobloch, the leader of the Jewish community, argues that they insult their memory because people walk on them and get them dirty. Instead, the city began to place markers on buildings, with photos and biographical details of the Jews who once lived there.

We made one other stop in Munich, to visit the site of the 1972 Summer Olympics. This was the first time the Olympics had been held in Germany since the notorious Nazi Olympics held in Berlin in 1936, when Jesse Owens's remarkable performance had embarrassed Hitler and put the lie to his notion of the superiority of the white Aryan race. It had nevertheless been a great propaganda success for Hitler, who had temporarily suspended the Nazis' persecution of the Jews to put on a display of German hospitality and warmth before the world.

The 1972 Games were supposed to put the memory of Hitler's time behind Germany. Instead, it was reinforced when Palestinian terrorists infiltrated the Olympic Village and took Israeli athletes hostage, and murdered eleven of them. At one point, news reports suggested that the hostages had been saved. I'll never forget watching Jim McKay, the anchor for ABC's coverage of the Olympics, announce at 3:00 a.m., on September 6, that the new reports were wrong. Teary-eyed, he said, "They're all gone." I was just a boy growing up in Los Angeles when that happened. But I remember it clear as day.

Munich, especially to Dachau, was miserable—hot and muggy and depressing. As necessary as it was to bring my family here, my daughter Baba finally reached her limit in Munich.

"I hate Europe," she said. "Ghettos everywhere."

I fought with Baba and begged her to stay. But Baba, by now, had had enough, and she bailed on the trip. I was disappointed that she left. I wanted her to stay until we reached Italy, especially Venice, where the mood would have been lighter, and we could have visited more tourist destinations. We were close to the Chabad Rabbi of Venice and his family, and Baba loves them. We would have had such an uplifting Sabbath together, there as a family. But try as I might, I could not persuade her to stay.

I didn't fully understand the depth of her anger and despair until a year later, when she said she was still bitter about the trip, and devastated by its implications.

Shaina had also had enough, so she and Baba both went home. I pleaded with Shaina to stay, but she had made up her mind. The rest of us went to Italy, and I missed them every single day.

CHAPTER 26

VENICE: THE FIRST GHETTO

We drove four hours to make it for Shabbos in Venice on July 23. After three weeks traveling on a hectic, nearly nonstop trek through Germany and Eastern Europe, our family had looked forward to a more relaxing tour through Italy. As we drove through the Dolomites, I could not escape my sadness over Baba and Shaina's decision to leave just as we were going to this beautiful country to see our wonderful friends and enjoy the food at Italy's wonderful kosher restaurants, and visit nice places that were not monuments to mass murder and evil. Instead, Baba and Shaina's memories were going to be just of horrible places. I also still felt the residual tension from the fight with Baba, and was afraid that a gulf was opening between us.

Nevertheless, I was cheered by the opportunity to visit our friends Rabbi Ramy Banin and his wife, Shachar. Ramy is the Chabad emissary, and Venice is one of places where Chabad really shines. Ramy and Shachar pioneered the idea of holding large Shabbat dinners in Europe. Years and years ago, they began with the practice with three hundred to four hundred people on a Friday night. They didn't charge a fee, asking only for donations. Now, Chabad hosts Shabbat dinners in other cities in Europe, such as Budapest and Munich. Ramy is really a miracle worker. He has established flourishing Jewish life in Venice, and people come from all over the world and benefit from his hospitality. El Al had five flights a week from Tel Aviv because Ramy created this incredible hub for Jewish tourism.

It was nice to see so many Jews, people with *yarmulkes* all speaking Hebrew. There were so many Israelis in Venice you would think Israel was a country of five hundred million Jews instead of six million.

In my guest Shabbat sermon at Chabad, I spoke about the Torah reading that discusses all the places the Israelites moved. We were a nomadic people. We did not want to be, but we were expelled, persecuted, locked up, and ghettoized by different enemies over the centuries. I spoke of all the times during this summer that we went to places where terrible things happened to the Jewish people.

Ramy and Shachar provided a home away from home for my children, who worked here in the summers as camp counselors, to help the Jewish community of Venice. He had a transformative impact on my children and their connection to a deeper Hasidic life, a Chabad life, and a love of the Lubavitcher Rebbe, our teacher and our leader. I'm grateful to them on a personal level. Everyone should support JewishVenice.org. Having a visible and inspirational Jewish presence in one of Europe's oldest Jewish communities is vital.

Venice might be the most beautiful city in the world—it's called "the most serene"—but even in this magnificent city, and this happy country, we could not escape the evils of the Holocaust. One of the reasons for adding Italy to our tour was to take my children to the place where the seeds of anti-Semitism were planted.

Jews first settled in Venice in the 13th century, and were limited in what professions they could practice. They were also heavily taxed. Christian merchants did not like competition from Jews, and placed additional restrictions on their activities.

In 1386, a Jewish cemetery was opened at the Lido di Venezia. Then, foreshadowing the Nazi persecution, Jews were required to wear distinctive clothing—first, a yellow badge, in 1394. Then, a yellow hat, in 1496. And finally, a red hat, in 1500. Jews were prohibited from owning land or building a synagogue, and were sometimes forced to attend Christian services or become baptized. Blood libels resulted in Jews being murdered in 1480 and 1506.

Unlike other parts of Europe, Jews were not expelled from Italy. Consequently, many Jews forced out of Spain and Portugal immigrated to Venice. Some were Marranos who had hidden their religion to escape the Inquisition, devoted to rooting out Jews and heretics, and returned to Judaism after moving to Venice.

The Italians actually invented the ghetto. On March 29, 1516, the Venetian authorities under Doge Leonardo Loredan decided to confine the

Jews to a small island where foundries had once been. It was referred to as a ghetto, from the Italian *getto,* meaning *casting.* Or Venetian *geto,* meaning *foundry.* This is the origin of the word, which first described Venice's Ghetto Nuova, and later, ghettos that would be established by the Nazis, for Jews throughout Europe.

It was essentially a prison. Jews could leave the ghetto during the day, but were locked inside at night. They had to wear distinctive clothing, such as a yellow circle or scarf. Christians came to the ghetto to shop, see doctors, and do their banking. Economically, Jews suffered. But spiritually, their lives were rich. In the 1500s, several synagogues were built, along with a school.

The situation improved in the 17th century as Jewish commerce, medicine, and scholarship flourished. Hundreds of Jews died when the plague ravaged the ghetto in 1630–31, but the community recovered, and the ghetto's boundary was extended. By around 1650, four thousand people lived in an area roughly two-and-a-half city blocks. New restrictions imposed at the end of the century led many Jews to leave the city. Some prominent religious scholars left to start communities in other parts of Europe. Exorbitant taxes started to take their toll on Jewish businesses, and the Jewish community was forced to declare bankruptcy in 1737.

The ghetto was abolished after Napoleon invaded Venice in 1797, and the city subsequently became part of the Hapsburg Empire. Some Jews lived around the ghetto. But now, those who could afford to live elsewhere, moved to nicer locations in the city. For the Jews in Italy, Napoleon was the person who tore down the gates of the ghetto. The hinges were left in place for a memento. For Italians, however, he was a conqueror who looted the city and ended the thousand-year Venetian republic.

Outside of Italy, the Jewish relationship with Napoleon was more complicated. He abolished the ghetto, promoted *liberté, égalité, and fraternité,* and emancipated the Jews of France. Nevertheless, many rabbis—including the founder of Chabad, Shneur Zalman of Liadi—opposed Napoleon because they felt he was a secularizer, and feared that if there was no barrier to keep Jews rooted in their own communities and traditions, the Jewish people would assimilate and disappear. Paradoxically, these rabbis supported Tsar Alexander I against Napoleon in their war of 1812, largely because he would preserve the status quo of treating Jews as second-class citizens.

I have often contemplated Rabbi Shneur Zalman's view. He was correct about how emancipation led to greater assimilation. I see it in America, as many Jews seem on their way to assimilating into oblivion. On the other hand, the Jewish people have not disappeared in the time since Shneur Zalman sided with the Tsar. To be sure, millions have perished. But millions have survived. And his seventh-generation successor, Rabbi Menachem Mendel Schneerson—our Rebbe who died in 1994—certainly believed that Judaism can win arguments in the marketplace of ideas, and that Jewish identity can be affirmed, even in the most secular environment. I also have a difficult time with the idea of supporting a totalitarian autocrat like Tsar Alexander, who was responsible for the worst pogroms. Napoleon was hardly a saint, and he certainly traded in the social anti-Semitism of his time. But he never persecuted the Jews. Also, emancipation was critical because it allowed Jews to embrace the dignity of more or less equal citizenship.

Full emancipation for the Jews of Italy came with unification in 1861. One Venetian Jew, Luigi Luzzatti, was elected to the parliament, where he served for fifty years, and was elected Italy's first Jewish Prime Minister, in 1910. This was indicative of the relatively positive environment for Jews in Italy, which continued even after King Vittorio Emanuele appointed the fascist leader Benito Mussolini as prime minister, in 1922.

The fascist government only began to impose anti-Jewish laws in 1938, two years after forming an alliance with Hitler. The situation of Italian Jews did not become precarious until the Nazi occupation began in September 1943. After Mussolini was deposed after a string of military defeats, the Allies took Sicily and landed on the Italian mainland at Anzio. The Nazis snatched him back and reinstalled him as a figurehead behind their lines. They were still in control as far south as Rome, and began to hunt for Jews to deport to concentration camps. Professor Giuseppe Jona, the leader of the Jewish community in Venice, chose suicide over providing the Nazis with a list of Jews, like the Warsaw Ghetto's Adam Czerniaków.

His sacrifice did not save his community. About twelve hundred Jews were living in Venice when German troops occupied the city in 1943. In November, Jews were declared "enemy aliens" who were to be arrested and have their property seized. Most Jews were detained in early December 1943, but the Nazis continued to hunt them through the beginning of 1945. Between November 9, 1943, and August 17, 1944, 246 people were deported to extermination camps, including Chief Rabbi Adolfo Ottolenghi. Only eight of those Jews returned.

Today, Venice has a Jewish population of about five hundred people, about the same as at the end of the war. Although, only thirty of them live in the former ghetto. That is where the city's major Jewish institutions are located. The ghetto is intact, and is a major tourist destination, with a water-taxi stop identified in Italian and Hebrew. Venice has a Jewish bookstore, a Jewish publishing house, a social center, a rest home, a museum, a yeshiva, a kosher grocery, and a terrific kosher restaurant called Gam Gam, once the location of the gatehouse where the Jews had to check in before they left the ghetto.

The ghetto consists of an open square surrounded by six-story buildings on three sides, where the Nazis gathered Jews for deportation. There are two bronze monuments there—one depicting the Last Train. And the other, Nazi brutality against the Jews.

The Jews were not permitted to build synagogues as independent structures, so most were located on the top floors of buildings, meeting the traditional requirement that nothing separate the synagogue and the sky so as to get the congregations nearer to heaven. Each represented a different ethnic group of Jews. Three of the synagogues are controlled by the Jewish Museum, which houses Jewish ritual objects and tells the story of the community in Venice.

On the fifth floor of the building, on one side of the museum, is the oldest synagogue in the ghetto—the Tedesca (German Synagogue), built in 1528. This is also the location of the Museum of Hebrew Art. On the other side of the Jewish Museum is the Canton Synagogue, which was built in 1531. The Italian Synagogue, built in 1575, served the Italians, the poorest group in the ghetto. The Spanish Synagogue, constructed in 1550, and the Levantine Synagogue, which was built on the ground rather than on top of another building, are the only two synagogues from the original ghetto still used for services. Chabad opened a rabbinical yeshiva in 1998, which holds three prayer services every day. Today, Chabad are the Jews who are most visible because of the way they wear their distinctive religious garb—black hats, *yarmulkes*, and *tzitzit*. Locals maintain a low profile.

In 2016, Venice observed the anniversary of the establishment of the ghetto. As Professor Donatella Calabi told *The New York Times*, "The 500th anniversary is an occasion not to celebrate—you don't have a festival for a ghetto—but to commemorate. An unbroken stretch of 500 years of history will not happen again soon."

Every time I come here, they tell me the place is going to be underwater. It makes you wonder why they built a city like this. If you had found swampy land a thousand years ago would you have thought, *Hey, great place to build a city of brick and stone?* That it has lasted this long is remarkable.

Like everyone else, I find Venice romantic. That image endures because the city has the three characteristics of erotic attraction I describe in my book *Kosher Lust*—unavailability, mysteriousness, and sinfulness. Principles of erotic attraction apply to places as well as to people. Venice seems to have that alluring and semi-erotic quality, with its world-famous annual Venice carnival, with its masks and costumes.

The city is unavailable in the sense that it is difficult to get to. No cars are allowed. You must park outside the city and take boats through the canals, or walk to get around. That it is not an easy place to visit increases the attraction.

Venice is also mysterious. There are endless labyrinthine alleyways and tiny canals. A certain monotony can set in when cities become known too well. That is not a problem in Venice. If not for Google Maps, I would have constantly been lost. And on Shabbat, when we could not use our phones, we *were* constantly lost.

The third rule of attraction is sinfulness. Venetians were seagoing merchants and traders, glorified pirates, much given to masked balls and secret liaisons. The famous libertine Giacomo Casanova was a Venetian. It gives the city an air of mysterious sinfulness.

I was happy to be in Italy. It's the cradle of Catholicism, and you might think it's where you would have the most anti-Semitism. But instead, you have the least. I believe that the Italian people have an affinity with the Jewish people, which I cannot fully understand or explain. They are passionate, using their hands to gesticulate, and animating their points with deliberation. They are also intensely spiritual and religious, which is why the seat of the Roman Catholic Church is in Italy. They are, at their core, a Mediterranean people, which may be why ancient Rome had an affinity with the Jews of ancient Israel—as long as they agreed to be subjugated to brutal Roman rule.

CHAPTER 27

MILAN: THE FATE OF THE ITALIAN JEWS

O n to Milan, one of the world's fashion capitals. This was the part of the trip meant to balance out the horrible places we'd gone earlier. There had been no balance before we got to Italy, and the reason was that it did not sit right with me. I just couldn't see myself going to places such as Auschwitz or Łódź during the day, before attending a concert or an art exhibition at night. Even in Italy, if we went to the beach, as people normally do on vacation, I couldn't spend more than an hour or two because it felt strange and inappropriate.

Jews have been in Milan since as early as 388, when records indicate their synagogue was destroyed by an "act of God." It was rebuilt and attacked by a Christian mob in the sixth century. Little else is known until 1320, when Jews were expelled. It is not clear how long they were banned from the city, but we do know Jews were permitted to live there after receiving permission from Pope Nicholas V in 1452. Nicholas also approved the construction of a synagogue, but the Jews were required to wear a yellow badge.

Pope Pius II imposed a tax on the Jews to subsidize a crusade in 1459, and thirty years later, the Jews were expelled again. At some point, they were allowed to return, but were banished again in 1597. It was apparently not until 1714 that Jews were allowed to return to Milan, after the area fell under the dominion of the Austrian Empire. The community grew to roughly five hundred, and a new synagogue was built in 1840. In 1859, Jews were finally granted full rights when Milan became part of the new Italian kingdom. The Jewish community grew rapidly as Milan became an industrial and commercial center. Before World War II, about twelve thousand Jews lived in Milan.

More than a decade before Hitler came to power, Benito Mussolini founded the Fascist Party in Milan, in 1919. By 1928, he was the absolute ruler of Italy, with the title Duce. In 1939, Mussolini signed the Tripartite Pact aligning Italy with Germany and Japan, much to the dismay of the Western Allies.

The conventional narrative is that Mussolini did not share Hitler's anti-Semitism to the same demented degree, and ordinary Italians didn't all buy it either, and so the Jews fared better in Italy than they did elsewhere. This view of Mussolini must be re-examined in light of the publication of the diaries of his mistress Claretta Petacci, in 2009. According to Petacci, Mussolini bragged that his hatred for Jews preceded Adolf Hitler's. He referred to Jews as "disgusting," "enemies," and "reptiles," and vowed to "destroy them all."

Following Hitler's lead, Mussolini enacted racial laws in 1938, which led to the dismissal of Jews from their jobs, students' removal from schools, and a drumbeat of denunciations in the media. In *The Italian Executioners: The Genocide of the Jews in Italy*, Simon Levis Sullam wrote that Italian civilians played a key role in identifying and informing on Jews after years of anti-Jewish incitement by the fascists.

"The majority of Italian executioners were not necessarily ideologically motivated," Sullam says. "The genocide was widely carried out by bureaucratic means, through police measures and actions: actions that represented political imperatives for some, for others simply orders from superiors, and for yet others an opportunity for profit or vendetta."

Profit and vendetta seem to have been the main motive; the Italians were never as ideologically motivated as the Germans. This makes little difference to the person betrayed or killed, as with the Italian guides who offered to smuggle Jews across the border into Switzerland. They would charge as much as $40,000 for their services, and then "double their earnings by betraying their clients."

When Allied forces invaded Italy in July 1943, Hitler refused to give Mussolini the support he asked for, and after a series of defeats, the people and the party turned against Mussolini. He was arrested on July 25, 1943, and a provisional Italian government was set up under General Pietro Badoglio, who began secret discussions with the Allies about an armistice. On October 13, 1943, one month after Italy surrendered to the Allies, it declared war on Germany.

Hitler sent more German troops into Italy to hold off the Allies on his southern flank. German paratroopers, in a daring raid, snatched Mussolini before he could be turned over to the Allies and set him up in a new Fascist state in the north.

The Nazis, now in direct control of most of the peninsula, also began to round up Jews and deport them. Today, underneath Milan's busy Central Train Station, is the secret track discovered in 1995, that was used to transport Italian Jews to Auschwitz. Jews from northern Italy were loaded into boxcars in the early morning hours when no one would see them. Altogether, approximately eight hundred Jews from Milan were deported. A Holocaust memorial was later built on platform 21.

About five thousand Italian Jews survived the war. In 1955, the Center of Jewish Contemporary Documentation opened for the study of contemporary Italian Judaism, the Holocaust, and anti-Semitism. The center also published a memorial book with the individual stories of every deportee from 1943 to 1945.

After the 1967 Six-Day War, approximately three thousand Jews fled from Libya and Egypt—where it was no longer safe for them to live—to Italy. Other Jews came later from Lebanon and Iran. Today, Milan has about ten thousand Jews, the second most in Italy, after Rome. The community has a Hebrew school and several modern synagogues. In 2016, a celebration was held to commemorate 150 years of Jewish life in Milan.

One of the best parts of the city for us was the availability of kosher food. There are three kosher restaurants in Milan, but two of them were closed because it was August and everyone goes to the seaside. There was a dairy restaurant open, and we had pizza and pasta. It may not sound like much. But to us, who were starving from lack of kosher food, it was absolute heaven.

We also took the opportunity to see what is perhaps the second-most famous painting in the world, after the *Mona Lisa*—*The Last Supper*, which is also by Leonardo da Vinci, and covers a wall in the refectory of the Convent of Santa Maria delle Grazie. Because of the crowds, guards cycle small groups through at fifteen-minute intervals, so you don't get to spend a lot of time studying the mural. What you do see is a picture of a Passover Seder—with the matzoh serving as the wafers, and the four cups of wine the beverage—which captures the moment when Jesus says that one of his followers is going to betray him. Judas is painted in dark tones that suggest he is a demonic figure. He is also holding a bag of money, presumably the thirty pieces of silver he supposedly received for selling Jesus out to the Romans.

Leonardo's portrayal seems to simply reflect the stereotype of Jews at the time, much like Shakespeare's character of Shylock. In the painting, Jesus seems to be saying, *"One of you is going to betray me, and if you're wondering who it is, it's the person I'm about to give bread to—the guy sitting here holding the money, who looks like the devil."*

In my book *Kosher Jesus*, I argue that Judas Iscariot was most likely an invention. He was a convenient scapegoat because he had the most identifiable Jewish name. The Christians needed to ingratiate themselves with the Romans after Jesus died, and the Jews had launched a disastrous and failed rebellion in 66–70, and were now the most hated group in the empire. The early Christians actually suffered from guilt by association with the Jews, so clearly they are saying to the Romans: *"You think the Jews weren't loyal to you? Look what they did to our Lord!"*

The attitudes of people as smart as Leonardo and Shakespeare just go to show the deep-dyed anti-Semitism of European culture. Jews were seen as money grubbing Christ-killers who rejected Jesus and would sell out anyone for personal gain. More than two thousand years of Christian anti-Judaism morphed into modern European anti-Semitism, which has more recently encompassed a strain of ideological anti-Zionism.

Decades of history have influenced people's stereotypes. That is why it is so important for Jews to be visible. Wearing *yarmulkes* and *tzitzit* makes people see Jews as normal people who may dress differently because of their religion. The invisibility of the Jewish community of Europe becomes a problem because so many Jews were murdered in Europe that there are not that many left. If we cloak ourselves when we visit, and invite this invisibility, we cannot negate these false stereotypes. Still, this is no excuse for European anti-Semitism, and it is obviously for the European societies to cure themselves of the age-old virus of anti-Semitism, rather than put the onus on the victims.

We visited the Sforza Museum in Sforza Castle to see the last sculpture Michelangelo created. It's unfinished. You can see the beginning of the image emerging from the stone, almost as if the figure is wrestling itself free. It was a reminder of the Chasidic view of the two types of creation. One is the creation of something from nothing—the way God created the world. There is also creation of something from something, as when you take a piece of marble and carve a sculpture, or fashion silver to make a beautiful goblet.

In Chasidic thought, there is always an image present within the form, even before it is revealed. You are not creating anything new when you make something beautiful from an existing object. You are merely exposing what was always there. This image we see in the museum was always in the rock, and Michelangelo exposed it.

Back in the center of town, I ruminated about the morality of the Allied bombing of Milan. So many people were killed, and buildings destroyed, all across Europe. It is a shame, but Hitler started the war with a blitzkrieg on Warsaw and other Polish cities. The Allies bombed cities primarily for strategic reasons: Milan, for example, was bombed because it was the industrial and economic heart of Italy. In Germany itself, and in Japan, the point was to break the enemy's will to resist, as with the firebombing of Dresden, and the dropping of atomic bombs on Japan.

World War II was total war. Hitler was engaged in genocide, with ten thousand Jews being murdered every single day. The tyranny of the Nazis had to be stopped. It is much easier in hindsight to question the necessity of bombing cities.

One landmark that did survive the war is the Arch of Peace. Napoleon wanted to build a monument like the Arc de Triomphe in Paris, to celebrate his wars and conquests. But he was toppled before it was done. It was later completed, and the new title bestowed upon it to mock the deposed Bonaparte.

We had to get up at 6:00 a.m. to catch a flight the next morning, and I said to my wife at 1:00 a.m., that I had to go to Piazzale Loreto, where Mussolini was hanged on April 29, 1945. Yes, crazy as it sounds, I had to fit one last war-related visit into our itinerary.

As the Allies moved toward Northern Italy, Mussolini, dressed as a German soldier, and his mistress, Claretta Petacci, set out for Switzerland in the hope of escaping to Spain. They, along with a number of other fascists, were caught by Italian partisans and taken to the Town Hall in Palazzo Manzi, in Dongo, a town near Lake Como. Today, the palace is the End of War Museum.

Fearing that Mussolini and Petacci might be rescued by fascist supporters, the partisans transferred them in the middle of the night, to a nearby farm. They were picked up there on April 28, 1945, and taken to the village of Giulino di Mezzegra, and told to stand against the wall at the entrance of the Villa Belmonte. There they were shot. The wall still has bullet holes. A black cross with Mussolini's name and the date of his execution marks the site.

On one hand, this is the type of marker I expect in places where historical events occurred. But on the other, it makes me wonder if the people living there are fascists. I can understand having a plaque, but why put a cross with his name, as if it were a memorial? And why isn't there any information about his life and crimes?

The Italians brought Mussolini's body, and that of Petacci and other fascists who were executed, to Piazza Loreto in Milan, and dumped them on the ground. This was the same square where fifteen partisans had been shot a year earlier. A crowd gathered, and their bodies were brutalized. One woman reportedly fired five shots into Mussolini's body, and shouted, "Five shots for my five assassinated sons!"

Later, they were hung upside down on meat hooks, from the roof of a gas station, to protect them from further abuse by the mob. There are pictures of the grisly scene. The gas station is gone, but we managed to find the exact spot where Mussolini was hung. There should be some sort of marker or exhibit explaining the events, but there is not.

I did a Facebook Live at 2:00 a.m., with my very patient wife holding the camera, and observed that Mussolini's death was one of the few instances where there was a little bit of justice—not that I approve of the people abusing the bodies. After Hitler learned what happened to Mussolini, he swore that he would not let the same thing happen to him. Just two days after Il Duce's execution, Hitler killed himself before his enemies could find him, and ordered that his body, and that of his wife of forty hours, Eva Braun, be burned.

American troops arrived in Milan the same day and had the bodies transferred to the city morgue. There is a grotesque photo taken by a US Army photographer of the disfigured body of Mussolini beside that of Petacci. An autopsy showed that he died of bullet wounds. No big surprise there. But samples of Mussolini's brain were also sent to America to see if he might have been insane as a result of syphilis. Apparently, this was not proven.

The story gets even more bizarre. After his body was buried in an unmarked grave in the Musocco cemetery, his body was dug up by some die-hard Fascist supporters, on Easter Sunday, 1946, and moved from place to place, before being found several months later, hidden in a trunk in a monastery just outside Milan, and mysteriously missing a leg. The body was then hidden by the government at a Capuchin monastery in Cerro Maggiore, for eleven years. Finally, in 1957, a new Italian government agreed to reinter his body in his birthplace of Romagna, in a family crypt with a marble bust above his sarcophagus. The tomb is decorated with fascist symbols, and has become a pilgrimage site for neo-Fascists, which just goes to show the difficulty in disposing of dictators and their effects.

CHAPTER 28

FLORENCE: A GREAT SYNAGOGUE

We spent a week in Tuscany, with three wonderful days in Florence at the end of July. Florence is a living museum of art, culture, and history in which the Jews play an important part. Jews settled in Florence in the late 14th century, and quickly became prominent in banking and moneylending, protected in turn by the pope and the powerful Medici family, who could be fickle friends. Lorenzo the Magnificent was one of their protectors, but both the Jews and the Medici were expelled in 1494, when a Catholic theocracy took power under the fanatical Dominican friar Girolamo Savonarola.

When the Medici returned to power in 1512, Jews were allowed to return. But they were expelled again in 1527. Four years later, Alessandro de' Medici rescinded the ban. He was succeeded by Cosimo de' Medici, who allowed Jews fleeing persecution in Spain, Portugal, and the papal states to settle in Florence. Cosimo, however, sought the favor of the anti-Jewish pope Pius V, to win the title of Grand Duke of Tuscany. To please the pontiff, he imposed various restrictions on the Jewish community, forcing them to wear badges, banning foreign Jews from the city, shutting down the Jewish banks, and establishing a ghetto in 1571.

Some restrictions were placed on the commercial activities of the Jews inside the ghetto, but otherwise they were largely allowed to govern themselves and to establish schools, a *mikveh*, a butcher and bakery, as well as two synagogues. Jews had to pay the gatekeepers to open and close the gate they had to pass through in order to work outside the ghetto walls. Later, some wealthy Jews were allowed to live outside the ghetto. Despite the relative tolerance of the Medicis, the community shrank to fewer than one thousand by the 18th century. Nothing remains today of the Florence Ghetto.

As in Venice, the Jews were emancipated when Napoleon's army entered the city on March 25, 1799. However, their freedom would be brief. When the grand dukes returned to power in 1814, Jews were forced back into the ghetto. It was finally abolished in 1848, and Jews were given equal rights by Grand Duke Leopold II. Jews became citizens of the kingdom of Italy when Florence was incorporated in 1861. A spectacular Moorish-style synagogue, inspired by Constantinople's Byzantine church of Hagia Sophia, was built in 1882. Florence is one of the few cities, if not the only city in the world, where a synagogue is one of the dominant features of the skyline.

Approximately three thousand Jews lived in Florence in 1931. In September 1943, anticipating the Nazis' arrival, Elia Dalla Costa, the Archbishop of Florence, instructed Father Cipriano Ricotti to deliver a letter to the heads of monasteries and convents in and around Florence, asking them to shelter Jews. The archbishop even allowed Jews to stay in his home for a short time.

Mother Sandra Busnelli from the convent of Suore Francescane Missionarie Di Maria, at Piazza del Carmine, said, "We hoped they would be safer in the religious houses. The Superior General of our order gladly gave her permission and immediately fifty women were brought to the main hall."

The Nazis came when Mussolini fell, and the first deportation took place on November 6, 1943, followed by a second, five days later. On November 26th, Fascists raided convents where Jewish women and children were hiding under the protection of the nuns. The Jews hiding at the Carmelite convent were abused and imprisoned. Only one woman survived the raid. The others were deported on December 6th, and murdered in Auschwitz.

Two boys, who were the sons of a rabbi, stayed in the Istituto di Santa Marta in Settignano, just outside Florence. Mother Marta Folcia said a special blessing she taught herself in Hebrew, and when all the children had to kiss the cross, Folcia would cover it with her fingers so that the two Jewish boys would kiss her hand instead. In April 1944, German soldiers took over part of the school, but the nuns kept the boys' identities secret. They safely emerged from hiding after the arrival of Allied forces in June, which included someone from the Jewish Brigade, who one of the boys recognized by the Star of David on his sleeve.

Like the Poles, the Italians claimed, after the war, that the persecution of the Jews had been solely the work of the Nazis, when in fact, the Fascists had been active collaborators. The local Carabinieri were responsible for arresting Jews, while the Germans carried out the deportations.

The death toll would have been much higher without these religious people who risked their lives to live their faith: Father Cipriano Ricotti, Mother Marta Folcia, Mother Benedetta Vespignani, Mother Sandra Busnelli, and Archbishop of Florence Elia Dalla Costa are remembered by Yad Vashem as Righteous Among the Nations.

A total of 284 Jews were deported from Florence. Only thirteen returned. A haunting monument outside the synagogue lists their names. There is also a memorial sculpture and plaque at platform 16 of the Santa Maria Novella train station, where most of the deportations occurred.

After the war, Florence's Jewish population numbered sixteen hundred. The Germans had used the Great Synagogue as a garage for military vehicles, and then tried to blow it up in August 1944. Italian resistance fighters defused most of the explosives, but the damage was extensive. The Torah scrolls were saved and hidden from the Nazis in the hills of Tuscany. The museum opened next to the synagogue, in 2007. It contains ritual objects and artifacts, and documents the Jewish community's history from 1437 to the present.

Today, approximately one thousand Jews live in Florence. In addition to the spectacular Sephardic temple, there is an Ashkenazi shul. The community has a kindergarten, an elementary school, a high school, a home for the elderly, a youth club, a Jewish cultural center, a sports club, and a museum. The city also has two outstanding Chabad houses, with one providing excellent Friday night and Saturday Shabbat meals, where we ate and heard inspiring words from the Torah.

We visited the home of Michelangelo. What's interesting is that before he died, he burned many of his papers because he did not want people to know that the perfection he achieved in his sculptures and paintings was a product of laborious effort. He did not want anyone to see his mistakes, errors, or flaws. He believed in perfection, and wanted his process to appear effortless, as if it were divinely inspired.

One of the main differences between Christianity and Judaism is that Christianity believes in perfection. Jesus is perfect. Judaism, by sharp contrast, believes in struggle—the fact that people wrestle with doing the right thing against a predilection to do otherwise. The righteousness in Judaism is defined not as perfection, but as struggle. Israel, he who strives with God, this is our model of righteousness. The Hebrew Bible retells so many stories of the failings of prophets and kings. There isn't a single perfect personality in the Bible. Michelangelo, influenced by Catholic society with its emphasis on worshipping a perfect god-man, wanted to transcend—or to make everyone believe he had transcended—his humanity, in the expression of his art.

Sometimes their religion got the better of the Florentines, as when they drove out the practical art-loving Medici, in favor of the delusional art-hating preacher Savonarola. He persuaded the people to burn the material possessions he considered sinful, in "bonfires of the vanities." Even the great artist Botticelli was bamboozled into burning many of his canvases, and undoubtedly, many great books, works of art, and other irreplaceable items were lost to history in the flames.

Many books that escaped the fires were kept in the library in San Lorenzo, where many of the Medicis are buried. Michelangelo was commissioned by Pope Clement VII to build the library, which today houses priceless manuscripts. I was particularly interested in the book of Esther on display. It must have been several hundred years old. The Florentines had a culture that appreciated study for its own sake; the library with the pews nearly on top of each other reminded me of yeshivas where students are crammed together.

When I list Jewish values, one is enlightenment—study for study's sake, and not just for the utilitarian purpose of getting a job or knowing a craft. I believe that curiosity is the most important thing for relationships and for life, because it means that you always want to know more. As we Jews say: *learning for knowledge's sake.*

In the great art of Florence, the influence of Judaism and the Hebrew Bible is plain to see. Consider Michelangelo's famous sculpture of David—the most famous sculpture in the world is of a Jewish shepherd boy who would become a king. The sculpture was commissioned in 1501, and placed outside the seat of government, the Palazzo Vecchio. David was a hero who could defeat the giant Goliath, and was the Bible's greatest king. He became a symbol of this small republic's struggle for spiritual freedom and ultimate political independence.

My children greatly enjoyed and appreciated the beauty of these great artworks, even amid—with the exception of David—their Christian orientation. Yes, there was some discomfort with all the Christian iconography, especially since they were raised to reject the divinity and messiahship of Jesus. But after first feeling disoriented by the overwhelming Christian character of the artwork, they learned to separate its beauty from the religious statement it might have been seeking to make. In fact, they drew pride from knowing that so much of the artwork is either based on, or inspired by, the Hebrew Bible.

The bronze doors of the Florence Baptistery, by Ghiberti, depict scenes from the Hebrew Bible, not the New Testament. At the top left is Adam and Eve being created. On the right is Cain killing Abel. Other panels tell the story of Noah, Abraham's sacrifice of Isaac, and Moses receiving the Ten Commandments. The Torah had such incredible influence on civilization and art and Christianity. How ironic and tragic that the continent of Europe, which has been so deeply influenced by Judaism and Jewish ideas, has, in turn, shown such unreasonable antipathy and persecution to the Jews, who have resided there for two millennia, rather than seeking to respect and learn from the Jewish communities who reside in their midst.

We prayed at the Great Synagogue, which holds services in the Portuguese and Spanish traditions. It was built, thanks to the bequest of the president of the Jewish community, who left his estate for the construction of a grand shul he felt would match the grandeur of Florence. It was guarded by many Italian soldiers in full combat gear, because of the ongoing global threat of terrorism against Jews, and the memory of the 1982 terrorist attack on the Great Synagogue in Rome.

By coincidence, it was Tisha B'Av, the saddest day of the Jewish calendar, when the First Temple was destroyed by the Babylonians, and many other calamities in Jewish history occurred. It is traditional to read from the Book of Lamentations, which was written by Jeremiah the prophet as he witnessed the destruction of the temple and Jerusalem. Jeremiah, some believe, spoke prophetically about the Holocaust when he wrote of an emaciated people. Everyone in the synagogue stood in the dark with candles. It was one the most eerie and moving services I've ever attended.

We had a beautiful Shabbos dinner with Rabbi Eli Bornstein, who has been a Chabad emissary for forty-one years, in Bologna and Florence. Chabad organizes meals for the thousands of Jewish tourists who want to see the grand sites of Europe, and families like ours on trips to painful places of Jewish history. You can feel dislocated after some time in Europe. But when you come to a Chabad house in Venice or Budapest or Florence, you feel uplifted and inspired. It is important to see thriving synagogues and Shabbos meals, and people putting on tefillin and lighting Shabbat candles, and houses with mezuzahs on the doors.

I was proud to be part of Chabad's work when I was the emissary of the rebbe at Oxford, for eleven years. It is vital that we invest more in European Jewish communities, and for people to support Chabad in all its work to revive them. Some in Israel's political leadership have written off the importance of a diaspora community. This is a mistake. I agree that it is important to encourage people to move to Israel, and I'm proud of my daughter Chana and son Mendy, both of whom emigrated to Israel and served nobly in the Israel Defense Forces. But it is equally vital to build up and strengthen local diaspora communities so Judaism is visible and flourishes everywhere. It is also vital for Israel's safety to have strong diaspora communities that stand up for Israel around the world, influencing local populations and pressing governments to support the only democracy in the Middle East.

CHAPTER 29

ALL ROADS LEAD TO ROME

On August 6th, we finally reached Rome. The Eternal City set on seven hills by the Tiber, built on the ruins of antiquity. The heart of Christendom, where the seeds of anti-Semitism were planted, nurtured, and spread around the globe.

When the world was ruled from Rome, the Jews were despised for their rebelliousness, which was said to proceed from their strict adherence to their religion. Jews have lived in Rome since the second century BCE. The first Jews are believed to have been sent by Judah Maccabee, as emissaries and traders.

Ancient Judea was the scene of two of the most ferocious rebellions against Roman rule. The last one ended with the utter destruction of Jerusalem, and thousands of rebels were crucified, their families sold into slavery. Approximately fifteen hundred Jewish prisoners were brought to Rome, and some eventually gained their freedom and stayed in Italy.

Unlike the Greeks, who had a problem with Jews practicing Judaism, the Romans were mainly interested in Jews being submissive. Rome had no state religion; all the gods in the world were honored there. Religious persecution of Jews only began when Christianity came to dominate. In the second century, Bishop Melito of Sardis accused them of betraying and killing their Lord and Savior Jesus Christ. This is the central Christian complaint against the Jews, the accusation of deicide. Once the Emperor Constantine made Christianity the state religion of the Roman Empire, it was perhaps inevitable that centuries of massacres of Jews should culminate in the Holocaust.

Jews outside of Israel had long made voluntary contributions of a shekel to the temple, but the Emperor Vespasian, the successor to Titus who destroyed Jerusalem, forced the Jews under his domain to pay the money to the public treasury. This tax remained in effect for roughly two centuries. Besides the tax, Jews, unlike Christians, were not mistreated under the Romans, even after the Bar Kokhba revolt in 132–135, which led to most of the Jewish community being massacred or scattered outside the Holy Land. Small numbers of Jews moved to other parts of Italy, but most stayed close to Rome.

Things got bad for the Jews following Constantine's acceptance of Christianity, and the spread of the religion throughout the empire. Suddenly, there was a new power—the Church—which began to impose or encourage laws that limited the practice of Judaism, restricted Jews' political rights, and prohibited their involvement in certain economic activities. Christians also sought to cajole Jews to convert, while Constantine prohibited conversion to Judaism and intermarriage.

Theodosius II went further, prohibiting the construction of new synagogues, and barring Jews from certain professions. Justinian later gave them the status of inferior citizens. Strangely, not much is known about the treatment of Jews for the next five hundred years, but it can be assumed that given the lack of a central political authority, the Church called most of the shots. Pope Gregory I gave them protection in Rome and other parts of Italy. Pope Calixtus II issued a papal bull that guaranteed Jews certain protections. But the Fourth Lateran Council, convened by Pope Innocent III in 1215, required Jews to wear badges on their clothes. By this time, approximately two hundred Jewish families lived in Rome, which had Talmudic academies and many Jewish scholars.

The Church's prohibition on usury led Jews into the field of moneylending starting at the end of the 13th century. Many Jews in Italy became prosperous bankers. As Jews became more successful, many assimilated and adopted the lifestyle of the elites of the Renaissance. Others became scholars, poets, doctors, kabbalists, artists, and printers.

The popes continued to issue proclamations to protect the Jews, but they were often ignored by the Franciscans, and others who increasingly persecuted the Jews in the 15th century. The Jews in Rome who were under the Vatican's direct sovereignty were less subject to the vicissitudes of the rulers of other parts of Italy. Thus, for example, when Spain controlled Sicily and Sardinia and expelled the Jews, those in Rome were unaffected.

The situation changed dramatically in the 16th century, with the rise of Protestantism. In an effort to prevent the spread of this new threat, the Roman Church instituted the inquisition in 1542, and staffed it with fanatics dedicated to stamping out dissent. The Jews were caught up in this counter-reformation which saw Judaism as another threat to Christianity.

In 1553, Pope Julius III ordered all copies of the Talmud in Italy to be burned. Two years later, Paul IV required the Jews in the Papal States to live in ghettos, and limited their commercial activity to selling rags. Pius V subsequently expelled the Jews from all of the Papal States, except Rome and Ancona. For most of the remainder of the century, Rome was one of the few places under Church control where Jews were allowed to live. They were confined, however, to an overcrowded ghetto not far from the Vatican in 1555, by Pope Paul IV. Within the ghetto, which was locked at night, Jews managed to make life bearable, creating social, cultural, religious, and educational institutions.

In 1729, the San Gregorio della Divina Pietà Church opened in what is today Piazza Gerusalemme. Until 1870, the pope required the Jews living in the nearby ghetto to attend compulsory sermons every Shabbat from priests who would tell them how sinful they were, how they killed Jesus, and how angry God was at them. The Jews put wax in their ears so they did not have to listen. The priests' response was to add an inscription to the façade of the church during its restoration, in 1858. Taken from a passage in the Book of Isaiah (65:2–3), where the Lord complains about the obstinacy of the Jews, it reads in Hebrew and Latin: "All day long I have stretched out my hands to a disobedient and faithless nation." I have pointed out the inscription to my children many times upon our visits to Rome, since the church lies directly across from the Great Synagogue of Rome, where we go to pray.

Approximately seven thousand Jews lived in Rome by the 18th century, roughly a quarter of the Jewish population of Italy. In 1848, Pope Pius IX ordered that the gates and walls of the ghettos be demolished in Rome and in other towns of the Papal States. He would also later end the requirement that Jews attend sermons where they were encouraged to convert.

Jews did not begin to achieve equality under law until Rome was incorporated in the Kingdom of Italy, in 1870. This ushered in a period of Christian tolerance toward Jews that has continued, with a brief interruption during the Fascist-Nazi era, to the present day. It also marked the end of restrictions on Jewish participation in various occupations. Hence, Jews became prominent in virtually every sphere of activity, from politics to art, scholarship, economics.

When Mussolini and his Fascist Party came to power in 1922, Jews were not mistreated. It was not until Italy and Nazi Germany became allied in 1938, and anti-Semitic measures limiting their participation in society came into effect, that many Jews chose to leave Italy as persecution grew more severe. In 1931, 47,485 Jews lived in Italy. By 1939, the number had fallen to 35,156.

After entering the war, Italy established forty-three concentration camps. These were nothing like the camps set up by the Nazis—families stayed together, and there were schools, cultural activities, and social events. And the prisoners were primarily enemy aliens and non-Italian Jews. Only about two hundred Italian Jews were interned. When the Allies captured southern Italy in July 1943, Jews in that part of the country were liberated.

The Jews of Rome, numbering some twelve thousand, were not so lucky. The Nazis quickly took over the administration of the Jews, with the intention of deporting them to the death camps. On October 16, 1943, the Germans surrounded the Jewish quarter and arrested 1,023 Jews who were sent to Auschwitz, whence only sixteen returned. Another 993 Jews were deported later, but that was it. Most of the city's Jews managed to hide, or were protected by non-Jews until American forces liberated Rome on June 4, 1944.

The SS officer responsible for the roundup of Jews was Herbert Kappler. Before sending the Jews to their deaths, he extorted fifty kilograms of gold from them in return for their safety. Pope Pius XII offered to loan the gold to Kappler without interest or payback date, but the Jews organized the gold ransom on their own.

Kappler was arrested and tried in 1948, for the massacre of 355 Italian civilians, including seventy-five Jews, in the Ardeatine Caves just outside Rome, on March 24, 1944, and sentenced to life imprisonment. But he escaped prison, in his second wife's suitcase, in 1977. They fled to Germany, where the government refused to extradite him.

According to Yad Vashem, 7,680 Italian Jews, out of nearly nine thousand who were deported, perished in the Holocaust, most in Auschwitz-Birkenau. But it is estimated that more than 80 percent of Italian Jews survived the war. The Italian military, so ineffective in battle, helped rescue forty thousand non-Italian Jews.

The Vatican was considered a neutral state, and the Germans did not violate their neutrality, which allowed 477 Jews to hide there and survive the war. Another 4,238 were protected in monasteries and convents (one would assume, with the tacit consent of the pope). Pius also appealed to Latin American governments in countries with large Catholic populations, to issue emergency passports. But he was discouraged from helping Jews emigrate, by some of his representatives there. The Vatican was especially opposed to Jewish emigration to Palestine because the land was "holier for Catholics than for Jews."

Despite the pope's cowardice, many devout Catholics put their lives on the line to save Jews. Thousands of Jewish survivors later went to Italy as refugees, a large number of whom boarded ships bound for Palestine. Rome remained home to the largest number of Jews.

Pope Pius's defenders argue that he did a great deal behind the scenes to help the Jews, and could not have done more without making the situation worse and endangering members of the Church. Critics like me say he could not possibly have made the situation worse, because how do you make *anything* worse than the Holocaust? Wholesale, continent-wide genocide, running crematoria day and night throughout Europe to exterminate every Jewish man, woman, and child that can be found—how could the leader of the world's largest religion, devoted to the sanctity of human life as created in God's image, hold his tongue? If he suffered for trying to save the Jews—even if he had been killed for it—isn't that the very symbol of Christianity; a suffering servant put to death by an oppressive occupier, for the horrid sins of mankind?

Pius had a lot of moral authority, and he chose not to use it. History must condemn him as a coward and a weakling, perhaps even an anti-Semite. Piux XII's predecessor, Pius XI, was going to issue a papal bull condemning the anti-Semitism of the Nazis, but he died before it was released. Pius XII decided not to publish it. There is other evidence as to where he stood. He excommunicated Catholics who embraced communism, but not those who became Nazis. He only found his voice when he begged the Allies not to bomb Rome.

Further evidence is the secret audience he granted Supreme SS Polizeiführer Karl Wolff, who had served as Himmler's chief of staff, and was, in 1943, the chief of SS operations in occupied Italy. Pius obviously knew he was doing something scandalous, and attested that the meeting took place in great secrecy, with Wolff in disguise. Years later, Wolff said, "From the Pope's own words I could sense the sincerity of his sympathy and how much he loved the German people."

Pius's lowest moment came on October 16, 1943, the day he watched—literally—as the Germans rounded up more than one thousand Roman Jews for extermination, right underneath his window. Nearly all would perish by gas just a few days later, at Auschwitz. A special SS contingent had been brought in for the roundup, and once they got the Jews in trucks, they did a little sightseeing in St. Peter's Square, where many of the trucks parked three hundred feet from Pius's window so the SS men could see the Vatican. Pius watched in silence.

In early 2005 came the revelation that Pius had ordered the mass kidnapping of hundreds of thousands of Jewish children who had been given to the Catholic Church for safekeeping, by refusing to hand them back to their rightful Jewish guardians after the war. "Children who have been baptized must not be entrusted to institutions that would not be in a position to guarantee their Christian upbringing," said a church document discovered in a French church archive, and dated October 23, 1946. "It should be noted that this decision taken by the Holy Congregation of the Holy Office has been approved by the Holy Father."

Some people, notably John Cornwell, author of the international bestseller *Hitler's Pope*, believe Pius was a deep anti-Semite. Having studied much of the history, I concur with his conclusions.

In 2007, the Vatican's ambassador to Israel, Archbishop Antonio Franco, threatened that he would refuse to attend the official Holocaust Remembrance Day ceremony at Yad Vashem to protest the museum's depiction of Pope Pius XII as a passive bystander to the Nazi extermination of European Jewry. In truth, Yad Vashem's characterization of Pius as someone who simply refused to intervene is vastly understated and does not communicate the full horror of the pope's complicity with evil through the duration of the Holocaust.

Yad Vashem's exhibit on Pius reads: "When Jews were deported from Rome to Auschwitz, the pope did not intervene. The pope maintained his neutral position throughout the war, with the exception of appeals to the rulers of Hungary and Slovakia towards its end. His silence and the absence of guidelines obliged churchmen throughout Europe to decide on their own how to react."

Pius's moral cowardice in refusing to condemn the Holocaust is well-established, and it is a shame that the Catholic Church is more offended by its revelation than by its occurrence.

Indeed, the inability of Pius XII to speak out against the destruction of European Jewry constitutes perhaps the greatest moral failure on the part of a religious leader in the history of the world. Books like *The Battle for Rome* by Robert Katz convincingly demonstrate that Pius's failure was indicative of a callous indifference to the value of human life, in favor of papal authority and the preservation of church property. An autocrat who repeatedly told the Roman curia that their job was not to give him advice, but to follow his orders, said there is ample evidence for Pius as a collaborator with the Nazi government in their occupation of Rome.

When, in reprisal for a partisan attack against German troops, the Nazis executed 335 Roman citizens—many of them Jews, but the vast majority Catholic—Pius was implored to protest the execution. As usual, he refused to say anything that might upset the Nazis. It seems that neither the love of God nor his fellow man could move him to publicly condemn Hitler, with whom he had famously negotiated, as papal nuncio, the 1933 concordat, which the Führer praised as being "especially significant in the urgent struggle against international Jewry."

But while he did not prize the lives of Jews, there was one thing that Pius did esteem: the bricks and mortar of his churches. As the British and American Armies geared up in the spring of 1944, for a massive offensive to capture Rome, Pius suddenly found his voice. He condemned the Allies for bombing the ancient city, and ordered his American bishops to launch public relations offensives in the United States to pressure the Roosevelt government not to cause destruction to the sacred monuments of the Church. But while his attention was turned toward his precious buildings, the Nazis continued to gas more than ten thousand Jews each day.

For all his white robes, Pius was a dark soul whose record is a stain against the Church, whose leadership was an affront to a great religion, and whose papacy was an outrage to holiness and decency.

Pius's defenders, and even some of his critics, dispute this. His wartime role was complex, they argue, and much remains secret because of the Vatican's refusal to completely open its archives. The debate has grown more heated since the Vatican began consideration of recognizing Pius XII as a saint, and the Church's claim that Pius saved the lives of many Jews—

something that only the Vatican archives might be able to corroborate. According to Church doctrine, the first step in sainthood is beatification, which requires verification that Pius performed one miracle. If the Church determines that he performed two miracles, he could be canonized—that is, made a saint.

In 2014, Pope Francis said, "I looked into it and no miracle has been found yet....So the process has stalled." This sounds like Pope Francis, who may himself feel scandalized by Pius's indifference to the genocide of European Jewry, is morally averse to declaring Pius a saint, and understands how fully it would compromise the moral authority of the Church. It would behoove Pope Francis, who has spoken up so boldly for the world to recognize the Armenian genocide, to bury any thought of canonizing Pius once and for all.

Jewish life is now thriving in Rome, with kosher restaurants that are full of tourists. The Jews of Rome have enjoyed a peaceful life in the post-war period, with the exception of two terrible incidents that occurred at the height of Palestinian terrorism, against Jewish targets outside Israel. On October 9, 1982, Palestinian terrorists attacked the Great Synagogue of Rome, killing a two-year-old boy and wounding forty others. Then, on December 27, 1985, terrorists attacked the El Al counter at Rome's airport, killing sixteen and wounding ninety-nine. One other incident occurred outside Italy, but involved an Italian cruise ship, the *Achille Lauro*. It was hijacked in October 1985, and Leon Klinghoffer, an elderly wheelchair-bound American Jew, was shot and thrown overboard. The Italians take no chances now, and have heavy security around synagogues and other Jewish institutions. To pray in the Great Synagogue, one must present one's passport, undergo a thorough security check, and answer questions.

On the surface, the situation in Rome, and in Italy more generally, seems excellent for Jews, and nothing like the climate in most of Europe. Nevertheless, a 2015 study found that 63 percent of Italian Jews believe anti-Semitism to be either a "very big" or a "fairly big" problem, and 68 percent said they felt anti-Semitism was increasing.

If not for my positive experience, I would expect more anti-Semitism in Italy—where Catholic teachings about the Jews have been poisoning the water for two thousand years—than anywhere else. Of course, it was possible for Jews to escape the curse of their faith by converting. But it wasn't guaranteed. The Nazis did not care if a Jew was a convert. What mattered was their blood, and if they sniffed any Jewish blood coursing through your veins, you were a parasite to be exterminated.

When people see me in the Czech Republic and other places in Europe, with a *yarmulke* and *tzitzit*, they stare for a moment. There are few, if any, Jews left in many parts of Europe, so we are looked at like unicorns. Here in Italy, however, people see you and they don't care. They are warm. It is a different mentality.

Most people who tour Italy and the magnificent ruins have little or no idea about the Jewish history behind them. How many people, for example, are aware that something in the region of ten thousand Jewish captives from Judea were transported to Rome as slaves, and that many of them schlepped the stones from the Tivoli quarry that built the magnificent Coliseum? Or that gold plundered from the Temple in Jerusalem helped to finance the largest amphitheater of the ancient world? It could hold more than eighty thousand people, and was so large that they not only had gladiator fights, they staged mock naval battles.

The Romans loved blood—the spectacle of human beings killing and disemboweling each other, or trying to defend themselves against wild animals. Watching extreme gore and violence on a regular basis desensitizes the population. You become inured to human death when it becomes entertainment. Is it really surprising that a culture that cheered the gladiators would produce a man like Hadrian, who killed a million Jews after the Bar Kokhba revolt?

In the Jewish religion, we are not even allowed to look at blood. When you slaughter an animal, according to ritual prescription, you have to pour the blood into the earth and say a special blessing, because we are supposed to be sickened by the sight of blood and abhor spilling it.

The intersection between Jewish and Roman history is clearest in the Arch of Titus in Rome. It was erected around 82 CE, by the Emperor Domitian, shortly after the death of his older brother Titus, to commemorate Titus's defeat of the Jews and destruction of the Temple in Jerusalem. Josephus, the turncoat Jewish historian, describes Titus as trying to save the temple from the fires set by Roman centurions. There's no truth to that. We know Titus wanted to inflict this on the Jews. And there was no need to destroy the temple. It was built by a vassal Roman king—Herod—and it was one of the great structures of the ancient world. He did it out of vindictiveness.

The arch is infamous for Jews because it shows the Romans taking away the spoils of the temple—the menorah, the fire pans that were used to remove the ash from the altar, and the table of showbread. The Lubavitcher Rebbe maintained that the depiction of the menorah was inaccurate. He said Rashi and Maimonides agreed that the menorah was not curved the way we understand it today, as it is in the symbol of the State of Israel. It was straight, so the image may have been one of the other candelabras in the temple, used for illumination. The arch also shows Jewish slaves being brought to Rome, many of whom died en route. Jews have a custom of not walking under the arch, because it is a symbol of Jewish subjugation. Now, Italian authorities don't let anyone walk under it, in the name of preservation.

It was a scorching hot day when we went to the Forum, and that is probably why there were fewer tourists than I have ever seen there. For me, the emptiness also represented the disappearance of Roman civilization. This greatest of civilizations died. The Romans are gone, but we Jews are still here, just as we outlasted the Babylonians, Persians, Assyrians, Greeks, and the other ancient civilizations who sought our destruction. Yes, for fifteen hundred years, Rome was the greatest civilization in the world. But it was based on values that could not sustain it indefinitely. Rome had a veneer of civilization, but the empire was sustained by brute force. You cannot live just for money and subjugating others. When you live for the internal virtues of getting along with people and inspiring them, the influence lasts forever. The Jewish people never had the kind of empire or power the Romans did. But look at the global influence we have deployed throughout our history.

Constantine has an arch, too, commemorating his victory over his rival emperor, Maxentius, on the Milvian Bridge, on October 28, 312 CE. Maxentius drowned in the Tiber during the battle. And with typical Roman brutality, his body was retrieved, and his head paraded through the streets. He had been vouchsafed a vision of victory, and he began to move the empire toward acceptance of Christianity as a way of unifying it under one banner. It was Constantine who built the Church of the Holy Sepulchre on the site where Jesus was crucified and buried in Jerusalem. Curiously, the official symbol of Rome remained the sun god. Constantine had been a sun worshipper. That is one of the reasons Christians celebrate Sunday instead of Saturday as their holy day, even though it is clear in the Bible that Sunday is the day God did the most work, creating heaven and earth, while God rested on Saturday.

Jews could not win. When Rome was a pagan empire, its legions destroyed the temple. When it became a Christian empire, Jews were subject to horrific religious persecution. All of this culminates in the Holocaust because Europe became suffused with Jew-hatred. The genesis of this history can be traced back to Arch of Titus.

Despite the centuries of persecution, Jews have never abandoned their faith. They were prepared to be slaughtered by the Romans, to be burned at the stake in Spain, to be victims of pogroms in Poland, Russia, and Ukraine, and ultimately, to be nearly annihilated by Hitler. Jews endured all these horrors, rather than give up Judaism or their Jewish identity.

As mentioned at the beginning of the book, anti-Semitism is not purely a European phenomenon that grew out of Christian doctrine. There is also a good deal of anti-Semitic sentiment expressed in the Koran. And modern Islamic radicals draw inspiration and license from these verses for their violence against Jews and Israel.

While we were touring, the Senate Foreign Relations Committee passed the Taylor Force Act, which President Trump later signed into law. This was an important measure, named for Taylor Force, an American non-Jewish West Point graduate and Afghanistan veteran, murdered by a Palestinian terrorist while he was visiting Jaffa. The law called for the United States to cut off aid to the Palestinian Authority unless it ceases its "pay for slay" policy, whereby terrorists in Israeli jails, and the families of suicide bombers, are paid salaries that are significantly higher than the wages the average Palestinian can obtain doing honest work. Essentially, American taxpayers have been subsidizing incentives for Palestinians to commit acts of terror that have claimed the lives of many Americans and hundreds of Israelis.

I apologize for the digression, but this was an important piece of legislation that I was proud to support. In May 2018, our World Values Network gala in New York honored the parents of Taylor Force with The Elie Wiesel Award—our highest honor, its recipient chosen by Marion and Elisha Wiesel—for their courage and commitment to ensuring that no one else dies because American funds are diverted to pay Palestinian terrorists and incentivize violence.

CHAPTER 30

HITLER BEER: THE TRIP COMES TO AN END

On our way to Naples, we had the one confrontation with anti-Semitism of the entire trip, in a little town called Paestum, where there are some beautifully preserved Greek temples from the epoch of the Parthenon in Athens.

We walked into a store to buy some cold drinks and snacks, and we saw they were selling beer with labels featuring pictures of historical figures. One of them was Adolf Hitler, and he was giving the *Sieg Heil* salute. The bottles come with a variety of poses. There were also labels with pictures of Lenin, Tito, Stalin, and Mussolini.

I started to do a Facebook Live from the store about the labels, and I became aware that a guy was watching me. He, and the store owner and his daughter, began speaking to each other in Italian while staring at me. The owner walked over to us and said, "History."

Debbie looked at him and said, "Do you know this man murdered my family?"

Then he pointed to the back of the bottle, and the name of the manufacturer and said, "Turin, Turin. You should speak to the company. I'm just selling it."

Then his daughter came over and said she was protective of her father, and asked, "Why are you making trouble?"

I said, "Trouble? We're not making trouble. You're glorifying someone who murdered six million Jews. How can you sell this?"

She said (and I'll never forget this for the rest of my life), "You have your opinion of Hitler, and other people have other opinions."

So the father's defense was, "I'm not doing anything." He was basically saying, *I have no idea what you are talking about. I'm just selling the stuff.*

His daughter's defense was, "People have different opinions of Hitler. You have a negative opinion, and others have a more positive outlook. Why should you force your opinion on others?"

It turns out that Vini Lunardelli is a winery that began selling the bottles as a joke, in 1995. But they became so popular, the company expanded the line. The Simon Wiesenthal Center protested to the company when the historical series first came out, and again, after renewed complaints in 2013. At that time, Alessandro Lunardelli, who heads the company, said the labels were "not meant to offend anyone," and rationalized that the monsters of history are not "unlike today's monsters, multinationals without faces, recognizable tyrants."

The company website says the company's historical series has received worldwide attention "for the originality of the idea and for the quality of the wines," as opposed to their despicable subject matter. "Today," the company boasts, "approximately half of the bottles of wine produced by the company are dedicated to the Historical Series, which by now amounts to over 50 different labels, and has become a cult object among the collectors."

Partly due to the uproar over the dictator labels, the company added others, including Che Guevara, Karl Marx, Napoleon, and Winston Churchill. But the company also expanded the disgusting *Der Führer* line, which now has fifty-four different labels. Besides more than a dozen images of Hitler, labels feature Eva Braun, Rudolf Hess, Hermann Göring, and others, some of them including Nazi slogans such as *Deutschland über alles* (Germany above all things), and *Ein Volk, ein Reich, Ein Führer!* (One People, One Empire, One Leader!). They are, apparently, very popular with tourists from Germany and Austria, where Nazi imagery is forbidden. We were not the first to be offended. The police confiscated twenty thousand of the bottles from the *Der Führer* line, but an Italian court ruled in 2007, that the company could continue to sell them. The company has ignored complaints because of the demand for the products. "It's history, not propaganda," Andrea Lunardelli says, of his cash cow.

Italians take these symbols seriously, and it is hard to imagine they appreciate seeing wine bottles bearing the images of these monsters. How many Italians were murdered by Hitler, by the fascists, by Mussolini? You have to separate between the legitimate study of history, and the grotesque commercialization of genocidal monsters.

Every reader of this book should reach out to the company to express how inappropriate this disgusting beer and wine line is, and demand that it be immediately withdrawn. Our experience was stomach-turning. Whether or not the owner meant anything by it, what he was doing was vulgar, insensitive, and utterly deplorable.

I did not want an ugly confrontation with the owner or his daughter. To the contrary, I wanted to show how different we Jews are from the kind of hate they were promoting for profit. I told them forcefully, but respectfully, that selling the Hitler beer was an abomination and a moral outrage. Debbie was even more forceful and disgusted.

We left without buying anything, obviously, and with a determination to show our children that they should never stand down from respectfully, but determinedly, combating anti-Semitism.

***

We were coming to the end of our trip, and I began having disturbing dreams about places we had visited. I had a dream of walking through one of the death camps that we'd visited, and feeling haunted by the spirits of the people who were there.

I also thought about whether I should be allowed to feel joy after visiting those terrible places. According to the Talmud, after the destruction of the temple, the rabbis said, "Does anyone deserve to have weddings anymore? Does anyone deserve to have celebrations anymore?"

Other tourists can see the beauty of the places we visited, and enjoy it. But Jews who are immersed in history know that a cloud hangs over all these places. We may feel guilty after bearing witness to the horrors of the Holocaust, but I believe we still have to choose life.

My children also grappled with how to react to what they saw on the trip. Baba's overriding and painful sentiments were that "Israel is a country of living Jews, and you brought me to Europe, where we are seeing all this destruction. It's a giant Jewish cemetery. It makes me question God." She also shared my belief, however, that "Judaism has to be a religion of life," and that "we can't forget the people who made the sacrifices to make places like America free." Baba wanted to pay homage to the brave American and Allied soldiers who liberated Europe and stopped the Holocaust.

I think it is important to take children to places of historical significance, even on a vacation to a beautiful holiday destination. We all have a responsibility to help our children understand that these blessings are not free—that people sacrificed to make it possible for us to enjoy them.

The trip gave me a lot to think about. The best part was that I shared it with my wife and children, and we were able to talk these things through as we went from place to place.

The idea was to immerse ourselves in the dark, hallowed sites of the Holocaust so as to remember the six million, and better understand genocide, its psychology, its causes, and the way it is remembered today. And yet, for all the places we went, and everything we saw, I realize we still saw just the tip of the iceberg. And it overwhelmed us.

Having been to many of the sites before, I did not expect my views to change. But they did. Perhaps my most significant insight was the importance of sustaining Jewish life in Europe. We visited too many towns where Hitler had succeeded in eradicating Jewish life, and where a small remnant that survived is tenuously clinging to its roots.

It is a cliché to say it is impossible to comprehend the magnitude of the Holocaust. One reason is the inability to fully appreciate not only its impact on the future of the Jewish people, but the irreparable harm it did to humanity. I thought about this after our trip, when the Nobel Prizes were announced. Jews have won a disproportionate number of the prizes—about 25 percent—while being not even 1 percent of the world's population. How many of the more than 1.5 million Jewish children murdered by the Nazis would have grown up to win Nobel Prizes? How many would have become great musicians, writers, and artists who might have changed our understanding of the world? How many could have cured diseases and ended hunger? Albert Einstein escaped the Nazis, but how many geniuses did not?

And what of the children who were never born to women who were killed? Some might have changed the world. Others might be nothing more than loving human beings who had their own families, made an honest living, and lived lives of loving kindness. But that, of course, would have been enough.

***

It is now three years later. I am sitting at the kitchen table with my children, all of whom are pursuing their respective interests. Shaina is married to Moshe, a fine young rabbi and scholar from New York who works with Jewish teenagers, deepening their knowledge and inspiring their identity. Baba is engaged to Itamar, a fine young rabbi and scholar from Israel who works for the Jewish community in Fort Lauderdale, Florida, including running a Rabbinical College. Yosef is about to move to Israel, where he plans to join the IDF. Dovid is in high school and has become an outstanding rock guitarist. Cheftziba has just been bat mitzvah-ed, in the midst of the coronavirus pandemic.

At my suggestion, we began to discuss our trip to the Holocaust sites of Europe. It was, to say the least, a stressful journey—partly due to the pace we set, and partly to the amount of horror that greeted us every day. We were going nonstop from one awful place to another, with little sleep and—because we're kosher—little access to regular meals.

Each of the kids recounts to me their memories.

Dovid, who was eleven, had a difficult time. He had to let loose in the fountain in Lublin just to cast off the feeling of deadness, and feel alive. Still, he says now, at the table: "I think every person in the world, anyone old enough to remember what they see, should go on a trip like this. When you're a kid, it will grow with you, knowing all that stuff. It's like learning a language; you're better learning a language when you're under fourteen or something like that. I just feel that now I understand it. Before, I was thinking the Holocaust was horrible. But I never really appreciated how crazy it was until I went to a shtetl, where everyone was shot, or where people were forced to dig their own graves, knowing they were about to be shot, and a whole community was wiped out in minutes."

Yosef, sixteen, said, "I knew I had to see the camps because it's important to see what happened. It doesn't mean we should do the same thing again." When I asked him if he enjoyed the trip, he replied, "It was eye-opening, but I didn't enjoy it."

I also asked him how he felt about his Judaism, *Yiddishkeit*, and God when he was on the trip. He said, "I felt stronger because I was never going to let any nation kill my people again. That's why I want to join the Israeli military. It says in the Talmud, that if someone is coming to kill you, you should stand up and kill them first." True to his word, Yosef has chosen to join a pre-IDF military academy which will give him the training, once he joins the Israel Defense Forces, to get into an elite combat unit where we pray Almighty God will always keep him safe.

Shaina probably had the most positive reaction. She was also the oldest of the children who were with us. Afterward, she said, "It was depressing as hell." Still, she told me, "It was inspirational because I was connecting with my murdered people, and that I was a Jew and part of an eternal people. In good times and bad times, these are my people, and I was there, and they knew that I was there. How can you not be inspired by the story of Janusz Korczak, even though it's so tragic?"

She even found the monuments in Treblinka inspiring. "It uplifts you to know that people have held on to their faith and identity so strongly that they would die for it," she said. "We don't want that to happen in the future. We want other sources of inspiration. But that doesn't change how moved I was to be in a place where my people laid down their lives simply for being Jewish."

Baba had the toughest time. "I loved being with my little siblings," she said, later. "But I was lashing out at everyone. I wasn't very nice. When I was happy, it was short-lived happiness. I remember my little sister, Cheftziba, writing in her diary: 'Today we went to Auschwitz. Yesterday, we went to Mauthausen.' I was like, this is such BS. I was so mad. I still can't wrap my head around what happened. I never will, 'til the *Moshiach* (Messiah) comes. I remember, there were a few points on the trip—I'm not joking—where I really thought I had lost my mind forever. I had just seen too much."

After Shaina talked about being inspired, Baba said, "I think the only inspiring thing is the Jews who are still there and wouldn't let Judaism die. But I would not say anything from the Holocaust was inspiring. Still, going to those places was something you need to do as a Jew."

A year after the trip, Baba put down her feelings in writing. She said the experience had been "psychological torture," and wrote about how difficult it was to have questions without answers, that led her to question her faith:

The hurt in thinking I've been lied to, living a ferociously dedicated life as a God-fearing Jewish woman, when all roads in Auschwitz lead to no God at all. The guilt after feeling that way. The running to a corner and crying, "Maybe I've lost it." The opening of a siddur, desperate to feel heard. The immediate thought that perhaps for once I can accept that I am speaking to no one at all. Betrayed by God if He exists. Betrayed by my parents, friends, family, and school if He doesn't. Lashing out at the people around me as the concentration camps afflicted my very soul. Walking through a quaint, beautiful town, thinking, *Finally, a break.* Learning quickly that there are no breaks in Poland, that two thousand Jews were rounded up in the synagogue ahead of me, and burned alive as the whole city listened to their bloodcurdling screeches.

She also related a story I had not heard before, that she said soothed her "burning wounds." She said that she had seen a man with long white braided hair and wide blue eyes, wearing a *yarmulke*, speaking to people in the Galicia Jewish Museum. She saw a number tattooed on his arm, and said, "How can you believe in God—at least, a God that is good—after Auschwitz?"

"I don't believe in the God that most people believe in," he replied. "I believe that God is much more accepting and kinder than most do. I don't think he's waiting to mete out punishment all day. He is a kinder, more loving God than we know."

Those words, she wrote, "to the extent they could, healed my subterranean brokenness."

Her faith was revived when she went back to Israel. She expressed it in the conclusion of her essay when she talked about the coming of the Moshiach. "I know for certain," she wrote, "that the day will come when 'Death will be swallowed up forever, and God will wipe the tears off every face.' When this will all be but a faint nightmare, and 'the whole world will know that there is a God in Israel.'"

Thankfully, Baba did not lose her deep relationship God. When we got home, she said, "You can't get away from having a relationship with God. You really can't. Every human being wants purpose, wants meaning, and the only thing in this world that gives true meaning is God." But there can be no question that it was jolted and shaken to its core, and it would take many months to repair. She would later publish a moving and renowned essay on how the trip affected her faith, and how she came through it. I have quoted from the essay, in part, here.

I asked Debbie what she thought of taking the family on this kind of trip. "Looking back," she said, "I think it was the right thing to do. I don't think the little kids were harmed in any way. Dovid's very curious. He's always asking questions. Cheftziba's personality is, she's very easygoing, and she's a naturally happy person. Some things upset her, but we didn't let her go into certain places, like the gas chambers and crematoria. I didn't go in the crematoria, either. Overall, I think it was educational and important."

The conversations we had during and after the trip reinforced for me how important it was to take the children on this pilgrimage. We are not going to arrive at any solid conclusions. But for children to think of moral issues at such an early age is critical for their development as ethical human beings who are sensitive to human life.

I've often debated with my kids about who plays the more important role in the Jewish community today—Israeli soldiers? Or rabbis, educators, and social workers. For Yosef, it was no contest: "If there was a town with a really inspirational rabbi, but there were terrorists around it, they would all be killed. But a soldier would protect them. Nowadays, we wouldn't survive without a military, without the IDF. We had people studying during the Holocaust, and it did nothing."

I have to agree with Yosef that soldiers in Israel have to come first, because without an army, our enemies would kill us. But without Judaism, we are a people without an identity. So both are essential and we should not choose between them, insisting on the robust harmony and co-existence of both groups.

It is up to every parent to decide whether their children can handle the experiences we had. But I believe this was easily the most important trip of my entire life.

In May 2019, I visited Birkenau for the 75th anniversary of the deportation of Elie Wiesel to Auschwitz. I accompanied his son, Elisha, for the special commemoration. Each of us brought our thirteen-year-old sons, Elijah and Dovid Chaim, for what was an unforgettable occasion.

This book has grappled with the difficult question of the extent to which children should be exposed to the Holocaust. I have visited Auschwitz many times over the past few years alone, and was present for the 75th anniversary of the liberation of the death camp in January 2020, just one month before the coronavirus lockdowns. Still, it scars and numbs me every time.

The six million victims of the Holocaust were our brothers and sisters, our children and parents, our wives and our mothers. They cry out from the grave to be remembered. We will never forget them, regardless of how empty or barren it makes us feel, and regardless of how it affects our relationship with God.

At Sighet, Elisha Wiesel gave a masterful speech—an instant classic—about the simple triumph he seeks as the son of a survivor, to lead a normal life, raise healthy children, preserve a loving marriage, incorporate Jewish tradition into daily living, and honor the murdered victims of his family. After he spoke, a young woman whose grandparents had likewise been deported from Sighet to Auschwitz, spoke of the PTSD she had suffered as a third-generation Holocaust survivor. She spoke of how a therapist had helped her identify the trauma of being the grandchildren of survivors, and how she has learned to cope.

As anti-Semitism now begins to spread throughout the world, we in the Jewish community should be aware of our own trauma of seeing it all reappear. That we must fight it is clear. But how we explain to our children is not as evident.

Should we tell our children to take off their *yarmulkes* when they visit Germany—as a German government official shockingly suggested in May 2019—in order to forestall attack? In Krakow, just after visiting Auschwitz, we came to an outdoor market where paintings were sold. Krakow is a city where Pope John Paul II is literally a saint, so it wasn't surprising to see paintings that captured the pontiff's piety in prayer. But what was shocking was seeing the paintings right next to him, of rabbis surrounded by money, holding gold coins—even holding bitcoins!—rather than praying or studying. It was a disgusting display of anti-Semitism so vulgar that had I not posted the pictures on my Facebook page, no one would have believed it. But even as I protested this overt display of anti-Jewish prejudice, I was careful to show my son Dovid Chaim—who had just had his bar mitzvah in Israel—that he dare never shirk in public from being a proud Jew. I tried to show him the same as we walked the streets of Nice and Marseilles two summers back, even as the local Jewish community told us how dangerous it was to wear *yarmulkes*.

We should not put our children in danger. But should we not also factor in the psychological harm of being too self-conscious, rather than acting naturally as Jews? Is fearing anti-Semitism not its own form of PTSD?

I believe we have to confront the slow creep of anti-Semitism just as soon as it starts making tracks—but without making our children feel like victims. Rather, empowered as modern Jews to serve as lights unto the nations.

CONCLUSION

FOUR QUESTIONS ABOUT THE HOLOCAUST

This book has taken the reader on a journey with my family, to the most horrible places on earth. The trip was, at times, enjoyable, even uplifting. But so much of it was dispiriting and soul-destroying. To be sure, it was an essential trip, and I have no regrets in taking it. You might even decide—having read of our experiences—to take your family on a similar excursion. I promise you, the price, while steep, is worth it.

But it does leave profound and painful questions. Questions which, to use the Talmudic expression, exist at "rumo shel Olam," the top of the world, the summit of existence. And as there are four essential questions on Passover, there are equally four essential questions about the Holocaust. They are questions that kept recurring to my mind throughout our journey. In this chapter, I attempt to answer them.

1. Where was God during the Holocaust?

If even the stones of the Warsaw Ghetto cried out at the murder of the children, and there was no response from God, it follows that God was either, a.) dead, b.) no longer imposing His will in human affairs the way He did in the Torah, or c.) angry at the Jews, and only mollified by the slaughter of six million of them and the destruction of their culture as part of European society—but no one can figure out why.

This is the biggest question surrounding the greatest genocide in the history of the world.

The Torah has sustained the Jewish people for two thousand years. That's why we are still here. Then in one cataclysmic event, it was almost proven that it didn't matter.

Traditional Jews had three responses to the Holocaust:

1. Abandon God, in the belief that God abandoned man.

2. Submit to the idea that God is always right, and we are always wrong. We brought the destruction on ourselves through—pick your poison—a lack of sufficient piety, a substitution of secularism for faith, a pursuit of the Zionist dream of a Jewish State before the arrival of the Messiah, or a desire to assimilate among the Germans and cease being Jewish.

3. Engage God, even if it involves expressing righteous indignation. Continue a relationship with God, but one that had substantially changed. Whereas, before He was God, and we were His obedient servants, there was now greater equality in the relationship. We were no longer obedient. Rather, we were furious. We believed in You. We continue to believe in You. So how could You? How could You just watch? We're not going to simply let You off the hook by pretending You don't exist. No, You do exist. You are all-powerful. And we are a righteous nation, not to mention the 1.5 million blameless children who were massacred. So where were You? You told us the righteous would prosper, and yet they were not protected from the Nazis. Is it any wonder people question Your existence and essential goodness if You do not seemingly live by Your own moral code? We're angered and shocked at Your seeming dereliction of responsibility as Creator and Ruler of the universe.

Of all the possible responses, only the last makes any sense to me, and I have dedicated two books to fleshing it out. The first, written while I was rabbi at Oxford University, is called *Wrestling with the Divine*. The second, penned just a few years ago, is *The Fed-Up Man of Faith*. Both titles capture the essence of religious righteous indignation in the face of the Holocaust.

The very name *Israel* means *He who wrestles with God*. Whereas, Islam means to submit, and Christianity, in the words of Kierkegaard, demands "a leap of faith," Judaism teaches us to challenge and wrestle with the Creator. After the Holocaust, we remain a people of deep, uncompromising faith. But we are fed up. Fed up with a God whom we love, and to whom we have been particularly devoted, while He has allowed terrible atrocities to befall His people.

We reject the theodicy of the simple-minded and the religiously arrogant who would somehow find divine casual meaning in the catastrophe. There is no conceivable place in the universe where the murder of six million innocent people would make sense. There is no God worthy of the name, who could ever wish for such immoral destruction. And there is no sin that could ever be committed that would warrant death by gassing of millions of people.

For my son Yosef, even this theological response was inadequate. The only thing that makes sense is the creation of a Jewish Army. "We need Jews who know how to defend themselves," he told me after the trip. "A Torah? If you bring a Torah to a gun fight, you're probably not going to survive. It's not going to help."

I responded by telling him he's right. We cannot rely on faith alone when there are Hitlers in the world. But it is our faith in life, and its infinite value, that gives us the inspiration to fight evil in the first instance. Likewise, it is my Judaism that prevents me from letting God off the hook for the Holocaust. My faith commands me to put God's children before God Himself, as every parent would want. The Holocaust gives us a reason to show righteous indignation toward God, but not to abandon Him.

Baba had a crisis of faith in the killing fields of Europe. Ultimately, she came to terms with God, and said she recognized that the Holocaust was not some form of punishment. Rather, she felt that those who continued to believe in God after the Holocaust were forced to alter their theology. "They had to decide God isn't so powerful, and that morality is in their own hands." But after first feeling theologically defeated by the Holocaust, Baba would later embrace the ferocious response of intensifying a defiant faith that would see Judaism flourish against all odds.

I was proud that Baba went to Sydney, Australia, as a Chabad emissary to teach Judaism to women. She has since achieved a certain social media celebrity as the creator of *The Thirsty Souls* series, where she inspires people with life-affirming spirituality, making sure people know God is with us, and teaching Torah to the masses.

For we orthodox Jews whose theology insists on God's omnipotence, a diminished god who was powerless in the face of the Holocaust was not in the cards. The smaller deity offered to us by thinkers, like my friend Rabbi

Harold Kushner, in his famous bestseller, *When Bad Things Happen to Good People*, where he says that God is powerless to stop evil, and submits to the immutable laws of nature, is as heretical as it is uncomforting. For what is a God who stands powerless in the face of evil, other than pathetic and unworthy of worship? No, God is omnipotent. God is good. And God, therefore, should never have allowed the Holocaust to occur. The same God who destroyed the legions of Pharaoh should have annihilated the Gestapo and the SS before they could annihilate the Jews.

God's omnipotence obligates Him. If you're all-powerful, then you have to protect the weak and the vulnerable. God had the same obligation during the Holocaust. We have a right to demand that He uphold the same moral standards that He imposes on His world. But we must also ask why humanity permitted it to happen.

In this book, I have provided examples of places where the Nazis carried out their atrocities in secret, but the people in surrounding areas undoubtedly knew what was happening. I did not talk about the killing fields in parts of Eastern Europe we didn't visit, where almost two million Jews were murdered in the open, by the *Einsatzgruppen*—the Nazis' mobile killing squads. Father Patrick Desbois published a book, *In Broad Daylight: The Secret Procedures Behind the Holocaust by Bullets,* that documents how thousands of non-Jews sometimes came to watch the slaughter in a carnival-like atmosphere. Children would watch as Jews were lined up and shot, with boys sometimes bringing the killers bullets. What Germany did in the Holocaust beggars the imagination. No human mind can possibly make sense of it, and sometimes I wonder whether even the mind of God can make sense of it.

I was reminded of Elie Wiesel's semi-autobiographical book, *The Town Beyond The Wall.* I was inspired by one of the book's characters, a Torah prodigy who challenges God. The protagonist, Varady, is a great scholar who, as the Talmud would describe it, "enters the orchard," studying esoteric mystical texts that reveal great mysteries. He cannot fully handle what he has studied, and his mind is unhinged by the revelations. He becomes a heretic, insisting that man is more powerful than God, and that man could bring God to heel. This, he believed, was the secret to the universe: for man to discover his infinite power and unlimited potential. His neighbors were scandalized, and he was ostracized. But through this incredible character, Elie reinforced the idea that humans have an obligation to always challenge God.

2. After the Holocaust, has redemption come in the form of the State of Israel? Is the Jewish State the redemption of God's promise?

Why didn't God intervene and stop the Holocaust? I suppose that those who wish to defend God could argue that He intervened at the last moment to prevent the total annihilation of the Jewish people. The creation of the state of Israel was miraculous as well. Israel provided a haven for the remnant who survived, and reinforced their hope that God would never let the Jews be destroyed.

There are, of course, schools of Orthodox thought, such as the followers of the Satmar rebbe, who believed a Jewish State would not be created until the arrival of the Messiah. But that is a defeatist attitude that the Holocaust utterly refutes. The Torah is clear that "God blesses you in all that you do." To defend ourselves after the slaughter of six million innocents, we have to create an army for our protection, which God can then oversee.

I believe that the establishment of the State of Israel is the beginning of a redemptive process. Had Israel come into existence just ten years earlier, there would not have been a Holocaust. There would have been a homeland that took in Europe's Jews when no one else wanted them. There would have been a Jewish Army to fight the Jewish people's genocidal enemies, as there is today against Hamas, Hezbollah, and Iran.

I also wonder what changed in the Jewish spirit and outlook between the Holocaust and the establishment of Israel, when Jews fought bravely to secure their homeland. To be sure, they fought bravely in many resistance movements during the Holocaust as well, as I've detailed throughout this book. But surely the cataclysm of the Holocaust taught the Jews, *as a people,* that they had no choice but to fight back.

The State of Israel changed the Jewish historical calculus. Jews have now rejected the idea that we serve God through martyrdom, unless it is forced upon us in a manner that can in no way be evaded. Otherwise, we have an obligation to fight, defend our land, and defend our lives. Now, thank God, there is a Jewish Army guaranteeing that "Never Again" is more than just a motto.

Though the Holocaust had a profound impact on Jews, it is wrong to conclude that experience shaped our fighting spirit. Yes, we vow, "Never Again," today. But the Jews in Palestine were fighting for independence long before the Second World War began. Also, Jews knew nothing about the Holocaust when they first volunteered for the Jewish Brigade that fought beside the British.

The modern State of Israel largely confronts the same challenge. Iran and Ayatollah Khamenei speak in the same genocidal cadences as Hitler and the Nazis, regularly threatening the Jewish State with total destruction. Annihilation of Israel would, of necessity, require a second Holocaust, which the Iranians seem perfectly willing to carry out. And so it continues, as we recite in the Passover Haggadah: "…in every generation, another enemy rises to try and annihilate us." The prayer continues: "…and the Holy One, blessed be He, saves us from their evil designs."

Perhaps, no better indication of the relevance of the Holocaust today is the fortress mentality in Israel. I am not one of those who believes that the creation of Israel was simply a response to the Holocaust. The rebirth of the independent state we lost more than two thousand years ago was in process long before the rise of Hitler. In fact, 2017 was the year we celebrated the centennial of the Balfour Declaration, when the British government pledged to support the establishment of a Jewish home and Jewish political self-determination. Certainly, sympathy for the Jewish victims of the Holocaust played a role in the UN's ultimate decision to partition Palestine into Jewish and Arab states. But by 1948, the infrastructure for statehood had already been created by the Jewish pioneers who had started settling the land in the late 19th century.

The Arabs rejected the UN Partition Plan, and five Arab nations invaded Israel within hours of its declaration, with the goal of driving the Jews into the sea. They failed, by the grace of God, who had seemingly returned from an inexplicable hiatus, and restored the strength of the Jewish people who had come from nearly every corner of the earth to fight for the land God had promised Abraham. The State of Israel has since survived four or five more wars and an international terror campaign from an enemy determined to destroy it. The Jews vowed, "Never Again," and the state of Israel is a bulwark against that voice in the back of our heads that tells us it could happen again, whether in an increasingly powerful Jewish State, or in America, the land of freedom. Hitler's shadow still looms over us. Other people like to drink beer in a bottle with his picture on it.

After spending three summers in the places where our people suffered their greatest catastrophe, I did find answers—if only partial—to some of my questions. But not all.

3. Does European Jewry have any future after the Holocaust? Should Jews leave their homes in Europe?

Two of the greatest Jewish leaders of the 20th century had opposing views on this question. Theodor Herzl concluded that anti-Semitism was unmovable, and the only hope for Jewish survival was the establishment of an independent Jewish State. He insisted on the necessity of using diplomacy to persuade the world that Jews have a right to self-determination in their historical homeland—Israel—and helped turn the centuries-old dream of returning to Zion into a reality.

Rabbi Menachem Mendel Schneerson, affectionately known as the Rebbe, believed that Jews should have no fear, and communities should be expanded to all parts of the globe. Judaism was a global religion with global influence. To assist in this goal, the Rebbe sent emissaries around the world to establish and strengthen Jewish communities, and spread the light of Jewish values and faith.

Our trip convinced me that both Herzl and the Rebbe were correct. We need a Jewish State in the eternal Jewish homeland of Israel, that is the axis and pivot of world Jewry, while maintaining a global Jewish community that both spreads the light of the Jewish people and supports the Jewish State.

How can I say this? Doesn't the fact that six million Jews were killed while the world watched prove Herzl's point? After all, no Jew was spared. Even the most assimilated Jew, and non-Jew with only a distant Jewish relative, was sentenced to death. The world's leaders shut the gates to their countries, offering few Jews an opportunity to escape.

If Israel had existed at that time, Jews would have had a haven, and a government that would have done everything in its power to save them. In fact, even without a state, Jews in Palestine did what they could to rescue their brethren. The Mossad was first created to organize illegal immigration to Palestine, bringing Jews to their homeland, despite the objections of the British mandatory government. Heroic figures, like Hannah Senesh (we visited the dungeon in Budapest where she was tortured), put their lives on the line to fight the Nazis.

In many of the towns my family visited, few, if any, Jews remained. It is a terrible thing to admit, but in these places, Hitler won. He eradicated whole Jewish communities. When I walked through them, wearing my *yarmulke* and *tzitzit*, people stared at me and my family as though we were apparitions. If synagogues survived, they were often museums rather than places of worship, because no one was left to pray in them. I thought, *Is this what we really want? For Jews to be historical oddities like the dinosaurs?*

No. Amid the central importance of Israel to every aspect of the Jewish future, we need a global Jewish community where our people thrive and flourish in every part of the world.

Then there are the Israeli tourists who flock to cities such as Venice, Rome, Warsaw, Munich, and Berlin. Do we want Israelis, especially former IDF soldiers, doing a travel year abroad, to arrive in a continent bereft of Jews, and find no place to feel at home? No Chabad houses? No shuls to pray in? No kosher restaurants? No *mikvehs*? No Jewish communities to visit and feel part of?

Yosef disagrees with me. He argued that, "When we're not together, we're weak and we're exposed. They kill us. When we're strong, as one, they can't. In Israel, we have an army. And if we are all there, it will be harder to defeat us."

I told him that the genocidal Iranian Mullahs make the same case, but for the opposite effect. "Israel is a one-bomb state," one of the murderers said. Because the Jews are all together, it's easier to annihilate the whole of the nation.

I was playing devil's advocate. But Yosef would have none of it. He agreed with Israeli leaders that all the European Jews should move to Israel, where they would be safe.

I believe that every Jew who wants to live in Israel should go there and be encouraged to do so. It is our eternal homeland. Despite terrorism and the threats of radical Islam in the region, Israel is strong and safe. The population is defended by a powerful military, a true people's army, composed mostly of courageous Jews with a fighting spirit. The government and the people are a flourishing democracy, and all citizens enjoy the freedoms we often take for granted in the United States, but which are a miracle in the Middle East.

On the other hand, the Jewish philosopher Emil Fackenheim formulated a 614th commandment that we should not give Hitler a posthumous victory. No Jew should be lost to his or her people or tradition. Abandoning the Jews of Europe, especially those who survived Hitler's genocidal war, is unacceptable. Allowing or encouraging Europe to become *judenrein* would violate that commandment and betray the ideals of both Herzl and the Rebbe.

But Israel has something else. Governed by Jewish values, it has an army that celebrates no victories or military glory, but only defense of human life. Judaism has no victory arches. You will find many things in Israel—the ruins of the ancient temple, ancient synagogues, and *mikvehs*. The Maccabees and King David had great military victories. But Jews don't celebrate them, because we do not believe in the glory of war. We do not believe societies are enhanced or ennobled by war. Precisely the opposite is true. We are a people who celebrate peace, and our God's name is Shalom (peace).

Jews believe the purpose of war is to protect life. We fight only because we are *forced* to fight. There is no glory in it. Even in modern Israel, which has seen the electrifying victories of the Six-Day War, when Israel conquered land three times its size. Or the more sobering Yom Kippur War, when Israel was almost annihilated, but rallied to threaten Cairo and Damascus and encircle the Egyptian Third Army. Even then, Israel made no celebratory military arches. Israel has no celebrations for its wars, only monuments to the fallen soldiers, and countless victims of terror, who gave their lives to defend their people.

Europe, of course, is different. Going back to ancient Greek and Roman times, rulers were celebrated not for peacemaking, but for war and conquest. Caesar and Augustus, Trajan and Constantine earned their places in the annals of history by dominating the enemy. Even in benign modern democracies, like Britain, the rulers—like King Charles and his two sons—get married in military garb.

For Baba, these values were something that had to be rejected. Europe had too much of a military history, and its victims were too often the Jews, to ever find true redemption. And whether or not they should be blamed, Poland was at the center of it. Baba reacted negatively toward the tragic history of Polish Jewry, and its worse incarnation (in her opinion), the city of Łódź. Łódź was an accursed place not fit for Jews. Baba did not understand why there was any community there at all. Shaina disagreed, playing yin to Baba's yang. Jews had to be everywhere. They are a people that must flourish with international influence.

Who's right? Baba's point of view had, unfortunately, a lot going for it. Why remain in places that have such dark history? Why not move to Israel and live safely among other Jews? But I could equally make the argument that forfeiting the Jewish right to live in Poland, or any other place in Europe, was exactly Hitler's dream. And while I'm, of course, not saying that defiance of Hitler should be the main argument guiding Jewish communal residence—neither should his squalid memory push us away.

More broadly, should the Jews of Europe stay in Europe, given the rise of anti-Semitism there? If they leave, where should they go? To America? Or make *aliyah* to Israel? Has the diaspora outlived its purpose? Or is it an important part of Jewish identity and destiny?

In the American Jewish Committee's 2018 survey, 69 percent of American Jews said, "A thriving Diaspora is vital for the long-term future of the Jewish people." Fair enough. It's the sort of thing you would expect from the American Jewish Committee and its members, nearly all of whom are Jews who live outside of Israel. But it's something with which I concur.

Despite the solicitation of Israeli officials, not all Jews will make *aliyah*, and should not be made to feel guilty for not doing so. You're not a bad Jew for not living in Israel, even as you might just be a more complete Jew for doing so. For those Jewish men and women who choose to live outside of the ancient Jewish homeland, they must be encouraged, inspired, and obligated to build Jewish life in their cities, and to support Israel vocally, politically, financially, and publicly from their respective countries.

A political argument can also be made for strengthening diaspora communities. In the United States, especially, Jewish communal support for Israel is vital to ensuring that the US-Israel Alliance endures. Jewish communities elsewhere may have much less influence, but how much will any government official care about Israel if they no longer have Jewish constituents?

The world Jewish community, as well as the State of Israel, should be investing in their welfare. Philanthropists should participate in reinvigorating Jewish communities in Eastern Europe, providing educational opportunities to build Jewish identity, and restoring synagogues and other Jewish institutions. Similarly, Israel should invest in these communities, just as it has committed millions of dollars to assist American organizations to strengthen Jewish education in the United States, and to support Birthright Israel (the program that offers young Jews who have never been to Israel, a free ten-day trip). I want to see living, flourishing communities throughout Europe, where Jews are proud, strong, and committed to Israel and Judaism.

Another questions arises. Given the increasing violence against Jews in Europe, should we hide our Jewishness when we travel there?

In April 2018, a Syrian asylum seeker shouting, "Jew!," in Arabic, attacked a man wearing a *yarmulke* in Berlin. The victim was an Israeli Arab who had put on the *yarmulke* to test whether it was dangerous to wear one in Germany.

This was not an isolated incident. In many European cities, Jews are warned not to wear *yarmulkes* or necklaces with Stars of David, or give any outward appearance of being Jewish. We were given the same caution when we first arrived in Germany. A survey in January 2018, found that 27 percent of Europeans felt insecure, and 51 percent said wearing Jewish symbols made them feel unsafe. Meanwhile, everywhere you go in Europe, you see men, women, and children proudly wearing clothes that identify them as Muslim, even though they themselves are vulnerable to attacks by bigots.

We Jews cannot allow ourselves to become invisible.

I can understand the fear many Jews feel, especially in countries such as Sweden, where anti-Semitism has surged, and the Jewish community is small and lacks the infrastructure to defend itself, or to be politically influential. Even in a place with a stronger community, such as France, Jews are justifiably afraid, given the number of attacks on Jews.

The Rebbe's message was not to give in to fear. We can make no concessions—not in our appearance, not in our names, not in any part of our identity—to those who would harm us. Chabad is successful around the world precisely because it doesn't cede an inch of Jewish identity. Jewish pride is the key to Chabad's success and inspiration.

Instead of hiding their Judaism, Jews must walk openly and proudly, including in Europe. I'm not a fearless person, but I walk around Europe with my *tzitzit* hanging out, and wearing a *yarmulke*. The Chabad guys do not hide their Jewishness. It is up to the political leaders of Europe, and the local police, to ensure that no Jew is endangered because they identify as Jews.

The outlooks of the Rebbe and Herzl now intersect. This is not the 1940s. Today, there is a Jewish State, and as the representative of the Jewish people everywhere, the Israeli government must say to the leaders of Europe:

We will hold you accountable in international forums, for your failure to protect your Jewish citizens. There will be a price to pay for your inaction.

The situation is different in Europe, where anti-Semitism is a perennial flower, and violence against Jews is on the rise. A CNN poll in December 2018, found that "more than a quarter of Europeans polled believe Jews have too much influence in business and finance. Nearly one in four said Jews have too much influence in conflict and wars across the world. One in five said they have too much influence in the media, and the same number believe they have too much influence in politics."

Most respondents significantly overestimated the Jewish population of the world and in their own countries. But "majorities or near-majorities in every country…said they were not aware of ever having met a Jewish person." This may help explain why our family was such a curiosity in these places. Of the Holocaust: 34 percent told CNN they knew "little or nothing" about the genocide. Not surprisingly, the results were worse for the younger generation. Significantly, perhaps only 10 percent of Europeans would admit to unfavorable views of Jews, compared to 37 percent who said they didn't like Muslims. But that's probably because they don't perceive Jews to be an active threat.

In March of 2018, the ADL issued a report where Jews in Germany said they "are worried about anti-Semitism among the new migrant and refugee population, many from Syria and Iraq, and by the rise of the far-right Alternative for Germany Party.

In the UK, the Labor Party has been accused of turning a blind eye to anti-Semitism, and its immediate past leader, Jeremy Corbyn, was an open anti-Semite. An overall tolerance for anti-Jewish and anti-Israel sentiment within the party continues seemingly unabated. The late British chief rabbi, Jonathan Sacks, accused Corbyn of giving "support to racists, terrorists and dealers of hate, who want to kill Jews and remove Israel from the map." He said that, for the first time in the 362 years Jews have lived in Britain, many questioned whether it is safe to raise children there. A 2017 survey found that almost one-third of British Jews considered leaving the United Kingdom due to anti-Semitism. If such a large, prosperous, and relatively powerful Jewish community—where I myself lived for eleven years—feels so threatened, what hope is there for Jews in towns in Eastern Europe where remnants of pre-war communities are struggling to survive?

The Polish Jewish community wrote an open letter in February 2018, stating that Polish Jews did not feel safe due to a wave of anti-Semitism that followed the adoption of a law providing fines and imprisonment for anyone who accused the Polish population of responsibility or complicity in war crimes. As of this writing, the government has partially repealed the law—the punishments have been removed—and the Jewish community seems safe from attack. Indeed, when I visit Poland, I feel safe wherever I travel, and have been treated with great kindness by the Polish government and its officials. I have many times throughout this book praised the Polish government for all it does to maintain the Nazi German extermination camp museums, and for its strong support of Israel. Still, it is incumbent upon the government to do all in its power to fight any form of Holocaust revisionism.

Two-thirds of Hungarian Jews said in June 2018, that anti-Semitism is a serious problem in their country. Paradoxically, the Jewish community's watchdog on anti-Semitism, TEV, found that anti-Semitic incidents in 2017, decreased 23 percent from 2016, to a total of thirty-seven. The perception that anti-Semitism is more widespread might be related to a campaign attacking George Soros, the Jewish billionaire philanthropist and Holocaust survivor, accusing him of supporting illegal immigration into the country. Some Hungarian Jews believe the propaganda is meant to appeal to an anti-Semitic segment of the population. Yet Hungary has a strong relationship with Israel, and its support for the Jewish State should be applauded.

The most serious incidents in recent years have occurred in France, which we did not visit on this trip, even though the collaborationist Vichy regime, headed by the Hitler toady Marshal Pétain, deported eighty thousand French Jews to their deaths—one of the most shameful episodes in all of French history. The French deported their Jews to Auschwitz and other concentration camps, thereby seemingly mitigating their collusion. But the ignominy of France's collaboration with the Nazis is an eternal stain on the country that promised the world liberty, equality, and fraternity.

Present-day France is a country where at least eleven Jews have been murdered in the past twelve years, including an eighty-five-year-old Holocaust survivor, in 2018. Assaults against Jews are occurring regularly. The influx of thousands of refugees from the Middle East has contributed to the spread of extremism in parts of France. Young Jews are particularly susceptible to harassment and assaults. Consequently, two-thirds of Jews (nearly 100 percent in and around Paris) attend private schools (Jewish and non-Jewish), whereas most once attended public schools. In September 2017, a former school principle in Marseille admitted that he advised Jews not to attend his school because of the danger that they would be attacked or harassed.

An indication of French sentiment was found in a May 2018 poll, which revealed that 52 percent of the French public believe that Zionism is a "racist ideology"; 54 percent believe that Zionism is an "international organization that seeks to influence the world and societies in favor of Jewish interests"; 26 percent said calls to boycott Israel were justified; and 57 percent agreed with the statement, "Israel is a threat to regional stability."

When in Paris, I love to walk the city, visiting its countless historical sites and museums. Although my family and I look unmistakably Jewish, by and large—with some exceptions of people who will give us menacing stares, and some who will even spit—we are treated warmly by the people we meet. Most Parisians exemplify the acceptance shown to Jews by leading French figures, from Émile Zola to Manuel Valls.

Yet when you wear a *yarmulke* in France, Jews come over to tell you, in whispers, a.) that they're Jewish too, as if you are in a secret society like the illuminati, and b.) that it's a bad idea to wear a *kippah* openly. You keep on getting advice to take off your *kippah*, lest you get attacked.

Having recently read Marc Weitzmann's masterful work, *Hate: The Rising Tide of Anti-Semitism in France*, I knew I couldn't blame these Jews for their fear and discretion. In 2018, there were 541 attacks against Jews, up 74 percent from the previous year.

In February 2019, after nearly one hundred Jewish tombstones got the "swastika treatment" in southeast France, French President Emmanuel Macron came before a Jewish communal conference to declare a war against the rising tide of Jew-hatred, as well as to concede—at last—that "anti-Zionism is one of the modern forms of antisemitism."

He said these things because they had finally become undeniable. For most of the past two decades, as social siege-engines have cornered the Jews of France, local authorities chose to forgo an aggressive policy of decrying anti-Semitism for a slothful one of denying it. When a synagogue was burned down amid a rush of Islamist demonstrations in the early 2000s, French justice officials, politicians, and journalists maintained "a virtual blackout on more than 500 cases of antisemitic violence" directed by Muslims, at Jews, according to Shmuel Trigano, a prominent scholar on the subject.

Then, in 2006, Ilan Halimi, a twenty-three-year-old Jewish cellular clerk, was abducted, held for twenty-four days, tortured, stabbed, doused with gasoline, burned alive, and murdered. Even after those who hatched the plot confessed to selecting their victim on the basis of his Jewishness (and presumed stores of gold), minister of the interior Nicolas Sarkozy would use the term "antisemitism by amalgam." There wasn't a philosopher in France who knew what that meant.

The worst part is that nearly fifty "uninvolved" locals—including many Christians—knew of Halimi's whereabouts. The doorman of the building even gave Halimi's captors the keys to a boiler room to use as their makeshift black site. Even as his disappearance became the most talked-about story in France, not one of these neighbors so much as picked up a phone to anonymously tip-off police.

Fast-forward ten years, and nothing would change. In 2016, Sarah Halimi (a distant cousin of Ilan's) was beaten and thrown out her window by a twenty-seven-year-old neighbor who noticed the mezuzah on her door. Just the sight of the sacred Jewish door parchment ignited within him—to quote the official psychiatric report—a "frantic outburst of hate." Despite that he admitted to targeting her out of hate, and for being a Jew, the murder has still not been classified as anti-Semitic. Though cleared of mental illness, Kobili Traoré is still considered "unfit for trial" because, at the time of the murder, he was—get this—in a state of "acute delirium" from smoking marijuana. This outcome makes a mockery of the nation that gave the world its first modern code of law.

Then, in March of 2018, an eighty-five-year-old Holocaust-survivor, Mireille Knoll, was stabbed eleven times in her apartment, before being "partly burned." The authorities classified the murder as being motivated by "membership, real or supposed, of the victim of a particular religion."

France's inability to face its anti-Semitism seems to have been pulled out of Parisian absurdist theater, whose Jew-hating founder, Jean Genet, once lionized Palestinian suicide bombers as "blowing up in thousands of pieces of laughter," achieving what he called "the joy of the hero" as they blew apart mothers and children.

Of course, all of this occurred before the Macron crackdown. Since his announcement, however, little has improved.

If France doesn't take action to combat growing anti-Semitism, they will continue to witness a mass exodus of Jews, and lose the goodwill of people like me, who love the beauty and culture of France, but are increasingly disgusted by the country's refusal to purge the Jew-hatred from within.

The rise of anti-Semitism and far-right parties in Europe has exacerbated the wider question as to whether Jews should remain on the continent. After the horrific terrorist attacks in Barcelona that killed thirteen people and injured more than one hundred, in August 2017, the chief rabbi said there was no future for the Jews in the city. After referring to Spain as a "hub of Islamist terror for all of Europe," he said, "I tell my congregants: Don't think we're here for good. And I encourage them to buy property in Israel. This place is lost. Don't repeat the mistake of Algerian Jews, of Venezuelan Jews. Better [get out] early than late." The next day, the leader of the Jewish community in that same city rebuked the rabbi and asserted that Jewish life in Barcelona was thriving. That Jews were not afraid, and would not be driven from their homes by fear stoked by Islamic fanatics.

While I respect the desire of the chief rabbi to protect his congregants, I still believe that what he said is unacceptable. His job is to inspire people, not scare them. Rather than pushing the Jewish community to exit, he should be leading marches in the streets, demanding that the authorities protect their Jewish citizens. He should be on every TV channel, shaming the government into action. And if need be, organizing the local Jewish community into security squads to make sure they protect themselves.

The terror in Barcelona was only the most recent manifestation of the danger posed by radical Islam. The rabbi's words echoed those of Jewish leaders in other parts of Europe who have argued that the rise in anti-Semitism has made life for Jews in Europe intolerable. Israeli leaders have repeatedly reinforced this sentiment, and encouraged European Jews to make *aliyah*.

While not all Jews are prepared to move to Israel, a growing number say that they may leave their homes. The European Union Agency for Fundamental Rights, which was established to uphold human rights and fight all forms of racism, surveyed 16,400 respondents from twenty-eight EU member nations. More than one-third (38 percent) said they are considering leaving Europe. This is not surprising, given that 85 percent reported that anti-Semitism is the most serious problem they face, and 89 percent said that anti-Semitism in the EU has risen significantly in the past five years.

Which leads us to the final question:

4. How should we teach our children about the Holocaust? Should we bring them to Treblinka? Should we teach them to hate the enemies of the Jews? Are we too obsessed with the Holocaust?

I took my children on a Holocaust holiday, strange as the juxtapositions of those two words may sound. The very phrase excites controversy. How could there be a Holocaust holiday? Isn't this expression a trivialization of the genocide? But that was my whole point. What diminishes the Holocaust is when we are afraid to take our children to the most horrible places on earth, lest it scar them. But putting blinders on their eyes will not protect them.

It is hard for me not to be immersed in the memory of the Holocaust. I never stop reading books and watching documentaries on World War II and the Holocaust. I do not believe that we Jews are obsessed. The very word is a pejorative. It would indicate that the time has come for us to move on from Holocaust memory, or not talk about it so much—that we've given the past too much attention, and now should focus on the future.

But if we hope to prevent the recurrence of genocide, we have to learn from our martyred brethren, the heroic Jews of Europe who did everything to keep their children alive. First and foremost, this means fighting back against those threatening genocide, long before the slaughter ever starts. What would have happened if the world had reacted more harshly to Hitler's persecution of the Jews, especially after *Kristallnacht*? What if the world had taken seriously Hitler's threat to exterminate the Jewish people? What if Chamberlain had refused to sign the Munich Agreement, and the Allies declared war on Hitler before he began his conquests, and while his *Wehrmacht* was still weak? What if countries had opened their doors to Jews seeking safe haven? What if Pope Pius XII had spoken out against the annihilation of European Jewry? What if the Allies had bombed the death camps? What if more Germans and citizens of other occupied countries had rescued Jews instead of being bystanders or collaborators? There are so many what-if's.

If anything, we must be over-vigilant, hyper-cautious, and have no tolerance for risk. There has to be a new spirit of defiance, which means we do not give one inch when it comes to opposing the words and plans of evil men. For in complacency lies the greatest danger.

The collective response to threats of genocide lately has not been so good. The failure to react to Syria's repeated use of chemical weapons against its own people, to its building a crematorium to dispose of and conceal the murder of prisoners, is pathetic. Israel reportedly considered bombing the crematorium. An Israel official said, "A country that lost millions of its people to crematoria cannot stand by when it happens to another people a few dozens of kilometers from our border," while most of the world "stands by and remains silent—exactly as it did 70 years ago." Ultimately, however, Israel decided not to act because of the possibility of escalating hostilities on its northern border, and upsetting Russia and the United States. The failure by any country to destroy the butcher Assad's crematorium is yet another indication that we have not learned the lessons of the Holocaust.

Israel reportedly considered a military strike on Iran's nuclear facilities. But the military objected, and the government feared a hostile response from the Obama administration. President Obama repeatedly said, "Nothing was off the table." But the Iranians had become confident that he would never use military force. So they made a deal to halt their nuclear program for only fifteen years, in exchange for the immediate removal of sanctions, and a windfall of tens of billions of dollars.

Genocidal rhetoric in our time must be resisted completely. That's why it was a disgrace that the United States negotiated the disastrous nuclear deal with Iran, while the mullahs in Tehran were speaking openly of killing all the Jews in Israel. I lost a lot of friends because I took such a strong position against the Iran deal. Did I overreact? Knowing what I do about the Holocaust, I believe that my response was measured, proportionate, and essential. If anything, it was underdone. Genocidal threats must be combated with all guns blazing. You can't let these maniacs talk about annihilating a people, because most genocides are incremental. They start with words, then the lies and deception build up, along with the body count.

The world has never stopped genocide, and we don't have to ask why. For the most part, we simply don't care. It doesn't touch us. It affects people across the sea, or beyond some towering mountain range. Perhaps we hear about it from a newspaper. But even the ink from a front-page headline, or a graphic photograph, is unable to penetrate our hearts.

This kind of apathy in the face of monstrous evil cannot continue. We must show the world that we have learned from the horrors of history.

Many Jews have asked whether we should hate the Nazis and the Germans of the World War II era. The answer is an emphatic *yes*. Not today's Germans, who did not perpetrate the Holocaust. But we should certainly blame and despise Hitler's Germany and those who voted him into power democratically, and enacted his genocide.

I reject any and all theological justifications for the Holocaust. We will always confront God over the Holocaust. I argue with my children, and I challenged Elie Wiesel. When Elie said we should not hate because it consumes the hater, I disagreed with this greatest of men. I believe we need to feel the same hate Churchill felt toward Hitler.

I realize we live in a liberal age. We want to show our love, not pass judgment, and to perfect the world. How then could it be that on our watch, six million Jews were murdered in the Holocaust; that Pol Pot killed more than 1.5 million Cambodians; and that eight hundred thousand people were slaughtered in the Rwandan genocide in just three short months? Have we learned any lessons from these examples of ultimate evil?

The progressive answer, for some, is that we do not love enough. They may excuse the evildoer's actions as having been motivated by some socioeconomic cause, and seek to *understand* rather than resist evil. They justify murderous actions based on poverty, persecution, or gullibility. We are often told the killers of Israeli Jews were humiliated at army checkpoints, were unemployed in Gaza, or felt their only option was to engage in terrorism.

Is it any wonder that today, we are witnessing Bashar Assad using chemical weapons against Syrian children; Hamas terrorists indiscriminately bombarding Israel with rockets; radical Muslims turning themselves into suicide bombs; and extremists murdering worshippers in mosques, churches, and synagogues? The Uighurs being persecuted by the Chinese in Xinjiang?

The failure of liberalism, and the reason why it often inspires a failed foreign policy of passivity, is rooted in its unwillingness to hate evil. Many say they derive this from Jesus's Sermon on the Mount, when he said, "If anyone slaps you on the right cheek, turn to them the other cheek also."

This noble sentiment is often misinterpreted by those who fail to distinguish between the petty grievances Jesus was referring to, and mass murder. Jesus did not mean to equate the person who stole your parking space with a mass murderer. He told his followers to love *their* enemies, not God's enemies. When I lived in the UK, I heard a man whose father was killed by the IRA, solely because he was a Protestant, tell the interviewer that, as a Christian, he was compelled to love and forgive his father's murderers. But no human being can confer such forgiveness. The act of taking a human life is a crime against God, who created life and endowed it with infinite worth. Individuals who have erased the image of God from their countenance, through savage acts of brutality, have removed themselves from the human family. Our love must be directed toward the victims of violence, not the victimizers.

Elie Wiesel, whom I never disagreed with on any issue under the sun save this, used to say to me, "We cannot hate our enemies. It seeps into our blood and poisons us." But what else can we do when we are talking about the enemies of humanity? Without despising their cruelty, how will we muster the will to oppose them?

How are we supposed to demonstrate our moral resolve to fight extremists who wish to exterminate Jews, Christians, or Muslims, if we don't hate them? How are we supposed to react to terrorists who indiscriminately bomb civilian areas; who use children as human shields against the defenders of the innocent; and who indoctrinate their youth with the belief they will reach a heavenly paradise by blowing themselves up, along with as many bystanders as possible? The greatest foreign policy failure of our time, and the reason that genocides continue to happen, is our refusal to hate evil.

The appropriate response to today's evil was expressed by French President François Hollande, following a horrific terrorist attack in Paris: "I despise these terrorists with every fiber of my being," he said. "I hate them and everything they stand for. And I will fight them to the last man."

We must passionately hate anti-Semitism, and other forms of bigotry, to summon the determination to fight them fervently. And we cannot wait for the evildoers to act before taking steps to stop them. The threat of genocide today becomes the reality of mass murder tomorrow.

The world, overall, refused to hate Hitler. Gandhi, the most respected man in the world, said of Hitler, "I do not believe him to be as bad as he is portrayed." George Bernard Shaw infamously said, "The Nazi movement is in many respects one which has my warmest sympathy." No doubt they felt foolish later. But by then, it was too late.

Gandhi's disciple Martin Luther King summed it up best: "He who passively accepts evil is as much involved in it as he who helps to perpetrate it. He who accepts evil without protesting against it is really cooperating with it."

If we hope to prevent the recurrence of genocide, we have to learn from our martyred brethren—the heroic Jews of Europe who did everything they could to keep their children alive. First and foremost, this means fighting back against those threatening genocide from the moment they voice their intentions. Genocidal rhetoric, expressly forbidden in the United Nations anti-Genocide Convention of 1948, must be treated with the utmost gravity, from its first utterance. When it comes to evil, our vigilance should know no bounds and have no tolerance for risk. For in even a fragment of naiveté toward the plans of evil men lies the greatest danger. After all, one cannot prevent what one does not properly anticipate.

Which brings us back to the question of how to educate about the Holocaust.

Obviously, we must teach our children, and all the children in the societies where they live, about the Holocaust. But what should we teach them?

It is difficult for anyone to grasp the enormity of the Holocaust. You hear the number *six million*, but it's meaningless until you visit the sites, and you understand that 3,000 were murdered here, 12,000 there, 270,000 somewhere else. Perhaps students could use virtual reality, YouTube videos, and other forms of modern technology to more directly experience the sites where Jews were murdered. We can also try to put that abstract number into some perspective that is easier to understand. For example, 2,890 Jews were killed *every day*, 120 were killed *per hour*, and 2 Jews were killed *every minute* of the war.

To put it in more immediate, yet painful perspective, the rate of killing can be compared to the time it would take to wipe out the town in which students live. For example, it would take only one day and nine hours to murder the entire population of Rochester, New York; eighty-three days for Orlando, 146 days for Atlanta, and 218 days for the District of Columbia.

One thing we need to do is to try to put students in the shoes of people at the time. What would you do in the same situation?

I thought about how important this is when I heard Yosef talking about the trip. He said, "I'm never going back there. Our people were massacred in the streets, and no one did anything about it. Our neighbors watched us being killed, and just said, 'Whatever.' I didn't understand how that could happen. How could you watch people die? I just don't understand it."

When I asked him what he would do, he said, "It's hard to say. But I think I would have helped. If I saw a neighbor being beaten and killed, I would stop the person who was hurting him. I wouldn't just stand there."

Brave and worthy sentiments, to be sure. But would it have been realistic in Nazi Germany, or Austria or Poland? These are questions students should confront.

There was a great movie, years ago, called *The Wave*. It was a true story about a high school class studying World War II, whose teacher decides to try an experiment to help his students better understand what life was like in Nazi Germany. The students create a club with uniforms and salutes and symbols, and it becomes exclusive. Over the course of time, the club begins to resemble the Hitler Youth. The teacher tells them various things about their leader, but never who it is until the school administrator decides the experiment has gotten out of hand. The teacher summons the students to the auditorium to reveal that their leader is Adolf Hitler. The movie offers a powerful answer to the oft-asked questions: How could this have happened? Could it ever happen here in America?

There are many resources for teaching about the Holocaust. Many high schools in America assign Anne Frank's diary and Elie Wiesel's book *Night*. It is essential that these books—especially *Night*, with its detailed firsthand description of what occurred at Auschwitz—remain part of the essential high school curriculum. It is important to expose students to memoirs that resonate more than dry history books.

High school textbooks, especially, need to be improved. A number of years ago, Mitchell Bard analyzed some of the most widely used high school history textbooks, and found their coverage of the Holocaust sorely inadequate. In one case, for example, the authors made this startling moral equivalence: "Nazi murder of the Jews and other groups was the foremost atrocity of the war, but the Allies also acted harshly."

Showing students movies can also be effective. Many important Holocaust-related films and plays are available. One that I found interesting was *The Last Supper*, about a Jewish family dinner in 1933, shortly after Hitler has come to power. It offers insight into the question of why the Jews didn't leave Germany. The members of the family, and guests, reflect the various opinions of Jews at the time. For example, the son thinks Hitler has the right ideas about returning Germany to its former glory. His sister is a Zionist who announces that she plans to go to Israel. Another family member is a Communist. The father is a businessman who can't imagine that Hitler will do anything to the Jews, and is committed to staying in Germany. This type of movie helps students get inside the heads of Jews who faced the dilemma of how to respond to Hitler's rise to power. Interestingly, the playwright is Ido Netanyahu, brother of the Prime Minister of Israel, and son of the renowned historian Benzion Netanyahu.

So yes, it is important for Americans—and especially American Jews—to learn about the history of the Holocaust. But it is even more desperately needed in Europe and other parts of the world.

So having made my decision to educate my children about the Holocaust, did I do it the right way? Do I have any regrets? Writing a few years after the fact, in the time that it has taken me to write this book, I have had significant time to reflect on the journey.

Yes, there are things I would have done differently. I would have interspersed more recreational activities in between visiting the killing fields, as incongruous as that may sound. I would have lightened the trip by making sure that we didn't only visit places of extermination, one after the other. In other words, I would have given the kids something of a breather.

But aside from that, I don't see what else could have been different. This was a once-in-a-lifetime journey, and my children need to know about what happened to their people. Not because suffering is an essential part of Jewish identity, and not because I thought it would make them more empathetic or humble. I believe that children should have a happy childhood, and we should do everything to ensure that they are not *unnecessarily* exposed to things which may upset or traumatize them. Rather, as Shaina said so eloquently to Baba, the trip was essential to remember the six million. They cry out to remembered. They cannot even cry out from their graves, for they have none, save being entombed in our memory.

My children were given the opportunity to pay homage to 1.5 million children who were brutally murdered. They were given the chance to pray at the sites where six million innocent souls were barbarously murdered. And they were afforded a journey to honor those who died in the sanctification of God's name. I believe my children emerged as better people as a result. I believe they became stronger, more resilient, more respectful, and more appreciative of life.

But even if that is not completely accurate—and I pray that it is—I am certain the six million martyred souls looked down upon us as we traveled from place to place to consecrate their memory, and knew the one thing they must always know—now and forever—is that they are never forgotten.

INDEX

ACKNOWLEDGMENTS

This book is consecrated to the sacred memory of the six million martyrs of the Holocaust. Would that it never had to be written and that they and their innumerable descendants would still be alive.

I have to thank my family for accompanying me on such an excruciating journey. Many of my friends still think I was insane to take my children, for weeks on end, to the major Holocaust sites. To this day, even my wife is not sure I made the right decision. But I believe I did. Still, my children deserve immense credit for their forbearance, patience, and willingness to absorb incalculable pain in order to pay homage to the six million Jews murdered by Hitler and the German Nazis. So to the children who participated, Mendy, Shaina, Baba, Yosef, Dovid, and little Cheftziba, thank you for being children so utterly devoted to the Jewish God, the Jewish Torah, and more than anything else, the Jewish people. (My daughters Mushki and Shterny were married and did not attend the trip, and our daughter Chana was serving in the Israeli army after having made *aliyah* to the holy land).

My wife Debbie shared the burden with me at all times, including the difficult planning and the logistics of such a complex trip where we never stopped moving. Coming from a Holocaust family herself, this journey was extremely valuable to her. Debbie is my soulmate and partner in all things, both personal and professional. And it means sharing my life and experiences, which we always pray and hope will be joyous and celebratory, even while others, like visiting the sites of Holocaust memory, can be excruciatingly painful.

Elie Wiesel devoted his life to bearing witness to the six million Jews who were murdered by the Nazi Germans, including his parents, his sister, and many other members of his family. He was a man of incomparable greatness, and one of the most inspirational Jewish figures of all time. I miss him every day, and I thank him for lending eternity to the memory of the six million. Today, his extraordinary wife, Marion, who is also a Holocaust survivor, and translated most of his books, continues his legacy through the monumental work of the Elie Wiesel Foundation for Humanity.

Elie's son, Elisha, is one of my closest friends, and one of the most decent and moral men I know. While many see Elie's legacy as his dozens of books, his global footprint, and winning the Nobel Peace Prize, his most important gift to the world is Elisha. Elisha showed me that the child of a survivor can choose life over death; a commitment to the Jewish future over a cynical defeatism at losses suffered; a passionate commitment to friendship, family, charity; and commitment over any excuse to abandon God after his seeming abandonment of Jewry during the war. Elisha and his wife, Lynn, and beautiful children Elijah and Shira, are family to us. And Elisha has helped reconcile me with the God of Israel—seeing His compassionate guidance in Jewish history, even when He seems to hide.

Miriam Adelson's family lost approximately eighty members in the Holocaust, and she has been a constant companion in helping me remember and mourn the six million. She and her husband, Sheldon, are not only the world's leading Jewish philanthropists. They are also, arguably, the leading contributors to Holocaust memory, in the world. And I thank them with all my heart for their unceasing love to six million Jewish souls whose only markers are our memory. Sheldon, a supernova of Jewish giving and commitment, passed away in the very last stages of my editing this book, and his passing was extremely painful for me personally and an irreplaceable loss to the Jewish people generally. I pray that his memory be an eternal blessing.

Mitchell Bard is a close friend and a brilliant scholar. Much of the expansive history contained in this volume comes from his encyclopedic knowledge and writings on the Holocaust, and he was instrumental in every step of this book's creation, writing, and editing. Without Mitchell's indefatigable scholarship, so much of the exhaustive history that has been incorporated into this book would not be present. Mitchell has been my indispensable partner in having this book written, in collating so many of my and my children's memories, in shaping the kaleidoscopic history of the Holocaust which I have attempted to present, and getting the manuscript into shape. I remain eternally grateful.

The Lubavitcher Rebbe, Rabbi Menachem Mendel Schneerson, was not only the greatest Jewish leader of the 20th century, he was a personality who lead millions of Jews back to their heritage, and gave comfort to millions more who could not make peace with God after the Holocaust. The Rebbe brought humanity, warmth, and love to a people who had endured the most savage assault in human history. That Judaism today is once again flourishing as a global and passionate faith is a result of his Herculean efforts. The Rebbe was my teacher and inspiration. I miss him every day.

My father, Yoav Botach, died during the writing of this book in May 2020, at the height of the coronavirus pandemic. His loss has been extremely painful to process and I am still making sense of it. My father taught me to be a proud Jew and to love my people. And while his family, having come from Iran and Israel, were not affected by the European holocaust, he spoke constantly of what the Germans had done to the Jews and how strong our nation must be to ensure it is never repeated. As I hope, God willing, to write a full-length book about the personal grief that a child experiences after the tragic loss of a parent, I will not here discuss my sentiments at length, other than to say that I miss him every day and it was my honor to dedicate this book to his memory.

Most of all, I thank Almighty God for giving me the strength, health, and opportunity to remember the six million. I pay homage to my Creator for my wife, children, grandchildren, friends, community, and the blessings He gave me, enabling me to serve my people. I trust that God will take care of the six million lost souls who are now with him in Heaven; comfort all the mourners of Zion; and never abandon His people again. Indeed, I ask God the Creator to send the Messiah speedily in our days, and usher in a world bereft of sorrow, death, and mourning in an era of eternal brotherhood and peace. And at that time, as I said at in my father's eulogy on the Mount of Olives in Jerusalem, we will be reunited with those we have lost who will reawaken to a world shining with particles of everlasting light.

Rabbi Shmuley Boteach
January, 2021
New York City, NY
United States of America